FROM REAL LIFE TO REEL LIFE
A Filmography of Biographical Films

by

Eileen Karsten

with the assistance of
Dorothy-Ellen Gross

The Scarecrow Press, Inc.
Metuchen, N.J., & London
1993

British Library Cataloguing-in-Publication data available

Library of Congress Cataloging-in-Publication Data

Karsten, Eileen, 1954–
    From real life to reel life : a filmography of biographical films /
by Eileen Karsten with the assistance of Dorothy-Ellen Gross.
        p.   cm.
    Includes bibliographical references (p.   ) and indexes.
    ISBN 0-8108-2591-0 (alk. paper)
    1. Biographical films—Catalogs.   I. Gross, Dorothy-Ellen,
1949–
II. Title.
PN1995.9.B55K37   1993
016.79143'651—dc20   93-9160

For my sons,

B.J. and Michael

CONTENTS

Introduction   vii

Filmography   1

Selected Bibliography   341

Performer Index   343

Film Title Index   391

Subject Index   421

Date of Release Index   455

About the Author   476

INTRODUCTION

This book is the end product of a discussion on whether a film was ever made on the life of George Washington. When I started to research the answer, I found that no single source exists that lists biographical films. So, after a long and frustrating search, I decided to compile a filmography of biographical films.

The history of biographical film is as varied as the subjects portrayed in the films. Biographical film, or "biopic," is defined as "a motion picture based on the life of a public figure, most commonly an individual struggling to achieve goals against considerable odds or to recover from a major setback which threatens an already successful career."[1] The early biographical films released in the 1930's and 1940's were this type of picture. These films were made about inspirational figures such as Louis Pasteur, Abraham Lincoln, and Thomas Edison. Emphasized in these pictures were their struggles to achieve goals that would benefit all humankind. Virtually all the early films emphasized the same "common characteristics [that were] the heroic elements of determination and personal courage."[2]

Biographical film subjects since the late 1940's have included such popular figures as athletes and entertainment personalities. These films have emphasized the personal lives of the subjects, often focusing on their love affairs and personal problems, such as drinking or drug abuse. In the earlier films, the subject would always overcome his or her problem and go on to greater heights. In later films, the subject does not always overcome the problem, but sometimes faces death or imprisonment. These films often serve to quench the public's curiosity about the intimate secrets and lives of celebrities.

With the advent of television, biographical films reached a new popularity, and were made not only about major current and historical personalities, but also about minor personalities who briefly made the headlines—films frequently limited to the event that made them famous. With television, too, the lives of major figures now could be made into mini-series lasting four to eight hours, stretching over two or three nights and exploring many aspects of their lives in detail. The focus of television films has varied from the inspirational to the exploitive.

In this book, I have tried to list all the major biographical films and documentaries shown in the United States since the advent of sound. Films were chosen by the following criteria:

—The film deals primarily with the life of a person.

—The person really exists or existed.

—The film was released in English or with English subtitles.

—The film was shown commercially either in a movie theater or on television.

—The quality of the film was not taken into consideration, and the films vary from such serious biographical studies as *Wilson* to such exploitive films as *The People Vs. Jean Harris*.

The book is arranged in alphabetical order by the subject of the film. Each entry includes the following information:

—Title. For foreign films, the U.S. title is listed.

—Date of release. For foreign films, I have tried to find the U.S. release date.

—Distribution or production company, when available.

—Director.

—Running time. In some cases, I found several different running times for one film. I have listed the running time I could verify in at least two sources.

—The biographical subject and the actor who portrayed him or her. In some films, the subject's name has been changed or a pseudonym has been used. In these cases, I have listed both the variant form and the proper form of the name.

—Other major figures who played prominent roles in the film or in the biographical subject's life and the actors who portrayed them. In biographical films of major figures, many well-known persons will appear only briefly, and these brief appearances are not listed.

—Other supporting actors who appear in the film.

—Cross-references from the main biographical subject to other entries in whose films the subject also has appeared.

EXAMPLE:

Liszt, Franz, 1811–1886. (Hungarian composer and pianist)

630. *Lisztomania* (1975). 105 min. Warner Bros. D: Ken Russell.
Liszt: Roger Daltrey
Lola Montes: Anulka Dziubinska
Richard Wagner: Paul Nicholas
Supporting cast: Sara Kestelman, Fiona Lewis, Veronica Quilligan.

SEE ALSO: **Grieg, Edvard.**

If a piece of information is not available, the abbreviation **N/A** has been used.

I have tried to make the book as comprehensive as possible, but there are films that I purposely excluded.

—Films were excluded if I could not verify the existence of the film's subject in a standard reference source.

—That the film attempted to be a biographical film had to be verified in at least two sources for inclusion in the book. Frequently in films, famous personalities or public figures were used as a plot device—e.g., Shirley Temple asking Abraham Lincoln to pardon her father in the *Little Colonel*. This is a common occurrence in films set in the past since it offers an aura of authenticity to the film.

—To quote Emerson, "There is properly no history; only biography."[3] Historical films include major figures from the period or event that they are portraying, but I have generally excluded these films. The purpose of a historical film generally is to recreate an event, not to tell the life stories of the people involved. Films dealing with major historical events are included only when they deal primarily with the personalities involved rather than the actual event.

—Western films were excluded when they contained no biographical information and the events portrayed could not be verified as actual events. The creators of western films frequently named their main characters after famous figures for the sake of name recognition. Billy the Kid has been featured in more than fifty westerns. If every film were biographical, then Billy shot more than a hundred men and dated Dracula's niece. (In real life, he killed twenty-seven men before being shot by Sheriff Pat Garrett at the age of twenty-one.)

—Mini-series were included on a limited basis through 1986 since many of them were not readily available in video format at the time of this writing. I have included mostly feature-length productions that were first shown either in a movie theater or on television.

—I have excluded all films released in a foreign language except those which I could verify as having been released with English subtitles or dubbed into English.

—All films made specifically for educational purposes have been excluded from the book because they ordinarily are geared toward children and young adults; they are usually less than an hour, in order to fit into a class period; frequently they are composed of still photographs and paintings, not live performers; and some are edited versions of longer, commercially produced films. Other good reference sources exist which provide access to these films.

As for the films that I might accidentally have missed, or any new ones, I would appreciate hearing from any kind readers about them. For the curious readers, I could find only two biographical films about George Washington. CBS has televised a two-part mini-series on George Washington starring Barry Bostwick. To my knowledge, they are the only commercial, noneducational, biographical films done on our first president. In a future edition, I plan to include all biographical mini-series, any new films released, or films brought to my attention by readers of this book.

Notes

1. Frank E. Beaver, *Dictionary of Film Terms* (New York: McGraw-Hill, 1983), 34.

2. Beaver, 34.

3. John Bartlett, *Familiar Quotations: A Collection of Passages, Phrases and Proverbs Traced to Their Sources in Ancient and Modern Literature,* 15th ed., ed. Emily Morison Beck et al. (Boston: Little, Brown and Company, 1980), 496.

FILMOGRAPHY

Abberline, Frederick, 1843–1929
  See **Jack The Ripper.**

Abbott, Bud, 1898–1974. (American comic actor of the 1940's and 1950's)

1. *Bud And Lou* (1978). 100 min. Bob Banner Assoc. D: Robert C. Thompson
   Abbott: Harvey Korman
   Lou Costello: Buddy Hackett
   Supporting cast: Arte Johnson, Michele Lee, Robert Reed

Abelard, Peter, 1079–1142. (French philosopher and theologian who was condemned for heresy in 1140)

1a *Stealing Heaven* (1989). 116 min. Scotti Brothers Pictures. D: Clive Donner.
   Abelard: Derek de Lint
   Heloise: Kim Thomson
   Supporting cast: Pasty Byrne, Kenneth Cranham, Denholm Elliott, Bernard Hepton

Abernathy, Ralph, 1926–
  See **King, Martin Luther, Jr.**

Abrahams, Harold, 1899–
  See **Liddell, Eric.**

Abubadika, Mwlina Imiri, 1935–
  See **Carson, Sonny.**

Adams, Edie, 1929–
See **Kovacs, Ernie.**

Adams, John, 1735–1826. (Second American president and signer of Declaration of Independence)

2. *1776* (1972). 141 min. Columbia Pictures. D: Peter Hunt.
   Adams: William Daniels
   Benjamin Franklin: Howard da Silva
   Thomas Jefferson: Ken Howard
   Supporting cast: Blythe Danner, Donald Madden, Roy Poole, Virginia Vestoff

   SEE ALSO: **Washington, George.**

Adams, Randall Dale, 1949–   (American wrongly convicted of murder who served twelve years in prison)

2a *The Thin Blue Line* (1988). 106 min. Miramax Films. D: Earl Morris.
   Documentary.

Adamson, George, 1906–1989
See **Adamson, Joy.**

Adamson, Joy, 1937–1980. (Austrian-born wildlife conservationist who worked with African lions)

3. *Born Free* (1966). 95 min. Columbia Pictures. D: James Hill.
   Joy Adamson: Virginia McKenna
   George Adamson: Bill Travers
   Supporting cast: Geoffrey Keen, Peter Lukoye

4. *Christian the Lion* (1976). 89 min. Lion International Films. D: Bill Travers, James Hill.
   Joy Adamson: Virginia McKenna
   George Adamson: Bill Travers
   Supporting cast: George Adamson, Terence Adamson, Anthony Bourke, John Rendall

5. *Living Free* (1972). 91 min. Columbia Pictures. D: Jack Couffer.
   Joy Adamson: Susan Hampshire
   George Adamson: Nigel Davenport
   Supporting cast: Shane De Louvres, Edward Judd, Geoffrey
   Keen, Peter Lukoye

Adler, Polly, 1900–1962. (New York's reigning madam in the
1920's and 1930's)

6. *A House Is Not a Home* (1964). 98 min. Paramount Pictures. D:
   Russel Rouse.
   Adler: Shelley Winters
   Supporting cast: Broderick Crawford, Cesar Romero, Ralph
   Taegar, Robert Taylor

Ahasuerus, King of Persia, c. 5th century B.C.
See **Esther,** Queen of Persia.

Albaret, Celeste, 1891–1984
See **Proust, Marcel.**

Albert, Prince, 1819–1861
See **Victoria,** Queen of England.

Aldrin, Edwin E. "Buzz," 1930–   (Second American astronaut
to walk on the moon)

7. *Return to Earth* (1976). 90 min. King-Hitzig Prod. D: Jud
   Taylor.
   Aldrin: Cliff Robertson
   Supporting cast: Ralph Bellamy, Charles Cioffi, Shirley
   Knight

Alexander, Grand-Duke of Vladimir, 1220–1263. (Russian prince
who successfully resisted an attempt by the Teutonic knights
to invade Russia in 1242)

7a *Alexander Nevsky* (1938). 91 min. Mosfilm Studios. D: Sergei Eisenstein.
Alexander: Nikolai Cherkasov
Supporting cast: A.L. Abrikossov, Vassily Novikov, N.P. Okhlopov, Dmitri Orlov

Alexander the Great, King of Macedonia, 356–323 B.C.

8. *Alexander the Great* (1956). 135 min. United Artists. D: Robert Rossen.
Alexander: Richard Burton
Supporting cast: Claire Bloom, Danielle Darrieux, Fredric March

Alexander, Grover Cleveland, 1887–1950. (American baseball player and star National League pitcher)

9. *The Winning Team* (1952). 98 min. Warner Bros. D: Lewis Seiler.
Alexander: Ronald Reagan
Supporting cast: Doris Day, Frank Lovejoy, Eve Miller

Alexandra, Empress of Russia, 1872–1918
See **Anderson, Anna; Nicholas II,** Emperor of Russia; **Rasputin, Grigori Efimovich.**

Alexis, Czarevitch, son of Peter I, Emperor of Russia, 1690–1718
See **Peter I,** Emperor of Russia.

Alfred the Great, King of England, 849–899.

10. *Alfred the Great* (1969). 125 min. MGM. D: Clive Donner.
Alfred: David Hemmings
Supporting cast: Colin Blakely, Julian Glover, Prunella Ransome, Michael York

Ali, Muhammad, 1942– (African-American who was three-time heavyweight boxing champion)

11. *AKA Cassius Clay* (1970). 85 min. United Artists. D: William Cayton.
    Documentary.

11a *Champions Forever* (1989). 87 min. Ion Pictures. D: Dimitri Logothetis.
    Documentary which includes segments on George Foreman, Joe Frazier, Larry Holmes and Ken Norton.

12. *The Greatest* (1977). 101 min. Columbia Pictures. D: Tom Gries.
    Ali: Muhammad Ali
    Sonny Liston: Roger E. Mosley
    Supporting cast: Ernest Borgnine, Robert Duvall, John Marley

Amin, Idi, 1925– (Ugandan military dictator; disposed)

13. *Amin, the Rise and Fall* (1981). 101 min. Intermedia Prod. D: Sharad Patel.
    Amin: Joseph Olita
    Supporting cast: Denis Hills, Geoffrey Keen, Leonard Trolley

13a *General Idi Amin Dada* (1974). 107 min. Mara Films. D: Barbet Schroeder.
    Documentary.

Amory, Cleveland, 1917–
    See **Cousins, Norman.**

Amundsen, Roald, 1872–1928. (Norwegian explorer who discovered the South Pole)

14. *The Red Tent* (1971). 121 min. Paramount Pictures. D: Mikhail Kalatozov.
    Amundsen: Sean Connery
    Umberto Nobile: Peter Finch
    Supporting cast: Claudia Cardinale, Massimo Girotti, Hardy Kruger

Andersen, Hans Christian, 1805–1875. (Danish poet and writer of fairy tales)

15. *The Daydreamer* (1966). 98 min. Arthur Rankin, Jr. D: Jules Bass.
    Andersen: Paul O'Keefe
    Supporting cast: Ray Bolger, Jack Gilford, Margaret Hamilton

16. *Hans Christian Andersen* (1952). 120 min. RKO. D: Charles Vidor.
    Andersen: Danny Kaye
    Supporting cast: Farley Granger, Zizi Jeanmaire, Philip Tonge, Joey Walsh

Anderson, Anna, 1901?–1984. (German woman who maintained for over thirty years that she was the Grand Duchess Anastasia Nikolaievna Romanov)

16a *Anastasia: The Mystery Of Anna* (1986). 208 min. Telecom Entertainment Inc. D: Marvin Chomsky.
    Anderson: Amy Irving
    Czar Nicholas: Omar Sharif
    Czarina Alexandra: Claire Bloom
    Supporting cast: Olivia de Havilland, Susan Lucci, Jan Niklas, Nicolas Surovy

Andre, John, 1751–1780
    See **Arnold, Benedict.**

Andree, Salomon August, 1854–1897. (Swedish explorer who died in an attempt to reach the North Pole in a hot air balloon)

17. *The Flight of the Eagle* (1982). 141 min. Bold Prod. D: Jan Troell.
    Andree: Max von Sydow
    Knut Fraenkel: Sverre Anker Ousdal
    Nils Strindberg: Goran Stangertz
    Supporting cast: Clement Harari, Lotta Larsson, Eva von Hanno

Andrews, James J., d. 1862. (Civil War Union spy and winner of Congressional Medal of Honor)

18. *The Great Locomotive Chase* (1956). 85 min. Walt Disney Prod. D: Francis D. Lyon.
    Andrews: Fess Parker
    Supporting cast: Jeffrey Hunter, Claude Jarman, Jr., John Lupton, Jeff York

Angelou, Maya, 1928– (African-American writer best known for her autobiographical work)

19. *I Know Why the Caged Bird Sings* (1979). 100 min. Tomorrow Entertainment. D: Fielder Cook.
    Angelou: Constance Good
    Supporting cast: Paul Benjamin, Diahann Carroll, Ruby Dee, Esther Rolle

Anglin, Clarence, 1931?–
See **Morris, Frank.**

Anglin, John, 1930?–
See **Morris, Frank.**

Anne of Cleves, 1515–1557
See **Henry VIII,** King of England.

Anthony, Marc, 83?–30 B.C.
See **Caesar, Julius,** Emperor of Rome; **Cleopatra,** Queen of Egypt.

Armstrong, Louis, 1900–1971. (African-American jazz trumpeter whose style of improvisation revolutionized jazz performance in the 1920s)

20. *Louis Armstrong, Chicago Style* (1976). 78 min. Stonehenge Prod. D: Lee Philips.
Armstrong: Ben Vereen
Supporting cast: Margaret Avery, Red Buttons, Janet MacLachlan

Arnold, Benedict, 1741–1801. (American Revolutionary War general and traitor)

21. *The Scarlet Coat* (1955). 101 min. MGM. D: John Sturges.
Arnold: Robert Douglas
John Andre: Michael Wilding
John Bolton: Cornel Wilde
Supporting cast: Bobby Driscoll, Anne Francis, John McIntire, George Sanders

Arouch, Salamo. (Greek Auschwitz Concentration Camp inmate who was middleweight boxing champion of the Balkans prior to World War II.)

21a *Triumph Of The Spirit* (1989). 120 min. Nova International Films. D: Robert M. Young.
Arouch: Willem Dafoe
Supporting cast: Harmut Becker, Wendy Gazelle, Robert Loggia, Edward James Olmos

Arruza, Carlos, 1920–1966. (Mexican bullfighter)

22. *Arruza* (1972). 75 min. Avco Embassy Corp. D: Budd Boetticher.
Documentary

Ashley, Merrill, 1950–
See **Balanchine, George.**

Ashton-Warner, Sylvia, 1908–1984. (New Zealand teacher who developed a radically successful new method of teaching Maori children in the 1940's)

22a *Sylvia* (1985). 98 min. Unitel International Ltd. D: Michael Firth.
Ashton-Warner: Eleanor David
Supporting cast: Joseph George, Mary Regan, Nigel Terry, Tom Wilkinson

Atahualpa, d. 1533
See **Pizarro, Francisco.**

Attila the Hun, Hunnish King, 406–453.

23. *The Sign of the Pagan* (1954). 92 min. Universal-International. D: Douglas Sirk.
Attila: Jack Palance
Supporting cast: Jeff Chandler, Rita Gam, Ludmilla Tcherina

Avalon, Frankie, 1940–
See **Marcucci, Robert.**

Aykroyd, Dan, 1952–
See **Belushi, John.**

Aylward, Gladys, 1902–1970. (British missionary to China, 1932–1949)

24. *The Inn of the Sixth Happiness* (1958). 156 min. 20th Century-Fox. D: Mark Robson.
Aylward: Ingrid Bergman
Supporting Cast: Michael David, Robert Donat, Curt Jurgens

B

Bacall, Lauren, 1924–
See **Bogart, Humphrey.**

Bach, Anna Magdalena, 1700–1760
See **Bach, Johann Sebastian.**

Bach, Johann Sebastian, 1685–1750. (German organist, composer, and master contrapuntist)

24a *The Chronicle Of Anna Magdalena Bach* (1967). 93 min. New York Films. D: Jean-Marie Straub.
Bach: Gustav Leonhardt
Anna Bach: Christiane Lang
Supporting cast: Hans-Peter Boye, Paolo Carlini, Ernst Castelli, Kathrien Leonhardt

Bader, Douglas, 1910–1982. (RAF fighter pilot who lost both legs in a flying accident)

25. *Reach for the Sky* (1956). 108 min. J. Arthur Rank. D: Lewis Gilbert.
Bader: Kenneth More
Supporting cast: Alexander Knox, Muriel Pavlow, Sydney Tafler

Bailey, F. Lee, 1933–
See **Sheppard, Sam.**

Bailey, James Anthony, 1847–1906
See **Barnum, P.T.** (Phineas Taylor).

Baker, Chesney "Chet", 1929–1988. (African American jazz trumpeter whose career was destroyed by drug addiction)

25a *Let's Get Lost* (1989). 119 min. Zeitgeist Films. D: Bruce Weber.
Documentary.

Baker, John, 1945–1970. (American runner and coach)

26. *A Shining Season* (1979). 100 min. Columbia Pictures Television. D: Stuart Margolin.
Baker: Timothy Bottoms
Supporting cast: Ed Begley, Jr., Constance Forslund, Allyn Ann McLerie, Rip Torn

Baker, Josephine, 1906–1975. (African-American dancer who became the toast of Paris in the 1920's and 1930's)

26a *The Josephine Baker Story* (1991). 130 min. HBO Pictures. D: Brian Gibson.
Baker: Lynn Whitfield
Supporting cast: Ruben Blades, David Dukes, Louis Gossett, Jr., Craig T. Nelson

Baker, Nicole, 1957?–
See **Gilmore, Gary.**

Balanchine, George, 1904–1983. (Russian-American choreographer, ballet master, and director of the New York City Ballet, 1948–1983)

26b *Dancing For Mr. B: Six Balanchine Ballerinas* (1989). 86 min. Seahorse Film. D: Anne Belle, Deborah Dickson.
Documentary.

Balin, Ina, 1957– (American actress who participated in the airlift of Vietnamese orphans from Saigon)

27. *The Children of An Lac* (1980). 100 min. Charles Fries Prod. D: John Llewellyn Moxey.
Balin: Ina Balin

Betty Tisdale: Shirley Jones
Supporting cast: Alan Fudge, Lee Paul, Ben Piazza, Beulah Quo

Ball, Ernest R., 1878–1927. (American vaudeville actor and composer of popular songs)

28. *Irish Eyes Are Smiling* (1944). 90 min. 20th Century-Fox. D: Gregory Ratoff.
Ball: Dick Haymes
Supporting cast: June Haver, Anthony Quinn, Monty Woolley

Balter, Marie, 1930– (American patient who survived twenty years in a mental institution to become a mental health administrator)

28a *Nobody's Child* (1986). 100 min. Gaylord Production Co. D: Lee Grant.
Balter: Marlo Thomas
Supporting cast: Blanche Baker, Kathy Baker, Ray Baker, Madeleine Sherwood

Barbie, Klaus, 1913– (French Nazi war criminal known as "The Butcher of Lyon")

28b *Hotel Terminus: The Life And Times Of Klaus Barbie* (1987). 267 min. Memory Pictures. D: Marcel Ophuls.
Documentary.

Barker, Arizona "Ma," 1880–1935. (American gangster of the 1930's)

29. *Bloody Mama* (1970). 90 min. American International Pictures. D: Roger Corman.
Barker: Shelley Winters
Supporting cast: Pat Hingle, Robert De Niro, Don Stroud

Barnes, Florence "Pancho", 1901–1975. (Pioneer American avia-
  trix)

29a *Pancho Barnes* (1988). 150 min. Orion Television. D: Richard
   T. Heffron.
   Barnes: Valerie Bertinelli
   Supporting cast: Cynthia Harris, Geoffrey Lewis, James
     Stephens, Ted Wass

Barnum, P.T. (Phineas Taylor), 1810–1891. (American showman and founder of the Barnum and Bailey Circus)

30. *Barnum* (1986). 100 min. Robert Halmi Prod. D: Lee Philips.
    Barnum (as a young man): John Roney
    Barnum: Burt Lancaster
    Jenny Lind: Hanna Schygulla
    Supporting cast: Kristen Bishop, Michael Higgins, Laura
      Press, Rob Roy

31. *The Mighty Barnum* (1934). 87 min. United Artists. D: Walter
    Lang.
    Barnum: Wallace Beery
    James Anthony Bailey: Adolphe Menjou
    Supporting cast: Janet Beecher, Virginia Bruce, Rochelle
      Hudson

    SEE ALSO: **Lind, Jenny.**

Barrett, Elizabeth, 1806–1861. (British poet and wife of poet
  Robert Browning)

32. *The Barretts of Wimpole Street* (1934). 110 min. MGM. D:
    Sidney Franklin.
    Barrett: Norma Shearer
    Robert Browning: Fredric March
    Supporting cast: Katherine Alexander, Ralph Forbes,
      Charles Laughton, Maureen O'Sullivan

33. *The Barretts Of Wimpole Street* (1956). 105 min. MGM. D:
    Sidney Franklin.
    Barrett: Jennifer Jones

Robert Browning: Bill Travers
Supporting cast: John Gielgud, Virginia McKenna

Barrow, Clyde, 1909–1934
See **Parker, Bonnie.**

Barrows, Sydney Biddle, 1952–   (American debutante who became the proprietor of an escort service)

33a *Mayflower Madam* (1987). 93 min. Quintex. D: Lou Antonio.
Barrows: Candice Bergen
Supporting cast: Jim Antonio, Caitlin Clarke, Chita Rivera, Chris Sarandon

Barry, Jan, 1941– (American rock singer who was famous for the surf sound of the 1960's)

34. *Deadman's Curve* (1978). 100 min. EMI Television. D: Richard Compton.
Barry: Richard Hatch
Dean Torrance: Bruce Davison
Supporting cast: Pamela Bellwood, Dick Clark, Wolfman Jack, Susan Sullivan

Barrymore, Diana, 1921–1960. (American actress and daughter of actor John Barrymore)

35. *Too Much Too Soon* (1958). 121 min. Warner Bros. D: Art Napoleon.
Barrymore: Dorothy Malone
John Barrymore: Errol Flynn
Supporting cast: Ray Danton, Neva Patterson, Efrem Zimbalist, Jr.

Barrymore, John, 1882–1942
See **Barrymore, Diana; Flynn, Errol.**

Barthel, Joan, 1932–
  See **Reilly, Peter.**

Bartholdi, Frederic Auguste, 1834–1904. (French sculptor who designed the Statue of Liberty)

35a *Liberty* (1986). 156 min. Robert Greenwald Productions. D: Richard Sarafian.
  Bartholdi: Frank Langella
  Supporting cast: Claire Bloom, Carrie Fisher, George Kennedy, Chris Sarandon

Bass, Sam, 1851–1878
  See **Canary, Martha Jane ("Calamity Jane").**

Bast, William, 1931–
  See **Dean, James.**

Bates, Charles, 1920–
  See **Hearst, Patty.**

Bathsheba, c. 10th century B.C.
  See **David,** King of Israel.

Baynes, Nora, 1880–1928. (American vaudeville singer)

36. *Shine On Harvest Moon* (1944). 112 min. Warner Bros. D: David Butler.
  Baynes: Ann Sheridan
  Jack Norworth: Dennis Morgan
  Supporting cast: Jack Carson, Irene Manning, S.Z. Sakall

Bazna, Elyesa, 1904–1970. (World War II spy)

37. *Five Fingers* (1952). 108 min. 20th Century-Fox. D: Joseph L. Mankiewicz.

Bazna/Cicero: James Mason
Supporting cast: Danielle Darrieux, Walter Hampden, Michael Rennie

Beach Boys. (American rock group known for California "surfin' " sound)

37a *The Beach Boys: An American Band* (1985). 103 min. Sharp Features. D: Malcolm Leo.
Documentary.

Beach, Sylvia, 1887–1962
See **Joyce, James.**

Beale, Edie, 1916–
See **Beale, Edith Bouvier.**

Beale, Edith Bouvier, 1896–1977. (Cousin of Jacqueline Bouvier Kennedy)

38. *Grey Gardens* (1976). 95 min. N/A. D: David Maysles, Albert Maysles.
Documentary.

Bean, Roy, 1825–1903. (American self-appointed justice of the peace in Texas during the late 1800's)

39. *The Life and Times of Judge Roy Bean* (1972). 120 min. Warner Bros. D: John Huston.
Bean: Paul Newman
Supporting cast: Jacqueline Bisset, Ava Gardner, Victoria Principal

40. *The Westerner* (1940). 100 min. United Artists. D: William Wyler.
Bean: Walter Brennan
Supporting cast: Gary Cooper, Doris Davenport, Fred Stone, Forrest Tucker

Beatles, The. (British rock group best known as the leaders of the British music invasion)

41. *Beatlemania* (1981). 86 min. This Is the Week That Beatle-mania Was Co., Inc. D: Joseph Manduke.
George Harrison: David Leon
John Lennon: Mitch Weissman
Paul McCartney: Ralph Castelli
Ringo Starr: Tom Teeley
This was a four-person show.

42. *The Birth of the Beatles* (1979). 100 min. Dick Clark Prod. D: Richard Marquand.
George Harrison: John Altman
John Lennon: Stephen McKenna
Paul McCartney: Rod Culbertson
Ringo Starr: Ray Ashcroft
Pete Best: Ryan Michael
Brian Epstein: Brian Jameson
Supporting cast: Nigel Havers, Wendy Morgan, Roy Storm, David Wilkinson

43. *The Compleat Beatles* (1982). 120 min. Teleculture, Inc. D: Patrick Montgomery.
Documentary

44. *Let It Be* (1970). 80 min. United Artists. D: Michael Lindsay-Hogg
Documentary

SEE ALSO: **Lennon, John.**

Beck, Martha. (American murderer who preyed on lonely women)

44a *The Honeymoon Killers* (1970). 115 min. Cinerama. D: Leonard Kastle.
Beck: Shirley Stoler
Ray Fernandez: Tony LoBianco
Supporting cast: Barbara Cason, Marilyn Chris, Mary Jane Higby, Kip McArdle

Becket, Thomas, 1118–1170. (Archbishop of Canterbury; murdered by order of King Henry II)

45. *Becket* (1964). 148 min. Paramount Pictures. D: Peter Glenville.
Becket: Richard Burton
Henry II: Peter O'Toole
Supporting cast: John Gielgud, Martita Hunt, Donald Wolfit

Beckett, Samuel, 1906–1989. (Irish Nobel Prize-winning author and playwright)

45a *Samuel Beckett: Silence To Silence* (1987). 80 min. Radio Telefis Eireann. D: Sean O'Mordha.
Documentary.

Beethoven, Johanna
See **Beethoven, Ludwig van.**

Beethoven, Karl, 1806-?
See **Beethoven, Ludwig van.**

Beethoven, Ludwig van, 1770–1827. (German composer famous for his development of the symphony)

45b *Beethoven's Great Love* (1936). 116 min. Generales Productions. D: Abel Gance.
Beethoven: Harry Baur
Supporting cast: Annie Ducaux, Jany Holt, Yoland Lafon, Lucien Rozemberg

45c *Beethoven's Nephew* (1985). 103 min. New World Pictures. D: Paul Morrissey.
Beethoven: Wolfgang Reichmann
Johanna van Beethoven: Jane Birkin
Karl van Beethoven: Dietmar Prinz
Supporting cast: Nathalie Baye, Ulrich Beer, Mathieu Carriere, Erna Korhel

46. *The Magnificent Rebel* (1962). 95 min. Walt Disney Prod. D:
Georg Tressler.
Beethoven: Karl Boehm
Supporting cast: Ivan Desny, Ernst Nadhering, Gabriele
Porks

SEE ALSO: **Schubert, Franz.**

Behan, Brendan, 1923–1964. (Irish author who is best known for
his works dramatizing his prison experiences)

46a *Hungry Feeling: The Life And Death Of Brendan Behan* (1985). 85
min. First Run Features. D: Allan Miller.
Documentary.

Beiderbecke, Leon Bismarck "Bix", 1903–1931. (American cor-
netist best known for his distinctive style of rhythmic
lyricism)

47. *Young Man With a Horn* (1950). 112 min. Warner Bros. D:
Michael Curtiz.
Beiderbecke: Kirk Douglas
Supporting cast: Lauren Bacall, Hoagy Carmichael, Doris
Day, Juano Hernandez

Belasco, David, 1854–1931
See **Carter, Leslie.**

Bell, Alexander Graham, 1847–1922. (American physicist who
invented the telephone)

48. *The Story of Alexander Graham Bell* (1939). 97 min. 20th
Century-Fox. D: Irving Cummings.
Bell: Don Ameche
Supporting cast: Charles Coburn, Henry Fonda, Loretta
Young

Belushi, John, 1949–1982. (American comic who rose to prominence on the televison program *Saturday Night Live*)

48a *Wired* (1989). 108 min. Taurus Entertainment. D: Larry Pearce.
Belushi: Michael Chiklis
Dan Aykroyd: Gary Groomes
Supporting cast: Patti D'Arbanville, Lucinda Jenney, Ray Sharkey, J.T. Walsh

Bembenek, Lawrencia "Bambi", 1959– (Former American police officer convicted of murder who escaped to Canada)

48b *Used Innocence* (1988). 95 min. First Run Features. D: James Benning.
Documentary.

Benton, Thomas Hart, 1782–1858
See **Fremont, John Charles.**

Berkowitz, David "Son of Sam," 1953–
See **Zigo, Ed.**

Bernadette, Saint, 1844–1879. (French visionary of Lourdes)

49. *Bernadette of Lourdes* (1961). 95 min. Janus Pictures. D: Robert Darene.
Bernadette: Daniele Ajoret
Supporting cast: Nadine Alari, Robert Arnoux, Blanchette Brunoy

50. *The Song Of Bernadette* (1943). 156 min. 20th Century-Fox. D: Henry King.
Bernadette: Jennifer Jones
Supporting cast: Charles Bickford, William Eythe, Vincent Price

Bernhardt, Sarah, 1844–1923. (French stage actress considered the greatest dramatic actress of the late 1800's)

51. *The Incredible Sarah* (1976). 106 min. Reader's Digest. D: Richard Fleischer.
Bernhardt: Glenda Jackson
Supporting cast: Daniel Massey, Yvonne Mitchell, Douglas Wilmer

Bernstein, Carl, 1944–
See **Ephron, Nora; Woodward, Bob.**

Berrigan, Daniel, 1921– (American priest and Vietnam War protestor who was arrested for destroying draft records)

51a *The Trial of the Catonsville Nine* (1972). 85 min. Melville Productions. D: Gordon Davidson.
Berrigan: Ed Flanders
Supporting cast: Gwen Arner, Burton Heyman, Richard Jordan, Nancy Malone

Berry, Chuck, 1926– (African-American rock musician)

51b *Chuck Berry Hail! Hail! Rock'N'Roll* (1987). 118 min. Universal Pictures. D: Taylor Hackford.
Documentary.

Best, Pete, 1941–
See **Beatles, The.**

Bethune, Norman, 1890–1939. (Canadian doctor who accompanied Mao Tse-tung on his "Great March")

51c *Bethune* (1977). 88 min. Trans World Entertainment. D: Eric Till.
Bethune: Donald Sutherland
Supporting cast: David Gardner, James Hong, Kate Nelligan

51d *Bethune, The Making Of A Hero* (1990). 115 min. Trans World Entertainment. D: Phillip Borsos.
Bethune: Donald Sutherland
Supporting cast: Anouk Aimee, Harrison Liu, Helen Mirren, Helen Shaver

Biddle, Ed, d.1902
See **Soffel, Kate.**

Big Bopper, 1932?-1959
See **Valens, Richie.**

Biko, Ntsiki
See **Biko, Steve.**

Biko, Steve, 1946–1977. (South African black anti-apartheid activist, founder and leader of the Black Consciousness Movement)

51e *Cry Freedom* (1987). 155 min. Universal Pictures. D: Richard Attenborough.
Biko: Denzel Washington
Ntsiki Biko: Juanita Waterman
Donald Woods: Kevin Kline
Wendy Woods: Penelope Wilton
Supporting cast: Kate Hardie, John Matshikiza, Josette Simon, Wabei Siyolwe

Billy the Kid, 1859–1881
See **Bonney, William** ("Billy the Kid").

Binder, Alvin
See **Williams, Wayne Bertram.**

Bingham, George Charles, 3rd Earl of Lucan, 1800–1888
See **Cardigan, James Thomas Brudenell.**

Blackbeard the Pirate, 1680–1718
    See **Teach, Edward** ("Blackbeard").

Blades, Ruben, 1948– (Panamanian musician known as the "King of Latin Salsa")

51f *The Return Of Ruben Blades* (1985). 90 min. Film Four International. D: Robert Mugge.
    Documentary.

Bleier, Robert Patrick "Rocky," 1946– (American football player and member of the Pittsburgh Steelers)

52. *Fighting Back* (1980). 100 min. MTM Enterprises. D: Robert Lieberman.
    Bleier: Robert Urich
    Supporting cast: Bonnie Bedelia, Art Carney, Howard Cosell, Richard Herd

Bligh, William, 1754–1817. (British naval officer who was captain of H.M.S. *Bounty*)

53. *The Bounty* (1984). 130 min. Orion Pictures. D: Roger Donaldson.
    Bligh: Anthony Hopkins
    Fletcher Christian: Mel Gibson
    Supporting cast: Edward Fox, Bernard Hill, Laurence Olivier

54. *Mutiny on the Bounty* (1935). 132 min. MGM. D: Frank Lloyd.
    Bligh: Charles Laughton
    Fletcher Christian: Clark Gable
    Supporting cast: Herbert Mundin, Eddie Quillan, Franchot Tone

55. *Mutiny on the Bounty* (1962). 179 min. MGM. D: Lewis Milestone.
    Bligh: Trevor Howard
    Fletcher Christian: Marlon Brando
    Supporting cast: Hugh Griffith, Richard Harris, Richard Haydn

Blixen, Bror, 1886–1946
  See **Blixen, Karen.**

Blixen, Karen, 1885–1962. (Danish novelist and storyteller)

56. *Out Of Africa* (1985). 150 min. Mirage Productions. D:
    Sydney Pollack.
    Blixen: Meryl Streep
    Bror Blixen Finecke: Klaus Maria Brandauer
    Denys Finch Hatton: Robert Redford
    Supporting cast: Mallick Bowens, Michael Gough, Rachel
      Kempson, Joseph Thiaka

Blunt, Anthony, 1907–1983. (British spy and art historian)

57. *Blunt* (1986). 120 min. N/A. D: John Glenister
    Blunt: Ian Richardson
    Guy Burgess: Anthony Hopkins
    Donald Maclean: Michael McStay
    Supporting cast: Geoffrey Chater, Rosie Kerslake, Albert
      Welling, Michael Williams

Bly, Nellie, 1867–1922. (American journalist)

58. *The Adventures of Nellie Bly* (1981). 100 min. Taft International
    Pictures. D: Henning Schellerup.
    Bly: Linda Purl
    Supporting cast: Gene Barry, Raymond Buktenica, J.D.
    Cannon, John Randolph

Boaz, c. 11th century B.C.
  See **Ruth.**

Bogart, Humphrey, 1899–1957. (American actor famous for
    tough-guy roles)

59. *Bogie* (1980). 100 min. Charles Fries Prod. D: Vincent Sher-
    man.

Bogart: Kevin O'Connor
Lauren Bacall: Kathryn Harrold
Mayo Methot: Ann Wedgeworth
Supporting cast: Patricia Barry, Richard Dysart, Donald May, Alfred Ryder

Boleyn, Anne, Queen of England, 1507–1536. (Second wife of Henry VIII and mother of Elizabeth I)

60. *Anne of the Thousand Days* (1969). 145 min. Universal Pictures. D: Charles Jarrott.
Boleyn: Genevieve Bujold
Henry VIII: Richard Burton
Supporting cast: John Colicos, Irene Papas, Anthony Quayle

SEE ALSO: **Henry VIII,** King of England.

Bolton, John, d. 1775
See **Arnold, Benedict.**

Bonaparte, Napoleon, 1769–1821
See **Napoleon Bonaparte,** Emperor of France.

Bonaparte, Paolina, 1780–1825. (Napoleon Bonaparte's sister and Duchess of Guastalla)

61. *Imperial Venus* (1962). 120 min. Rizzoli Film. D: Jean Delannoy.
Bonaparte: Gina Lollobrigida
Napoleon: Raymond Pellegrin
Supporting cast: Stephen Boyd, Gabriele Ferzetti, Massimo Girotti, Micheline Presle

Bonner, Elena, 1923–
See **Sakharov, Andrei.**

Bonney, Anne, 1700–1720. (Eighteenth-century British pirate captain)

62. *Anne of the Indies* (1951). 87 min. 20th Century-Fox. D: Jacques Tourneur.
Bonney: Jean Peters
Edward Teach: Thomas Gomez
Supporting cast: Louis Jourdan, Herbert Marshall, Debra Paget

Bonney, William "Billy the Kid," 1859–1881. (American outlaw and Wild West legend). Billy the Kid is a prime example of the heroic myth in biography. On film, Billy has been portrayed from being a misunderstood youth protecting his mother's honor, to being a murderous psychopath. What kind of person Billy was, or was not, will probably remain a mystery, but Hollywood will continue to make films on his life, portraying him as angel and devil. The films listed below are examples of cinematic portrayals of Billy the Kid.

63. *Billy the Kid* (1930). 90 min. MGM. D: King Vidor.
Bonney: John Mack Brown
Supporting cast: Roscoe Ates, Wallace Beery, Karl Dane, Kay Johnson

64. *Billy the Kid* (1941). 95 min. MGM. D: David Miller.
Bonney: Robert Taylor
Supporting cast: Brian Donlevy, Mary Howard, Ian Hunter

65. *Billy the Kid Returns* (1938). 54 min. Republic Pictures. D: Joseph Kane.
Bonney: Roy Rogers
Supporting cast: Smiley Burnette, Mary Hart, Morgan Wallace

66. *Dirty Little Billy* (1972). 100 min. Columbia Pictures. D: Stan Dragoti.
Bonney: Michael J. Pollard
Supporting cast: Charles Aidman, Richard Evans, Lee Purcell

66a *Gore Vidal's Billy The Kid* (1989). 96 min. Turner Network
Television, Inc. D: William Graham.
Bonney: Val Kilmer
Supporting cast: Rene Auberjonois, Wilford Brimley, Julie
Carmen, Duncan Regehr

67. *The Kid From Texas* (1950). 78 min. Universal-International.
D: Kurt Newman.
Bonney: Audie Murphy
Pat Garrett: Frank Wilcox
Supporting cast: Albert Dekker, Gale Storm, Shepperd
Strudwick

68. *The Law Vs. Billy the Kid* (1954). 73 min. Columbia Pictures.
D: William Castle.
Bonney: Scott Brady
Supporting cast: Paul Cavanagh, Alan Hale, Jr., Betta St.
John

69. *The Left-Handed Gun* (1958). 102 min. Warner Bros. D: Arthur
Penn.
Bonney: Paul Newman
Supporting cast: John Dehner, Hurd Hatfield, Lita Milan

70. *The Outlaw* (1943). 103 min. RKO. D: Howard Hughes.
Bonney: Jack Buetel
John H. Holliday: Walter Huston
Supporting cast: Thomas Mitchell, Jane Russell, Joe Sawyer

71. *The Parson and the Outlaw* (1957). 71 min. Columbia Pictures.
D: Oliver Drake.
Bonney: Anthony Dexter
Supporting cast: Buddy Rogers, Sonny Tufts, Marie Windsor

72. *Pat Garrett and Billy the Kid* (1973). 106 min. MGM. D: Sam
Peckinpah.
Bonney: Kris Kristofferson
Pat Garrett: James Coburn
Supporting cast: Richard Jaeckel, Katy Jurado, Jason Ro-
bards, Jr.

72a *Young Guns* (1988). 97 min. Twentieth Century Fox Film. D:
Christopher Cain.

Bonney: Emilio Estevez
Pat Garrett: Patrick Wayne
Supporting cast: Dermot Mulroney, Lou Diamond Philips, Charlie Sheen, Kiefer Sutherland

SEE ALSO: **Chisum, John Simpson.**

Boone, Daniel, 1735–1820. (American frontiersman and founder of Boonesborough, Kentucky)

73. *Daniel Boone* (1936). 80 min. RKO. D: David Howard.
Boone: George O'Brien
Supporting cast: Heather Angel, Ralph Forbes, Clarence Muse, George Regas

74. *Daniel Boone, Trail Blazer* (1956). 76 min. Republic Pictures. D: Albert C. Gannaway, Ismael Rodriquez.
Boone: Bruce Bennett
Supporting cast: Lon Chaney, Kem Dibbs, Faron Young

75. *Young Daniel Boone* (1950). 71 min. Monogram Prod. D: Reginald LeBorg.
Boone: David Bruce
Supporting cast: Don Beddoe, Kristine Miller, Damian O'Flynn, Mary Treen

Booth, Edwin, 1833–1893. (American stage actor and brother of John Wilkes Booth)

76. *Prince of Players* (1955). 102 min. 20th Century-Fox. D: Philip Dunne.
Booth: Richard Burton
John Wilkes Booth: John Derek
Supporting cast: Charles Bickford, Raymond Massey, Maggie McNamara

Booth, John Wilkes, 1839–1865
See **Booth, Edwin; Mudd, Samuel.**

Borden, Lizzie, 1860–1927. (American murder suspect acquitted of the ax slaying of her father and stepmother)

77. *The Legend of Lizzie Borden* (1975). 100 min. Paramount Pictures. D: Paul Wendkos.
Borden: Elizabeth Montgomery
Supporting cast: Fionnula Flanagan, Ed Flanders, Katherine Helmond

Borgia, Cesare, 1475–1507. (Italian prince and politician, son of Pope Alexander VI)

78. *Bride of Vengeance* (1949). 91 min. Paramount Pictures. D: Mitchell Leisen.
Borgia: Macdonald Carey
Lucretia Borgia: Paulette Goddard
Supporting cast: Raymond Burr, Albert Dekker, Rose Hobart, John Lund

79. *Prince of Foxes* (1949). 111 min. 20th Century-Fox. D: Henry King.
Borgia: Orson Welles
Supporting cast: Marina Berti, Wanda Hendrix, Tyrone Power

Borgia, Lucretia, 1480–1519. (Italian patron of the arts and sister of Cesare Borgia)

80. *Lucretia Borgia* (1952). 105 min. United Artists. D: Christian Jaque.
Borgia: Martine Carol
Supporting cast: Pedro Armendariz, Massimo Serato, Ventine Tessier

SEE ALSO: **Borgia, Cesare.**

Bowie, Jim, c. 1790–1836. (American frontiersman and inventor of the Bowie knife)

81. *The Alamo* (1960). 192 min. United Artists. D: John Wayne.
    Bowie: Richard Widmark
    Davy Crockett: John Wayne
    Sam Houston: Richard Boone
    William Travis: Laurence Harvey
    Supporting cast: Carlos Arruza, Frankie Avalon, Pat Wayne

81a *The Alamo: Thirteen Days to Glory* (1987). 156 min. Fries
    Entertainment Inc. D: Burt Kennedy.
    Bowie: James Arness
    Davy Crockett: Brian Keith
    Sam Houston: Lorne Greene
    Antonio Santa Anna: Raul Julia
    William Travis: Alec Baldwin
    Supporting cast: Gene Evans, David Ogden Stiers, Isela
        Vega, Ethan Wayne

82. *Comanche Territory* (1950). 76 min. Universal-International.
    D: George Sherman.
    Bowie: Macdonald Carey
    Supporting cast: Charles Drake, Will Geer, Maureen O'Hara

83. *The Iron Mistress* (1952). 110 min. Warner Bros. D: Gordon
    Douglas.
    Bowie: Alan Ladd
    Supporting cast: Joseph Calleia, Phyllis Kirk, Virginia Mayo

    SEE ALSO: **Houston, Sam.**

Boyce, Christopher John, 1953– (American technician who sold
    secret high technology information to the Russians)

83a *The Falcon and the Snowman* (1985). 131 min. Orion Pictures.
    D: John Schlesinger.
    Boyce: Timothy Hutton
    Andrew Daulton Lee: Sean Penn
    Supporting cast: Richard Dysart, Pat Hingle, David Suchet,
        Joyce Van Patten

Boyle, Richard, 1941?– (American photojournalist)

84. *Salvador* (1986). 123 min. Cinema 85. D: Oliver Stone.
Boyle: James Woods
Supporting cast: James Belushi, Elpedia Carrillo, Michael Murphy, John Savage

Boyle, William Anthony "Tony," 1904–1985
See **Yablonski, Joseph A. ("Jock").**

Bradlee, Ben, 1921–
See **Woodward, Bob.**

Bradley, Omar, 1893–1981
See **Patton, George.**

Brady, James "Diamond Jim," 1856–1917. (American financier infamous for his appetite for food and diamonds)

85. *Diamond Jim* (1935). 91 min. Universal-International. D: A. Edward Sutherland.
Brady: Edward Arnold
Lillian Russell: Binnie Barnes
Supporting cast: Jean Arthur, Eric Blore, Cesar Romero

SEE ALSO: **Russell, Lillian.**

Brady, James S. (American press secretary who was shot during Hinckley's attempted assassination of President Reagan)

85a *Without Warning: The James Brady Story* (1991). 90 min. HBO Pictures. D: Michael Toshiyuki Uno.
Brady: Beau Bridges
Sarah Brady: Joan Allen
Ronald Reagan: Bryan Clark
Supporting cast: Steven Flynn, David Strathairn

Brady, Sarah, 1942?–
    See **Brady, James S.**

Brahms, Johannes, 1833–1897
    See **Schumann, Clara.**

Braun, Eva, 1910–1945
    See **Hitler, Adolf.**

Brice, Fanny, 1891–1951. (American singer-comedienne and Ziegfeld star)

86. *Funny Girl* (1968). 153 min. Columbia Pictures. D: William Wyler.
    Brice: Barbra Streisand
    Flo Ziegfeld: Walter Pidgeon
    Supporting cast: Anne Francis, Kay Medford, Omar Sharif

87. *Funny Lady* (1975). 140 min. Columbia Pictures. D: Herbert Ross.
    Brice: Barbra Streisand
    Billy Rose: James Caan
    Supporting cast: Roddy McDowall, Omar Sharif, Ben Vereen

88. *Rose of Washington Square* (1939). 86 min. 20th Century-Fox. D: Gregory Ratoff.
    Brice: Alice Faye
    Supporting cast: William Frawley, Al Jolson, Moroni Olsen, Tyrone Power

Brico, Antonia, 1902–1989. (Dutch-American pianist who became the first woman symphonic conductor)

89. *Antonia: A Portrait of the Woman* (1974). 58 min. Phoenix Films. D: Judy Collins, Jill Godmilow.
    Documentary

Bridger, Jim, 1804–1881. (American pioneer and scout, the first white man to see the Great Salt Lake)

90. *Bridger* (1976). 100 min. Universal Television. D: David Lowell Rich.
Bridger: James Wainwright
Kit Carson: Ben Murphy
Supporting cast: Dirk Blocker, Sally Field, William Windom

SEE ALSO: **Fremont, John Charles.**

Brimmer, Gabriela, 1947– (Mexican cerebral palsy victim who overcame near-total paralysis to become a college graduate and acclaimed author)

90a *Gaby—A True Story* (1987). 114 min. Tri-Star Pictures. D: Luis Mandoki.
Brimmer: Rachel Levin
Brimmer (age 3): Paulina Gomez
Michel Brimmer: Robert Loggia
Sari Brimmer: Liv Ullmann
Supporting cast: Norma Aleandro, Robert Beltran, Tony Goldwyn, Lawrence Monoson

Brimmer, Michel
See **Brimmer, Gabriela.**

Brimmer, Sari
See **Brimmer, Gabriela.**

Bronte, Anne, 1820–1849
See **Bronte, Charlotte.**

Bronte, Bramwell, 1817–1848
See **Bronte, Charlotte.**

Bronte, Charlotte, 1816–1855. (British gothic novelist best known for her novel *Wuthering Heights*)

91. *Bronte* (1983). 88 min. N/A. D: Delbert Mann.
   Bronte: Julie Harris
   This was a one-woman show.

92. *The Bronte Sisters* (1979). 115 min. Gaumont. D: Andre Techine.
   Bronte: Marie-France Pisier
   Anne Bronte: Isabelle Huppert
   Bramwell Bronte: Pascal Gregory
   Emily Bronte: Isabelle Adjani
   Supporting cast: Roland Bertin, Patrick Magee, Helen Surgere

93. *Devotion* (1946). 107 min. Warner Bros. D: Curtis Bernhardt.
   Bronte: Ida Lupino
   Anne Bronte: Nancy Coleman
   Bramwell Bronte: Arthur Kennedy
   Emily Bronte: Olivia de Havilland
   Supporting cast: Victor Francen, Paul Henreid, Dame May Whitty

Bronte, Emily, 1818–1848
See **Bronte, Charlotte.**

Brooks, Herb, 1937– (American coach of the 1980 Olympic gold medal hockey team)

94. *Miracle on Ice* (1981). 150 min. Moonlight Prod. D: Steven Hillard Stern.
   Brooks: Karl Malden
   Mike Eruzione: Andrew Stevens
   Supporting cast: Steve Guttenberg, Jerry Houser, Robert F. Lyons, Allan Miller

Broughton, Diana, 1913–
See **Erroll, Josslyn Hay.**

Broughton, Henry John Delves "Jock," 1884–1942
    See **Erroll, Josslyn Hay.**

Brown, A. Roy, 1894?–1944
    See **Richthofen, Manfred von.**

Brown, Christy, 1932–1981. (Irish artist, writer and cerebral palsy victim)

94a *My Left Foot* (1989). 103 min. Miramax Films. D: Jim Sheridan.
    Brown: Daniel Day-Lewis
    Brown (as a boy): Hugh O'Conor
    Supporting cast: Cyril Cusack, Brenda Fricker, Ray McAnally, Fiona Shaw

Brown, Lew, 1893–1958
    See **DeSylva, Buddy.**

Browne, Coral, 1913–
    See **Burgess, Guy.**

Browning, Elizabeth Barrett, 1806–1861
    See **Barrett, Elizabeth.**

Browning, Robert, 1812–1889
    See **Barrett, Elizabeth.**

Bruce, Honey Harlowe
    See **Bruce, Lenny.**

Bruce, Lenny, 1925–1966. (American comic prominent on the 1960's nightclub circuit)

95. *Lenny* (1974). 112 min. United Artists. D: Bob Fosse.
    Bruce: Dustin Hoffman
    Honey Harlowe: Valerie Perrine
    Supporting cast: Stanley Beck, Jan Miner, Gary Morton

Brummel, George Bryan "Beau," 1778–1840. (British dandy and
   arbiter of dress in Regency England)

96. *Beau Brummel* (1954). 111 min. MGM. D: Curtis Bernhardt.
    Brummel: Stewart Granger
    George III: Robert Morley
    George, Prince of Wales: Peter Ustinov
    Supporting cast: James Donald, Rosemary Harris, Paul
       Rogers, Elizabeth Taylor

Brutus, c. 85–42 B.C.
   See **Caesar, Julius,** Emperor of Rome.

Bryan, William Jennings, 1860–1925
   See **Darrow, Clarence.**

Bryant, Louise, 1890–1936
   See **Reed, John.**

Bryant, Paul "Bear," 1913–1983. (American collegiate football
   coach at the University of Alabama)

97. *The Bear* (1984). 110 min. Embassy Pictures. D: Richard
    Sarafian.
    Bryant: Gary Busey
    Supporting cast: Cary Guffey, Cynthia Leake, Harry Dean
       Stanton, Carmen Thomas

Brzeska, Sophie, 1871?–1922?
   See **Gaudier-Brzeska, Henri.**

Buchalter, Louis, 1897–1944
See **Lepke, Louis.**

Bugliosi, Vincent, 1934–
See **Manson, Charles.**

Bundy, Theodore Robert "Ted," 1947–1989. (American murderer believed by the F.B.I. to be the most prolific serial killer in the United States)

97a *The Deliberate Stranger* (1986). 200 min. Lorimar Television Inc. D: Marvin J. Chomsky.
Bundy: Mark Harmon
Supporting cast: Frederic Forrest, George Grizzard, Ben Masters, Glynnis O'Connor

Buonarroti, Michelangelo, 1475–1564. (Italian sculptor, painter, architect and poet of the High Renaissance)

98. *The Agony and the Ecstasy* (1965). 140 min. 20th Century-Fox. D: Carol Reed.
Buonarroti: Charlton Heston
Julius II: Rex Harrison
Supporting cast: Harry Andrews, Adolfo Celi, Diane Cilento, Alberto Lupo

Burgess, Guy, 1911–1963. (British diplomat and spy)

99. *Another Country* (1984). 90 min. Orion Pictures. D: Marek Kanievska.
Burgess/Bennett: Rupert Everett
Supporting cast: Robert Addie, Colin Firth, Michael Jenn, Anna Massey

99a *An Englishman Abroad* (1985). 63 min. BBC Enterprises Ltd. D: John Schlesinger.
Burgess: Alan Bates
Coral Browne: Coral Browne
This was a two-person show.

SEE ALSO: **Blunt, Anthony.**

Burke, Billie, 1885–1970
See **Ziegfeld, Florenz.**

Burke, Robert O'Hara, 1821–1861. (Irish explorer who led the first expedition to cross the Australian continent from south to north)

99b *Burke & Wills* (1987). 140 min. Hoyts Edgley. D: Graeme Clifford.
Burke: Jack Thompson
William John Wills: Nigel Havers
Supporting cast: Ralph Cotterill, Matthew Farger, Chris Haywood, Greta Scacchi

Burns, Robert Elliot, 1890–1955. (American drifter who was wrongly convicted of robbery and sentenced to a Georgia chain gang)

99c *The Man Who Broke 1,000 Chains* (1987). 114 min. Lorimar Televison Inc. D: Daniel Mann.
Burns: Val Kilmer
Supporting cast: Sonia Braga, Elisha Cook, Charles Durning, Kyra Sedgewick

Burr, Aaron, 1756–1836
See **Madison, Dolley.**

Burroughs, William S., 1914– (American author and exemplar of the Beat Generation)

100. *Burroughs* (1984). 86 min. Citifilmworks, Inc. D: Howard Brookner.
Documentary

Burton, Richard Francis, 1821–1890. (British explorer who led expedition which discovered the source of the Nile River)

100a *Mountains Of The Moon* (1990). 135 min. Tri-Star Pictures. D: Bob Rafelson.
Burton: Patrick Bergin
John Hanning Speke: Iain Glen
Supporting cast: Richard E. Grant, Fiona Shaw, John Savident, James Villiers

Butler, James, 1837–1876
See **Hickok, James Butler** ("Wild Bill").

Butsicaris, Jimmy. (American restaurant owner and foster parent)

101. *Jimmy B and Andre* (1980). 105 min. Georgian Bay Prod. D: Guy Green.
Butsicaris: Alex Karras
Andre Reynolds: Curtis Yates
Supporting cast: Joby Baker, Eddie Barth, Susan Clark, Madge Sinclair

Butterfield, Tom, 1940–1982. (American social welfare and youth leader)

102. *The Children Nobody Wanted* (1981) 100 min. Warner Bros. Television. D: Richard Michaels
Butterfield: Frederic Lehne
Supporting cast: Barbara Barrie, Matt Clark, Michelle Pfeiffer, Noble Willingham

Byrd, Richard, 1888–1957. (American rear admiral and polar explorer)

103. *The Secret Land* (1948). 71 min. Orville O. Dull. D: N/A. Documentary

Byron, George, 1788–1824. (British poet and satirist of the 19th century)

104. *Bad Lord Byron* (1951). 85 min. J. Arthur Rank. D: David Macdonald.
    Byron: Dennis Price
    Caroline Lamb: Joan Greenwood
    Supporting cast: Sonia Holm, Mai Zetterling

    SEE ALSO: **Lamb, Caroline; Shelley, Percy Bysshe.**

C

Caesar, Julius, Emperor of Rome, 100 or 102–44 B.C.

105. *Caesar the Conqueror* (1962). 100 min. Matheus Films. D: Amerigo Anton.
    Caesar: Cameron Mitchell
    Marc Anthony: Bruno Tocci
    Supporting cast: Rick Battaglia, Raffaella Carra, Ivo Payer, Dominique Wilms

106. *Julius Caesar* (1950). 90 min. David Bradley. D: David Bradley.
    Caesar: Harold Tasker
    Brutus: David Bradley
    Cassius: Grosvenor Glenn
    Marc Anthony: Charlton Heston
    Supporting cast: Theodore Cloak, Cornelia Peeples, Frederick Roscoe, Arthur Sus

107. *Julius Caesar* (1953). 121 min. MGM. D: Joseph L. Mankiewicz.
    Caesar: Louis Calhern
    Brutus: James Mason
    Cassius: John Gielgud
    Marc Anthony: Marlon Brando
    Supporting cast: Greer Garson, Deborah Kerr, Edmond O'Brien

108. *Julius Caesar* (1970). 117 min. Peter Snell Prod. D: Stuart Burge.
    Caesar: John Gielgud
    Brutus: Jason Robards

Cassius: Richard Johnson
Marc Anthony: Charlton Heston
Supporting cast: Richard Chamberlain, Diana Rigg, Robert Vaughn

SEE ALSO: **Cleopatra,** Queen of Egypt.

Calamity Jane, 1850–1903
See **Canary, Martha Jane** ("Calamity Jane").

Caldicott, Helen, 1938– (American pediatrician and antinuclear activist)

109. *Eight Minutes to Midnight* (1981). 60 min. Mary Benjamin. D: Mary Benjamin.
Documentary

Caligula, Emperor of Rome, A.D. 12–41.

110. *Caligula* (1980). 156 min. Penthouse Films International. D: Tinto Brass.
Caligula: Malcolm McDowell
Supporting cast: John Gielgud, Helen Mirren, Peter O'Toole, Teresa Ann Savoy

Callas, Maria, 1923–1977. (Celebrated American opera singer of the late 1950's and the 1960's)

110a *Maria* (1987). 90 min. London Trust Productions. D: Tony Palmer.
Documentary.

Campanella, Roy, 1921– (American baseball player whose career was cut short by an automobile accident)

111. *It's Good to Be Alive* (1974). 100 min. Metromedia. D: Michael Landon.
Campanella: Paul Winfield
Supporting cast: Ramon Bieri, Ruby Dee, Louis Gossett

Campbell, Alan, 1905–1963
   See **Parker, Dorothy.**

Campbell, Ian, 1931–1963
   See **Hettinger, Karl.**

Campbell, Joseph, 1904–1987. (Leading American expert on mythology)

111a *Hero's Journey: The World Of Joseph Campbell* (1987). 58 min. Mythology Limited. D: Janelle Balnicke, William Free. Documentary.

Canada, Lena, 1942– (Canadian nurse)

112. *Touched by Love* (1984). 95 min. The Elvis Company. D: Gus Trikonis.
   Canada: Deborah Raffin
   Supporting cast: John Amos, Diane Lane, Michael Learned, Cristina Raines

Canaris, Wilhelm, 1887–1945. (German admiral who was head of Nazi counter-intelligence)

112a *Canaris, Master Spy* (1954). 92 min. Europa Film. D: Alfred Weidenmann.
   Canaris: O.E. Hasse
   Supporting cast: Martin Held, Adrian Hoven, Wolfgang Preiss, Barbara Ruetting

Canary, Martha Jane "Calamity Jane," 1850–1903. (American horsewoman and frontier character)

113. *Calamity Jane* (1953). 101 min. Warner Bros. D: David Butler.
   Canary: Doris Day
   Bill Hickok: Howard Keel
   Supporting cast: Philip Carey, Allyn McLerie, Gale Robbins

114. *Calamity Jane* (1984). 100 min. CBS Entertainment. D: James Goldstone.
Canary: Jane Alexander
Bill Hickok: Frederic Forrest
Supporting cast: David Hemmings, Ken Kercheval, Walter Olkewicz

115. *Calamity Jane and Sam Bass* (1949). 85 min. Universal-International. D: George Sherman.
Canary: Yvonne De Carlo
Sam Bass: Howard Duff
Supporting cast: Lloyd Bridges, Dorothy Hart, Milburn Stone

SEE ALSO: **Hickok, James Butler.**

Cantor, Eddie, 1892–1964. (American singer, comic and film actor famous for his banjo eyes)

116. *The Eddie Cantor Story* (1953). 116 min. Warner Bros. D: Alfred E. Green.
Cantor: Keefe Brasselle
Flo Ziegfeld: William Forrest
Supporting cast: Ann Doran, Marilyn Erskine, Aline MacMahon, Hal March

Capone, Alphonse, 1898–1947. (American Prohibition era gangster)

117. *Al Capone* (1959). 105 min. Allied Artists. D: Richard Wilson.
Capone: Rod Steiger
Supporting cast: James Gregory, Nehemiah Persoff, Fay Spain, Murvyn Vye

118. *Capone* (1975). 101 min. 20th Century-Fox. D: Steve Carver.
Capone: Ben Gazzara
Supporting cast: Susan Blakely, John Cassavetes, Harry Guardino, Sylvester Stallone

119. *The St. Valentine's Day Massacre* (1967). 100 min. 20th Century-Fox. D: Roger Corman.
    Capone: Jason Robards, Jr.
    Supporting cast: Jean Hale, Ralph Meeker, Clint Ritchie, George Segal

    SEE ALSO: **Ness, Eliot; Nitti, Francesco Saverio; Raft, George.**

Cappelletti, Joey, 1962–
    See **Cappelletti, John.**

Cappelletti, John, 1952– (American football player, Heisman Trophy winner, and member of the Los Angeles Rams)

120. *Something for Joey* (1977). 120 min. MTM Prod. D: Lou Antonio.
    Cappelletti: Marc Singer
    Joey Cappelletti: Jeff Lynas
    Supporting cast: Linda Kelsey, Gerald S. O'Loughlin, Geraldine Page

Caputo, Philip, 1941– (American Pulitzer Prize-winning author and Vietnam veteran)

120a *A Rumor of War* (1980). 240 min. Charles Fries Production. D: Richard T. Heffron.
    Caputo: Brad Davis
    Supporting cast: Richard Bradford, Keith Carradine, Brian Dennehy, Michael O'Keefe

Caravaggio, Michelangelo Merisi de, 1573–1610. (Italian painter, founder of naturalistic school)

120b *Caravaggio* (1986). 93 min. BFI Film. D: Derek Jarman.
    Caravaggio: Nigel Terry
    Caravaggio (as a boy): Noam Almaz
    Caravaggio (as a young man): Dexter Fletcher

Supporting cast: Sean Bean, Garry Cooper, Spencer Leigh, Tilda Swinton

Cardigan, James Thomas Brudenell, 1797–1868. (British general who led the charge of the Light Brigade)

121. *The Charge of the Light Brigade* (1968). 130 min. United Artists. D: Tony Richardson
Cardigan: Trevor Howard
George Charles Bingham: Harry Andrews
Fitzroy James Henry Somerset Raglan: John Gielgud
Supporting cast: Jill Bennett, Peter Bowles, David Hemmings, Vanessa Redgrave

Carlotta, Empress of Mexico, 1840–1927.

122. *The Mad Empress* (1939). 72 min. Warner Bros. D: Miguel C. Torres.
Carlotta: Medea Novara
Benito Juarez: Jason Robards, Sr.
Maximilian: Conrad Nagel
Supporting cast: Lionel Atwill, Evelyn Brent, Guy Bates Post

SEE ALSO: **Juarez, Benito.**

Carnes, Clarence, d. 1988. (American criminal and youngest man sentenced to Alcatraz Prison)

123. *Alcatraz: The Whole Shocking Story* (1980). 200 min. Pierre Cossette Prod. D: Paul Krasny.
Carnes: Michael Beck
Robert Stroud: Art Carney
Supporting cast: Ronny Cox, Alex Karras, Telly Savalas, Will Sampson

Carney, Bill. (American quadriplegic who sued for the custody of his children)

124. *The Ordeal of Bill Carney* (1981). 100 min. The Belle Company. D: Jerry London.
Carney: Ray Sharkey
Mason Rose: Richard Crenna
Supporting cast: Ana Alicia, Vincent Baggetta, Betty Buckley, Jeremy Licht

Carroll, Lewis, 1832–1898
See **Hargreaves, Alice Pleasance Liddell.**

Carson, Kit, 1809–1868. (American trapper, scout, and Indian agent)

125. *Kit Carson* (1940). 97 min. Edward Small Prod. D: George B. Seitz.
Carson: Jon Hall
Supporting cast: Dana Andrews, Lynn Bari, Harold Huber

SEE ALSO: **Bridger, Jim; Fremont, John Charles.**

Carson, Sonny, 1935– (African-American writer)

126. *The Education of Sonny Carson* (1974). 105 min. Paramount Pictures. D: Michael Campus.
Carson: Rony Clanton
Supporting cast: Paul Benjamin, Don Gordon, Ram John Holder, Joyce Walker

Carter, Leslie, 1862–1937. (American actress)

127. *The Lady With Red Hair* (1941). 81 min. Warner Bros. D: Curtis Bernhardt.
Carter: Miriam Hopkins
David Belasco: Claude Rains
Supporting cast: Richard Ainley, Laura Hope Crews, Helen Westley

Caruso, Enrico, 1874–1921. (Italian opera singer and a leading tenor of the Metropolitan Opera company)

128. *The Great Caruso* (1951). 109 min. MGM. D: Richard Thorpe.
Caruso: Mario Lanza
Supporting cast: Ann Blyth, Richard Hageman, Dorothy Kirsten, Jarmila Novotna

Carver, Ellsworth "Sonny," 1931?– (American teenager, known as the "Woo Woo Kid", who made headlines during the 1940's because of his affairs with two older women)

128a *In the Mood* (1987). 98 min. Lorimar Motion Pictures. D: Phil Alden Robinson.
Wisecarver: Patrick Dempsey
Judy Cusimano: Talia Balsam
Francine Glatt: Beverly D'Angelo
Supporting cast: Michael Constantine, Kathleen Freeman, Peter Hobbs, Betty Jinnette

Casanova, Giovanni, 1725–1798. (Italian adventurer and reputed great lover)

129. *The Adventures of Casanova* (1948). 83 min. Eagle-Lion Prod.
D: Roberto Gavaldon.
Casanova: Arturo de Cordova
Supporting cast: Turhan Bey, Lucille Bremer, John Sutton

130. *Fellini's Casanova* (1977). 158 min. TCF/PEA. D: Federico Fellini.
Casanova: Donald Sutherland
Supporting cast: Tina Aumont, Daniel Emilfork Berenstein, Cicely Browne, Jim Karlsen

Cash, Johnny, 1932– (American country and western singer known as the "man in black")

130a *Johnny Cash! The Man, His World, His Music* (1970). 94 min.
Verite Production. D: Robert Elfstrom.
Documentary.

Cassady, Carolyn, 1923-
  See **Kerouac, Jack.**

Cassady, Neal, 1926–1968
  See **Kerouac, Jack.**

Cassidy, Robert Parker "Butch," 1866–1908?. (American outlaw)

131. *Butch and Sundance: The Early Days* (1979). 110 min. 20th
  Century-Fox. D: Richard Lester.
  Cassidy: Tom Berenger
  Harry Longabaugh/Sundance Kid: William Katt
  Supporting cast: Jeff Corey, Brian Dennehy, Michael C.
    Gwynne, John Schuck

132. *Butch Cassidy and the Sundance Kid* (1969). 110 min. 20th
  Century-Fox. D: George Roy Hill.
  Cassidy: Paul Newman
  Harry Longabaugh/Sundance Kid: Robert Redford
  Etta Place: Katharine Ross
  Supporting cast: Jeff Corey, George Furth, Henry Jones,
    Strother Martin

Cassius, d. 42 B.C.
  See **Caesar, Julius,** Emperor of Rome.

Castle, Irene, 1893–1969
  See **Castle, Vernon.**

Castle, Vernon, 1887–1918. (British dancer who revolutionized
  modern dancing)

133. *The Story of Vernon and Irene Castle* (1939). 93 min. RKO. D:
  H.C. Potter.
  Castle: Fred Astaire
  Irene Castle: Ginger Rogers
  Supporting cast: Walter Brennan, Lew Fields, Etienne
    Girardot, Edna May Oliver

Castro, Fidel, 1927-
 See **Guevara, Ernesto ("Che").**

Catharine of Aragon, Queen of England, 1485–1536
 See **Henry VIII,** King of England.

Catherine I, Empress of Russia, 1684?–1796
 See **Peter I,** Emperor of Russia.

Catherine II, "the Great," Empress of Russia, 1729–1796.

134. *Catherine the Great* (1934). 93 min. United Artists. D: Paul Czinner.
 Catherine: Elisabeth Bergner
 Supporting cast: Gerald du Maurier, Douglas Fairbanks, Jr., Joan Gardner, Flora Robson

135. *The Great Catherine* (1968). 98 min. Warner Bros. D: Gordon Flemyng.
 Catherine: Jeanne Moreau
 Peter: Zero Mostel
 Supporting cast: Jack Hawkins, Peter O'Toole, Akim Tamiroff

136. *A Royal Scandal* (1945). 94 min. 20th Century-Fox. D: Otto Preminger.
 Catherine: Tallulah Bankhead
 Supporting cast: Anne Baxter, William Eythe, Charles Coburn

137. *The Scarlet Empress* (1934). 109 min. Paramount Pictures. D: Josef von Sternberg.
 Catherine: Marlene Dietrich
 Peter: Sam Jaffe
 Supporting cast: Louise Dresser, John Lodge, C. Aubrey Smith

137a *Young Catherine* (1991). 186 min. Turner Pictures. D: Michael Anderson.
 Catherine: Julia Ormond
 Elizabeth, Empress of Russia: Vanessa Redgrave

Supporting cast: Marthe Keller, Franco Nero, Christopher Plummer, Maximilian Schell

SEE ALSO: **Jones, John Paul; Pugachev, Emelyan Ivanovich.**

Catherine of Valois, Queen of England, 1401–1437
See **Henry V,** King of England.

Cavanaugh, Florence, 1885?–1947
See **Cavanaugh, Frank.**

Cavanaugh, Frank, 1866–1933. (American World War I hero and collegiate football coach)

138. *The Iron Major* (1943). 85 min. RKO. D: Ray Enright.
Cavanaugh: Pat O'Brien
Florence Cavanaugh: Ruth Warrick
Supporting cast: Leon Ames, Bruce Edwards, Robert Ryan, Russell Wade

Cavell, Edith, 1865–1915. (British nurse who worked in Belgium during World War I and was executed by the Germans for assisting Allied refugees)

139. *Nurse Edith Cavell* (1939). 95 min. RKO. D: Herbert Wilcox.
Cavell: Anna Neagle
Supporting cast: Edna May Oliver, Zasu Pitts, May Robson, George Sanders

Cellini, Benvenuto, 1500–1571. (Italian Renaissance goldsmith, sculptor and engraver)

140. *The Affairs of Cellini* (1934). 90 min. United Artists. D: Gregory LaCava.
Cellini: Fredric March
Supporting cast: Vince Barnett, Constance Bennett, Frank Morgan, Fay Wray

Cerdan, Marcel, 1916–1949
  See **Piaf, Edith.**

Cermak, Anton, 1873–1933. (Chicago mayor fatally wounded by a bullet intended for Franklin D. Roosevelt)

141. *The Man Who Dared* (1933). 75 min. 20th Century-Fox. D: Hamilton McFadden.
  Cermak/Novak: Preston Foster
  Supporting cast: Zita Johann, Joan Marsh, Frank Sheridan

Cervantes, Miguel de, 1547–1616. (Spanish novelist whose masterpiece was *Don Quixote)*

142. *Cervantes* (1968). 111 min. Commonwealth United. D: Vincent Sherman.
  Cervantes: Horst Buchholz
  Supporting cast: Jose Ferrer, Louis Jourdan, Gina Lollobrigida

Chagall, Marc, 1887–1985. (Russian painter identified with the impressionist and cubist schools best known for his fanciful paintings influenced by Russian folklore)

142a *Homage to Chagall—The Colours of Love* (1976). 88 min. Kino International Corp. D: Henry Rasky.
  Documentary.

Chamberlain, Lindy, 1948– (Australian woman accused of murdering her infant daughter)

142b *A Cry in the Dark* (1988). 121 min. Warner Bros. D: Fred Schepisi.
  Chamberlain: Meryl Streep
  Michael Chamberlain: Sam Neill
  Supporting cast: Lewis Fitz-gerald, Neil Fitzpatrick, Brendan Higgins, Dennis Miller

Chamberlain, Michael
　　See **Chamberlain, Lindy.**

Chambers, Whittaker, 1901–1961
　　See **Hiss, Alger.**

Champion, Bob, 1948– (British jockey and Grand National winner)

143. *Champions* (1983). 115 min. Ladbroke Entertainment, Ltd. D: John Irvin.
　　Champion: John Hurt
　　Supporting cast: Jan Francis, Ben Johnson, Edward Woodward

Chanel, Coco, 1883–1971. (French fashion designer)

144. *Chanel Solitaire* (1981). 120 min. United Film. D: George Kaczender.
　　Chanel: Marie-France Pisier
　　Supporting cast: Karen Black, Timothy Dalton, Brigitte Fossey, Rutger Hauer

Chaney, Lon, 1883–1930. (American actor known for his ability to distort his face and body)

145. *Man of a Thousand Faces* (1957). 122 min. Universal- International. D: Joseph Pevney.
　　Chaney: James Cagney
　　Lon Chaney, Jr.: Roger Smith
　　Supporting cast: Jane Greer, Dorothy Malone, Marjorie Rambeau

Chaney, Lon, Jr., 1906–1973
　　See **Chaney, Lon.**

Chapayev, Vasilii Ivanovich, 1887–1919. (Russian military hero and leader of Red Army during 1918 civil war)

145a *Chapayev* (1934). 94 min. Lenfilm. D: Georgy Vassiliev, Sergei Vassiliev.
Chapayev: Boris Babochkin
Supporting cast: Boris Blinov, Leonid Kmit, Varvara Myasnikova, Illarion Pevtsov

Chapman, Edward Arnold, 1916?– (British safecracker who was a double agent in World War II)

146. *Triple Cross* (1967). 126 min. Warner Bros. D: Terence Young.
Chapman: Christopher Plummer
Supporting cast: Gert Frobe, Trevor Howard, Romy Schneider

Charles I, King of England, 1600–1649
See **Cromwell, Oliver.**

Charles II, King of England, 1630–1685.

147. *The Exile* (1947). 95 min. Universal-International. D: Max Ophuls.
Charles: Douglas Fairbanks, Jr.
Supporting cast: Paule Croset, Henry Daniell, Maria Montez

148. *Forever Amber* (1947). 137 min. 20th Century-Fox. D: Otto Preminger.
Charles: George Sanders
Supporting cast: Linda Darnell, Richard Greene, Cornel Wilde

149. *The King's Thief* (1955). 78 min. MGM. D: Robert Z. Leonard.
Charles: George Sanders
Supporting cast: Ann Blyth, David Niven, Edmund Purdom

SEE ALSO: **Gwyn, Nell; Penn, William; Radisson, Pierre Esprit.**

Charles VII, King of France, 1403–1461
See **Joan of Arc,** Saint.

Charles XII, King of Sweden, 1682–1718
See **Peter I,** Emperor of Russia.

Charles, Prince of Wales, 1948–

150. *Charles and Diana: A Royal Love Story* (1982). 100 min. St. Lorraine Prod. D: James Goldstone.
Charles: David Robb
Diana Spencer: Caroline Bliss
Elizabeth II: Margaret Tyzack
Philip: Christopher Lee
Supporting cast: Charles Gray, David Langton, Rod Taylor, Mona Washbourne

151. *The Royal Romance of Charles and Diana* (1982). 100 min. Chrysalis-Yellen Prod. D: Peter Levin.
Charles: Christopher Baines
Diana Spencer: Catherine Oxenberg
Elizabeth II: Dana Wynter
Philip: Stewart Granger
Supporting cast: Barbara Caruso, Olivia de Havilland, Ray Milland, Holland Taylor

Charriere, Henri, 1906–1973. (Venezuelan criminal sentenced to Devil's Island)

152. *Papillon* (1973). 150 min. Allied Artists. D: Franklin J. Schaffner.
Charriere: Steve McQueen
Supporting cast: Don Gordon, Dustin Hoffman, Victor Jory

Chennault, Claire Lee, 1890–1958
    See **Scott, Robert Lee.**

Chessman, Caryl W., 1922–1960. (American author and convict who received eight stays of execution)

153. *Cell 2455, Death Row* (1955). 77 min. Columbia Pictures. D: Fred F. Sears.
    Chessman: William Campbell
    Supporting cast: Marian Carr, Vince Edwards, Kathryn Grant

154. *Kill Me If You Can* (1977). 100 min. NBC-TV. D: Buzz Kulik.
    Chessman: Alan Alda
    Supporting cast: John Hillerman, Walter McGinn, Talia Shire

Chisum, John Simpson, 1824–1884. (American rancher and major figure in the Lincoln County War)

155. *Chisum* (1970). 111 min. Warner Bros. D: Andrew V. McLaglen.
    Chisum: John Wayne
    William Bonney/Billy the Kid: Geoffrey Deuel
    Pat Garrett: Glenn Corbett
    Supporting cast: Bruce Cabot, Christopher George, Ben Johnson, Forrest Tucker

Chopin, Frederic, 1810–1849. (Polish composer and pianist)

156. *A Song to Remember* (1945). 113 min. Columbia Pictures. D: Charles Vidor.
    Chopin: Cornel Wilde
    Franz Liszt: Stephen Bekassy
    George Sand: Merle Oberon
    Supporting cast: Sig Arno, George Coulouris, Nina Foch, Paul Muni

    SEE ALSO: **Liszt, Franz; Sand, George.**

Christian, Fletcher, 1764–1793
See **Bligh, William.**

Christiane F.
See **F., Christiane.**

Christie, Agatha, 1891–1976. (British mystery writer best known for her works featuring the characters, Miss Jane Marple and Hercule Poirot)

157. *Agatha* (1979). 98 min. Warner Bros. D: Michael Apted.
Christie: Vanessa Redgrave
Supporting cast: Timothy Dalton, Celia Gregory, Dustin Hoffman, Helen Morse

Christie, John Reginald, 1898–1953. (British murderer whose trial led to the abolishment of the death penalty in England)

158. *10 Rillington Place* (1971). 111 min. Columbia Pictures. D: Richard Fleischer.
Christie: Richard Attenborough
Timothy Evans: John Hurt
Supporting cast: Gabrielle Days, Judy Geeson, Andre Morell

Christina, Queen of Sweden, 1626–1689.

159. *The Abdication* (1974). 103 min. Warner Bros. Television International. D: Anthony Harvey.
Christina: Liv Ullmann
Supporting cast: Graham Crowden, Cyril Cusack, Peter Finch, Paul Rogers

160. *Queen Christina* (1933). 97 min. MGM. D: Rouben Mamoulian
Christina: Greta Garbo
Supporting cast: John Gilbert, Ian Keith, Lewis Stone

Christo, 1935– (Bulgarian-American sculptor known for his use of fabrics to wrap and tie objects, urban buildings and landscape sites)

160a *Islands* (1987). 58 min. Maysles Film. D: Albert Maysles, David Maysles, Charlotte Zwerin
Documentary.

Christy, Edwin P., 1815–1862
See **Foster, Stephen.**

Churchill, Odette, 1912– (French World War II spy)

161. *Odette* (1951). 100 min. United Artists. D: Herbert Wilcox.
Churchill: Anna Neagle
Supporting cast: Marius Goring, Trevor Howard, Peter Ustinov

Churchill, Winston, 1874–1965. (British prime minister during World War II)

161a *The Finest Hours* (1964). 114 min. Macmillan Films. D: Peter Baylis.
Documentary.

162. *Young Winston* (1972). 145 min. Columbia Pictures. D: Richard Attenborough.
Churchill: Simon Ward
Supporting cast: Anne Bancroft, John Mills, Robert Shaw

SEE ALSO: **Simpson, Wallis Warfield.**

Ciano, Edda Mussolini, 1911–
See **Mussolini, Benito.**

Ciano, Galeazzo, 1903–1944
See **Mussolini, Benito.**

Cid, El, c. 1043–1099
    See **Diaz, Rodrigo** ("El Cid").

Cimo, Tony, 1945?– (American bricklayer who was convicted of hiring a hit man to avenge the brutal slaying of his parents)

162a *Vengeance: The Story of Tony Cimo* (1986). 100 min. Robirdie Pictures Inc. D: Marc Daniels.
    Cimo: Brad Davis
    Supporting cast: Michael Beach, Brad Dourif, William Conrad, Roxanne Hart

Clairmont, Clara, 1798–1879
    See **Shelley, Percy Bysshe.**

Clapton, Eric, 1945– (British rock musician considered a virtuoso on the electric guitar)

163. *Eric Clapton and His Rolling Hotel* (1981). 62 min. N/A. D: Rex Pyke.
    Documentary

Clare of Assisi, Saint, 1194–1253
    See **Francis of Assisi,** Saint.

Clark, Charles Dismas, 1901–1963. (American priest known for his work with ex-convicts in St. Louis)

164. *The Hoodlum Priest* (1961). 101 min. United Artists. D: Irvin Kershner.
    Clark: Don Murray
    Supporting cast: Keir Dullea, Larry Gates, Logan Ramsey, Cindi Wood

Clark, Joe, 1939– (American high school principal best known for his radical disciplinary methods)

164a *Lean On Me* (1989). 108 min. Warner Bros. D: John G. Avildsen.
Clark: Morgan Freeman
Supporting cast: Robert Guillaume, Alan North, Lynne Thigpen, Beverly Todd

Clark, William, 1770–1838
See **Lewis, Meriwether.**

Claudel, Camille, 1864–1943. (French sculptor specializing in figures who was an assistant, mistress and student of Rodin)

164b *Camille Claudel* (1988). 149 min. Orion Pictures. D: Bruno Nuytten.
Claudel: Isabelle Adjani
Paul Claudel: Laurent Grevill
Claude Debussy: Maxime Leroux
Auguste Rodin: Gerard Depardieu
Supporting cast: Katrine Boorman, Philippe Clevenot, Alain Delon, Danielle Lebrun

Claudel, Paul, 1868–1955
See **Claudel, Camille.**

Clay, Cassius, 1942–
See **Ali, Muhammad.**

Clemens, Olivia Langdon, 1842–1904
See **Twain, Mark.**

Clemens, Samuel Langhorne, 1835–1910
See **Twain, Mark.**

Cleopatra, Queen of Egypt, 69–30 B.C.

165. *Antony and Cleopatra* (1972). 160 min. Folio Films. D: Charlton Heston.

Cleopatra: Hildegard Neil
Marc Anthony: Charlton Heston
Supporting cast: John Castle, Freddie Jones, Eric Porter, Fernando Rey

166. *Caesar and Cleopatra* (1946). 127 min. J. Arthur Rank. D: Gabriel Pascal.
Cleopatra: Vivien Leigh
Marc Anthony: Stewart Granger
Julius Caesar: Claude Rains
Supporting cast: Cecil Parker, Flora Robson, Francis L. Sullivan

167. *Cleopatra* (1934). 101 min. Paramount Pictures. D: Cecil B. De Mille
Cleopatra: Claudette Colbert
Marc Anthony: Henry Wilcoxon
Julius Caesar: Warren William
Supporting cast: Ian Keith, Gertrude Michael, Joseph Schildkraut

168. *Cleopatra* (1963). 243 min. 20th Century-Fox. D: Joseph L. Mankiewicz.
Cleopatra: Elizabeth Taylor
Marc Anthony: Richard Burton
Julius Caesar: Rex Harrison
Supporting cast: Pamela Brown, George Cole, Hume Cronyn

169. *Serpent of the Nile* (1953). 81 min. Columbia Pictures. D: William Castle.
Cleopatra: Rhonda Fleming
Marc Anthony: Raymond Burr
Julius Caesar: William Lundigan
Supporting cast: Michael Ansara, Julie Newmar

Cline, Patsy, 1932–1963. (American country-western singer whose career was ended by her untimely death in an airplane crash)

170. *Sweet Dreams* (1985). 115 min. Silver Screen Partners, L.P. D: Karel Reisz.

Cline: Jessica Lange
Charlie Dick: Ed Harris
Supporting cast: David Clennon, Gary Basaraba, James Staley, Ann Wedgeworth

Clive, Robert, 1725–1774. (British soldier and founder of the empire of British India)

171. *Clive of India* (1935). 90 min. United Artists. D: Richard Boleslawski.
Clive: Ronald Colman
Supporting cast: Colin Clive, Francis Lister, Loretta Young.

Clooney, Rosemary, 1928– (American singer and actress)

172. *Rosie: The Rosemary Clooney Story* (1982). 100 min. Charles Fries Prod. D: Jackie Cooper.
Clooney: Sondra Locke
Jose Ferrer: Tony Orlando
Supporting cast: Cheryl Anderson, John Karlen, Penelope Milford, Robert Ridgely

Cochise, d. 1874. (Apache chief)

173. *Broken Arrow* (1950). 93 min. 20th Century-Fox. D: Delmer Daves.
Cochise: Jeff Chandler
Supporting cast: Will Geer, Debra Paget, Basil Ruysdael, James Stewart

174. *Conquest Of Cochise* (1953). 78 min. Columbia Pictures. D: William Castle.
Cochise: John Hodiak
Supporting cast: John Crawford, Joy Page, Robert Stack

Cody, William "Buffalo Bill," 1846–1917. (American scout and showman)

175. *Buffalo Bill* (1944). 89 min. 20th Century-Fox. D: William Wellman.
     Cody: Joel McCrea
     Supporting cast: Linda Darnell, Thomas Mitchell, Maureen O'Hara, Anthony Quinn

176. *Buffalo Bill* (1963). 95 min. Solly V. Bianco. D: Mario Costa.
     Cody: Gordon Scott
     Supporting cast: Mario Brega, Mirco Ellis, Catherine Ribeiro

177. *Buffalo Bill and the Indians* (1976). 120 min. United Artists. D: Robert Altman.
     Cody: Paul Newman
     Supporting cast: Geraldine Chaplin, Joel Grey, Burt Lancaster, Kevin McCarthy

178. *Buffalo Bill Rides Again* (1947). 70 min. Screen Guild. D: Bernard B. Ray.
     Cody: Richard Arlen
     Supporting cast: Jennifer Holt, Gil Patrick, Lee Shumway

179. *Young Buffalo Bill* (1940). 59 min. Republic Pictures. D: Joseph Kane.
     Cody: Roy Rogers
     Supporting cast: George Haynes, Pauline Moore, Hugh Sothern

     SEE ALSO: **Hickok, James Butler** ("Wild Bill").

Cohan, George M., 1878–1942. (American stage actor, playwright, and producer)

180. *Yankee Doodle Dandy* (1942). 126 min. Warner Bros. D: Michael Curtiz.
     Cohan: James Cagney
     Supporting cast: Rosemary DeCamp, Walter Huston, Joan Leslie, Irene Manning

Cohen, Elie, d. 1965. (Egyptian-born Israeli government agent who infiltrated the highest levels of the Syrian government for Israel)

180a *The Impossible Spy* (1987). 96 min. BBC-TV. D: Jim Goddard.
Cohen: John Shea
Supporting cast: Michal Bat-Adam, Sasson Gaby, Chaim
Girafi, Eli Wallach

Cohn, Roy, 1927–1986. (American lawyer who was special
assistant to Senator Joseph McCarthy during his communist witch-hunts)

180b *Citizen Cohn* (1992). 110 min. HBO Pictures. D: Frank
Pierson.
Cohn: James Woods
J. Edgar Hoover: Pat Hingle
Joseph McCarthy: Joe Don Baker
Walter Winchell: Joseph Bologna
Supporting cast: Frederic Forrest, David Marshal Grant,
Lee Grant, Josef Sommer

Cole, Nat King, 1919?–1965. (African-American pianist, singer
and founder of the King Cole Trio)

180c *The Unforgettable Nat King Cole* (1989). 90 min. Pioneer
Artists. D: Alan Lewens.
Documentary.

Coleman, Wayne Carl, 1947?–
See **Isaacs, William Carroll**

Coll, Vincent "Mad Dog," 1909–1932. (American gangster
during the 1920's, executed by order of Dutch Schultz)

181. *Mad Dog Coll* (1942). 126 min. Columbia Pictures. D: Burt
Balaban.
Coll: John Chandler
Dutch Schultz: Vincent Gardenia
Supporting cast: Joy Harmon, Brooke Hayward, Neil
Nephew, Jerry Orbach

Collins, Marva, 1936– (American teacher who has gained national recognition for her work with ghetto youngsters)

182. *The Marva Collins Story* (1981). 100 min. NRW Features. D: Peter Levin.
Collins: Cicely Tyson
Supporting cast: Morgan Freeman, Mashaune Hardy, Roderick Wimberly

Colson, Charles, 1931– (Aide to President Richard Nixon and Watergate conspirator)

183. *Born Again* (1978). 110 min. Robert L. Munger. D: Irving Rapper.
Colson: Dean Jones
Richard M. Nixon: Harry Spillman
Supporting cast: Dana Andrews, Anne Francis, Jay Robinson

SEE ALSO: **Dean, John.**

Columbus, Christopher, 1451–1506. (Italian explorer and discoverer of the New World)

184. *Christopher Columbus* (1949). 104 min. Universal- International. D: David Macdonald.
Columbus: Fredric March
Ferdinand: Francis Lister
Isabella: Florence Eldridge
Supporting cast: James Robertson Justice, Kathleen Ryan, Francis L. Sullivan, Nora Swinburne

184a *Christopher Columbus* (1985). 360 min. Lorimar Productions. D: Alberto Lattuada.
Columbus: Gabriel Byrne
Ferdinand: Nicol Williamson
Isabella: Faye Dunaway
Supporting cast: Rossano Brazzi, Virna Lisi, Oliver Reed, Raf Vallone

Comaneci, Nadia, 1962– (Rumanian Olympic gymnast who received the first perfect score in international competition)

185. *Nadia* (1984). 100 min. Dave Bell Prod. D: Alan Cooke.
    Comaneci: Talia Balsam
    Bela Karolyi: Jonathan Banks
    Supporting cast: Joe Bennett, Simone Blue, Johann Carlo, Conchata Ferrell

Connolly, Maureen, 1934–1969. (American tennis player and Grand Slam champion)

186. *Little Mo* (1978). 150 min. Worldvision Enterprises. D: Daniel Haller.
    Connolly: Glynnis O'Connor
    Supporting cast: Claude Akins, Anne Baxter, Michael Learned

Conroy, Pat, 1946– (American schoolteacher to underprivileged children in South Carolina)

187. *Conrack* (1974). 107 min. 20th Century-Fox. D: Martin Ritt.
    Conroy: Jon Voight
    Supporting cast: Hume Cronyn, Madge Sinclair, Paul Winfield

Constantine I, Emperor of Rome, c. 274–337.

188. *Constantine and the Cross* (1962). 120 min. Jonia Films. D: Lionello DeFelice.
    Constantine: Cornel Wilde
    Supporting cast: Elisa Cegani, Christine Kaufman, Belinda Lee, Massimo Serato

Cook, Frederick Albert, 1865–1940. (American physician and arctic explorer who claimed to have been the first person to reach the North Pole)

189. *Cook & Peary: The Race to the Pole* (1983). 100 min. Robert Halmi Prod. D: Robert Day.
Cook: Richard Chamberlain
Robert Edwin Peary: Rod Steiger
Supporting cast: Michael Gross, Diane Venora, Samm-Art Williams

Corbett, James "Gentleman Jim," 1866–1933. (American heavyweight boxer and world champion)

190. *Gentleman Jim* (1942). 104 min. Warner Bros. D: Raoul Walsh.
Corbett: Errol Flynn
John L. Sullivan: Ward Bond
Supporting cast: William Frawley, Alan Hale, Alexis Smith

SEE ALSO: **Sullivan, John L.**

Corrigan, Douglas, 1907– (American pilot who flew from New York to California via Ireland)

191. *Flying Irishman* (1939). 72 min. RKO. D: Leigh Jason.
Corrigan: Douglas Corrigan
Supporting cast: Robert Armstrong, Paul Kelly, Donald MacBride, Gene Reynolds

Cortez, Gregorio, 1875–1916. (Mexican criminal)

192. *The Ballad of Gregorio Cortez* (1982). 99 min. Embassy Pictures. D: Robert M. Young.
Cortez: Edward James Olmos
Supporting cast: Tom Bower, James Gammon, Bruce McGill

Cortez, Hernando, 1485–1547. (Spanish conqueror of Mexico)

193. *Captain From Castile* (1947). 140 min. 20th Century-Fox. D: Henry King.
Cortez: Cesar Romero

Supporting cast: Lee J. Cobb, Jean Peters, Tyrone Power, John Sutton

Costello, Lou, 1906–1959
  See **Abbott, Bud.**

Cousins, Norman, 1915– (American writer and editor)

194. *Anatomy of an Illness* (1984). 120 min. Hamner Prod. D: Richard T. Heffron.
   Cousins: Edward Asner
   Cleveland Amory: David Ogden Stiers
   William Hitzig: Eli Wallach
   Supporting cast: Lelia Goldoni, Haunani Minn, Julie Montgomery, Millie Perkins

Coward, Charles. (British soldier and World War II German prisoner of war)

195. *The Password Is Courage* (1962). 116 min. MGM. D: Andrew L. Stone.
   Coward: Dirk Bogarde
   Supporting cast: Alfred Lynch, Maria Perschy, Nigel Stock

Coward, Noel, 1899–1973
  See **Lawrence, Gertrude.**

Cowley, R Adams, 1917– (American physician and shock-trauma specialist)

196. *Shocktrauma* (1982). 100 min. Glen-Warren Prod. D: Eric Till.
   Cowley: William Conrad
   Supporting cast: Lawrence Dane, Scott Hylands, Kerrie Keane, Linda Sorenson

Cox, Don
    See **Ginsberg, Allen.**

Cox, Jack, 1922– (American journalist)

197. *Last Plane Out* (1984). 98 min. CBS/Fox. D: David Nelson.
    Cox: Jan-Michael Vincent
    Anastasio Somoza: Lloyd Battista
    Supporting cast: Julie Carmen, Mary Crosby, David
    Huffman, William Windom

Crabtree, Lotta, 1847–1924. (American singer)

198. *Golden Girl* (1951). 108 min. 20th Century-Fox. D: Lloyd
    Bacon.
    Crabtree: Mitzi Gaynor
    Supporting cast: James Barton, Dennis Day, Dale Rob-
    ertson

Crandall, Prudence, 1803–1890. (American schoolteacher who
    was prosecuted in 1833 for running a school for African-
    American girls)

198a *She Stood Alone* (1991). 100 min. Walt Disney Prod. D: Jack
    Gold
    Crandall: Mare Winningham
    Supporting cast: Ben Cross, Daniel Davis, Robert Desid-
    erio, Lisa Maria Russell

Crawford, Christina, 1939–
    See **Crawford, Joan.**

Crawford, Joan, 1908–1977. (American Academy Award- win-
    ning actress)

199. *Mommie Dearest* (1981). 129 min. Paramount Pictures. D:
    Frank Perry.
    Crawford: Faye Dunaway

Christina Crawford (as a child): Mara Hobel
Christina Crawford (as an adult): Diana Scarwid
Supporting cast: Rutanya Alda, Howard da Silva, Steve Forrest

Crazy Horse, 1842–1877. (Sioux chief)

200. *Chief Crazy Horse* (1955). 86 min. Universal-International. D: George Sherman.
Crazy Horse: Victor Mature
Supporting cast: Suzan Ball, Ray Danton, Keith Larsen, John Lund

SEE ALSO: **Sitting Bull.**

Crick, Francis, 1916– (Nobel Prize-winning British scientist who constructed a molecular model of the complex genetic material deoxyribonucleic acid with James D. Watson)

200a *The Double Helix* (1987). 107 min. Arts & Entertainment Network. D: Mick Jackson.
Crick: Tim Pigott-Smith
Rosalind Franklin: Juliet Stevenson
James D. Watson: Jeff Goldblum
Maurice Wilkins: Alan Howard

Crippen, Hawley Harvey, 1862–1910. (American physician living in England who murdered his wife by poisoning her)

200b *Dr. Crippen* (1963). 97 min. Warner Bros. D: Robert Lynn.
Crippen: Donald Pleasence
Supporting cast: Coral Browne, Samantha Eggar, James Robertson Justice, Geoffrey Toone

Crockett, Davy, 1786–1836. (American frontiersman, Congressman and humorist)

201. *Davy Crockett and the River Pirates* (1956). 81 min. Walt Disney Prod. D: Norman Foster.

Crockett: Fess Parker
Supporting cast: Clem Bevans, Buddy Ebsen, Kenneth Tobey, Jeff York

202. *Davy Crockett, Indian Scout* (1950). 71 min. United Artists. D: Lew Landers.
Crockett: George Montgomery
Supporting cast: Noah Beery, Jr., Ellen Drew, Philip Reed, Chief Thundercloud

203. *Davy Crockett, King of the Wild Frontier* (1955). 93 min. Walt Disney Prod. D: Norman Foster.
Crockett: Fess Parker
Supporting cast: William Bakewell, Hans Conried, Buddy Ebsen, Basil Ruysdael

SEE ALSO: **Bowie, Jim.**

Cromwell, Oliver, 1599–1658. (Lord Protector of England)

204. *Cromwell* (1970). 141 min. Columbia Pictures. D: Ken Hughes.
Cromwell: Richard Harris
Charles I: Alec Guinness
Supporting cast: Timothy Dalton, Frank Finlay, Robert Morley, Dorothy Tutin

Crossley, Rosemary, 1945–
See **McDonald, Anne.**

Curie, Marie, 1867–1934. (Nobel Prize-winning Polish physicist and discoverer of radium)

205. *Madame Curie* (1943). 124 min. MGM. D: Mervyn LeRoy.
Curie: Greer Garson
Pierre Curie: Walter Pidgeon
Supporting cast: Victor Francen, C. Aubrey Smith, Robert Walter

Curie, Pierre, 1859–1906
    See **Curie, Marie.**

Curley, James M., 1874–1958 (American politician and mayor of Boston)

206. *The Last Hurrah* (1958). 121 min. Columbia Pictures. D: John Ford.
    Curley/Skeffington: Spencer Tracy
    Supporting cast: Dianne Foster, Jeffrey Hunter, Basil Rathbone

207. *The Last Hurrah* (1977). 110 min. O'Connor-Becker Prod. D: Vincent Sherman.
    Curley/Skeffington: Carroll O'Connor
    Supporting cast: John Anderson, Dana Andrews, Jack Carter

Curtiz, Michael, 1888–1962
    See **Flynn, Errol.**

Cusimano, Judy, 1923?–
    See **Wisecarver, Ellsworth.**

Custer, George Armstrong, 1839–1876. (American general defeated by Sitting Bull at Little Big Horn)

208. *Custer of the West* (1968). 144 min. Security Pictures Prod. D: Robert Siodmak.
    Custer: Robert Shaw
    Supporting cast: Jeffrey Hunter, Robert Ryan, Mary Ure

208a *Son of the Morning Star* (1991). 192 min.
    Custer: Gary Cole
    Supporting cast: Stanley Anderson, Rosanna Arquette, Terry O'Quinn, David Strathairn

209. *They Died With Their Boots On* (1942). 138 min. Warner Bros. D: Raoul Walsh.

Custer: Errol Flynn
Supporting cast: Olivia de Havilland, Charles Grapewin, Arthur Kennedy

Cvetic, Matthew, 1909–1962. (American spy who infiltrated the Communist party)

210. *I Was a Communist for the FBI* (1951). 83 min. Warner Bros. D: Gordon Douglas.
Cvetic: Frank Lovejoy
Supporting cast: Philip Carey, Dorothy Hart, James Millican

D

Dafoe, Allan Roy, 1883–1943. (Canadian physician who delivered the Dionne quintuplets)

211. *The Country Doctor* (1936). 110 min. 20th Century-Fox. D: Henry King.
Dafoe: Jean Hersholt
Supporting cast: June Lang, Slim Summerville, Michael Whalen

212. *Five of a Kind* (1938). 83 min. 20th Century-Fox. D: Herbert I. Leeds.
Dafoe: Jean Hersholt
Dionne Quintuplets: Dionne Quintuplets
Supporting cast: Cesar Romero, Claire Trevor

213. *Reunion* (1936). 80 min. 20th Century-Fox. D: Norman Taurog.
Dafoe: Jean Hersholt
Dionne Quintuplets: Dionne Quintuplets
Supporting cast: Rochelle Hudson, Helen Vinson

Dahl, Roald, 1916–
See **Neal, Patricia.**

Dallas, Claude. (American mountain man whose capture and escape from prison have become local folklore)

213a *Manhunt For Claude Dallas* (1986). 104 min. Prism Entertainment. D: jerry London.
Dallas: Matt Salinger
Supporting cast: Claude Akins, Pat Hingle, Lois Nettleton, Rip Torn

Dalley, John, 1935–
See **Guarneri String Quartet.**

Dalton, Bob, 1867–1937. (American outlaw)

214. *The Last Ride of the Dalton Gang* (1979). 150 min. Dan Curtis Prod. D: Dan Curtis.
Dalton: Cliff Potts
Em Dalton: Larry Wilcox
Grat Dalton: Randy Quaid
Supporting cast: Sharon Farrell, Jack Palance, Dale Robertson, Harris Yulin

Dalton, Emmett, 1871–1937
See **Dalton, Bob.**

Dalton, Gratton, 1862–1892
See **Dalton, Bob.**

Daltrey, Roger, 1944–
See **Who, The**.

D'Amboise, Jacques, 1934–   (African-American ballet dancer)

214a *He Makes Me Feel Like Dancin'* (1983). 90 min. NBC Television Network. D: Emile Ardolino.
Documentary.

Damien de Veuster, Joseph "Father Damien," 1840–1889. (Belgian missionary renowned for his work with lepers in Hawaii)

215. *Damien, the Leper Priest* (1982). 100 min. Tomorrow Entertainment. D: Steven Gethers.
Damien: Ken Howard
Supporting cast: William Daniels, Mike Farrell, Wilfrid Hyde-White, David Ogden Stiers

Damita, Lily, 1901–
See **Flynn, Errol.**

Danton, Georges, 1759–1794. (Political leader of the French Revolution)

216. *Danton* (1982). 136 min. Triumph Films. D: Andrzej Wajda.
Danton: Gerard Depardieu
Maximilien Robespierre: Wojciech Pszoniak
Supporting cast: Anne Alvaro, Ronald Blanche, Patrice Chereau

Darby, William, 1911–1945. (American World War II soldier)

217. *Darby's Rangers* (1958). 121 min. Warner Bros. D: William A. Wellman.
Darby: James Garner
Supporting cast: Edward Byrnes, Etchika Choreau, Jack Warden, Stuart Whitman

Darrow, Clarence, 1857–1938. (American defense lawyer in several controversial trials)

218. *Inherit the Wind* (1960). 127 min. United Artists. D: Stanley Kramer.
Darrow/Drummond: Spencer Tracy
William Jennings Bryan/Brady: Fredric March
John T. Scopes/Cates: Dick York
H.L. Mencken/Hornbeck: Gene Kelly

Supporting cast: Claude Akins, Donna Anderson, Florence Eldridge, Elliott Reid

SEE ALSO: **Leopold, Nathan.**

Darwin, Charles, 1809–1882. (British naturalist and proponent of the theory of natural selection)

219. *The Darwin Adventure* (1972). 91 min. 20th Century-Fox. D: Jack Couffer.
Darwin: Nicholas Clay
Supporting cast: Robert Flemyng, Susan Macready, Ian Richardson

David, King of Israel, c. 1010–970 B.C.

220. *David and Bathsheba* (1951). 116 min. 20th Century-Fox. D: Henry King.
David: Gregory Peck
Bathsheba: Susan Hayward
Goliath: Walter Talun
Supporting cast: James Robertson Justice, Raymond Massey, Kieron Moore

221. *David and Goliath* (1961). 95 min. Allied Artists. D: Richard Pottier, Ferdinando Baldi.
David: Ivo Payer
Goliath: Kronos
Supporting cast: Edward Hilton, Eleanora Rossi-Drago, Massimo Serato, Orson Welles

222. *King David* (1985). 114 min. Paramount Pictures. D: Bruce Beresford.
David: Richard Gere
Supporting cast: Niall Buggy, Alice Krige, Denis Quilley, Edward Woodward

223. *The Story of David* (1976). 250 min. ABC-TV. D: Alex Segal, David Lowell Rich.
David: Timothy Bottoms
Bathsheba: Jane Seymour

Supporting cast: Susan Hampshire, Keith Michell, Anthony Quayle

Davidman, Joy, 1915–1960
See **Lewis, C.S.**

Davies, Joseph E., 1876–1958. (American ambassador to the USSR, 1936–1938)

224. *Mission to Moscow* (1943). 123 min. Warner Bros. D: Michael Curtiz.
Davies: Walter Huston
Joseph Stalin: Manart Kippen
Supporting cast: Ann Harding, Eleanor Parker, Vladimir Sokoloff

Davies, Marion, 1897–1961
See **Hearst, William Randolph.**

Davis, Angela, 1944– (African-American activist, author and Communist leader)

225. *Brothers* (1977). 104 min. Warner Bros. D: Arthur Barron.
Davis/Paula: Vonetta McGee
George Jackson/Thomas: Bernie Casey
Supporting cast: Stu Gilliam, Ron O'Neal, Ronny Roker

Davis, Bette, 1908–1989
See **Flynn, Errol.**

Davis, John William, 1873–1955
See **Marshall, Thurgood.**

Davis, Nan, 1961–
See **Petrofsky, Jerrold.**

Day, Clarence, 1845?–1927. (American businessman, forty-year member of New York Stock Exchange and director of railroads)

226. *Life With Father* (1947). 118 min. Warner Bros. D: Michael Curtiz.
Day: William Powell
Clarence Day, Jr.: James Lydon
Supporting cast: Irene Dunne, Edmund Gwenn, Zasu Pitts, Elizabeth Taylor

Day, Clarence, Jr., 1874–1935
See **Day, Clarence.**

De Havilland, Olivia, 1916–
See **Flynn, Errol.**

De Lesseps, Ferdinand, 1805–1894. (French diplomat and promoter of Suez Canal)

227. *Suez* (1938). 100 min. 20th Century-Fox. D: Allan Dwan.
De Lesseps: Tyrone Power
Eugenie: Loretta Young
Supporting cast: Annabella, J. Edward Bromberg, Joseph Schildkraut

De Sade, Donatien Alphonse, Marquis, 1740–1814. (French writer infamous for his perversions)

228. *De Sade* (1969). 113 min. American International Pictures. D: Cy Endfield.
De Sade: Keir Dullea
Supporting cast: Senta Berger, John Huston, Anna Massey, Lilli Palmer

De Salvo, Albert, 1931–1973. (American murderer who strangled thirteen women in Boston between 1962 and 1964)

228a *The Boston Strangler* (1968). 120 min. 20th Century-Fox. D: Richard Fleischer.
De Salvo: Tony Curtis
Supporting cast: Henry Fonda, George Kennedy, Mike Kellin

De Soto, Hernando, c. 1496–1542
See **Pizarro, Francisco.**

Dean, James, 1931–1955. (American actor famous for his young-rebel roles)

229. *James Dean* (1976). 100 min. Jozak Company. D: Robert Butler.
Dean: Stephen McHattie
William Bast: Michael Brandon
Supporting cast: Candy Clark, Dane Clark, Meg Foster

230. *The James Dean Story* (1957). 82 min. Warner Bros. D: George W. George, Robert Altman.
Documentary

Dean, Jay Hanna "Dizzy," 1911–1974. (American baseball player and star National League pitcher)

231. *The Pride of St. Louis* (1952). 93 min. 20th Century-Fox. D: Harmon Jones.
Dean: Dan Dailey
Paul Dean: Richard Crenna
Supporting cast: Joanne Dru, Richard Hylton, Hugh Sanders

Dean, Jerome, 1911–1974
See **Dean, Jay Hanna** ("Dizzy").

Dean, John, 1938– (American political advisor to Richard Nixon who was a prominent figure in the Watergate scandal)

231a *Blind Ambition* (1979). 480 min. Time-Life Productions Inc.
D: George Schaefer.
Dean: Martin Sheen
Charles Colson: Michael Callan
Maureen Dean: Theresa Russell
John Ehrlichman: Graham Jarvis
H.R. Haldeman: Lawrence Pressman
G. Gordon Liddy: William Daniels
Jeb Stuart Magruder: Christopher Guest
John Mitchell: John Randolph
Richard Nixon: Rip Torn
Supporting cast: Lonny Chapman, Clifford David, Ed Flanders, Fred Grandy

SEE ALSO: **Liddy, G. Gordon.**

Dean, Maureen, 1946?–
See **Dean, John.**

Dean, Paul, 1937–1981
See **Dean, Jay Hanna** ("Dizzy").

Debussy, Claude, 1862–1918
See **Claudel, Camille.**

Delford, Alexandra, 1971–1980. (American victim of cystic fibrosis)

231b *Alex: The Life of a Child* (1986). 104 min. Mandy Films Inc. D: Robert Markowitz.
Delford: Gennie James
Carole Delford: Bonnie Bedelia
Frank Delford: Craig T. Nelson
Supporting cast: Brenda Bazinet, Danny Corkill, Melanie Mazman, Mark Withers

Delford, Carole
See **Delford, Alexandra.**

Delford, Frank, 1938–
   See **Delford, Alexandra.**

Delilah, c. 12th cent. B.C.
   See **Samson.**

Demara, Ferdinand, 1921–1982. (American fantasist)

232. *The Great Imposter* (1960). 112 min. Universal-International.
   D: Robert Mulligan.
   Demara: Tony Curtis
   Supporting cast: Gary Merrill, Edmond O'Brien, Arthur
   O'Connell

Dempsey, Jack, 1895–1983. (American world heavyweight boxing champion)

233. *Dempsey* (1983). 150 min. Charles Fries Prod. D: Gus
   Trikonis.
   Dempsey: Treat Williams
   Estelle Taylor: Victoria Tennant
   Supporting cast: Sally Kellerman, Peter Mark Richman,
   Jesse Vint, Sam Waterston

Dennis, Gerard Graham, 1920– (American jewel thief)

234. *The Great Jewel Robber* (1950). 91 min. Warner Bros. D: Peter
   Godfrey.
   Dennis: David Brian
   Supporting cast: John Archer, Jacqueline de Wit, Marjorie
   Reynolds

Dennis, Rocky, 1961–1978. (American victim of craniodiaphyseal dysplasia)

235. *Mask* (1985). 120 min. Universal Pictures. D: Peter
   Bogdanovich.
   Dennis: Eric Stoltz

Rusty Dennis: Cher
Supporting cast: Laura Dern, Richard Dysart, Sam Elliott,
Estelle Getty

Dennis, Rusty
See **Dennis, Rocky.**

Denton, Jeremiah, 1924– (U.S. Navy pilot and Vietnam War
POW)

236. *When Hell Was in Session* (1979). 100 min. Aubrey/Hamner
Prod. D: Paul Krasny.
Denton: Hal Holbrook
Supporting cast: Ronny Cox, Renne Jarrett, Mako, Eva
Marie Saint

Dershowitz, Alan M., 1938–
See **Von Bulow, Claus.**

Desideria, Queen of Sweden and Norway, 1781–1860
See **Napoleon Bonaparte,** Emperor of France.

Destinn, Emma, 1878–1930. (Bohemian operatic soprano)

238. *The Divine Emma* (1983). 107 min. United Artists. D: Jiri
Krejcik.
Destinn: Bozidara Turonovova
Supporting cast: Jiri Adamira, Milos Kopecky, Juraj Kukura

DeSylva, Buddy, 1895–1970. (American songwriter)

239. *The Best Things in Life Are Free* (1956). 103 min. 20th
Century-Fox. D: Michael Curtiz.
DeSylva: Gordon MacRae
Lew Brown: Ernest Borgnine
Ray Henderson: Dan Dailey
Supporting cast: Sheree North, Tommy Noonan, Murvyn
Vye

Devlin, Anne, 1778–1851. (Irish patriot who fought against British oppression in Ireland in the 1800's)

240. *Anne Devlin* (1984). 120 min. Aeon. D: Pat Murphy.
Devlin: Brid Brennan
Supporting cast: Gillian Hackett, Bosco Hogan, Des McAleer

Diaghilev, Serge, 1872–1929
See **Nijinsky, Waslaw.**

Diamond, Jack "Legs," 1895–1931. (American gangster in 1920's Albany, New York)

241. *The Rise and Fall of Legs Diamond* (1960). 101 min. Warner Bros. D: Budd Boetticher.
Diamond: Ray Danton
Supporting cast: Karen Steele, Elaine Stewart, Jesse White

Diana, Princess of Wales, 1961–
See **Charles,** Prince of Wales.

Diaz, Rodrigo "El Cid," c. 1043–1099. (Spanish soldier and legendary hero in Spanish literature)

242. *El Cid* (1961). 184 min. Allied Artists. D: Anthony Mann.
Diaz: Charlton Heston
Supporting cast: Sophia Loren, Genevieve Page, Raf Vallone

Dick, Charlie, 1933?–
See **Cline, Patsy.**

Didrickson, Babe, 1911–1956
See **Zaharias, Babe Didrickson.**

Diener, George Richard "Richie," 1954–1972. (American teen-age drug addict)

243. *The Death of Richie* (1977). 100 min. Henry Jaffe Enterprises.
   D: Paul Wendkos.
   Diener: Robby Benson
   Supporting cast: Eileen Brennan, Charles Fleischer, Ben
      Gazzara, Clint Howard

Dietrich, Marlene, 1901–1992. (German actress known for her glamourous image and husky singing voice)

243a *Marlene* (1984). 96 min. OKO-Filmproduktion. D: Maximilian Schell.
   Documentary.

Dietrich, Noah, 1888–1982
   See **Hughes, Howard.**

Dillinger, John, 1903–1934. (American gangster specializing in armed bank robberies)

244. *Dillinger* (1945). 89 min. United Artists. D: Max Nosseck.
   Dillinger: Lawrence Tierney
   Supporting cast: Elisha Cook, Jr., Anne Jeffreys, Edmund
      Lowe

245. *Dillinger* (1973). 107 min. American International Pictures.
   D: John Milius.
   Dillinger: Warren Oates
   Supporting cast: Ben Johnson, Cloris Leachman, Michelle
      Phillips

246. *Young Dillinger* (1965). 102 min. Allied Artists. D: Terry O.
   Morse.
   Dillinger: Nick Adams
   Supporting cast: John Ashley, Robert Conrad, Mary Ann
      Mobley

   SEE ALSO: **Sage, Anna.**

DiMaggio, Joe, 1914–
  See **Monroe, Marilyn.**

Dinessen, Isak, 1885–1962
  See **Blixen, Karen.**

Dionne Quintuplets, 1934–
  See **Dafoe, Allan Roy.**

Disraeli, Benjamin, 1804–1881. (British prime minister during the reign of Queen Victoria)

247. *Disraeli* (1929). 89 min. Warner Bros. D: Alfred E. Green.
  Disraeli: George Arliss
  Victoria: Margaret Mann
  Supporting cast: Florence Arliss, Joan Bennett, Anthony Bushnell

248. *The Prime Minister* (1942). 94 min. Warner Bros. D: Thorold Dickinson.
  Disraeli: John Gielgud
  Victoria: Faye Compton
  Supporting cast: Stephen Murray, Owen Nares, Diana Wynyard

  SEE ALSO: **Victoria,** Queen of England.

Dobkin, Mary, d. 1987. (American Little League coach, child benefactor and humanitarian)

249. *Aunt Mary* (1979). 100 min. Henry Jaffe Enterprises. D: Peter Werner.
  Dobkin: Jean Stapleton
  Supporting cast: Martin Balsam, Harold Gould, Robbie Rist, Dolph Sweet

Doel, Frank, d. 1968
  See **Hanff, Helene.**

Dolly, Jennie, 1892–1941. (American dancer and Ziegfeld star)

250. *The Dolly Sisters* (1945). 114 min. 20th Century-Fox. D: Irving Cummings.
Dolly: Betty Grable
Rosie Dolly: June Haver
Supporting cast: Reginald Gardiner, John Payne, S.Z. Sakall

Dolly, Rosie, 1892–1970
See **Dolly, Jennie.**

Don Juan, 1547–1578. (Spanish rake)

251. *The Adventures of Don Juan* (1949). 89 min. United Artists. D: Alexander Korda.
Don Juan: Douglas Fairbanks, Jr.
Supporting cast: Binnie Barnes, Joan Gardner, Merle Oberon

252. *Don Juan* (1926). 111 min. Warner Bros. D: Alan Crosland.
Don Juan: John Barrymore
Supporting cast: Mary Astor, Willard Louis, Estelle Taylor

253. *The Private Life of Don Juan* (1934). 110 min. Warner Bros. D: Vincent Sherman.
Don Juan: Errol Flynn
Supporting cast: Robert Douglas, Alan Hale, Viveca Lindfors

Donahue, Jack, 1892–1930
See **Miller, Marilyn.**

Donovan, Jean, 1953–1980. (American lay missionary murdered in El Salvador)

254. *Choices of the Heart* (1983). 100 min. Metromedia. D: Joseph Sargent.
Donovan: Melissa Gilbert
Supporting cast: Mike Farrell, Helen Hunt, Martin Sheen

Doolittle, James, 1896– (American general who led bombing raid over Tokyo)

255. *Thirty Seconds Over Tokyo* (1944). 138 min. MGM. D: Mervyn LeRoy.
Doolittle: Spencer Tracy
Ted Lawson: Van Johnson
Supporting cast: Scott McKay, Phyllis Thaxter, Robert Walker

Dorsey, Jimmy, 1904–1957. (American band leader during the Big Band era)

256. *The Fabulous Dorseys* (1947). 91 min. United Artists. D: Alfred E. Green.
Dorsey: Jimmy Dorsey
Tommy Dorsey: Tommy Dorsey
Supporting cast: Janet Blair, William Lundigan, Paul Whiteman

Dorsey, Tommy, 1905–1956
See **Dorsey, Jimmy.**

Dos Santos, Lucia, 1907– (Portuguese peasant girl who witnessed the Miracle of Fatima)

257. *The Miracle of Our Lady of Fatima* (1952). 102 min. Warner Bros. D: Crane Wilbur.
Dos Santos: Susan Whitney
Francisco Marto: Sammy Ogg
Jacinta Marto: Sherry Jackson
Supporting cast: Angela Clarke, Jay Novello, Gilbert Roland, Frank Silvera

Doss, Carl, 1914–1963
See **Doss, Helen.**

Doss, Helen, 1918– (American author and adoptive parent of twelve children)

258. *The Family Nobody Wanted* (1975). 90 min. Universal Television. D: Ralph Senesky.
    Doss: Shirley Jones
    Carl Doss: James Olson
    Supporting cast: Beeson Carroll, Katherine Helmond, Woodrow Parfrey

Downs, Elizabeth Diane, 1956– (American mother convicted of shooting her three children)

258a *Small Sacrifices* (1989). 200 min. Fries Entertainment, Inc. D: David Greene.
    Downs: Farrah Fawcett
    Supporting cast: Gordon Clapp, Ryan O'Neal, Emily Perkins, John Shea

Drake, Francis, Sir, 1540–1596. (British navigator and sea captain during the reign of Elizabeth I)

259. *Drake of England* (1935). 99 min. Assoc. British-Pathe, Ltd. D: Arthur Woods
    Drake: Matheson Lang
    Elizabeth: Athene Seyler
    Supporting cast: Jane Baxter, Donald Wolfit

260. *Seven Seas to Calais* (1963). 103 min. Adelphia Prod. D: Rudolph Mate.
    Drake: Rod Taylor
    Elizabeth: Irene Worth
    Supporting cast: Anthony Dawson, Basil Dignam, Keith Michell

Dresser, Paul, 1857–1906. (American songwriter best known for his sentimental ballads)

261. *My Gal Sal* (1942). 103 min. 20th Century-Fox. D: Irving Cummings.

Dresser: Victor Mature
Supporting cast: Rita Hayworth, Carole Landis, John Sutton

Drew, Daniel, 1797–1879
See **Fisk, James.**

Dreyfus, Alfred, c. 1859–1935. (French army officer accused of treason)

262. *I Accuse* (1958). 99 min. MGM. D: Jose Ferrer.
Dreyfus: Jose Ferrer
Emile Zola: Emlyn Williams
Supporting cast: Leo Genn, Viveca Lindfors, Anton Walbrook

SEE ALSO: **Zola, Emile.**

Dubarry, Marie, 1741–1793. (Mistress of Louis XV, King of France)

263. *Dubarry, Woman of Passion* (1930). 90 min. United Artists. D: Sam Taylor.
Dubarry: Norma Talmadge
Louis XV: William Farnum
Supporting cast: Hobart Bosworth, Ulrich Haupt, Conrad Nagel, Edgar Norton

264. *Madame Dubarry* (1934). 77 min. Warner Bros. D: William Dieterle.
Dubarry: Dolores Del Rio
Louis XV: Reginald Owen
Armand Richelieu: Osgood Perkins
Supporting cast: Victor Jory, Anita Louise, Verree Teasdale

Duchin, Eddy, 1909–1951. (American pianist)

265. *The Eddy Duchin Story* (1956). 123 min. Columbia Pictures. D: George Sidney.

Duchin: Tyrone Power
Supporting cast: Kim Novak, Victoria Shaw, Shepperd Strudwick, James Whitmore

Duco, Joyce. (American nun and social worker)

266. *The Weekend Nun* (1972). 90 min. Paramount Pictures. D: Jeannot Szwarc.
Duco/Damien: Joanna Pettet
Supporting cast: James Gregory, Vic Morrow, Ann Sothern

Duffy, Clinton T., 1898–1982. (American prison warden at San Quentin 1940–1952)

267. *Duffy of San Quentin* (1954). 78 min. Warner Bros. D: Walter Doniger.
Duffy: Paul Kelly
Supporting cast: Joanne Dru, Louis Hayward, Maureen O'Sullivan

Dummar, Melvin, 1944– (American claimant to Howard Hughes fortune)

268. *Melvin and Howard* (1980). 95 min. Universal Pictures. D: Jonathan Demme.
Dummar: Paul LeMat
Howard Hughes: Jason Robards
Supporting cast: Jack Kehoe, Pamela Reed, Mary Steenburgen

Duncan, Isadora, 1878–1927. (American dancer and freethinker)

269. *Isadora* (1969). 131 min. Universal Pictures. D: Karel Reisz.
Duncan: Vanessa Redgrave
Supporting cast: James Fox, Jason Robards, Ivan Tchenko

Dungee, George Elder, 1937?–
See **Isaacs, William Carroll.**

Dunnock, Mildred, 1906–
See **Neal, Patricia.**

Dupuy, Diane, 1948– (Canadian woman who founded Famous People Players puppet troupe)

269a *Special People* (1984). 120 min. Joe Cates Productions. D: Marc Daniels.
Dupuy: Brooke Adams
Supporting cast: Lesleh Donaldson, Ron James, Joseph Kelly, Susan Roman

Dux, Frank. (American martial arts expert who was the first westerner to win the Kumite)

269b *Bloodsport* (1987). 92 min. Cannon International. D: Newt Arnold.
Dux: Jean Claude Van Damme
Supporting cast: Leah Ayres, Norman Burton, Donald Gibb, Forest Whitaker

E

Eagels, Jeanne, 1894–1929. (American film actress)

270. *Jeanne Eagels* (1957). 109 min. Columbia Pictures. D: George Sidney.
Eagels: Kim Novak
Supporting cast: Jeff Chandler, Gene Lockhart, Agnes Moorehead

Eareckson, Joni, 1960– (American writer, artist and paraplegic)

271. *Joni* (1980). 108 min. World Wide Pictures. D: James F. Collier.
Eareckson: Joni Eareckson
Supporting cast: Katherine De Hetre, Cooper Huckabee, John Milford, Bert Remsen

Earhart, Amelia, 1898–1937. (American pilot and first woman to cross the Atlantic in an airplane)

272. *Amelia Earhart* (1976). 156 min. Universal Television. D: George Schaefer.
Earhart: Susan Clark
Supporting cast: Catherine Burns, John Forsythe, Stephen Macht, Susan Oliver

273. *Flight for Freedom* (1943). 101 min. RKO. D: Lothar Mendes.
Earhart/Carter: Rosalind Russell
Supporting cast: Eduardo Ciannelli, Walter Kingsford, Fred MacMurray, Herbert Marshall

Earp, Josephine Marcus, 1869?–1944. (American actress and wife of Wyatt Earp)

274. *I Married Wyatt Earp* (1983). 100 min. Osmond Television Prod. D: Michael O'Herlihy.
Earp: Marie Osmond
Wyatt Earp: Bruce Boxleitner
Supporting cast: Jeffrey DeMunn, Ross Martin, John Bennett Perry

Earp, Wyatt, 1848–1929. (American lawman)

275. *Frontier Marshal* (1939). 70 min. 20th Century-Fox. D: Allan Dwan.
Earp: Randolph Scott
John H. Holliday: Cesar Romero
Supporting cast: Binnie Barnes, John Carradine, Nancy Kelly

276. *Gunfight at the O.K. Corral* (1957). 122 min. Paramount Pictures. D: John Sturges.
Earp: Burt Lancaster
John H. Holliday: Kirk Douglas
Supporting cast: Rhonda Fleming, John Ireland, Jo Van Fleet

277. *Hour of the Gun* (1967). 100 min. United Artists. D: John Sturges.
Earp: James Garner
John H. Holliday: Jason Robards, Jr.
Supporting cast: Steve Ihnat, Robert Ryan, Albert Salmi

278. *Law and Order* (1932). 70 min. Universal-International. D: Edward L. Cahn.
Earp/Johnson: Walter Huston
Holliday/Brandt: Harry Carey
Supporting cast: Raymond Hatton, Russell Hopton, Russell Simpson

279. *My Darling Clementine* (1946). 97 min. 20th Century-Fox. D: John Ford.
Earp: Henry Fonda
John H. Holliday: Victor Mature
Supporting cast: Walter Brennan, Linda Darnell, Cathy Downs

280. *Tombstone, the Town Too Tough to Die* (1942). 80 min. Paramount Pictures. D: William McGann.
Earp: Richard Dix
John H. Holliday: Kent Taylor
Supporting cast: Edgar Buchanan, Frances Gifford, Victor Jory

SEE ALSO: **Earp, Josephine Marcus; Holliday, John H.** ("Doc"); **Masterson, William Barclay** ("Bat").

Eaton, Peggy O'Neal, 1796–1879. (Wife of a cabinet member during Andrew Jackson's administration)

281. *The Gorgeous Hussy* (1936). 102 min. MGM. D: Clarence Brown.
Eaton: Joan Crawford
Andrew Jackson: Lionel Barrymore
Supporting cast: Louis Calhern, Melvyn Douglas, James Stewart, Robert Taylor, Franchot Tone

Edison, Thomas, 1847–1931. (American inventor)

282. *Edison, the Man* (1940). 107 min. MGM. D: Clarence Brown.
Edison: Spencer Tracy
Supporting cast: Charles Coburn, Rita Johnson, Gene
Lockhart, Lynne Overman

283. *Young Tom Edison* (1940). 82 min. MGM. D: Norman
Taurog.
Edison: Mickey Rooney
Supporting cast: Fay Bainter, George Bancroft, Eugene
Palette, Virginia Weidler

Edward IV, King of England, 1442–1483
See **Richard III,** King of England.

Edward VIII, King of England, 1894–1972
See **Windsor, Edward.**

Edward, the Black Prince, 1330–1376.

284. *The Warriors* (1955). 85 min. 20th Century-Fox. D: Henry
Levin.
Edward: Errol Flynn
Supporting cast: Joanne Dru, Peter Finch, Yvonne
Furneaux

Edwardes, George, 1852–1915. (British impresario and owner of
the Gaiety Theatre)

285. *Gaiety George* (1946). 98 min. Embassy Pictures. D: George
King.
Edwardes/Howard: Richard Greene
Supporting cast: Hazel Court, Peter Graves, Ursula Jeans,
Ann Todd

Edwards, Buster. (British criminal who was involved in the
largest robbery in the British Isles)

285a *Buster* (1988). 93 min. Hemdale Releasing Corporation. D: David Green.
Edwards: Phil Collins
Supporting cast: Ellen Beaven, Larry Lamb, Stephanie Lawrence, Julie Walters

Edwards, Gus, 1879–1945. (American songwriter)

286. *The Star Maker* (1939). 94 min. Paramount Pictures. D: Roy Del Ruth.
Edwards: Bing Crosby
Supporting cast: Louise Campbell, Laura Hope Crews, Ned Sparks

Egan, Eddie, 1920– (New York police officer and film actor)

287. *Badge 373* (1973). 116 min. Paramount Pictures. D: Howard W. Koch.
Egan: Robert Duvall
Supporting cast: Verna Bloom, Henry Darrow, Eddie Egan

288. *The French Connection* (1971). 104 min. 20th Century-Fox. D: William Friedkin.
Egan/Doyle: Gene Hackman
Sonny Grosso/Russo: Roy Scheider
Supporting cast: Arlene Farber, Tony Lo Bianco, Fernando Rey

Ehrlich, Paul, 1854–1915. (German bacteriologist and Nobel Prize winner in physiology and medicine)

289. *Dr. Ehrlich's Magic Bullet* (1940). 103 min. Warner Bros. D: William Dieterle.
Ehrlich: Edward G. Robinson
Supporting cast: Donald Crisp, Ruth Gordon, Otto Kruger, Sig Rumann

Ehrlichman, John, 1925–
See **Dean, John.**

Eichmann, Adolf, 1906–1962. (Nazi war criminal and SS officer who implemented the "Final Solution")

290. *The Man in the Glass Booth* (1975). 117 min. Ely Landau. D: Arthur Hiller.
Eichmann/Goldman: Maximilian Schell
Supporting cast: Luther Adler, Lois Nettleton, Lawrence Pressman

291. *Operation Eichmann* (1961). 93 min. Allied Artists. D: R.G. Springsteen.
Eichmann: Werner Klemperer
Supporting cast: John Banner, Donald Buke, Ruta Lee, Barbara Turner

SEE ALSO: **Harel, Isser; Wallenberg, Raoul.**

Eisenhower, Dwight "Ike," 1890–1969. (World War II hero and thirty-fourth American president)

292. *Ike: The War Years* (1978). 196 min. ABC Circle Films. D: Boris Sagal, Melville Shavelson.
Eisenhower: Robert Duvall
Kay Summersby: Lee Remick
Supporting cast: Dana Andrews, J.D. Cannon, Darren McGavin

El Cid, c. 1043–1099
See **Diaz, Rodrigo** ("El Cid").

El Greco, 1541–1614
See **Greco, El.**

Elder, Katie
See **Holliday, John H.** ("Doc").

Elder, Lauren, 1947– (American artist and sole survivor of airplane crash in the Sierra Nevada)

293. *And I Alone Survived* (1978). 100 min. OJL Productions. D: William A. Graham.
     Elder: Blair Brown
     Supporting cast: David Ackroyd, Vera Miles, James G. Richardson, G.D. Spradlin

Eleanor of Aquitaine, 1122–1204
    See **Henry II,** King of England.

Elizabeth I, Queen of England, 1533–1603.

294. *Fire Over England* (1937). 89 min. J. Arthur Rank. D: William K. Howard.
     Elizabeth: Flora Robson
     Supporting cast: Vivien Leigh, Raymond Massey, Laurence Olivier

295. *The Private Lives of Elizabeth and Essex* (1939). 106 min. Warner Bros. D: Michael Curtiz.
     Elizabeth: Bette Davis
     Robert Devereux, earl of Essex: Errol Flynn
     Supporting cast: Donald Crisp, Olivia de Havilland, Alan Hale

296. *The Virgin Queen* (1955). 92 min. 20th Century-Fox. D: Henry Koster.
     Elizabeth: Bette Davis
     Walter Raleigh: Richard Todd
     Supporting cast: Joan Collins, Herbert Marshall, Jay Robinson

297. *Young Bess* (1953). 112 min. MGM. D: George Sidney.
     Elizabeth: Jean Simmons
     Henry VIII: Charles Laughton
     Supporting cast: Stewart Granger, Cecil Kellaway, Deborah Kerr

     SEE ALSO: **Drake, Francis,** Sir; **Mary Stuart,** Queen of Scotland.

Elizabeth II, Queen of England, 1926–
See **Charles,** Prince of Wales.

Elizabeth, Empress of Austria, 1837–1898
See **Franz Joseph,** Emperor of Austria.

Elizabeth, Empress of Russia, 1709–1763
See **Catherine II,** Empress of Russia.

Ellis, Ruth, 1926–1971. (British murderer and the last woman executed in England)

298. *Dance With a Stranger* (1985). 101 min. National Trustee Co., Ltd. D: Mike Newell.
Ellis: Miranda Richardson
Supporting cast: Jane Bertish, Matthew Carroll, Rupert Everett, Ian Holm

Emerson, Keith, 1948–
See **Emerson, Lake & Palmer.**

Emerson, Lake & Palmer. (American rock group)

299. *Emerson, Lake & Palmer in Concert* (1981). 91 min. N/A. D: Ron Kantor.
Documentary

Emmett, Dan, 1815–1904. (American songwriter and minstrel)

300. *Dixie* (1943). 89 min. Paramount Pictures. D: A. Edward Sutherland.
Emmett: Bing Crosby
Supporting cast: Billy De Wolfe, Dorothy Lamour, Lynne Overman, Marjorie Reynolds

Ensslin, Gudrun, 1940– (German socialist)

301. *Marianne and Juliane* (1982). 106 min. New Yorker Films. D:
Margarethe von Trotta.
Gudrun Ensslin/Marianne: Barbara Sukowa
Supporting cast: Jutta Lampe, Franz Rudnick, Doris
Schade, Rudiger Vogler

Entwistle, John, 1944–
See **Who, The.**

Ephron, Nora, 1941– (American playwright)

302. *Heartburn* (1986). 108 min. Paramount Pictures. D: Mike
Nichols.
Ephron/Samstat: Meryl Streep
Carl Bernstein/Forman: Jack Nicholson
Supporting cast: Stockard Channing, Jeff Daniels, Richard
Masur, Maureen Stapleton

Epstein, Brian, 1934–1967
See **Beatles, The.**

Erroll, Josslyn Hay, Earl of, 1901–1941. (British expatriate to
Kenya murdered by a jealous husband)

302a *White Mischief* (1988). 105 min. Columbia Pictures. D:
Michael Radford.
Erroll: Charles Dance
Diana Broughton: Greta Scacchi
Henry John Delves "Jock" Broughton: Joss Ackland
Supporting cast: Alan Dobie, Susan Fleetwood, John Hurt,
Sarah Miles

Eruzione, Mike, 1955–
See **Brooks, Herb.**

Esau, c. 17th cent. B.C.
    See **Jacob.**

Escalante, Jaime, 1930?– (Hispanic-American mathematics
    teacher who inspired his underprivileged students to pass
    the Advanced Placement Calculus Test)

302b *Stand and Deliver* (1988). 103 min. Warner Bros. D: Ramon
    Menendez.
    Escalante: Edward James Olmos
    Supporting cast: Rosana DeSoto, Andy Garcia, Virginia
        Paris, Lou Diamond Phillips

Essex, Robert Devereux, *2nd Earl of,* 1566–1601
    See **Elizabeth I,** Queen of England.

Esther, Queen of Persia, c. 5th century B.C.

303. *Esther and the King* (1960). 109 min. 20th Century-Fox. D:
    Raoul Walsh.
    Esther: Joan Collins
    Ahasuerus: Richard Egan
    Supporting cast: Rick Battaglia, Sergio Fantoni, Denis
        O'Dea

Etting, Ruth, 1897–1978. (American nightclub and Ziegfeld
    singer in the 1920's)

304. *Love Me or Leave Me* (1955). 122 min. MGM. D: Charles
    Vidor.
    Etting: Doris Day
    Martin Snyder: James Cagney
    Supporting cast: Harry Bellaver, Robert Keith, Cameron
        Mitchell

Eudoxie Fedorovna, Empress, consort of Peter I, Emperor of
    Russia, 1669–1731
    See **Peter I,** Emperor of Russia.

Eugenie, Empress of France, 1826–1920
   See **De Lesseps, Ferdinand.**

Evans, Timothy, 1924–1950
   See **Christie, John Reginald.**

Everingham, John, 1949– (Australian photojournalist)

305. *Love Is Forever* (1983). 150 min. 20th Century-Fox Television
    D: Hall Bartlett.
    Everingham: Michael Landon
    Keo Sirisomphene: Moira Chen
    Supporting cast: David Leonard, Priscilla Presley, Jurgen
       Prochnow, Edward Woodward

Evers, Medgar Wiley, 1925–1963. (Assassinated African- American civil rights activist)

305a *For Us the Living: The Medgar Evers Story* (1983). 90 min.
    Charles Fries Production. D: Michael Schultz.
    Evers: Howard Rollins, Jr.
    Supporting cast: Margaret Avery, Roscoe Lee Browne,
       Irene Cara, Paul Winfield

F

F., Christiane. (German prostitute and drug addict)

306. *Christiane F.* (1984). 131 min. New World Pictures. D: Ulrich
    Edel.
    Christiane F.: Natja Brunkhorst
    Supporting cast: Thomas Haustein, Jens Kuphal, Rainer
       Wolk

Fabian, 1943–
   See **Marcucci, Robert.**

Farmer, Frances, 1914–1970. (American film actress and leading lady during the 1930's whose career was cut short by ill-health)

307. *Frances* (1982). 140 min. Universal Pictures. D: Graeme Clifford.
Farmer: Jessica Lange
Lillian Farmer: Kim Stanley
Supporting cast: Bart Burns, Jeffrey DeMunn, Sam Shepard

308. *Will There Really Be a Morning?* (1983). 150 min. Jaffe-Blakely Prod. D: Fielder Cook.
Farmer: Susan Blakely
Lillian Farmer: Lee Grant
Supporting cast: Royal Dano, John Heard, Joseph Maher, Melanie Mayron

Farmer, Lillian
See **Farmer, Frances.**

Farnon, Siegfried
See **Herriot, James.**

Fassbinder, Rainer Werner, 1946–1982. (German film director known for his negative films about the current state of society)

308a *The Wizard of Babylon* (1982). 83 min. New Yorker Films. D: Dieter Schidor.
Documentary.

Faulk, John Henry, 1913– (American radio and television personality blacklisted during the 1950's)

309. *Fear on Trial* (1975). 100 min. Alan Landsburg Prod. D: Lamont Johnson.
Faulk: William Devane
Louis Nizer: George C. Scott

Supporting cast: Judd Hirsch, John Houseman, Lois Nettleton, Dorothy Tristan

Fenelon, Fania, 1918–1983. (Jewish World War II concentration camp survivor)

310. *Playing for Time* (1980). 150 min. Syzgy Productions. D: Daniel Mann.
Fenelon: Vanessa Redgrave
Supporting cast: Maud Adams, Jane Alexander, Shirley Knight

Ferdinand V, King of Spain, 1452–1516
See **Columbus, Christopher.**

Fernandez, Ray
See **Beck, Martha.**

Ferrer, Jose, 1909–
See **Clooney, Rosemary.**

Fields, Benny, 1894–1959
See **Seeley, Blossom.**

Fields, W.C., 1879–1946. (American comic and film actor best known for his con man roles)

311. *W.C. Fields and Me* (1976). 111 min. Universal Pictures. D: Arthur Hiller.
Fields: Rod Steiger
Carlotta Monti: Valerie Perrine
Supporting cast: Billy Barty, Jack Cassidy, John Marley, Bernadette Peters

SEE ALSO: **West, Mae.**

Filartiga, Joel. (Paraguayan activist physician who tried to expose the human rights violations of his government)

311a *One Man's War* (1991). 100 min. HBO Video. D: Sergio Toledo.
Filartiga: Anthony Hopkins
Supporting cast: Norma Aleandro, Ruben Blades, Sergio Bustamonte, Fernanda Torres

Finch Hatton, Denys, 1887–1931
See **Blixen, Karen.**

Finecke, Bror Blixen, 1886–1946
See **Blixen, Karen.**

First, Ruth, 1925–1982. (South African journalist and activist in the anti-apartheid movement)

311b *A World Apart* (1988). 113 min. Atlantic Entertainment Group. D: Chris Menges.
First/Diane Roth: Barbara Hershey
Shawn Slovo/Molly Roth: Jodhi May
Supporting cast: Rosalie Crutchley, Paul Freeman, Jeroen Krabbe, David Suchet

Fisher, Fred, 1875–1942. (American songwriter)

312. *Oh You Beautiful Doll* (1949). 93 min. 20th Century-Fox. D: John M. Stahl.
Fisher: S.Z. Sakall
Supporting cast: Charlotte Greenwood, June Haver, Mark Stevens

Fisher, Mel, 1922– (American treasure hunter who discovered in 1985 the sunken 17th-century Spanish galleon, *Nuestra Senora de Atocha,* which yielded treasure worth $200 million)

312a *Dreams of Gold: The Mel Fisher Story* (1986). 100 min. Inter Plantary Prod. D: James Goldstone.
Fisher: Cliff Robertson
Supporting cast: Judi Evans, Ed O'Ross, Scott Paulin, Loretta Swit

Fisk, James, 1835–1872. (American stock-market speculator)

313. *The Toast of New York* (1937). 109 min. RKO. D: Rowland V. Lee.
Fisk: Edward Arnold
Daniel Drew: Donald Meek
Cornelius Vanderbilt: Clarence Kolb
Supporting cast: Frances Farmer, Cary Grant, Thelma Leeds, Jack Oakie

Fitzgerald, F. Scott, 1896–1940. (American novelist whose works captured the spirit of the Roaring Twenties)

314. *Beloved Infidel* (1959). 123 min. 20th Century-Fox. D: Henry King.
Fitzgerald: Gregory Peck
Sheilah Graham: Deborah Kerr
Supporting cast: Eddie Albert, Philip Ober, Herbert Rudley, John Sutton

315. *F. Scott Fitzgerald and "The Last of the Belles"* (1974). 100 min. Viacom Enterprises. D: Anthony Page.
Fitzgerald: Richard Chamberlain
Zelda Fitzgerald: Blythe Danner
Supporting cast: David Huffman, Susan Sarandon, Ernest Thompson

316. *F. Scott Fitzgerald in Hollywood* (1976). 100 min. Titus Prod. D: Anthony Page.
Fitzgerald: Jason Miller
Zelda Fitzgerald: Tuesday Weld
Sheilah Graham: Julia Foster
Supporting cast: Suzanne Benton, Michael Lerner, Tom Ligon, Dolores Sutton

Fitzgerald, Zelda, 1900–1948
    See **Fitzgerald, F. Scott.**

Flanagan, Edward James, 1886–1948. (American priest and founder of Boys Town)

317. *Boys Town* (1938). 90 min. Loew's, Inc. D: Norman Taurog.
    Flanagan: Spencer Tracy
    Supporting cast: Henry Hull, Sidney Miller, Gene Reynolds, Mickey Rooney

Flores, Ralph
    See **Klaben, Helen.**

Floyd, Charles "Pretty Boy," 1901–1934. (American gangster who committed a string of bank robberies in the early 1930's)

318. *A Bullet for Pretty Boy* (1970). 88 min. American International. D: Larry Buchanan.
    Floyd: Fabian Forte
    Supporting cast: Michael Haynes, Jocelyn Lane, Astrid Warner

319. *Pretty Boy Floyd* (1960). 96 min. Le-Sac. D: Herbert J. Leder.
    Floyd: John Ericson
    Supporting cast: Herb Evers, Joan Harvey, Barry Newman

320. *The Story of Pretty Boy Floyd* (1974). 78 min. Universal-Public Arts, Ltd. D: Clyde Ware.
    Floyd: Martin Sheen
    Supporting cast: Ellen Corby, Kim Darby, Michael Parks

    SEE ALSO: **Purvis, Melvin.**

Flynn, Errol, 1909–1959. (Tasmanian actor best known for his swashbuckler roles)

320a *My Wicked, Wicked Ways* (1985). 143 min. CBS Fox Video. D: Don Taylor.
  Flynn: Duncan Regehr
  John Barrymore: Barrie Ingham
  Michael Curtiz: Stefan Gierasch
  Lily Damita: Barbara Hershey
  Bette Davis: Elissa Leeds
  Olivia De Havilland: Lee Purcell
  Hal Wallis: Michael Callan
  Raoul Walsh: Michael C. Gwynne
  Jack Warner: Hal Linden
  Supporting cast: George Coe, Deborah Harmon, John Dennis Johnston, Darren McGavin

Ford, Bob, 1862–1892. (American outlaw and killer of Jesse James)

321. *I Shot Jesse James* (1949). 83 min. Weiss Global Enterprises. D: Samuel Fuller.
  Ford: John Ireland
  Jesse James: Reed Hadley
  Supporting cast: Barbara Britton, J. Edward Bromberg, Preston Foster

Foreman, George, 1948–
  See **Ali, Muhammad.**

Fortas, Abe, 1910–1982
  See **Gideon, Clarence.**

Forte, Fabian, 1943–
  See **Marcucci, Robert.**

Fosse, Bob, 1927–1987. (American film director, dancer and choreographer)

322. *All That Jazz* (1979). 123 min. 20th Century-Fox. D: Bob Fosse.

Fosse/Gideon: Roy Scheider
Supporting cast: Cliff Gorman, Jessica Lange, Leland Palmer, Ann Reinking

Fossey, Dian, 1932?–1985. (American primatologist, leading authority on the mountain gorilla and founder of the Karisoke Research Center)

322a *Gorillas in the Mist* (1988). 125 min. Warner Bros. D: Michael Apted.
Fossey: Sigourney Weaver
Louis Leakey: Iain Cuthbertson
Supporting cast: Constantin Alexandrov, Bryan Brown, Julie Harris, John Omirah Miluwi

Foster, Gregory, 1949–1972. (American police officer killed in the line of duty)

323. *Foster and Laurie* (1975). 100 min. Charles Fries Prod. D: John Llewellyn Moxey
Foster: Dorian Harewood
Rocco Laurie: Perry King
Supporting cast: Jonelle Allen, Roger Aaron Brown, Talia Shire

Foster, Stephen, 1826–1864. (American writer of minstrel songs)

324. *I Dream of Jeannie* (1951). 90 min. Republic Pictures. D: Allan Dwan.
Foster: Bill Shirley
Supporting cast: Lynn Bari, Muriel Lawrence, Ray Middleton

325. *Swanee River* (1939). 84 min. 20th Century-Fox. D: Sidney Lanfield.
Foster: Don Ameche
Edwin P. Christy: Al Jolson
Supporting cast: Felix Bressart, Chick Chandler, Andrea Leeds

Fox, Terry, 1959–1981. (Canadian with cancer who ran across Canada to raise funds for cancer research)

326. *The Terry Fox Story* (1983). 97 min. Robert Cooper Films II, Inc. D: Ralph L. Thomas.
Fox: Eric Fryer
Supporting cast: Rosalind Chao, Robert Duvall, Elva Mai Hoover, Chris Makepeace

Foy, Eddie, 1854–1928. (American actor, vaudeville comic and dancer)

327. *The Seven Little Foys* (1955). 95 min. Paramount Pictures. D: Melville Shavelson
Foy: Bob Hope
Supporting cast: Angela Clarke, George Tobias, Milly Vitale

Fraenkel, Knut, 1872–1897
See **Andree, Salomon August.**

Fralick, Cindy. (American firefighter and the first woman member of the Los Angeles Fire Department)

327a *Firefighter* (1986). 96 min. Embassy TV. D: Robert Lewis.
Fralick: Nancy McKeon
Supporting cast: Guy Boyd, Barry Corbin, Vince Irizarry, Amanda Wyss

Frame, Janet, 1924– (New Zealand author who was misdiagnosed as schizophrenic and spent eight years in a mental hospital)

327b *An Angel at My Table* (1989). 157 min. New Line Cinema Corporation. D: Jane Campion.
Frame: Kerry Fox
Supporting cast: Iris Churn, Karen Ferguson, Alexia Keogh, K.J. Wilson

Francis of Assisi, Saint, 1181–1226. (Italian monk and founder of the Order of Friars Minor)

328. *Brother Sun, Sister Moon* (1973). 121 min. Paramount Pictures. D: Franco Zeffirelli.
Francis: Graham Faulkner
Clare of Assisi: Judi Bowker
Innocent III: Alec Guinness
Supporting cast: Valentina Cortese, Leigh Lawson, Lee Montague

329. *Francis of Assisi* (1961). 107 min. 20th Century-Fox. D: Michael Curtiz.
Francis: Bradford Dillman
Clare of Assisi: Dolores Hart
Innocent III: Finlay Currie
Supporting cast: Pedro Armendariz, Eduard Franz, Cecil Kellaway, Stuart Whitman

Frank, Anne, 1929–1945. (Jewish World War II attempted escapee from, and victim of, Nazi persecution)

330. *The Diary of Anne Frank* (1959). 170 min. 20th Century-Fox D: George Stevens.
Frank: Millie Perkins
Otto Frank: Joseph Schildkraut
Supporting cast: Richard Beymer, Lou Jacobi, Shelley Winters, Ed Wynn

331. *The Diary of Anne Frank* (1980). 100 min. 20th Century-Fox Television. D: Boris Sagal.
Frank: Melissa Gilbert
Otto Frank: Maximilian Schell
Supporting cast: James Coco, Joan Plowright, Clive Revill, Doris Roberts

SEE ALSO: **Gies, Miep.**

Frank, Leo, 1884–1915. (Jewish American factory manager unjustly convicted in 1913 of murdering a female employee in Atlanta, Georgia)

331a *The Murder of Mary Phagan* (1987). 222 min. Century Towers
       Productions Inc. D: Billy Hale.
       Frank: Peter Gallagher
       Mary Phagan: Wendy J. Cooke
       John M. Slaton: Jack Lemmon
       Supporting cast: Richard Jordan, Rebecca Miller, Robert
          Prosky, Kathryn Walker

Frank, Morris, 1907– (First American to use a Seeing Eye dog)

332. *Love Leads the Way* (1984). 99 min. Walt Disney Prod. D:
      Delbert Mann.
      Frank: Timothy Bottoms
      Supporting cast: Ralph Bellamy, Susan Dey, Arthur Hill,
         Eva Marie Saint

Frank, Otto, 1889–1980
    See **Frank, Anne; Gies, Miep.**

Franklin, Benjamin, 1706–1790
    See **Adams, John; Jones, John Paul.**

Franklin, Rosalind, 1920–1958
    See **Crick, Francis.**

Franz Josef, Emperor of Austria, 1830–1913.

333. *Forever My Love* (1962). 147 min. Paramount Pictures. D:
      Ernest Marischka.
      Franz Josef: Karl Boehm
      Elizabeth: Romy Schneider
      Supporting cast: Vilma Degischer, Magda Schneider

Fraser, Dawn, 1937– (Australian four-time Olympic gold
    medalist swimmer)

333a *Dawn* (1979). 111 min. Aquataurus. D: Ken Hannam.
Fraser: Bronwyn Mackay-Payne
Supporting cast: Bunney Brooke, John Diedrich, Ron Haddrick, Tom Richards

Fray, Ivan
See **Fray, Lucile.**

Fray, Lucile. (American farm wife and cancer victim)

334. *Who Will Love My Children?* (1983). 100 min. ABC Circle
Films. D: John Erman.
Fray: Ann-Margret
Ivan Fray: Frederic Forrest
Supporting cast: Cathryn Damon, Tracey Gold, Donald Moffat, Patricia Smith

Frazier, Joe, 1944–
See **Ali, Muhammad.**

Frece, Walter de, 1871–1935
See **Tilley, Vesta.**

Freed, Alan, 1922–1965. (American disc jockey who coined the phrase "rock 'n' roll")

335. *American Hot Wax* (1978). 91 min. Paramount Pictures. D:
Floyd Mutrux.
Freed: Tim McIntire
Supporting cast: Fran Drescher, John Lehne, Jay Leno, Laraine Newman

336. *Mr. Rock and Roll* (1957). 86 min. Paramount Pictures. D:
Charles Dubin.
Freed: Alan Freed
Supporting cast: Chuck Berry, Little Richard, Clyde McPhatter

SEE ALSO: **Valens, Richie.**

Fremont, Jessie Benton, 1824–1902
See **Fremont, John Charles.**

Fremont, John Charles, 1813–1890. (American explorer who demonstrated the feasibility of an overland route across the continental United States)

336a *Dream West* (1986). 420 min. Sunn Classic Pictures. D: Dick Lowry.
Fremont: Richard Chamberlain
Thomas Hart Benton: Fritz Weaver
Jim Bridger: Ben Johnson
Kit Carson: Rip Torn
Jessie Benton Fremont: Alice Krige
Abraham Lincoln: F. Murray Abraham
Supporting cast: Rene Enriquez, Jerry Orbach, G.D. Spradlin, Anthony Zerbe

Freud, Sigmund, 1856–1939. (Austrian founder of psychoanalysis)

337. *Freud* (1962). 120 min. Universal Pictures. D: John Huston.
Freud: Montgomery Clift
Supporting cast: Eileen Herlie, Susan Kohner, Larry Parks, Susannah York

Friedrich, Caspar David, 1774–1840. (German artist who specialized in landscapes and was a major painter in the German Romanticism school)

337a *Caspar David Friedrich* (1987). 84 min. Allianz Filmverlag. D: Peter Schamoni.
Friedrich: The artist never appears in the film.
Supporting cast: Helmut Griem, Hans Peter Hallwachs, Walter Schmidinger, Sabine Sinjen

Friendly, Fred, 1915–
See **Murrow, Edward R.**

Friese-Greene, William, 1855–1921. (British inventor of the motion picture)

338. *The Magic Box* (1951). 103 min. J. Arthur Rank. D: John Boulting.
Friese-Greene: Robert Donat
Supporting cast: Robert Beatty, Margaret Johnston, Maria Schell

Frisch, Max, 1911– (Swiss playwright and novelist)

339. *Max Frisch: Journal I–III* (1981). 122 min. Richard Dindo-Saga Production. D: Richard Dindo.
Documentary

Froman, Jane, 1910– (American radio and stage singer, even though crippled in an airplane crash, during World War II performed for U.S. combat troops)

340. *With a Song in My Heart* (1952). 117 min. 20th Century-Fox D: Walter Lang.
Froman: Susan Hayward
Supporting cast: Rory Calhoun, Thelma Ritter, Robert Wagner, David Wayne

Fuggate, Caril Ann, 1944?–
See **Starkweather, Charles.**

Fulton, Robert, 1765–1815. (American inventor of steam engine)

341. *In Old New York* (1940). 100 min. 20th Century-Fox. D: Henry King.
Fulton: Richard Greene
Supporting cast: Alice Faye, Brenda Joyce, Fred MacMurray

G

Gable, Clark, 1901–1960. (American Academy Award-winning actor)

342. *Gable and Lombard* (1976). 131 min. Universal Pictures. D: Sidney J. Furie.
Gable: James Brolin
Carole Lombard: Jill Clayburgh
Supporting cast: Red Buttons, Allen Garfield, Joanne Linville, Melanie Mayron

Gage, Nicholas, 1939– (Greek-American journalist for the *New York Times*)

343. *Eleni* (1985). 117 min. CBS, Inc. D: Peter Yates.
Gage: John Malkovich
Eleni Gatzoyiannis: Kate Nelligan
Supporting cast: Oliver Cotton, Rosalie Crutchley, Linda Hunt, Ronald Pickup

Galilei, Galileo, 1564–1642. (Italian astronomer and physicist who discovered the laws of motion)

344. *Galileo* (1973). 145 min. A.F.T. Distributing Corp. D: Joseph Losey.
Galileo: Topol
Supporting cast: Colin Blakely, Georgia Brown, Edward Fox, Clive Revill

Gallo, Joe, 1929–1972. (American gangster during the late 1940's and early 1950's)

345. *Crazy Joe* (1974). 100 min. Columbia Pictures. D: Carlo Lizzani.
Gallo: Peter Boyle
Supporting cast: Paula Prentiss, Rip Torn, Eli Wallach, Fred Williamson

Gandhi, Mahatma, 1869–1948. (Hindu nationalist and spiritual leader)

346. *Gandhi* (1982). 188 min. Columbia Pictures. D: Richard Attenborough.
Gandhi: Ben Kingsley
Supporting cast: Candice Bergen, Edward Fox, John Gielgud

Garbo, Greta, 1905?–1990. (Swedish film actress of the late 1920's and early 1930's best known for her reclusive behavior)

347. *The Silent Lovers* (1980). 105 min. Warner Bros. Television. D: John Erman.
Garbo: Kristina Wayborn
John Gilbert: Barry Bostwick
Supporting cast: Harold Gould, Brian Keith, John Rubinstein

Garland, Judy, 1922–1969. (American singer and film actress best known for her portrayal of Dorothy in *The Wizard of Oz*)

348. *Rainbow* (1978). 100 min. Ten-Four Prod. D: Jackie Cooper.
Garland: Andrea McArdle
Mickey Rooney: Moosie Drier
Supporting cast: Rue McClanahan, Don Murray, Michael Parks

Garrett, Pat, 1854–1908
See **Bonney, William** ("Billy the Kid"); **Chisum, John Simpson.**

Garrick, David, 1717–1779. (British actor who effected a radical change in acting by introducing a more natural form of speech)

349. *The Great Garrick* (1937). 91 min. Warner Bros. D: James Whale.
    Garrick: Brian Aherne
    Supporting cast: Lionel Atwill, Melville Cooper, Olivia de Havilland, Edward Everett Horton

    SEE ALSO: **Woffington, Peg.**

Gary, Romain, 1914–1980. (Russian-born French writer and diplomat)

350. *Promise at Dawn* (1970). 102 min. Avco. D: Jules Dassin.
    Gary (as an adult): Assaf Dayan
    Gary (as a teenager): Didier Haudepin
    Gary (as a child): Francois Raffoul
    Nina Kacew: Melina Mercouri
    Supporting cast: Despo, Fernand Gravey, Jean Martin, Jacqueline Porel

Gatrell, Ashby. (American Civil War conscientious objector who spent three years living in a cave rather than fight in the war)

350a *No Drums, No Bugles* (1971). 85 min. Jud Lee Productions. D: Clyde Ware.
    Gatrell: Martin Sheen
    Supporting cast: Davey Davidson, Rod McCarey, Denine Terry

Gatzoyiannis, Eleni, 1907–1948
    See **Gage, Nicholas.**

Gaudi, Antonio, 1852–1926. (Spanish architect who was the most famous exponent of the Catalan "modernisme")

350b *Antonio Gaudi* (1984). 97 min. Teshigahara Productions. D: Hiroshi Teshigahara.
    Documentary.

Gaudier-Brzeska, Henri, 1891–1915. (French sculptor of the ultramodern movement vorticism)

351. *Savage Messiah* (1972). 100 min. MGM. D: Ken Russell.
Gaudier-Brzeska: Scott Antony
Sophie Brzeska: Dorothy Tutin
Supporting cast: John Justin, Lindsay Kemp, Helen Mirren

Gauguin, Paul, 1848–1903. (French Postimpressionist artist whose best known works were from his sojourn in Tahiti)

352. *Gauguin the Savage* (1980). 125 min. Nephi Prod. D: Fielder Cook.
Gauguin: David Carradine
Vincent Van Gogh: Barrie Houghton
Supporting cast: Michael Hordern, Lynn Redgrave, Ian Richardson, Flora Robson

353. *The Moon and Sixpence* (1942). 89 min. United Artists. D: Albert Lewin.
Gauguin/Strickland: George Sanders
Somerset Maugham: Herbert Marshall
Supporting cast: Eric Blore, Doris Dudley, Heather Thatcher, Elena Verdugo

353a *Wolf at the Door* (1987). 92 min. Dagmar Film Prod. D: Henning Carlsen.
Gauguin: Donald Sutherland
August Strindberg: Max von Sydow
Supporting cast: Fanny Basdtien, Sofie Graboel, Valerie Morea, Merete Voldstedlund

SEE ALSO: **Van Gogh, Vincent**.

Gauzenko, Igor, 1915–1982. (Russian defector)

353b *Iron Curtain* (1948). 87 min. 20th Century Fox. D: William Wellman.
Gauzenko: Dana Andrews
Supporting cast: Eduard Franz, June Havoc, Berry Kroeger, Gene Tierney

Gehrig, Eleanor, 1905–1984
  See **Gehrig, Lou.**

Gehrig, Lou, 1903–1941. (American baseball player, first baseman for the New York Yankees, 1925–1939)

354. *A Love Affair: The Eleanor and Lou Gehrig Story* (1978). 96 min. Stonehenge Prod. D: Fielder Cook.
  Gehrig: Edward Herrmann
  Eleanor Gehrig: Blythe Danner
  Supporting cast: Patricia Neal, Gerald S. O'Loughlin, Jane Wyatt

355. *The Pride of the Yankees* (1942). 128 min. RKO. D: Sam Wood.
  Gehrig: Gary Cooper
  Eleanor Gehrig: Teresa Wright
  Supporting cast: Walter Brennan, Dan Duryea, Elsa Janssen, Ludwig Stossel

Genghis Khan, 1162–1227
  See **Khan, Genghis.**

George III, King of England, 1738–1820
  See **Brummel, George Bryan ("Beau"); Pitt, William.**

George, Prince of Wales, 1762–1830
  See **Brummel, George Bryan ("Beau").**

Geronimo, 1829–1909. (Apache chief who led a band of renegades along the Mexican border during the late 1800's)

356. *Geronimo* (1939). 89 min. Paramount Pictures. D: Paul Sloane
  Geronimo: Chief Thundercloud
  Supporting cast: Ellen Drew, Preston Foster, William Henry

357. *Geronimo* (1962). 101 min. United Artists. D: Arnold Laven.
Geronimo: Chuck Connors
Supporting cast: Kamala Devi, Ross Martin, Adam West

Gershwin, George, 1898–1937. (American composer of musical comedies and orchestral works)

358. *Rhapsody in Blue* (1945). 139 min. Warner Bros. D: Irving Rapper.
Gershwin: Robert Alda
Ira Gershwin: Herbert Rudley
Oscar Levant: Oscar Levant
Supporting cast: Anne Brown, Joan Leslie, Alexis Smith

Gershwin, Ira, 1896–1983
See **Gershwin, George.**

Geter, Lenell. (American engineer wrongly convicted of armed robbery and sentenced to life imprisonment)

358a *Guilty of Innocence: The Lenell Geter Story* (1987). 104 min. Embassy Communications. D: Richard T. Heffron.
Geter: Dorian Harewood
Supporting cast: Hoyt Axton, Dabney Coleman, Victor Love, Debbi Morgan

Giancana, Antoinette, 1935?– (Daughter of Chicago gangster Salvatore Giancana)

359. *Mafia Princess* (1986). 100 min. Group W Productions. D: Robert Collins.
Giancana: Susan Lucci
Salvatore Giancana: Tony Curtis
Supporting cast: Tony De Santis, Louie DiBianco, David McIlwraith, Kathleen Widdoes

Giancana, Salvatore "Sam," 1908–
See **Giancana, Antoinette.**

Gibb, Lois. (American activist who led the campaign for government relocation of residents of the polluted Love Canal area)

360. *Lois Gibb and the Love Canal* (1982). 100 min. Moonlight Prod. D: Glenn Jordan.
Gibb: Marsha Mason
Supporting cast: Penny Fuller, Robert Gunton, Roberta Maxwell, James Ray

Gibson, Guy, 1918–1944. (British World War II wing commander and Victoria Cross recipient)

361. *The Dam Busters* (1955). 102 min. Warner Bros. D: Michael Anderson.
Gibson: Richard Todd
Barnes N. Wallis: Michael Redgrave
Supporting cast: Patrick Barr, Derek Farr, Ursula Jeans, Basil Sydney

Gibson, Johnnie Mae. (First African-American woman F.B.I. agent)

361a *Johnnie Mae Gibson* (1986). 104 min. Foolscap Productions. D: Bill Dulce.
Gibson: Lynn Whitfield
Supporting cast: Richard Lawson, John Lehne, Howard E. Rollins, Jr., William Allen Young

Gideon, Clarence, 1910–1972. (American criminal whose appeal of his conviction for robbery led to the Supreme Court ruling guaranteeing the right to counsel in all criminal prosecutions)

362. *Gideon's Trumpet* (1980). 104 min. Worldvision Enterprises. D: Robert Collins.
Gideon: Henry Fonda
Abe Fortas: Jose Ferrer
Supporting cast: John Houseman, Dean Jagger, Sam Jaffe, Fay Wray

Gies, Jan
  See **Gies, Miep.**

Gies, Miep, 1909– (Dutch woman who hid the Frank family from the Nazis)

362a *The Attic: The Hiding of Anne Frank* (1988). 100 min.
  Gies: Mary Steenburgen
  Anne Frank: Lisa Jacobs
  Otto Frank: Paul Scofield
  Jan Gies: Huub Stapel
  Supporting cast: Eleanor Bron, Frances Cuka, Miriam Karlin, Ronald Pickup

Gilbert, John, 1897–1936
  See **Garbo, Greta.**

Gilbert, Ronnie, 1927–
  See **Weavers, The.**

Gilbert, W.S., 1836–1911. (British playwright famous for his comic opera librettos)

363. *The Great Gilbert and Sullivan* (1953). 105 min. Copert. D: Sidney Gilliat.
  Gilbert: Robert Morley
  Arthur Sullivan: Maurice Evans
  Supporting cast: Peter Finch, Martyn Green, Eileen Herlie

Gilbreth, Frank Bunker, 1868–1924. (American industrial engineer and pioneer in scientific management)

364. *Cheaper by the Dozen* (1950). 85 min. 20th Century-Fox. D: Walter Lang.
  Gilbreth: Clifton Webb
  Lillian Gilbreth: Myrna Loy
  Supporting cast: Barbara Bates, Edgar Buchanan, Jeanne Crain, Betty Lynn

Gilbreth, Lillian, 1878–1972. (American industrial engineer and pioneer in scientific management)

365. *Belles on Their Toes* (1952). 85 min. 20th Century-Fox. D: Henry Levin.
Gilbreth: Myrna Loy
Supporting cast: Edward Arnold, Jeanne Crain, Jeffrey Hunter, Debra Paget

SEE ALSO: **Gilbreth, Frank Bunker.**

Gillespie, John Birks "Dizzy," 1917– (African-American jazz trumpeter, bandleader and co-founder of the bebop style)

365a *Night in Havana: Dizzy Gillespie in Cuba* (1989). 84 min. Cinephile USA. D: John Holland.
Documentary.

SEE ALSO: **Parker, Charlie.**

Gilligan, Mary, 1943– (American nun who left the convent to marry and raise a family)

365b *Shattered Vows* (1984). 120 min. River City Productions. D: Jack Bender.
Gilligan: Valerie Bertinelli
Supporting cast: Leslie Ackerman, David Morse, Patricia Neal, Millie Perkins

Gilmore, Gary, 1941–1977. (American murderer who refused appeals to stay his execution)

366. *The Executioner's Song* (1982). 200 min. Lawrence Schiller Prod. D: Lawrence Schiller.
Gilmore: Tommy Lee Jones
Nicole Baker: Rosanna Arquette
Supporting cast: Jordan Clark, Christine Lahti, Eli Wallach

Gilmore, Thomas E., 1936– (American civil rights activist and sheriff)

367. *This Man Stands Alone* (1979). 90 min. EMI Television. D: Jerrold Freedman.
Gilmore/Haywood: Louis Gossett, Jr.
Supporting cast: Mary Alice, Barry Brown, Clu Gulager

Ginsberg, Allen, 1926– (American poet and sixties anti-war demonstrator considered the leading apostle of the "Beat Generation")

367a *Growing Up in America* (1989). 90 min. Cinephile Pictures. D: Morley Markson.
Documentary which includes segments on Don Cox, Fred Hampton, Fred Hampton, Jr., Abbie Hoffman, Deborah Johnson, William Kunstler, Timothy Leary, Jerry Rubin, and John Sinclair.

Giuliano, Salvatore, 1922–1950. (Sicilian folk hero who tried to promote Sicily's secession from Italy in the late 1940's)

367b *Salvatore Giuliano* (1961). 125 min. Lux Productions. D: Francesco Rosi.
Giuliano: Pietro Cammarata
Supporting cast: Fernando Cicero, Salvo Randone, Frank Wolff, Federico Zardi

367c *The Sicilian* (1987). 115 min. Twentieth Century-Fox. D: Michael Cimino.
Giuliano: Christopher Lambert
Supporting cast: Joss Ackland, Richard Bauer, Terence Stamp, John Turturro

Gladney, Edna, 1886?–1961. (American children's rights activist)

368. *Blossoms in the Dust* (1941). 100 min. MGM. D: Mervyn LeRoy.
Gladney: Greer Garson

Supporting cast: Felix Bressart, Marsha Mason, Walter Pidgeon

Gladstone, William Ewart, 1809–1898
See **Victoria,** Queen of England.

Glatt, Francine, 1920?–
See **Carver, Ellsworth.**

Glatzle, Mary, 1942– (American police officer)

369. *Muggable Mary, Street Cop* (1982). 100 min. CBS Entertainment. D: Sandor Stern.
Glatzle: Karen Valentine
Supporting cast: Robert Christian, Anne DeSalvo, John Getz

Goebbels, Joseph, 1897–1945. (German politician and minister of propaganda for the Third Reich)

370. *Enemy of Women* (1944). 86 min. Monogram Prod. D: Alfred Zeisler.
Goebbels: Paul Andor
Supporting cast: Claudia Drake, Sigrid Gurie, H.B. Warner, Donald Woods

Goldman, Emma, 1869–1940
See **Reed, John.**

Goliath, c. 11th century
See **David,** King of Israel.

Goodman, Benny, 1909–1986. (American band leader and clarinetist known as the "King of Swing")

371. *The Benny Goodman Story* (1955). 116 min. Universal- International. D: Valentine Davies.
     Goodman: Steve Allen
     Supporting cast: Sammy Davis, Jr., Harry James, Gene Krupa, Donna Reed

Gordon, Barbara, 1935– (American documentary filmmaker and television producer)

372. *I'm Dancing As Fast As I Can* (1982). 107 min. Paramount Pictures. D: Jack Hofsiss.
     Gordon: Jill Clayburgh
     Supporting cast: Joe Pesci, Dianne Wiest, Nicol Williamson

Gordon, Charles, 1833–1885. (British Army general killed during the siege of Khartoum)

373. *Khartoum* (1966). 128 min. United Artists. D: Basil Dearden.
     Gordon: Charlton Heston
     Mohammed Ahmed "Mahdi": Laurence Olivier
     Supporting cast: Richard Johnson, Alexander Knox, Ralph Richardson

Gordon, Patrick, 1635–1699
     See **Peter I,** Emperor of Russia.

Gordon, Ruth, 1896–1985. (American stage and film actress and author)

374. *The Actress* (1953). 91 min. MGM. D: George Cukor.
     Gordon: Jean Simmons
     Supporting cast: Anthony Perkins, Spencer Tracy, Ian Wolfe, Teresa Wright

Gortner, Marjoe, 1944– (American evangelist and film actor)

375. *Marjoe* (1972). 88 min. Cinema Prod. D: Howard Smith, Sarah Kernochan.
     Documentary

Goya y Lucientes, Francisco de, 1746–1828. (Spanish painter, etcher, and lithographer)

376. *The Naked Maja* (1959). 111 min. United Artists. D: Henry Koster.
Goya: Anthony Franciosa
Supporting cast: Gino Cervi, Ava Gardner, Amedeo Nazzari, Massimo Serato

Grafton, John. (American police officer)

377. *Trackdown: Finding the Goodbar Killer* (1983). 100 min. Grosso-Jacobson Prod. D: Bill Persky.
Grafton: George Segal
Supporting cast: Shelley Hack, Alan North, Tracy Pollan, Shannon Presby

Graham, Barbara, 1923–1955. (American murderer sent to the gas chamber)

378. *I Want to Live* (1958). 120 min. United Artists. D: Robert Wise.
Graham: Susan Hayward
Supporting cast: Theodore Bikel, Simon Oakland, Virginia Vincent

379. *I Want to Live* (1983). 100 min. United Artists Television. D: David Lowell Rich.
Graham: Lindsay Wagner
Supporting cast: Martin Balsam, Pamela Reed, Harry Dean Stanton

Graham, Calvin L., 1930?– (American sailor and World War II hero unjustly convicted of desertion)

379a *Too Young the Hero* (1988). 86 min. Pierre Cossette Productions. D: Buzz Kulik.
Graham: Ricky Schroder
Supporting cast: John De Vries, John Linton, Debra Mooney, Mary Louise Parker

Graham, Sheilah, 1908–
    See **Fitzgerald, F. Scott.**

Graham, Stan. (New Zealand farmer who committed seven of
    the grisliest murders in history)

379b *Bad Blood* (1987). 104 min. Academy Home Entertainment.
    D: Mike Newell.
    Graham: Jack Thompson
    Supporting cast: Donna Akersten, Carol Burns, Dennis
      Lill, Martyn Sanderson

Grant, Cary, 1904–1986
    See **Loren, Sophia.**

Gray, Pete, 1915– (Disabled American baseball player who
    played outfield for the St. Louis Browns during World War
    II)

379c *A Winner Never Quits* (1986). 104 min. Columbia Pictures
    Television. D: Mel Damski.
    Gray: Keith Carradine
    Supporting cast: G.W. Bailey, Fionnula Flanagan, Dennis
      Weaver, Mare Winningham

Graziani, Rodolfo, 1882–1955
    See **Mukhtar, Omar.**

Graziano, Rocky, 1922– (American heavyweight boxer who
    retired from the ring undefeated)

380. *Somebody Up There Likes Me* (1956). 113 min. MGM. D:
    Robert Wise.
    Graziano: Paul Newman
    Supporting cast: Pier Angeli, Eileen Heckart, Harold J.
      Stone

Great Vance, The, 1840–1888
   See **Leybourne, George.**

Greco, El, 1541–1614. (Spanish painter and exponent of mysticism in art)

381. *El Greco* (1966). 95 min. 20th Century-Fox. D: Luciano Salce.
   El Greco: Mel Ferrer
   Supporting cast: Adolfo Celi, Franco Giacobini, Renzo Giovampietro, Rossanna Schiaffino

Green, Hannah, 1932– (American writer)

382. *I Never Promised You a Rose Garden* (1977). 96 min. Warner Bros. D: Anthony Page.
   Green: Kathleen Quinlan
   Supporting cast: Bibi Andersson, Signe Hasso, Reni Santoni, Susan Tyrrell

Greenberg, Dave, 1943– (American police officer)

383. *The Super Cops* (1974). 94 min. MGM. D: Gordon Parks.
   Greenberg: Ron Leibman
   Bob Hantz: David Selby
   Supporting cast: Dan Frazer, Sheila Frazier, Pat Hingle

Greenberg, Joanne, 1932–
   See **Green, Hannah.**

Greenberg, Stanley R.
   See **Pelosi, James.**

Gregory, Jim, 1950– (American collegiate football player, first white player on Grambling College's team)

384. *Grambling's White Tiger* (1981). 100 min. Jenner/Wallach Prod. D: Georg Stanford Brown.

Gregory: Bruce Jenner
Eddie Robinson: Harry Belafonte
Supporting cast: LeVar Burton, Dennis Haysbert, Deborah
   Pratt, Ray Vitte

Grey, Jane, Queen of England, 1537–1554.

385. *Lady Jane* (1985). 142 min. Paramount Pictures. D: Trevor
   Nunn.
   Grey: Helena Bonham Carter
   Supporting cast: Jill Bennett, Cary Elwes, Michael Hor-
      dern, John Wood

Grieg, Edvard, 1843–1907. (Leading Norwegian composer
   known for the strongly pronounced nationalism of his
   music)

386. *Song of Norway* (1970). 142 min. ABC Pictures. D: Andrew
   L. Stone.
   Grieg: Torval Maursted
   Nina Hagerup Grieg: Florence Henderson
   Henrik Ibsen: Frederick Jaeger
   Franz Liszt: Henry Gilbert
   Rikard Nordraak: Frank Porretta
   Supporting cast: Robert Morley, Edward G. Robinson,
      Christina Schollin, Harry Secombe

Grieg, Nina Hagerup, 1845–1935
   See **Grieg, Edvard.**

Griffith, Corinne, 1896– (American film actress)

387. *Papa's Delicate Condition* (1963). 98 min. Paramount Pic-
   tures. D: George Marshall.
   Griffith: Linda Bruhl
   Supporting cast: Jackie Gleason, Glynis Johns, Charles
      Ruggles

Grimaldi, Rainier de, 1923–
    See **Kelly, Grace.**

Grimble, Arthur, 1888–1956. (British colonial administrator on Central Pacific Islands)

388. *Pacific Destiny* (1956). 97 min. British-Lion Prod. D: Wolf Rilla.
    Grimble: Denholm Elliott
    Supporting cast: Felix Felton, Michael Hordern, Gordon Jackson, Susan Stephen

Grimm, Jacob, 1786–1859
    See **Grimm, Wilhelm.**

Grimm, Wilhelm, 1785–1863. (German philologist and collector of traditional folktales)

389. *The Wonderful World of the Brothers Grimm* (1963). 129 min. MGM. D: Henry Levin, George Pal.
    Grimm: Laurence Harvey
    Jacob Grimm: Karl Boehm
    Supporting cast: Claire Bloom, Oscar Homolka, Walter Slezak

Groda-Lewis, Mary, 1949– (American award-winning physician who overcame dyslexia, reform school, and a stroke to achieve her dream of becoming a physician)

389a *Love, Mary* (1985). 120 min. CBS Entertainment. D: Robert Day.
    Groda-Lewis: Kristy McNichol
    Supporting cast: Matt Clark, Piper Laurie, David Paymer, Rachel Ticotin

Grosso, Salvatore "Sonny," 1938?–
    See **Egan, Eddie.**

Groves, Leslie R., 1896–1970
 See **Oppenheimer, J. Robert.**

Guarneri String Quartet. (American musical group which is the oldest "original" string quartet in the world)

389b *High Fidelity—The Adventures of the Guarneri String Quartet* (1989). 85 min. Four Oaks Foundation. D: Allan Miller. Documentary.

Guerre, Martin, fl. 1560. (French imposter)

390. *The Return of Martin Guerre* (1982). 111 min. European International. D: Daniel Vigne.
 Guerre: Gerard Depardieu, Bernard-Pierre Donnadieu, Stephane Peau
 Supporting cast: Maurice Barrier, Nathalie Baye, Sylvie Meda, Isabelle Sadoyan

Guevara, Ernesto "Che," 1928–1967. (Latin American revolutionary leader)

391. *Che* (1969). 96 min. 20th Century-Fox. D: Richard Fleischer.
 Guevara: Omar Sharif
 Fidel Castro: Jack Palance
 Supporting cast: Cesare Danova, Robert Loggia, Barbara Luna, Woody Strode

Guinan, Mary "Texas," 1888?–1933. (1920's New York nightclub queen)

392. *Incendiary Blonde* (1945). 113 min. Paramount Pictures. D: George Marshall.
 Guinan: Betty Hutton
 Supporting cast: Arturo de Cordova, Barry Fitzgerald, Charles Ruggles

Gunn, Mrs. Aeneas, 1870–1961. (Australian pioneer and first white woman to travel to the Never-Never, the Northern Territory populated by aborigines, of which she wrote an account in her book *We of the Never-Never*)

393. *We of the Never-Never* (1983). 132 min. Triumph Films. D: Igor Auzins.
Gunn: Angela Punch McGregor
Supporting cast: Tony Barry, Arthur Dignam, Lewis Fitz-Gerald, Tommy Lewis

Gunther, Frances, 1897?–1964
See **Gunther, John.**

Gunther, John, 1901–1970. (American journalist and European correspondent)

394. *Death Be Not Proud* (1975). 100 min. Westfall Productions. D: Donald Wrye.
Gunther: Arthur Hill
Frances Gunther: Jane Alexander
John Gunther, Jr.: Robby Benson
Supporting cast: Linden Chiles, Ralph Clanton, Wendy Phillips

Gunther, John, Jr., 1929–1947
See **Gunther, John.**

Gurdjieff, Georges Ivanovitch, 1872–1949. (Famed Russian cult leader)

394a *Meetings With Remarkable Men* (1979). 107 min. Remar Libra. D: Peter Brook.
Gurdjieff: Dragan Maksimovic
Gurdjieff (as a young man): Mikica Dimitrijevic
Supporting cast: Athol Fugard, Bruce Myers, Terence Stamp, Gerry Sundquist

Guthrie, Woody, 1912–1967. (American Depression era folk-singer and composer)

395. *Bound for Glory* (1976). 147 min. United Artists. D: Hal Ashby.
Guthrie: David Carradine
Supporting cast: Ronny Cox, Melinda Dillon, John Lehne, Gail Strickland

395a *A Vision Shared: A Tribute to Woody Guthrie and Leadbelly* (1988). 72 min. CBS Music Video Enterprises. D: Jim Brown.
Documentary.

Gwyn, Nell, 1650–1687. (British comedy actress and mistress of Charles II)

396. *Nell Gwyn* (1934). 87 min. United Artists. D: Herbert Wilcox.
Gwyn: Anna Neagle
Charles II: Cedric Hardwicke
Samuel Pepys: Esme Percy
Supporting cast: Laurence Anderson, Jeanne de Casalis, Miles Malleson, Helena Pickard

Gypsy Rose Lee, 1914–1970. (American stripper)

397. *Gypsy* (1962). 149 min. Warner Bros. D: Mervyn LeRoy.
Gypsy: Natalie Wood
June Havoc: Suzanne Cupito, Ann Jillian, Diane Pace
Supporting cast: Parley Baer, Karl Malden, Rosalind Russell, Paul Wallace

H

Hagerup, Nina, 1845–1935
See **Grieg, Edvard.**

Haggart, David, 1801–1821. (Scottish highwayman)

398. *Sinful Davey* (1969). 95 min. United Artists. D: John Huston.
Haggart: John Hurt

Supporting cast: Nigel Davenport, Pamela Franklin, Ronald Fraser, Robert Morley

Halbert, Frederic, 1945– (American farmer whose son and cattle were among poison victims of an industrial accident)

399. *Bitter Harvest* (1981). 100 min. Charles Fries Prod. D: Roger Young.
Halbert/DeVries: Ron Howard
Sandra Halbert/DeVries: Tarah Nutter
Supporting cast: Art Carney, Barry Corbin, Richard Dysart, David Knell

Halbert, Sandra, 1943–
See **Halbert, Frederic.**

Haldeman, H.R., 1926–
See **Dean, John.**

Halliwell, Kenneth, 1926?–1967
See **Orton, Joe.**

Halsey, William F., 1882–1959 (Admiral and commander of U.S. 3rd Fleet in the Pacific)

400. *The Gallant Hours* (1960). 115 min. United Artists. D: Robert Montgomery.
Halsey: James Cagney
Supporting cast: Richard Jaeckel, Les Tremayne, Dennis Weaver

Hambleton, Iceal E., 1919?– (American Air Force colonel shot down over Vietnam who survived in the jungle for twelve days before being rescued)

400a *Bat 21* (1988). 105 min. Tri-Star Pictures. D: Peter Markle.
Hambleton: Gene Hackman

Supporting cast: David Marshall Grant, Danny Glover, Jerry Reed, Clayton Rohner

Hamilton, Alexander, 1757–1804. (First American Secretary of the Treasury)

401. *Alexander Hamilton* (1931). 73 min. Warner Bros. D: John Adolfi.
Hamilton: George Arliss
John Jay: Charles Middleton
Thomas Jefferson: Montagu Love
George Washington: Alan Mowbray
Supporting cast: Lionel Belmore, Doris Kenyon, Gwendolin Logan, John T. Murray

SEE ALSO: **Washington, George.**

Hamilton, Emma, 1761–1815. (British mistress of Admiral Nelson)

402. *Lady Hamilton* (1969). 98 min. Rapid-P.E.A.-S.N.C. D: Christian Jaque.
Hamilton: Michele Mercier
Horatio Nelson: Richard Johnson
Supporting cast: Robert Hundar, Harald Leipnitz, John Mills, Nadja Tiller

403. *That Hamilton Woman* (1941). 125 min. Korda Prod. D: Alexander Korda.
Hamilton: Vivien Leigh
Horatio Nelson: Laurence Olivier
Supporting cast: Sara Allgood, Gladys Cooper, Alan Mowbray

SEE ALSO: **Nelson, Horatio.**

Hamilton, Polly
See **Sage, Anna.**

Hammett, Dashiell, 1894–1961. (American mystery writer best known for creating the fictional detectives "Nick and Nora Charles")

404. *Hammett* (1983). 97 min. Warner Bros. D: Wim Wenders.
   Hammett: Frederic Forrest
   Supporting cast: Peter Boyle, Marilu Henner, Roy Kinnear

   SEE ALSO: **Hellman, Lillian.**

Hampton, Fred, 1948–1969. (African-American Black Panther leader who was killed during a police raid on Black Panther headquarters)

404a *The Murder of Fred Hampton* (1971). 88 min. Mike Gray & Associates. D: Michael Gray, Howard Alk.
   Documentary.

   SEE ALSO: **Ginsberg, Allen.**

Hampton, Fred, Jr.
   See **Ginsberg, Allen.**

Handel, George Frideric, 1685–1759. (German-born English composer best known for his oratorios)

405. *The Great Mr. Handel* (1942). 103 min. J. Arthur Rank. D: Norman Walker.
   Handel: Wilfrid Lawson
   Supporting cast: Elizabeth Allan, Malcolm Keen, Max Kirby, Michael Shepley

Handy, W.C., 1873–1958. (African-American musician and composer known as "father of the blues")

406. *St. Louis Blues* (1958). 93 min. Paramount Pictures. D: Allen Reisner.
   Handy: Nat King Cole
   Supporting cast: Pearl Bailey, Ruby Dee, Eartha Kitt

Hanff, Helene. (American writer and book collector)

406a *84 Charing Cross Road* (1987). 99 min. Columbia Pictures. D: David Jones.
   Hanff: Anne Bancroft
   Frank Doel: Anthony Hopkins
   Supporting cast: Eleanor David, Jean De Baer, Judi Dench, Maurice Denham

Hanlan, Edward "Ned," 1855–1908. (Canadian rowing champion who set records that have stood for a hundred years)

406b *The Boy in Blue* (1986). 98 min. 20th Century-Fox. D: Charles Jarrott.
   Hanlan: Nicolas Cage
   Supporting cast: Cynthia Dale, David Naughton, Christopher Plummer, Sean Sullivan

Hannibal, 247–183 B.C. (Carthaginian general)

407. *Hannibal* (1960). 103 min. Warner Bros. D: Edgar G. Ulmer.
   Hannibal: Victor Mature
   Supporting cast: Gabriele Ferzetti, Rita Gam, Milly Vitale

Hanson, Marla, 1961– (American model whose face was seriously disfigured when attacked by hired assailants)

407a *The Marla Hanson Story* (1991). 96 min. Citadel Entertainment. D: John Gray.
   Hanson: Cheryl Pollack
   Supporting cast: Kirk Baltz, Madison Mason, Dale Midkiff, Jennifer Van Dyke

Hantz, Robert, 1945?–
   See **Greenberg, Dave.**

Hardin, John Wesley, 1853–1895. (American lawyer and outlaw)

408. *The Lawless Breed* (1952). 83 min. Universal-International. D: Raoul Walsh.

Hardin: Rock Hudson
Supporting cast: Julia Adams, Michael Ansara, Hugh O'Brian

Harel, Isser, 1912–1963. (Head of Israeli intelligence)

409. *The House on Garibaldi Street* (1979). 100 min. Charles Fries Prod. D: Peter Collinson.
Harel: Martin Balsam
Adolf Eichmann: Alfred Burke
Supporting cast: Nick Mancuso, Janet Suzman, Topol

Hargitay, Mickey, 1929?–
See **Mansfield, Jayne.**

Hargreaves, Alice Pleasance Liddell, 1852–1934. (British girl who was the inspiration for Alice in Lewis Carroll's *Alice In Wonderland*)

409a *Dreamchild* (1985). 90 min. Thorn EMI Screen Entertainment. D: Gavin Millar.
Hargreaves: Coral Browne
Hargreaves (as a child): Amelia Shankley
Lewis Carroll: Ian Holm
Supporting cast: Jane Asher, Caris Corfman, Nicola Cowper, Peter Gallagher

Harlow, Jean, 1911–1937. (American film actress and the first of the Hollywood blonde sex symbols)

410. *Harlow* (1965). 125 min. Paramount Pictures. D: Gordon Douglas.
Harlow: Carroll Baker
Supporting cast: Red Buttons, Michael Connors, Peter Lawford

411. *Harlow* (1965). 109 min. Magna Pictures. D: Alex Segal.
Harlow: Carol Lynley
Supporting cast: Hurd Hatfield, Barry Sullivan, Efrem Zimbalist, Jr.

Harlowe, Honey
See **Bruce, Lenny.**

Harmon, Leola Mae. (U.S. Air Force nurse)

412. *Why Me?* (1984). 100 min. Lorimar Prod. D: Fielder Cook.
Harmon: Glynnis O'Connor
James Stallings: Armand Assante
Supporting cast: Bruce Abbott, Annie Potts, Michael Sacks,
Craig Wasson

Harris, David, 1960–
See **Adams, Randall Dale.**

Harris, Frank, 1855–1931. (American writer)

413. *Cowboy* (1958). 92 min. Columbia Pictures. D: Delmer
Daves.
Harris: Jack Lemmon
Supporting cast: Brian Donlevy, Glenn Ford, Anna Kashfi,
Dick York

Harris, Jean, 1924– (American teacher and murderer)

414. *The People Vs. Jean Harris* (1981). 150 min. PKO Television,
Ltd. D: George Schaefer.
Harris: Ellen Burstyn
Supporting cast: Martin Balsam, Peter Coyote, Richard
Dysart, Priscilla Morrill

Harris, Townsend, 1804–1878. (American ambassador and first
U.S. consul to Japan)

415. *The Barbarian and the Geisha* (1958). 104 min. 20th Century-
Fox. D: John Huston.
Harris: John Wayne
Supporting cast: Eiko Ando, Sam Jaffe, Soh Yamamura

Harrison, George, 1943–
   See **Beatles, The.**

Hart, Lorenz, 1895–1943
   See **Rodgers, Richard.**

Hart, Moss, 1904–1961. (American librettist and playwright)

416. *Act One* (1963). 110 min. Warner Bros. D: Dore Schary.
   Hart: George Hamilton
   George S. Kaufman: Jason Robards
   Supporting cast: Ruth Ford, Jack Klugman, Sam Levene,
   Eli Wallach

Harte, Bret, 1836–1902
   See **Twain, Mark.**

Hassan, Concetta. (American mother who became an Army
   helicopter pilot)

416a *A Time to Triumph* (1986). 120 min. Phoenix Entertainment
   Group. D: Noel Black.
   Hassan: Patty Duke
   Supporting cast: Joseph Bologna, Julie Bovasso, Denise
   Mickelbury, Dara Modglin

Hastings, Beatrice, 1879–1943
   See **Modigliani, Amedeo.**

Hauptmann, Bruno Richard, 1899–1935
   See **Lindbergh, Charles.**

Hauser, Kaspar, 1812–1833. (German youth who was isolated in
   a dark cellar from birth to age seventeen years)

416b *The Mystery of Kaspar Hauser* (1975). 109 min. Libra Cinema 5 Films. D: Werner Herzog.
      Hauser: Bruno S.
      Supporting cast: Walter Ladengast, Brigitte Mira, Hans Musaus, Willy Semmelrogge

Havoc, June, 1916–
      See **Gypsy Rose Lee.**

Hawksworth, Henry. (American victim of multiple personalities)

417. *The Five of Me* (1981). 100 min. Jack Farren Prod. D: Paul Wendkos.
      Hawksworth: David Birney
      Supporting cast: John McLiam, Mitchell Ryan, Dee Wallace, James Whitmore, Jr.

Hayden, Melissa, 1928–
      See **Balanchine, George.**

Hayes, Billy, 1947?– (American who served a prison sentence in Turkey for drug smuggling)

418. *Midnight Express* (1978). 121 min. Columbia Pictures. D: Alan Parker.
      Hayes: Brad Davis
      Supporting cast: Bo Hopkins, Irene Miracle, Randy Quaid

Hayes, Ira Hamilton, 1922–1955. (Native American Marine who fought at Iwo Jima)

419. *The Outsider* (1961). 108 min. Universal-International. D: Delbert Mann.
      Hayes: Tony Curtis
      Supporting cast: Bruce Bennett, James Franciscus, Gregory Walcott

Hays, Lee, 1914–1981
  See **Weavers, The.**

Hayward, Bridget, 1939?–1960
  See **Hayward, Leland.**

Hayward, Brooke, 1937–
  See **Hayward, Leland.**

Hayward, Leland, 1902–1971. (American producer and theatrical agent)

420. *Haywire* (1980). 200 min. Warner Bros. Television. D: Michael Tuchner.
  Hayward: Jason Robards
  Bridget Hayward: Dianne Hull
  Brooke Hayward: Deborah Raffin
  William Hayward: Hart Bochner
  Margaret Sullavan: Lee Remick
  Supporting cast: Linda Gray, Christopher Guest, Dean Jagger, Richard Johnson

Hayward, William, 1941–
  See **Hayward, Leland.**

Hayworth, Rita, 1918–1987. (American film actress of the 1940's best known for her sultry film image)

421. *Rita Hayworth: The Love Goddess* (1983). 100 min. The Susskind Co. D: James Goldstone.
  Hayworth: Lynda Carter
  Orson Welles: Edward Edwards
  Supporting cast: John Considine, Jane Hallaren, Michael Lerner, Alejandro Rey

Hearst, Patty, 1954– (American kidnap victim and convicted bank robber)

422. *The Ordeal of Patty Hearst* (1979). 150 min. Finnegan Assoc.
   D: Paul Wendkos.
   Hearst: Lisa Eilbacher
   Charles Bates: Dennis Weaver
   Supporting cast: Stephen Elliott, David Haskell, Dolores
      Sutton

422a *Patty Hearst* (1988). 108 min. Atlantic Entertainment. D:
   Paul Schrader.
   Hearst: Natasha Richardson
   Supporting cast: Frances Fisher, William Forsythe, Jodi
      Long, Ving Rhames

Hearst, William Randolph, 1863–1951. (American newspaper
   magnate)

423. *The Hearst and Davies Affair* (1985). 100 min. ABC Circle
   Films. D: David Lowell Rich.
   Hearst: Robert Mitchum
   Marion Davies: Virginia Madsen
   Supporting cast: Doris Belack, Fritz Weaver

Heartfield, John, 1891–1968. (German photomontagist)

424. *John Heartfield, Photomontagist* (1981). 63 min. British Film
   Institute. D: Helmut Herbst.
   Documentary

Hecht, Ben, 1894–1964. (American writer, frequent collaborator
   with Charles MacArthur)

425. *Gaily, Gaily* (1969). 107 min. United Artists. D: Norman
   Jewison.
   Hecht/Harvey: Beau Bridges
   Supporting cast: Hume Cronyn, Brian Keith, George Ken-
      nedy, Melina Mercouri

Hefner, Hugh, 1926–
   See **Stratten, Dorothy.**

Held, Anna, 1873–1918
See **Ziegfeld, Florenz.**

Hellerman, Fred, 1927–
See **Weavers, The.**

Hellman, Lillian, 1905–1984. (American playwright)

426. *Julia* (1977). 118 min. 20th Century-Fox. D: Fred Zinnemann.
Hellman: Jane Fonda
Dashiell Hammett: Jason Robards
Dorothy Parker: Rosemary Murphy
Supporting cast: John Glover, Hal Holbrook, Vanessa Redgrave, Maximilian Schell, Meryl Streep

Helmsley, Harry, 1909–
See **Helmsley, Leona.**

Helmsley, Leona, 1919– (American real estate investor known as the "Queen of Mean" who was convicted of tax evasion)

426a *Leona Helmsley: The Queen of Mean* (1990). 96 min. Charles Fries Entertainment. D: Richard Michaels.
Helmsley: Suzanne Pleshette
Harry Helmsley: Lloyd Bridges
Supporting cast: Joe Regalbuto, Raymond Singer, Bruce Weitz

Heloise, 1101–1164
See **Abelard, Peter.**

Helton, Jacquelyn. (American cancer victim)

427. *Sunshine* (1973). 150 min. Universal Pictures. D: Joseph Sargent.

Helton/Hayden: Cristina Raines
Supporting cast: Cliff De Young, Meg Foster, Brenda Vaccaro

Hemingway, Ernest, 1899–1961. (American journalist, novelist and short-story writer)

428. *Hemingway's Adventures of a Young Man* (1962). 145 min. 20th Century-Fox. D: Martin Ritt.
Hemingway/Adams: Richard Beymer
Supporting cast: Diane Baker, Paul Newman, Eli Wallach

Henderson, Ray, 1896–1970
See **DeSylva, Buddy.**

Hendrix, Jimi, 1942–1970. (African-American rock musician)

429. *Jimi Hendrix* (1973). 102 min. Warner Bros. D: Joe Boyd, John Head, Gary Weis.
Documentary

429a *Jimi Plays Monterey* (1989). 55 min. Movie Visions. D: D.A. Pennebaker, Chris Hegedus
Documentary.

Henry II, King of England, 1133–1189.

430. *The Lion in Winter* (1968). 135 min. Embassy Pictures. D: Anthony Harvey.
Henry: Peter O'Toole
Eleanor: Katharine Hepburn
Supporting cast: Timothy Dalton, Anthony Hopkins, Jane Merrow

SEE ALSO: **Becket, Thomas.**

Henry V, King of England, 1387–1422.

431. *Henry V* (1945). 137 min. United Artists. D: Laurence Olivier.

Henry: Laurence Olivier
Catherine of Valois: Renee Asherson
Supporting cast: Leslie Banks, Leo Genn, Esmond Knight, Robert Newton

431a *Henry V* (1989). 135 min. Samuel Goldwyn Home Entertainment. D: Kenneth Branagh.
Henry: Kenneth Branagh
Catherine of Valois: Emma Thompson
Supporting cast: Brian Blessed, Ian Holm, Derek Jacobi, Alec McCowen

Henry VIII, King of England, 1491–1547.

432. *Henry VIII and His Six Wives* (1973). 125 min. Levitt-Pickman Film Corp. D: Waris Hussein.
Henry: Keith Michell
Catherine of Aragon: Frances Cuka
Anne Boleyn: Charlotte Rampling
Jane Seymour: Jane Asher
Catherine Howard: Lynne Frederick
Anne of Cleves: Jenny Bos
Catherine Parr: Barbara Leigh-Hunt
Supporting cast: Donald Pleasence

433. *The Private Life of Henry VIII* (1933). 97 min. United Artists. D: Alexander Korda.
Henry: Charles Laughton
Anne Boleyn: Merle Oberon
Jane Seymour: Wendy Barrie
Catherine Howard: Binnie Barnes
Anne of Cleves: Elsa Lanchester
Catherine Parr: Everley Gregg
Supporting cast: Claude Allister, Robert Donat, Franklin Dyall, Miles Mander

SEE ALSO: **Boleyn, Anne; Elizabeth I,** Queen of England; **More, Thomas; Tudor, Mary.**

Hensler, Paul G., 1947– (U.S. soldier in Vietnam War)

434. *Don't Cry, It's Only Thunder* (1981). 120 min. Sanrio Co., Ltd. D: Peter Werner.
Hensler/Anderson: Dennis Christopher
Supporting cast: Roger Aaron Brown, Lisa Lu, Susan Saint James, James Whitmore, Jr.

Hepburn, Katharine, 1909–
See **Hughes, Howard.**

Herbert, Victor, 1859–1924. (Irish-American composer and conductor best known for his light operas)

435. *The Great Victor Herbert* (1939). 84 min. Paramount Pictures. D: Andrew L. Stone.
Herbert: Walter Connolly
Supporting cast: Susanna Foster, Allan Jones, Mary Martin

SEE ALSO: **Kern, Jerome.**

Herman, Victor, 1915–1985. (American incarcerated in a Siberian prison in the late 1930's)

436. *Coming Out of the Ice* (1982). 100 min. Konigsberg Company. D: Waris Hussein.
Herman: John Savage
Supporting cast: Francesca Annis, Ben Cross, Willie Nelson, Frank Windsor

Herod the Great, King of Judea, 73–4 B.C.

437. *Herod the Great* (1959). 93 min. Samuel Schneider. D: Arnaldo Genoino.
Herod: Edmund Purdom
Supporting cast: Sylvia Lopez, Alberto Lupo, Sandra Milo

Herriot, James, 1916– (British veterinarian and author best known for his autobiographical works)

438. *All Creatures Great and Small* (1974). 92 min. Talent Assoc. D: Claude Whatham.
Herriot: Simon Ward
Siegfried Farnon: Anthony Hopkins
Supporting cast: Lisa Harrow, Freddie Jones, Brian Stirner

439. *All Things Bright and Beautiful* (1979). 94 min. World Pictures. D: Eric Till.
Herriot: John Alderton
Siegfried Farnon: Colin Blakely
Supporting cast: Lisa Harrow, Bill Maynard, Richard Pearson

Hettinger, Karl. (American police officer)

440. *The Onion Field* (1979). 122 min. Avco Embassy Corp. D: Harold Becker.
Hettinger: John Savage
Ian Campbell: Ted Danson
Supporting cast: Ronny Cox, David Huffman, Franklyn Seales, James Woods

Heydrich, Reinhard, 1904–1942. (Deputy chief of Gestapo; assassinated)

441. *Hangmen Also Die* (1943). 131 min. United Artists. D: Fritz Lang.
Heydrich: Hans V. Twardowski
Supporting cast: Walter Brennan, Brian Donlevy, Anna Lee

442. *Hitler's Hangman* (1943). 84 min. MGM. D: Douglas Sirk.
Heydrich: John Carradine
Supporting cast: Alan Curtis, Ralph Morgan, Patricia Morison

443. *Operation Daybreak* (1975). 102 min. Warner Bros. D: Lewis Gilbert.
Heydrich: Anton Diffring
Supporting cast: Joss Ackland, Timothy Bottoms, Martin Shaw

Hickock, Richard, 1931–1965
   See **Smith, Perry.**

Hickok, James Butler "Wild Bill," 1837–1876. (Frontier scout and U.S. marshal)

444. *Badlands of Dakota* (1941). 74 min. Universal Pictures. D: Alfred E. Green.
   Hickok: Richard Dix
   Supporting cast: Frances Farmer, Ann Rutherford, Robert Stack

445. *Frontier Scout* (1938). 61 min. Fine Arts/Grand National. D: Sam Newfield.
   Hickok: George Houston
   Supporting cast: Guy Chase, Beth Marion, Al St. John

446. *I Killed Wild Bill Hickok* (1956). 63 min. Associated Artists. D: Richard Talmadge.
   Hickok: Tom Brown
   Supporting cast: Frank Carpenter, John Forbes, Helen Westcott

447. *The Plainsman* (1937). 113 min. Paramount Pictures. D: Cecil B. DeMille.
   Hickok: Gary Cooper
   Martha Jane Canary/Calamity Jane: Jean Arthur
   William Cody/Buffalo Bill: James Ellison
   Supporting cast: Charles Bickford, Porter Hall, Victor Varconi

448. *The Plainsman* (1966). 92 min. Universal Pictures. D: David Lowell Rich.
   Hickok: Don Murray
   Martha Jane Canary/Calamity Jane: Abby Dalton
   William Cody/Buffalo Bill: Guy Stockwell
   Supporting cast: Bradford Dillman, Leslie Nielsen, Henry Silva

449. *Pony Express* (1953). 101 min. Paramount Pictures. D: Jerry Hopper.
   Hickok: Forrest Tucker

William Cody/Buffalo Bill: Charlton Heston
Supporting cast: Rhonda Fleming, Jan Sterling

450. *The White Buffalo* (1977). 97 min. United Artists. D: J. Lee Thompson.
Hickok: Charles Bronson
Supporting cast: Kim Novak, Will Sampson, Jack Warden

451. *Wild Bill Hickok Rides* (1942). 81 min. Warner Bros. D: Ray Enright.
Hickok: Bruce Cabot
Supporting cast: Constance Bennett, Ward Bond, Warren William

452. *Young Bill Hickok* (1940). 59 min. Republic Pictures. D: Joseph Kane.
Hickok: Roy Rogers
Supporting cast: George Hayes, John Miljan, Jacqueline Wells

SEE ALSO: **Canary, Martha Jane ("Calamity Jane").**

Hill, Ann Kurth
See **Hill, John Robert.**

Hill, Barney, 1922?– (American UFO observer)

453. *The UFO Incident* (1975). 120 min. Universal Pictures. D: Richard A. Colla.
Hill: James Earl Jones
Betty Hill: Estelle Parsons
Supporting cast: Beeson Carroll, Barnard Hughes, Dick O'Neill

Hill, Betty, 1920?–
See **Hill, Barney.**

Hill, Joan Robinson, 1931–1969
See **Hill, John Robert.**

Hill, Joe, 1879–1915. (Swedish labor activist)

454. *Joe Hill* (1971). 114 min. Paramount Pictures. D: Bo Widerberg.
Hill: Thommy Berggren
Supporting cast: Evert Anderson, Kelvin Malave, Ania Schmidt, Cathy Smith

Hill, John Robert, 1931–1972. (American plastic surgeon and chief suspect in the death of his wife)

455. *Murder in Texas* (1981). 200 min. Billy Hale Films. D: Billy Hale.
Hill: Sam Elliott
Ann Kurth Hill: Katharine Ross
Joan Robinson Hill: Farrah Fawcett
Supporting cast: Dimitra Arliss, Andy Griffith, Craig T. Nelson

Hill, Virginia, 1916–1966. (Mistress of gangster Bugsy Siegel)

456. *The Virginia Hill Story* (1974). 90 min. RSO Films, Inc. D: Joel Schumacher.
Hill: Dyan Cannon
Benjamin "Bugsy" Siegel: Harvey Keitel
Supporting cast: Herbert Anderson, Allen Garfield, John Vernon

SEE ALSO: **Siegel, Benjamin** ("Bugsy")

Hirsch, Elroy, 1924– (American football player)

457. *Crazylegs* (1953). 87 min. Republic Pictures. D: Francis D. Lyon.
Hirsch: Elroy Hirsch
Supporting cast: Louise Lorimer, Lloyd Nolan, Joan Vohs

Hiss, Alger, 1904– (American State Department official accused of passing secret documents to a Communist spy in 1949)

457a *The Trials of Alger Hiss* (1980). 166 min. A History of Film Production. D: John Lowenthal.
Documentary.

Hitler, Adolf, 1889–1945. (German chancellor and architect of the Third Reich)

458. *The Black Fox* (1962). 89 min. Capri Films. D: Louis Clyde Stouman.
Documentary

459. *The Bunker* (1981). 150 min. Time-Life Prod. D: George Schaefer.
Hitler: Anthony Hopkins
Eva Braun: Susan Blakely
Supporting cast: Cliff Gorman, Martin Jarvis, Richard Jordan, Piper Laurie

460. *Hitler* (1962). 107 min. Allied Artists. D: Stuart Heisler.
Hitler: Richard Basehart
Supporting cast: Maria Emo, Martin Kosleck, Cordula Trantow

461. *Hitler—Dead or Alive* (1943). 64 min. Ben Judell. D: Nick Grinde.
Hitler: Bobby Watson
Supporting cast: Ward Bond, Bruce Edwards, Dorothy Tree

462. *The Hitler Gang* (1944). 101 min. Paramount Pictures. D: John Farrow.
Hitler: Bobby Watson
Supporting cast: Martin Kosleck, Alexander Pope, Victor Varconi

463. *Hitler: The Last Ten Days* (1973). 108 min. Paramount Pictures. D: Ennio de Concini.
Hitler: Alec Guinness
Supporting cast: Adolfo Celi, Diane Cilento, Simon Ward

464. *The Last Ten Days* (1956). 113 min. Columbia Pictures. D: G.W. Pabst.
Hitler: Albin Skoda

Supporting cast: Willy Krause, Lotte Tobisch, Oskar Werner

465. *Our Hitler* (1980). 450 min. Omni Zoetrope. D: Hans-Jurgen Syberberg.
   Documentary, with characters portrayed by actors in certain sections.

466. *The Strange Death of Adolf Hitler* (1943). 72 min. Universal-International. D: James Hogan.
   Hitler: Ludwig Donath
   Supporting cast: George Dolenz, Fritz Kortner, Gale Sondergaard

   SEE ALSO: **Mussolini, Benito; Speer, Albert.**

Hitzig, William, 1904–1983
   See **Cousins, Norman.**

Hockney, David, 1937– (British painter associated with the pop-art movement)

467. *A Bigger Splash* (1974). 105 min. Buzzy Enterprises, Ltd. D: Jack Hazan.
   Hockney: David Hockney
   Supporting cast: Celia Birtwell, Ossie Clark, Mo McDermott, Peter Schlesinger

Hoffa, Jimmy, 1913–1975? (American labor leader who mysteriously disappeared in 1975)

468. *Power* (1980). 200 min. Columbia Pictures Television. D: Barry Shear, Virgil Vogel.
   Hoffa/Vanda: Joe Don Baker
   Supporting cast: Ralph Bellamy, Karen Black, Howard da Silva

   SEE ALSO: **Kennedy, Robert F.**

Hoffman, Abbie, 1936–1989
  See **Ginsberg, Allen.**

Hogan, Ben, 1912– (American golfer who won all three U.S major titles in 1948 and in 1953 won every major world championship)

469. *Follow the Sun* (1951). 93 min. 20th Century-Fox. D: Sidney Lanfield.
  Hogan: Glenn Ford
  Supporting cast: Anne Baxter, June Havoc, Dennis O'Keefe

Holder, Maryse, 1941?–1977. (American university professor and writer who was murdered while visiting Mexico City)

469a *A Winter Tan* (1988). 91 min. Circle Films. D: Jackie Burroughs.
  Holder: Jackie Burroughs
  Supporting cast: Diane D'Aquila, Erando Gonzalez, Anita Olanick, Javier Torres Zarragoza

Holiday, Billie, 1915–1959. (African-American blues singer known as "Lady Day")

470. *Lady Sings the Blues* (1972). 144 min. Paramount Pictures. D: Sidney J. Furie.
  Holiday: Diana Ross
  Supporting cast: Sid Melton, Richard Pryor, Billy Dee Williams

Hollander, Xaviera, 1943– (New York madam in the 1960's)

471. *The Happy Hooker* (1975). 96 min. Cannon Films. D: Nicholas Sgarro.
  Hollander: Lynn Redgrave
  Supporting cast: Jean-Pierre Aumont, Tom Poston, Lovelady Powell

472. *My Pleasure Is My Business* (1974). 85 min. August Film
     Prod. D: Al Waxman.
     Hollander: Xaviera Hollander
     Supporting cast: Colin Fox, Kenneth Lynch, Henry Ramer

Holliday, John H. "Doc," 1849–1885. (American outlaw)

473. *Doc* (1971). 96 min. United Artists. D: Frank Perry.
     Holliday: Stacy Keach
     Wyatt Earp: Harris Yulin
     Katie Elder: Faye Dunaway
     Supporting cast: Denver John Collins, Dan Greenburg,
     Mike Whitney

   SEE ALSO: **Bonney, William ("Billy the Kid"); Earp,
   Wyatt; Masterson, William Barclay ("Bat").**

Holly, Buddy, 1936–1959. (American rock musician whose
career was cut short by a fatal airplane crash)

474. *The Buddy Holly Story* (1978). 114 min. Columbia Pictures.
     D: Steve Rash.
     Holly: Gary Busey
     Supporting cast: Amy Johnston, Maria Richwine, Charles
     Martin Smith, Don Stroud

   SEE ALSO: **Valens, Richie.**

Holmes, Fanny, d. 1929
   See **Holmes, Oliver Wendell.**

Holmes, Larry, 1949–
   See **Ali, Muhammad.**

Holmes, Oliver Wendell, 1841–1935. (American Supreme Court
justice, 1902–1932)

475. *The Magnificent Yankee* (1950). 80 min. MGM. D: John Sturges.
Holmes: Louis Calhern
Fanny Holmes: Ann Harding
Supporting cast: Eduard Franz, Philip Ober, Ian Wolfe

Hoover, J. Edgar, 1895–1972. (Director of the FBI, 1924–1972)

475a *J. Edgar Hoover* (1987). 120 min. Finnegan Company. D: Robert Collins.
Hoover: Treat Williams
Lyndon B. Johnson: Rip Torn
John F. Kennedy: Art Hindle
Robert F. Kennedy: James F. Kelly
Richard M. Nixon: Anthony Palmer
Supporting cast: Andrew Duggan, Louise Fletcher, Robert Harper, David Ogden Stiers

476. *The Private Files of J. Edgar Hoover* (1977). 112 min. American International Pictures. D: Larry Cohen.
Hoover (as an older man): Broderick Crawford
Hoover (as a younger man): James Wainwright
Robert F. Kennedy: Michael Parks
Martin Luther King: Raymond St. Jacques
Louis Lepke: Gordon Zimmerman
Supporting cast: Ronee Blakley, Dan Dailey, Jose Ferrer, Rip Torn

SEE ALSO: **Cohn, Roy; Karpis, Alvin; Kennedy, John F.; Kennedy, Robert F.; King, Martin Luther, Jr.; Lepke, Louis.**

Hopper, Edward, 1882–1967. (American painter best known for his portrayals of American urban life)

477. *Hopper's Silence* (1981). 46 min. Brian O'Doherty. D: Brian O'Doherty.
Documentary

Hopper, Hedda, 1890–1966
  See **Parsons, Louella.**

Horman, Beth
  See **Horman, Edmund.**

Horman, Charles, 1942–1973
  See **Horman, Edmund.**

Horman, Edmund. (American businessman whose son was killed by government forces in Chile)

478. *Missing* (1982). 122 min. Universal Pictures. D: Constantin Costa-Gavras.
  Horman: Jack Lemmon
  Beth Horman: Sissy Spacek
  Charles Horman: John Shea
  Supporting cast: Charles Cioffi, David Clennon, Melanie Mayron

Horn, Tom, 1860–1903. (American bounty hunter)

479. *Mr. Horn* (1979). 200 min. Lorimar Prod. D: Jack Starrett.
  Horn: David Carradine
  Al Sieber: Richard Widmark
  Supporting cast: Karen Black, Richard Masur, Clay Tanner

480. *Tom Horn* (1980). 98 min. Warner Bros. D: William Wiard.
  Horn: Steve McQueen
  Supporting cast: Elisha Cook, Linda Evans, Richard Farnsworth

Horowitz, Vladmir, 1904–1989. (Russian-American pianist whose name has become synonymous with pianistic excellence)

480a *Vladmir Horowitz, The Last Romantic* (1985). 90 min. Maysles Brothers. D: David Maysles, Albert Maysles.
  Documentary.

Horton, James Edwin, 1878–1973 (American judge who presided at the controversial 1931 Scottsboro rape trial)

481. *Judge Horton and the Scottsboro Boys* (1976). 100 min. Tomorrow Entertainment. D: Fielder Cook.
Horton: Arthur Hill
Supporting cast: Ken Kercheval, Vera Miles, Lewis J. Stadlen

Hoskins, John, 1898–1964. (American World War II admiral)

482. *The Eternal Sea* (1954). 103 min. Republic Pictures. D: John H. Auer.
Hoskins: Sterling Hayden
Supporting cast: Virginia Grey, Dean Jagger, Alexis Smith

Houdini, Bess, 1876?–1943
See **Houdini, Harry.**

Houdini, Harry, 1874–1926. (American magician and escape artist)

483. *The Great Houdinis* (1976). 100 min. ABC Circle Film. D: Melville Shavelson.
Houdini: Paul Michael Glaser
Bess Houdini: Sally Struthers
Supporting cast: Adrienne Barbeau, Ruth Gordon, Vivian Vance

484. *Houdini* (1953). 106 min. Paramount Pictures. D: George Marshall.
Houdini: Tony Curtis
Bess Houdini: Janet Leigh
Supporting cast: Angela Clarke, Stefan Schnabel, Torin Thatcher, Ian Wolfe

484a *Young Harry Houdini* (1987). 100 min. Walt Disney Productions. D: James Orr.
Houdini: Wil Wheaton
Houdini (as an adult): Jeffrey DeMunn

Supporting cast: Barry Corbin, Roy Dotrice, Jose Ferrer, Kerri Green

Houston, Jeanne Wakatuski, 1934– (Japanese-American World War II detention camp inmate)

485. *Farewell to Manzanar* (1976). 105 min. Universal Television. D: John Korty.
Houston (as a child): Oori Takeshita
Houston (as an adult): Nobu McCarthy
Supporting cast: Clyde Kasatu, Akemi Kikumura, Yuki Shimoda

Houston, Sam, 1793–1863. (American statesman and first president of the Republic of Texas)

486. *The First Texan* (1950). 82 min. Allied Artists. D: Byron Haskin.
Houston: Joel McCrea
Supporting cast: Felicia Farr, Wallace Ford, Jeff Morrow

486a *Houston: The Legend of Texas* (1986). 156 min. Taft Entertainment Television. D: Peter Levin.
Houston: Sam Elliot
Jim Bowie: Michael Beck
Antonio Santa Ana: Richard Yniguez
Supporting cast: Devon Ericson, Michael C. Gwynne, Bo Hopkins, Donald Moffat

487. *Man of Conquest* (1939). 105 min. Republic Pictures. D: George Nicholls, Jr.
Houston: Richard Dix
Supporting cast: Edward Ellis, Joan Fontaine, Gail Patrick

SEE ALSO: **Bowie, Jim.**

Hovick, Louise, 1914–1970
See **Gypsy Rose Lee.**

Howard, Catherine, Queen of England, 1520–1542
See **Henry VIII,** King of England.

Howard, Joseph E., 1878–1961. (American songwriter)

488. *I Wonder Who's Kissing Her Now* (1947). 104 min. 20th
Century-Fox. D: Lloyd Bacon.
Howard: Mark Stevens
Supporting cast: Reginald Gardiner, June Haver, Martha
Stewart

Hoxsey, Harry, 1901–1973. (American homeopathic medicine
practitioner who claimed to have a cure for cancer and
whose clinics were closed by the Food and Drug Administration after lengthy court battle)

488a *Hoxsey: Quacks Who Cure Cancer* (1988). 100 min. Realidad
Productions. D: Ken Ausabel.
Documentry.

Huckaby, Elizabeth, 1905– (American principal at first Southern school to be integrated in 1957)

489. *Crisis at Central High* (1981). 125 min. Time-Life Prod. D:
Lamont Johnson.
Huckaby: Joanne Woodward
Supporting cast: Charles Durning, Henderson Forsythe,
Shannon John, Tamu

Hughes, Francine, 1947– (American woman who murdered her
abusive husband)

490. *The Burning Bed* (1985). 95 min. Tisch/Avnet Financial. D:
Robert Greenwald.
Hughes: Farrah Fawcett
Supporting cast: James Callahan, Paul LeMat, Richard
Masur, Grace Zabriskie

Hughes, Howard, 1905–1976. (Eccentric American business-man)

491. *The Amazing Howard Hughes* (1977). 215 min. EMI TV. D: William A. Graham.
Hughes: Tommy Lee Jones
Noah Dietrich: Ed Flanders
Katharine Hepburn: Tovah Feldshuh
Supporting cast: Jim Antonio, Sorrell Booke, James Hampton, Lee Purcell

SEE ALSO: **Dummar, Melvin.**

Hughes, Langston, 1902–1967. (African-American poet and novelist)

491a *Looking For Langston* (1989). 40 min. Sankofa Film. D: Isaac Julien.
Documentary.

Hugo, Adele, 1830–1915. (Daughter of French author Victor Hugo)

492. *The Story of Adele H* (1976). 97 min. Warner Bros. D: Francois Truffaut.
Hugo: Isabelle Adjani
Supporting cast: Reubin Dorey, Sylvia Marriott, Bruce Robinson

Hurok, Sol, 1888–1974. (American impresario)

493. *Tonight We Sing* (1953). 109 min. 20th Century-Fox. D: Mitchell Leisen.
Hurok: David Wayne
Supporting cast: Roberta Peters, Ezio Pinza, Tamara Toumanova

Huston, John, 1906–1987. (American film director best known for his films *The Maltese Falcon* and *Treasure of Sierra Madre)*

493a *John Huston and the Dubliners* (1987). 60 min. Liffey Films. D: Lilyan Sievernich.
Documentary.

I

Ibsen, Henrik, 1828–1906
See **Grieg, Edvard.**

Innocent III, Pope, 1161–1216
See **Francis of Assisi,** Saint.

Isaacs, Carl Junior, 1953–
See **Isaacs, William Carroll.**

Isaacs, William Carroll "Billy," 1958?– (American teenager who helped his convict brother escape from prison and accompanied him on a twelve day murder spree in 1973 from Maryland to Georgia)

494a *Murder One* (1988). 90 min. Miramax Films. D: Graeme Campbell.
Isaacs: Henry Thomas
Wayne Coleman: Stephen Shellen
George Dungee: Errol Slue
Carl Isaacs: James Wilder

Isabella I, Queen of Spain, 1451–1504
See **Columbus, Christopher.**

Ishi, 1861?–1916. (Chief and last member of Yana tribe)

495. *Ishi: The Last of His Tribe* (1978). 150 min. Edward and Mildred Lewis Prod. D: Robert Ellis Miller.
Ishi: Eloy Phil Casados
Ishi: Joseph Running Fox

Supporting cast: Devon Ericson, Geno Silva, Dennis Weaver

Itard, Jean, 1775–1838. (French physician)

496. *The Wild Child* (1970). 85 min. Films du Carrosse. D: Francois Truffaut.
Itard: Francois Truffaut
Supporting cast: Jean-Pierre Cargol, Jean Daste, Francoise Seigner, Paul Ville

Ivan IV, "the Terrible," Emperor of Russia, 1530–1584.

497. *Ivan the Terrible, Part 1* (1943). 96 min. Janus Prod. D: Sergei Eisenstein.
Ivan: Nikolai Cherkasov
Supporting cast: Serafina Birman, Ludmila Tselikovskaya

498. *Ivan the Terrible, Part 2* (1946). 84 min. Janus Prod. D: Sergei Eisenstein.
Ivan: Nikolai Cherkasov
Supporting cast: Serafina Birman, Piotr Kadochnikev

J

Jack the Ripper, late 1800's. (British murderer of six women in London in 1888). Jack the Ripper did exist and terrorized the East End of London from August 7, 1888, to November 10, 1888. The London police never caught Jack, nor were they able to discover his true identity. Where Jack came from and where he went are still mysteries. The following movies recreate Jack's crimes and offer filmmakers' opinions as to who Jack was and what happened to him.

499. *Jack the Ripper* (1959). 88 min. Paramount Pictures. D: Robert Baker.
Jack: John Le Mesurier
Supporting cast: Betty McDowall, Lee Patterson, George Rose, Ewen Solon

499a *Jack the Ripper* (1988). 192 min. Euston Films Production. D:
David Wickes.
Jack: No actor was credited with playing Jack.
Frederick Abberline: Michael Caine
Supporting cast: Armand Assante, Susan George, Ray
McAnally, Jane Seymour

500. *The Lodger* (1944). 84 min. 20th Century-Fox. D: John
Brahm.
Jack: Laird Cregar
Supporting cast: Sara Allgood, Merle Oberon, George
Sanders

501. *The Man in the Attic* (1954). 82 min. 20th Century-Fox. D:
Hugo Fregonese.
Jack: Jack Palance
Supporting cast: Frances Bavier, Byron Palmer, Constance
Smith

502. *Murder by Decree* (1979). 121 min. Avco Embassy Pictures.
D: Bob Clark.
Jack: Peter Jonfield
Supporting cast: James Mason, Christopher Plummer,
Donald Sutherland

503. *A Study in Terror* (1965). 94 min. Columbia Pictures. D:
James Hill.
Jack: John Fraser
Supporting cast: Georgia Brown, Donald Houston, John
Neville

504. *Time After Time* (1979). 112 min. Orion Pictures. D: Nicholas
Meyer.
Jack: David Warner
H.G. Wells: Malcolm McDowell
Supporting cast: Charles Cioffi, Mary Steenburgen, Kent
Williams

Jackson, Andrew, 1767–1845. (Hero of the Battle of New Orleans
and seventh American president)

505. *The President's Lady* (1953). 96 min. 20th Century-Fox. D: Henry Levin.
Jackson: Charlton Heston
Rachel Jackson: Susan Hayward
Supporting cast: Fay Bainter, Carl Betz, Ellen Drew

SEE ALSO: **Eaton, Peggy O'Neal; Lafitte, Jean.**

Jackson, George, 1941–1971
See **Davis, Angela.**

Jackson, Rachel, 1767–1828
See **Jackson, Andrew.**

Jacob, c. 16th century B.C. (Hebrew herdsman, father of Joseph, who stole his brother Esau's birthright)

505a *The Story of Jacob and Joseph* (1974). 120 min. Columbia Pictures Television. D: Michael Cacoyannis.
Jacob: Keith Michell
Esau: Julian Glover
Joseph: Tony LoBianco
Supporting cast: Harry Andrews, Herschel Bernardi, Colleen Dewhurst, Yona Elian

Jahnke, Richard, Jr., 1967– (American teenager who killed his abusive father to save the family from further harm)

505b *Right to Kill?* (1985). 104 min. Telepictures Corporation. D: John Erman.
Jahnke: Christopher Collet
Richard Jahnke, Sr.: Frederic Forrest
Supporting cast: Justine Bateman, Karmin Murcelo, Terrance O'Quinn, Ann Wedgeworth

Jahnke, Richard, Sr.
See **Jahnke, Richard, Jr.**

James, Frank, 1843–1915. (American outlaw, brother of Jesse James)

506. *The Return of Frank James* (1940). 92 min. 20th Century-Fox. D: Fritz Lang.
James: Henry Fonda
Supporting cast: Jackie Cooper, Henry Hull, Gene Tierney

SEE ALSO: **James, Jesse.**

James, Jesse, 1847–1882. (American outlaw credited with committing the first daytime bank robbery)

507. *The Great Jesse James Raid* (1953). 73 min. Lippert Pictures. D: Reginald LeBorg.
James: Willard Parker
Supporting cast: Wallace Ford, Tom Neal, Barbara Payton

508. *The Great Missouri Raid* (1950). 83 min. Paramount Pictures. D: Gordon Douglas.
James: Macdonald Carey
Frank James: Wendell Corey
Cole Younger: Bruce Bennett
Supporting cast: Ward Bond, Ellen Drew, Anne Revere

509. *The Great Northfield Minnesota Raid* (1972). 91 min. Universal Pictures. D: Philip Kaufman.
James: Robert Duvall
Frank James: John Pearce
Cole Younger: Cliff Robertson
Supporting cast: R.G. Armstrong, Luke Askew, Dana Elcar

510. *Jesse James* (1939). 105 min. 20th Century-Fox. D: Henry King.
James: Tyrone Power
Frank James: Henry Fonda
Supporting cast: Henry Hull, Nancy Kelly, Randolph Scott

511. *The Kansas Raiders* (1950). 80 min. Universal-International. D: Ray Enright.
James: Audie Murphy
Frank James: Richard Long

Supporting cast: Richard Arlen, Tony Curtis, Brian Donlevy

512. *The Last Days of Frank and Jesse James* (1986). 100 min. Joe Cates Prod. D: William A. Graham.
James: Kris Kristofferson
Frank James: Johnny Cash
Supporting cast: Ed Bruce, June Carter Cash, Willie Nelson, Gail Youngs

513. *The Long Riders* (1980). 100 min. United Artists. D: Walter Hill.
James: Stacy Keach
Frank James: James Keach
Cole Younger: David Carradine
Supporting cast: Keith Carradine, Robert Carradine, Dennis Quaid, Randy Quaid

514. *The True Story of Jesse James* (1957). 92 min. 20th Century-Fox. D: Nicholas Ray.
James: Robert Wagner
Frank James: Jeffrey Hunter
Supporting cast: Alan Hale, Hope Lange, Agnes Moorehead

515. *Young Jesse James* (1960). 73 min. 20th Century-Fox. D: William Claxton.
James: Ray Stricklyn
Frank James: Robert Dix
Supporting cast: Merry Anders, Emile Meyer, Willard Parker

SEE ALSO: **Ford, Bob; Starr, Belle.**

Jardine, Al, 1942–
See **Beach Boys.**

Jay, John, 1745–1829
See **Hamilton, Alexander.**

Jefferson, Thomas, 1743–1826
   See **Adams, John; Washington, George.**

Jensen, Andrew, 1928– (U.S. Navy chaplain court-martialed for adultery)

516. *The Trial of Chaplain Jensen* (1975). 90 min. 20th Century-Fox. D: Robert Day.
   Jensen: James Franciscus
   Supporting cast: Lynda Day George, Joanna Miles, Dorothy Tristan

Jesus Christ, 4(?) B.C.–A.D. 28(?). (Founder of Christianity)

517. *The Day Christ Died* (1980). 150 min. 20th Century-Fox Television. D: James Cellan Jones.
   Christ: Chris Sarandon
   Supporting cast: Colin Blakely, Hope Lange, Keith Michell

518. *The Gospel According to St. Matthew* (1966). 136 min. Alfredo Bini. D: Pier Paolo Pasolini.
   Christ: Enrique Irazoque
   Supporting cast: Margherita Caruso, Marcello Morante, Susanna Pasolini, Mario Socrate

519. *Gospel Road* (1973). 83 min. World Wide Pictures. D: Robert Elfstrom.
   Christ: Robert Elfstrom
   Supporting cast: June Carter Cash, Alan Dater, Larry Lee, Paul Smith

520. *The Greatest Story Ever Told* (1965). 195 min. United Artists. D: George Stevens.
   Christ: Max von Sydow
   Supporting cast: Charlton Heston, Robert Loggia, Dorothy McGuire

521. *Jesus* (1979). 117 min. Genesis Project. D: Peter Sykes, John Krish.
   Christ: Brian Deacon
   Supporting cast: David Goldberg, Niko Nitai, Rivka Noiman, Yossef Shiloah

522. *Jesus Christ Superstar* (1973). 103 min. Universal Pictures. D: Norman Jewison.
Christ: Ted Neeley
Supporting cast: Carl Anderson, Bob Bingham, Barry Dennen, Yvonne Elliman

523. *Jesus of Nazareth* (1976). 376 min. RAI/ITC Entertainment. D: Franco Zeffirelli.
Christ: Robert Powell
Supporting cast: Anne Bancroft, Ernest Borgnine, Valentina Cortese, James Earl Jones

524. *King of Kings* (1961). 168 min. MGM. D: Nicholas Ray.
Christ: Jeffrey Hunter
Virgin Mary: Siobhan McKenna
Supporting cast: Hurd Hatfield, Ron Randell, Robert Ryan

524a *The Last Temptation of Christ* (1988), 160 min. Universal Pictures. D: Martin Scorsese.
Christ: Willem Dafoe
Supporting cast: Gary Basaraba, Verna Bloom, Barbara Hershey, Harvey Keitel

SEE ALSO: **Pontius Pilate.**

Jillian, Ann, 1950– (American actress and singer who survived a battle with breast cancer)

524b *The Ann Jillian Story* (1987). 96 min. ITC Entertainment Group. D: Corey Allen.
Jillian: Ann Jillian
Andy Murcia: Tony LoBianco
Supporting cast: Diane D'Aquila, Thomas Hauff, Viveca Lindfors, George Touliatos

Joan of Arc, Saint, 1412–1431. (French peasant girl and martyr who, guided by divine voices, led the French army against the English)

525. *Joan of Arc* (1948). 100 min. RKO. D: Victor Fleming.
Joan: Ingrid Bergman

Charles VII: Jose Ferrer
Supporting cast: Ward Bond, J. Carrol Naish, Francis L. Sullivan

526. *Saint Joan* (1957). 110 min. United Artists. D: Otto Preminger.
Joan: Jean Seberg
Charles VII: Richard Widmark
Supporting cast: Felix Aylmer, John Gielgud, Richard Todd, Anton Walbrook

526a *The Trial of Joan of Arc* (1962). 65 min. Pathe Contemporary. D: Robert Bresson.
Joan: Florence Carrez
Supporting cast: Jean-Claude Fourneau, Jean Gillibert, Roger Honorat, Marc Jacquier

Jogiches, Leo, 1867–1919
See **Luxemburg, Rosa.**

John XXIII, Pope, 1881–1963.

526b *I Would Be Called John* (1987). 90 min. WNET Educational Broadcasting Co. D: Charles Jarrott.
John: Charles Durning
This was a one-man show.

527. *A Man Named John* (1968). 94 min. CCM Films. D: Ermano Olmi.
Documentary

John of Gaunt, Duke of Lancaster, 1340–1399
See **Wycliffe, John.**

John Paul II, Pope, 1920–

528. *From a Far Country: Pope John Paul II* (1981). 100 min. Trans World Films. D: Krzysztof Zanussi.
John Paul/Karol Wojtyla: Cezary Morawski

Supporting cast: Christopher Cazenove, Warren Clarke, Lisa Harrow, Sam Neill

529. *Pope John Paul II* (1984). 150 min. Coopeman-DePaul Prod. D: Herbert Wise.
John Paul: Albert Finney
Supporting cast: Michael Crompton, Nigel Hawthorne, Jonathan Newth

John the Baptist, 4 B.C.–A.D. 30
See **Salome.**

Johnson, Albert. (Canadian trapper)

530. *Death Hunt* (1981). 96 min. 20th Century-Fox. D: Peter Hunt.
Johnson: Charles Bronson
Supporting cast: Angie Dickinson, Ed Lauter, Lee Marvin, Andrew Stevens

Johnson, Amy, 1903–1941. (British pilot, first woman to make a solo flight from London to Australia)

531. *Wings and the Woman* (1942). 103 min. RKO. D: Herbert Wilcox.
Johnson: Anna Neagle
Jim Mollison: Robert Newton
Supporting cast: Charles Carson, Edward Chapman, Joan Kemp-Welch, Nora Swinburne

Johnson, Andrew, 1808–1875. (Seventeenth American president, whom Congress attempted to impeach in 1868)

532. *Tennessee Johnson* (1942). 103 min. MGM. D: William Dieterle.
Johnson: Van Heflin
Supporting cast: Lionel Barrymore, Ruth Hussey, Regis Toomey

Johnson, Bill, 1960– (American Olympic gold medal skier)

533. *Going for Gold: The Bill Johnson Story* (1985). 100 min. ITC Productions. D: Don Taylor.
Johnson: Anthony Edwards
Supporting cast: Wayne Northrop, Sarah Jessica Parker, Deborah Van Valkenburgh, Dennis Weaver

Johnson, Claudia "Lady Bird" 1912–
See **Johnson, Lyndon Baines.**

Johnson, Deborah, 1951–
See **Ginsberg, Allen.**

Johnson, Jack, 1878–1946. (African-American heavyweight boxing champion)

534. *The Great White Hope* (1970). 102 min. 20th Century-Fox. D: Martin Ritt.
Johnson/Jefferson: James Earl Jones
Supporting cast: Jane Alexander, Joel Fluellen, Lou Gilbert

535. *Jack Johnson* (1971). 90 min. Macmillan Films. D: William Cayton.
Documentary

Johnson, Lyndon Baines, 1908–1973. (Thirty-sixth American president responsible for the passage of the Civil Rights Act (1964) and the Voting Rights Act (1965))

535a *LBJ: The Early Years* (1987). 156 min. LBJ Productions. D: Peter Werner.
Johnson: Randy Quaid
Claudia "Lady Bird" Johnson: Patti LuPone
Robert F. Kennedy: James F. Kelly
Sam Rayburn: Pat Hingle
Supporting cast: Morgan Brittany, Barry Corbin, Charles Frank, Kevin McCarthy

SEE ALSO: **Hoover, J. Edgar.**

Johnson, Ray, 1927– (American criminal)

536. *Dangerous Company* (1982). 100 min. The Dangerous Company. D: Lamont Johnson.
Johnson: Beau Bridges
Supporting cast: Carlos Brown, Karen Carlson, Kene Holiday, Jan Sterling

Johnston, Reginald, 1874–1938
See **Pu Yi.**

Jolson, Al, 1886–1950. (American singer and actor who starred in the first sound film)

537. *Jolson Sings Again* (1950). 96 min. Columbia Pictures. D: Henry Levin.
Jolson: Larry Parks
Supporting cast: William Demarest, Ludwig Donath, Barbara Hale

538. *The Jolson Story* (1946). 128 min. Columbia Pictures. D: Alfred E. Green.
Jolson: Larry Parks
Supporting cast: William Demarest, Bill Goodwin, Evelyn Keyes

Jones, George, 1931–
See **Wynette, Tammy.**

Jones, Jim, 1931–1978. (American cult leader of the People's Temple)

539. *Guyana: Cult of the Damned* (1980). 90 min. Universal Pictures. D: Rene Cardona, Jr.
Jones/Johnson: Stuart Whitman
Leo J. Ryan/O'Brien: Gene Barry
Supporting cast: Jennifer Ashley, Joseph Cotten, Yvonne De Carlo, Bradford Dillman

540. *The Guyana Tragedy: The Story of Jim Jones* (1980). 192 min. Konigsberg Company. D: William A. Graham.
Jones: Powers Boothe
Leo J. Ryan: Ned Beatty
Supporting cast: Irene Cara, Veronica Cartwright, Rosalind Cash

Jones, John Paul, 1747–1792. (U.S. Navy officer and Revolutionary War hero)

541. *John Paul Jones* (1959). 126 min. Warner Bros. D: John Farrow.
Jones: Robert Stack
Catherine the Great: Bette Davis
Benjamin Franklin: Charles Coburn
Supporting cast: Jean-Pierre Aumont, Macdonald Carey, Erin O'Brien, Marisa Pavan

Jones, Kenny, 1949–
See **Who, The.**

Jones, Quincy, 1933– (Versatile African-American musician who has made his mark as a pianist, trumpeter, bandleader, recording executive, composer, and film producer)

541a *Listen Up: The Lives of Quincy Jones* (1990). 114 min. Warner Bros. D: Ellen Weissbrod.
Documentary.

Joplin, Janis, 1943–1970. (American rock and blues singer best known for her *Pearl* album)

542. *Janis* (1975). 96 min. Universal Pictures. D: Howard Alk, Seaton Findlay.
Documentary

Joplin, Scott, 1868–1917. (American pianist and ragtime composer)

543. *Scott Joplin* (1977). 96 min. Universal Pictures. D: Jeremy Paul Kagan.
Joplin: Billy Dee Williams
Supporting cast: Godfrey Cambridge, Clifton Davis, David Healy

Jorgensen, Christine, 1926– (First male to have a sex-change operation)

544. *The Christine Jorgensen Story* (1970). 89 min. United Artists. D: Irving Rapper.
Jorgensen: John Hansen
Supporting cast: Ellen Clark, John W. Hines, Quinn Redeker, Joan Tompkins

Joseph, c. 16th century B.C.
See **Jacob.**

Joseph, Chief, 1840–1904. (Nez Perce chief)

545. *I Will Fight No More Forever* (1975). 100 min. David Wolper Prod. D: Richard T. Heffron.
Joseph: Ned Romero
Supporting cast: Sam Elliott, Nick Ramus, James Whitmore

Joseph, Saint
See **Mary.**

Joseph II, Emperor of Austria, 1741–1790
See **Mozart, Wolfgang Amadeus.**

Joseph, of Cupertino, Saint, 1603–1663. (Italian Franciscan monk who exhibited preternatural powers)

545a *The Reluctant Saint* (1962). 105 min. Davis-Regal. D: Edward Dmytryk.
Joseph: Maximilian Schell

Supporting cast: Harold Goldblatt, Ricardo Montalban, Lea Padovani, Akim Tamiroff

Josephine, Empress of France, 1763–1814
See **Napoleon Bonaparte,** Emperor of France.

Joyce, James, 1882–1941. (Irish author best known for translating to the art of writing the conception and technique of the art of musical composition)

545b *James Joyce's Women* (1985). 88 min. Rejoicing Company. D: Michael Pearce.
Joyce: Chris O'Neill
Sylvia Beach: Fionnula Flanagan
Nora Barnacle Joyce: Fionnula Flanagan
Harriet Shaw Weaver: Fionnula Flanagan
Supporting cast: Paddy Dawson, Martin Dempsey, Timothy E. O'Grady, Tony Lyons

Joyce, Nora Barnacle, 1884–1951
See **Joyce, James.**

Juarez, Benito, 1806–1872. (President of Mexico during the mid-to late 1800's)

546. *Juarez* (1939), 132 min. Warner Bros. D: William Dieterle.
Juarez: Paul Muni
Carlotta: Bette Davis
Maximilian: Brian Aherne
Supporting cast: Joseph Calleia, Donald Crisp, Gale Sondergaard

SEE ALSO: **Carlotta,** Empress of Mexico.

Julius II, Pope, 1443–1513
See **Buonarroti, Michelangelo.**

Julius Caesar, 100 or 102 B.C.–44 B.C.
See **Caesar, Julius,** Emperor of Rome.

Jung, Carl Gustav, 1875–1961. (Swiss psychiatrist who is considered the father of analytical psychology)

546a *A Matter of Heart* (1986). 107 min. Image Entertainment Inc.
D: Mark Whitney.
Documentary.

K

Kacew, Nina
See **Gary, Romain.**

Kahlo, Frida, 1910–1954. (Mexican painter who is considered Latin America's greatest woman artist)

547. *Frida: Naturaleza Vida* (1988). 108 min. New Yorker Films. D: Paul Leduc.
Kahlo: Ofelia Medina
Kahlo (as a child): Valentina Leduc
Diego Rivera: Juan Jose Gurrola
Leon Trotsky: Max Kerlow
Supporting cast: Claudio Brook, Lolita Cortes, Salvador Sanchez, Cecilia Toussaint

Kahn, Gus, 1886–1941. (German-American songwriter)

547a *I'll See You in My Dreams* (1952). 110 min. Warner Bros. D: Michael Curtiz.
Kahn: Danny Thomas
Supporting cast: Doris Day, Frank Lovejoy, Mary Wickes

Kalitta, Conrad "Connie," 1939?–
See **Muldowney, Shirley.**

Kalmar, Bert, 1884–1947. (American songwriter)

548. *Three Little Words* (1950). 102 min. MGM. D: Richard
Thorpe.
Kalmar: Fred Astaire
Harry Ruby: Red Skelton
Supporting cast: Arlene Dahl, Gloria De Haven, Vera-Ellen

Kappler, Herbert, 1907–1978
See **O'Flaherty, Hugh.**

Karolyi, Bela
See **Comaneci, Nadia.**

Karpis, Alvin, 1908– (American gangster who was Public Enemy Number One on the FBI's most wanted list in 1935)

549. *The FBI Story: The FBI Versus Alvin Karpis, Public Enemy
Number One* (1974). 100 min. Warner Bros.-TV. D: Marvin
Chomsky.
Karpis: Robert Foxworth
J. Edgar Hoover: Harris Yulin
Supporting cast: Anne Francis, Kay Lenz, Gary Lockwood,
David Wayne

SEE ALSO: **Purvis, Melvin.**

Kassab, Freddy
See **MacDonald, Jeffrey.**

Kaufman, Barry, 1942– (American author and parent of an
autistic child)

550. *Son Rise: A Miracle of Love* (1979). 96 min. Filmways. D:
Glenn Jordan.
Kaufman: James Farentino
Raun Kaufman: Michael and Casey Adams
Suzie Kaufman: Kathryn Harrold

Supporting cast: Stephen Elliott, Henry Olek, Kerry Sherman

Kaufman, George S., 1889–1961
See **Hart, Moss.**

Kaufman, Raun
See **Kaufman, Barry.**

Kaufman, Suzie
See **Kaufman, Barry.**

Keaton, Joseph Francis "Buster," 1895–1966. (American comic film actor, known as the "Great Stoneface")

551. *Buster Keaton: A Hard Act to Follow* (1987). 180 min. Thames Television, Ltd. D: David Gill, Kevin Brownlow.
Documentary.

551a *The Buster Keaton Story* (1957). 91 min. Paramount Pictures. D: Sidney Sheldon.
Keaton: Donald O'Connor
Supporting cast: Ann Blyth, Rhonda Fleming, Peter Lorre

Keeler, Christine, 1941– (British prostitute who was involved in a major political scandal)

552. *The Christine Keeler Affair* (1964). 90 min. Topaz Film Corp. D: Robert Spafford.
Keeler: Yvonne Buckingham
Supporting cast: John Drew Barrymore, Alicia Brandet, Mimi Heinrich, Mel Welles

552a *Scandal* (1989). 115 min. Miramax Films. D: Michael Caton-Jones.
Keeler: Joanne Whalley-Kilmer
John Profumo: Ian McKellen
Mandy Rice-Davies: Bridget Fonda

Stephen Ward: John Hurt
Supporting cast: Britt Ekland, Roland Gift, Daniel Massey, Leslie Phillips

Keith, Agnes Newton, 1901– (British writer and inmate of a Japanese concentration camp)

553. *Three Came Home* (1950). 106 min. 20th Century-Fox. D: Jean Negulesco.
Keith: Claudette Colbert
Supporting cast: Florence Desmond, Sessue Hayakawa, Patric Knowles

Keller, Helen, 1880–1968. (American writer and lecturer on behalf of the blind)

554. *Helen Keller: The Miracle Continues* (1984). 100 min. 20th Century-Fox Television. D: Alan Gibson.
Keller: Mare Winningham
John Macy: Perry King
Anne Sullivan: Blythe Danner
Supporting cast: Peter Cushing, Alexander Knox, Vera Miles, Jack Warden

555. *The Miracle Worker* (1962). 107 min. United Artists. D: Arthur Penn.
Keller: Patty Duke
Anne Sullivan: Anne Bancroft
Supporting cast: Victor Jory, Andrew Prine, Inga Swenson

556. *The Miracle Worker* (1979). 100 min. Katz-Gallin/Half-Pint Prod. D: Paul Aaron.
Keller: Melissa Gilbert
Anne Sullivan: Patty Duke Astin
Supporting cast: Diana Muldaur, Anne Seymour, Charles Siebert

Kellerman, Annette, 1886–1975. (Australian swimmer who became a vaudeville hit in the early 1900's)

557. *The Million Dollar Mermaid* (1952). 115 min. MGM. D: Mervyn LeRoy.
Kellerman: Esther Williams
Supporting cast: David Brian, Victor Mature, Walter Pidgeon

Kelly, George R. "Machine Gun," 1897–1954. (American gangster whose reputation was mostly fiction created by his wife)

558. *Machine Gun Kelly* (1958). 80 min. American International. D: Roger Corman.
Kelly: Charles Bronson
Supporting cast: Susan Cabot, Wally Campo, Connie Gilchrist, Barboura Morris

SEE ALSO: **Purvis, Melvin.**

Kelly, Grace, 1929–1982. (American film actress who married the Crown Prince of Monaco)

559. *Grace Kelly* (1983). 100 min. Embassy Television. D: Anthony Page.
Kelly: Cheryl Ladd
Rainier: Ian McShane
Supporting cast: Lloyd Bridges, Diane Ladd, Alejandro Rey

Kelly, Hugh
See **Nitti, Francesco Saverio.**

Kelly, Ned, 1855–1880. (Australian outlaw during the 1870's gold rush)

560. *Ned Kelly* (1970). 103 min. United Artists. D: Tony Richardson.
Kelly: Mick Jagger
Supporting cast: Allen Bickford, Geoff Gilmour, Mark McManus

Kennedy, Edward Moore, 1932–
  See **Kennedy, Edward Moore, Jr.**

Kennedy, Edward Moore, Jr. "Ted," 1961– (American teen-ager, scion of the Kennedy family, who lost a leg to cancer)

560a *The Ted Kennedy Jr. Story* (1986). 104 min. Entertainment
  Partners Inc. D: Delbert Mann.
  Kennedy: Kimber Shoop
  Edward Kennedy: Craig T. Nelson
  Joan Kennedy: Susan Blakely
  Supporting cast: Dennis Creaghan, Jeff Harding, David
    Healy, Michael J. Shannon

Kennedy, Ethel, 1928–
  See **Kennedy, Robert F.**

Kennedy, Jacqueline Bouvier, 1929– (Wife of the thirty-fifth
  American president)

561. *Jacqueline Bouvier Kennedy* (1981). 150 min. ABC Circle
  Films. D: Stephen Gethers.
  Kennedy: Jaclyn Smith
  John F. Kennedy: James Franciscus
  Supporting cast: Stephen Elliott, Claudette Nevins, Rod
    Taylor

Kennedy, Joan, 1937?–
  See **Kennedy, Edward Moore, Jr. ("Ted")**

Kennedy, John F., 1917–1963. (World War II naval hero and
  assassinated thirty-fifth American president)

562. *Four Days in November* (1964). 120 min. United Artists. D:
  Mel Stuart.
  Documentary

563. *John F. Kennedy: Years of Lightning, Days of Drums* (1966). 85 min. U.S. Information Agency. D: Bruce Herschensohn. Documentary

564. *Johnny, We Hardly Knew Ye* (1977). 100 min. Talent Assoc., Ltd. D: Gilbert Cates.
Kennedy: Paul Rudd
Joseph P. Kennedy: William Prince
Supporting cast: Kevin Conway, Burgess Meredith, Shirley Rich, Richard Venture

564a *Kennedy* (1983). 420 min. Alan Landsburg Productions. D: Jim Goddard.
Kennedy: Martin Sheen
J. Edgar Hoover: Vincent Gardenia
Lyndon Johnson: Nesbitt Blaisdell
Jacqueline Kennedy: Blair Brown
Joseph P. Kennedy: E.G. Marshall
Robert F. Kennedy: John Shea
Rose Kennedy: Geraldine Fitzgerald
Martin Luther King, Jr.: Charles Brown
Supporting cast: Peter Boyden, James Burge, Veronica Castang, Kevin Conroy

565. *Missiles of October* (1974). 156 min. Viacom International. D: Anthony Page.
Kennedy: William Devane
Robert F. Kennedy: Martin Sheen
Supporting cast: Ralph Bellamy, Howard da Silva, Dana Elcar

566. *Prince Jack* (1984). 100 min. LMF Productions, Inc. D: Bert Lovitt.
Kennedy: Robert Hogan
Lyndon Johnson: Kenneth Mars
Joseph P. Kennedy: Lloyd Nolan
Robert F. Kennedy: James F. Kelly
Martin Luther King: Robert Guillaume
Supporting cast: Dana Andrews, Theodore Bikel, Cameron Mitchell, William Windom

567. *PT 109* (1963). 140 min. Warner Bros. D: Leslie H. Martinson.

Kennedy: Cliff Robertson
Supporting cast: Robert Culp, James Gregory, Ty Hardin

SEE ALSO: **Hoover, J. Edgar; Kennedy, Jacqueline Bouvier; Kennedy, Joseph, Jr.; Kennedy, Robert F.; King, Martin Luther, Jr.**

Kennedy, Joseph, Jr., 1915–1944. (American Navy pilot killed in a flying accident during World War II)

568. *Young Joe, the Forgotten Kennedy* (1977). 100 min. ABC Circle Films. D: Richard T. Heffron.
Kennedy: Peter Strauss
John F. Kennedy: Sam Chew, Jr.
Joseph P. Kennedy: Stephen Elliott
Robert F. Kennedy: Shane Kerwin
Rose Kennedy: Gloria Stroock
Supporting cast: Asher Brauner, Darleen Carr, Simon Oakland, Barbara Parkins

Kennedy, Joseph P., 1888–1969
See **Kennedy, John F.; Kennedy, Joseph, Jr.; Kennedy, Robert F.**

Kennedy, Robert F., 1925–1968. (U.S. Attorney General and senator from New York; assassinated)

569. *Blood Feud* (1983). 200 min. 20th Century-Fox Television. D: Mike Newell.
Kennedy: Cotter Smith
Jimmy Hoffa: Robert Blake
John F. Kennedy: Sam Groom
Supporting cast: Danny Aiello, Edward Albert, Brian Dennehy

569a *Robert Kennedy and His Times* (1985). 420 min. Columbia Pictures Television. D: Marvin J. Chomsky.
Kennedy: Brad Davis
Jimmy Hoffa: Trey Wilson
J. Edgar Hoover: Ned Beatty

Ethel Kennedy: Veronica Cartwright
John F. Kennedy: Cliff DeYoung
Joseph P. Kennedy: Jack Warden
Rose Kennedy: Beatrice Straight
Joseph McCarthy: Harris Yulin
Supporting cast: George Grizzard, Joe Pantoliano, Mitchell Ryan, Jeffrey Tambor

570. *The Unfinished Journey of Robert Kennedy* (1969). 75 min. David Wolper Prod. D: Mel Stuart.
Documentary

SEE ALSO: **Hoover, J. Edgar; Kennedy, John F.; Kennedy, Joseph, Jr.; King, Martin Luther, Jr.**

Kennedy, Rose Fitzgerald, 1890–
See **Kennedy, John F.; Kennedy, Joseph, Jr.; Kennedy, Robert F.**

Kenny, Elizabeth, 1886–1954. (Australian nurse who developed a successful method of treating polio)

571. *Sister Kenny* (1946). 116 min. RKO. D: Dudley Nichols.
Kenny: Rosalind Russell
Supporting cast: Beulah Bondi, Dean Jagger, Alexander Knox, Philip Merivale

Kent, Allegra, 1938–
See **Balanchine, George.**

Kern, Jerome, 1885–1945. (American composer, considered to be the father of modern musical theater)

572. *Till the Clouds Roll By* (1946). 137 min. MGM. D: Richard Whorf.
Kern: Robert Walker
Victor Herbert: Paul Maxey
Supporting cast: Lucille Bremer, Van Heflin, Dorothy Patrick

Kerouac, Jack, 1922–1969. (American writer whose works expressed the discontent of the Beat Generation)

573. *Heart Beat* (1980). 109 min. Orion Pictures. D: John Byrum.
Kerouac: John Heard
Carolyn Cassady: Sissy Spacek
Neal Cassady: Nick Nolte
Supporting cast: Anne Dusenberry, Ray Sharkey, Kent Williams

573a *Kerouac* (1984). 73 min. Jack Kerouac's America. D: John Antonelli.
Documentary.

573b *What Happened To Kerouac?* (1986). 96 min. New Yorker Films. D: Richard Lerner, Lewis MacAdams.
Documentary.

Khan, Genghis, 1162–1227. (Mongol conqueror who created an empire stretching from the Pacific Ocean to the Black Sea)

574. *The Conqueror* (1956). 111 min. RKO. D: Dick Powell.
Khan: John Wayne
Supporting cast: Pedro Armendariz, Susan Hayward, Agnes Moorehead

575. *Genghis Khan* (1965). 124 min. Columbia Pictures. D: Henry Levin.
Khan: Omar Sharif
Supporting cast: Stephen Boyd, James Mason, Eli Wallach

Kidd, William, 1645–1701. (Scottish sea captain who turned to piracy)

576. *Captain Kidd* (1945). 89 min. United Artists. D: Rowland V. Lee.
Kidd: Charles Laughton
Supporting cast: Barbara Britton, John Carradine, Gilbert Roland, Randolph Scott

Kimbrough, Emily, 1899–1989
See **Skinner, Cornelia Otis.**

King, Coretta Scott, 1927–
See **King, Martin Luther, Jr.**

King, Martin Luther, Jr., 1929–1968. (African-American minister and civil rights activist; assassinated)

577. *King* (1977). 300 min. Abby Mann Productions. D: Abby Mann.
King: Paul Winfield
Ralph Abernathy: Ernie Banks
J. Edgar Hoover: Dolph Sweet
John F. Kennedy: William Jordan
Robert F. Kennedy: Cliff DeYoung
Coretta King: Cicely Tyson
Martin Luther King, Sr.: Ossie Davis
Supporting cast: Tony Bennett, Roscoe Lee Browne, Lonny Chapman, Dick Anthony Williams

578. *King: A Filmed Record . . . Montgomery to Memphis* (1970). 153 min. Film Images. D: Joseph L. Mankiewicz, Sidney Lumet.
Documentary.

SEE ALSO: **Hoover, J. Edgar; Kennedy, John F.**

King, Martin Luther, Sr., 1899–1984
See **King, Martin Luther, Jr.**

Kinmont, Jill, 1936– (American skier and Olympic hopeful paralyzed in an accident)

579. *The Other Side of the Mountain* (1975). 101 min. Universal Pictures. D: Larry Pearce.
Kinmont: Marilyn Hassett
Supporting cast: Beau Bridges, Nan Martin, Belinda J. Montgomery

580. *The Other Side of the Mountain, Part 2* (1978). 100 min. Universal Pictures. D: Larry Pearce.
Kinmont: Marilyn Hassett
Supporting cast: Timothy Bottoms, Nan Martin, Belinda J. Montgomery

Kistler, Darci, 1964–
See **Balanchine, George.**

Klaben, Helen, 1941– (American airplane crash survivor who was left stranded after the crash in the wilderness for forty-nine days)

581. *Hey, I'm Alive* (1975). 78 min. Worldvision Enterprises. D: Lawrence Schiller.
Klaben: Sally Struthers
Ralph Flores: Edward Asner
Supporting cast: Hagan Beggs, Maria Hernandez, Milton Selzer

Klarsfeld, Beate, 1939– (German housewife who became involved in the search for Nazi war criminals and was instrumental in bringing Klaus Barbie to justice)

581a *Nazi Hunter: The Beate Klarsfeld Story* (1986). 104 min. Orion Television. D: Michael Lindsay-Hogg.
Klarsfeld: Farrah Fawcett
Klaus Barbie (in 1944): Vincent Gauthier
Klaus Barbie (in 1983): Claude Vernier
Supporting cast: Catherine Allegret, Tom Conti, Geraldine Page

Knievel, Evel, 1938– (American motorcycle stuntman)

582. *Evel Knievel* (1972). 90 min. Fanfare. D: Martin Chomsky.
Knievel: George Hamilton
Supporting cast: Rod Cameron, Bert Freed, Sue Lyon

Komitas, 1869–1935. (Armenian monk, ethnomusicologist and composer best known for utilitizing Armenian motifs in his music)

582a *Komitas* (1988). 96 min. Margarita Woskanjan Filmpro-
duktion. D: Don Asharian.
Komitas: Samuel Ovasapian
Supporting cast: Onig Saadetian, Sybille Vogelsang, Margarita Woskanjan

Kovacs, Ernie, 1919–1962. (American 1950's television comic)

583. *Ernie Kovacs: Between the Laughter* (1984). 100 min. ABC
Circle Films. D: Lamont Johnson.
Kovacs: Jeff Goldblum
Edie Adams: Melody Anderson
Supporting cast: Jordan Charney, John Glover, Cloris
Leachman, Madolyn Smith

Kovic, Ron, 1946– (Paralyzed American Vietnam vet who became active in the anti-war movement after his return from
Vietnam)

583a *Born on the Fourth of July* (1989). 144 min. Universal City
Studios, Inc. D: Oliver Stone.
Kovic (as an adult): Tom Cruise
Kovic (as a boy): Byran Larkin
Supporting cast: Raymond J. Barry, Willem Dafoe, Caro-
line Kava, Kyra Sedgwick

Kray, Reginald, 1933– (British gangster who, with his twin
brother, ruled London's underworld in the 1960's)

583b *The Krays* (1990). 119 min. Fugitive Features. D: Peter
Medak.
Kray: Gary Kemp
Ronald Kray: Martin Kemp
Supporting cast: Charlotte Cornwell, Susan Fleetwood,
Jimmy Jewel, Billie Whitelaw

Kray, Ronald, 1933–
    See **Kray, Reginald.**

Krents, Harold, 1944–1987. (Blind American law student)

584. *To Race the Wind* (1980). 100 min. Walter Grauman Prod. D: Walter Grauman.
    Krents: Steve Guttenberg
    Supporting cast: Barbara Barrie, Lisa Eilbacher, Randy Quaid, Mark L. Taylor

Kruger, Paul, 1825–1904
    See **Rhodes, Cecil.**

Krupa, Gene, 1909–1973. (American jazz drummer who popularized the drums with his extended solos)

585. *The Gene Krupa Story* (1959). 101 min. Columbia Pictures. D: Don Weis.
    Krupa: Sal Mineo
    Supporting cast: Yvonne Craig, James Darren, Susan Kohner, Susan Oliver

Kublai Khan, 1216–1294
    See **Polo, Marco.**

Kudirka, Simas, 1930– (Lithuanian seaman who tried to defect in 1970)

586. *The Defection of Simas Kudirka* (1978). 100 min. Paramount Pictures. D: David Lowell Rich.
    Kudirka: Alan Arkin
    Supporting cast: Richard Jordan, Shirley Knight, John McMartin, Donald Pleasence

Kunstler, William, 1919–
    See **Ginsberg, Allen.**

Kurth, Ann
See **Hill, John Robert.**

Kutcher, James, 1913?– (American soldier who was a victim of the 1950's Communist witch-hunt)

587. *The Case of the Legless Veteran* (1981). 65 min. Howard Patrick. D: Howard Patrick.
Documentary

L

Lafayette, Marie Joseph Paul Yves Roch Gilbert du Motier, Marquis de, 1757–1834. (French reformer, statesman, and major general in the Continental Army)

588. *Lafayette* (1963). 110 min. Maco Film Corp. D: Jean Dreville.
Lafayette: Michel Le Royer
George Washington: Howard St. John
Supporting cast: Vittorio De Sica, Jack Hawkins, Wolfgang Preiss, Orson Welles

SEE ALSO: **Washington, George.**

Lafitte, Jean, 1780–1854? (French pirate who played a major role in the Battle of New Orleans)

589. *The Buccaneer* (1938). 90 min. Paramount Pictures. D: Cecil B. De Mille.
Lafitte: Fredric March
Andrew Jackson: Hugh Sothern
Supporting cast: Franciska Gaal, Margot Grahame, Akim Tamiroff

590. *The Buccaneer* (1958). 121 min. Paramount Pictures. D: Anthony Quinn.
Lafitte: Yul Brynner
Andrew Jackson: Charlton Heston
Supporting cast: Claire Bloom, Henry Hull, Inger Stevens

591. *The Last of the Buccaneers* (1950). 79 min. Columbia Pictures. D: Lew Landers.
Lafitte: Paul Henreid
Supporting cast: Mary Anderson, John Dehner, Jack Oakie

Lahr, John, 1941–
See **Orton, Joe.**

Lake, Greg, 1948–
See **Emerson, Lake & Palmer.**

Lamb, Caroline, 1785–1828. (British novelist and mistress of Lord Byron)

592. *Lady Caroline Lamb* (1972). 118 min. United Artists. D: Robert Bolt.
Lamb: Sarah Miles
George Byron: Richard Chamberlain
Supporting cast: Jon Finch, Margaret Leighton, John Mills

SEE ALSO: **Byron, George.**

La Motta, Jake, 1921– (American boxer who was middleweight champion from 1949–1951)

593. *Raging Bull* (1980). 119 min. United Artists. D: Martin Scorsese.
La Motta: Robert De Niro
Ray Robinson: Johnny Barnes
Supporting cast: Cathy Moriarty, Joe Pesci, Theresa Saldana, Frank Vincent

Lamson, David Albert, 1903–1975. (American who was tried four times for the murder of his wife in the 1930's)

594. *We Who Are About to Die* (1937). 82 min. RKO. D: Christy Cabanne.
Lamson: John Beal

Supporting cast: Ann Dvorak, Preston Foster, Gordon Jones, Ray Mayer

Landon, Michael, 1937–1991. (American actor, director and producer known primarily for his television work)

595. *Sam's Son* (1984). 104 min. Worldvision. D: Michael Landon.
Landon/Orowitz: Timothy Patrick Murphy
Landon/Orman: Michael Landon
Supporting cast: Alan Hayes, Anne Jackson, Hallie Todd, Eli Wallach

Landru, Henri-Desire, 1869–1922. (French murderer, known as Bluebeard, who killed ten women)

596. *Bluebeard's Ten Honeymoons* (1960). 93 min. Allied Artists. D: W. Lee Wilder.
Landru: George Sanders
Supporting cast: Corinne Calvet, Ingrid Hafner, Jean Kent

597. *Landru* (1962). 114 min. Embassy Pictures. D: Claude Chabrol.
Landru: Charles Denner
Supporting cast: Danielle Darrieux, Michele Morgan, Hildegarde Neff

Lang, Donald, 1945– (American deaf-mute murder suspect)

598. *Dummy* (1979). 100 min. Warner Bros. D: Frank Perry.
Lang: LeVar Burton
Lowell Myers: Paul Sorvino
Supporting cast: Paul Butler, Brian Dennehy, Rose Gregorio, Gregg Henry

Langsdorff, Hans, 1890–1939. (German naval officer and captain of the battleship *Graf Spee*)

599. *The Battle of the River Plate* (1956). 106 min. Viacom Enterprises. D: Michael Powell, Emeric Pressburger.
Langsdorff: Peter Finch
Supporting cast: John Gregson, Ian Hunter, Anthony Quayle

Lansky, Meyer, 1902–
See **Siegel, Benjamin.**

Latour, Marie, d. 1943. (French abortionist executed during World War II)

599a *Story of Women* (1989). 110 min. MK2/New Yorker Films. D: Claude Chabrol.
Latour: Isabelle Huppert
Supporting cast: Dominique Blanc, Marie Bunel, Francois Cluzet, Nils Tavernier

Laurie, Rocco, 1948–1972
See **Foster, Gregory.**

Lawrence, D.H., 1885–1930. (British novelist who was prosecuted for obscenity in 1915 for *The Rainbow* and in 1928 for *Lady Chatterley's Lover*)

600. *The Priest of Love* (1981). 125 min. Filmways, Inc. D: Christopher Miles.
Lawrence: Ian McKellen
Frieda Lawrence: Janet Suzman
Mabel Dodge Luhan: Ava Gardner
Supporting cast: John Gielgud, Penelope Keith, Jorge Rivero

Lawrence, Frieda, 1879–1956
See **Lawrence, D.H.**

Lawrence, Gertrude, 1898?–1952. (British actress known primarily for her singing and dancing stage roles)

601. *Star!* (1968). 175 min. 20th Century-Fox. D: Robert Wise.
Lawrence: Julie Andrews
Noel Coward: Daniel Massey
Supporting cast: Michael Craig, Richard Crenna, Robert Reed

Lawrence, Marjorie, 1907–1979. (Australian opera singer whose career was curtailed by polio)

602. *Interrupted Melody* (1955). 106 min. MGM. D: Curtis Bernhardt.
Lawrence: Eleanor Parker
Supporting cast: Glenn Ford, Cecil Kellaway, Roger Moore

Lawrence, T.E., 1888–1935. (World War I British Army officer famous for uniting the Arab tribes against the Turks)

603. *Lawrence of Arabia* (1962). 222 min. Columbia Pictures. D: David Lean.
Lawrence: Peter O'Toole
Supporting cast: Alec Guinness, Jack Hawkins, Anthony Quinn

Lawson, Ted, 1917–
See **Doolittle, James.**

Leadbelly, 1885–1949
See **Ledbetter, Huddie.**

Leakey, Louis, 1903–1972
See **Fossey, Dian.**

Leander, Zarah, 1907–1981. (Swedish-German actress who starred in the German UFA Nazi films)

603a *My Life for Zarah Leander* (1987). 90 min. Christian Blackwood Prod., Inc. D: Christian Blackwood.
Documentary.

Lear, Harold Alexander, 1920–1978
See **Lear, Martha.**

Lear, Martha, 1930– (American writer whose husband suffered a series of debilitating heart attacks)

603b *Heartsounds* (1984). 128 min. Embassy Television. D: Glenn Jordan.
Lear: Mary Tyler Moore
Harold Lear: James Garner
Supporting cast: Wendy Crewson, David Gardner, Carl Marotte, Sam Wanamaker

Leary, Timothy, 1920– (American psychologist known as the "Messiah of LSD" who encouraged youth to use mind expanding drugs during the 1960's)

603c *Return Engagement* (1983). 89 min. Island Pictures. D: Alan Rudolph.
Documentary.

SEE ALSO: **Ginsberg, Allen.**

Ledbetter, Huddie, 1885–1949. (African-American blues musician and master of the twelve-string guitar)

604. *Leadbelly* (1976). 126 min. Paramount Pictures. D: Gordon Parks.
Ledbetter: Roger E. Mosley
Supporting cast: Paul Benjamin, Alan Manson, Madge Sinclair

SEE ALSO: **Guthrie, Woody.**

Lee, Andrew Daulton, 1953–
  See **Boyce, Christopher.**

Lee, Ethel. (Legally blind American woman who battled the establishment for the right to adopt a child)

604a *Eye on the Sparrow* (1987). 94 min. Republic Pictures. D: John Korty.
  Lee (as an adult): Mare Winningham
  Lee (as a child): Bianca Rose
  James Lee: Keith Carradine
  Supporting cast: Conchata Ferrell, Kaaren Lee, Sandy McPeak, Kathleen Turco-Lyon

Lee, Gypsy Rose, 1914–1970
  See **Gypsy Rose Lee.**

Lee, James
  See **Lee, Ethel.**

Lee, Laurel, 1945– (American victim of Hodgkin's disease)

605. *Walking Through the Fire* (1979). 100 min. Time-Life TV. D: Robert Day.
  Lee: Bess Armstrong
  Supporting cast: Swoosie Kurtz, Tom Mason, Richard Masur

Lee, Linda, d. 1954
  See **Porter, Cole.**

Lee, Lois. (American psychologist who opened a half-way house for rehabilitation of teenage prostitutes)

605a *Children of the Night* (1985). 104 min. Robert Guenette Prod. D: Robert Markowitz.
  Lee: Kathleen Quinlan

Supporting cast: Nicholas Campbell, Lar Park-Lincoln, Mario Van Peebles, Wally Ward

LeFlore, Ron, 1950– (American baseball player who overcame a criminal past to become a member of the Detroit Tigers)

606. *One in a Million: The Ron LeFlore Story* (1978). 100 min. EMI Television. D: William A. Graham.
LeFlore: LeVar Burton
Supporting cast: Paul Benjamin, James Luisi, Madge Sinclair

Lennon, John, 1940–1980. (British rock singer and former member of the Beatles; murdered)

607 *Imagine: John Lennon* (1988). 103 min. Warner Bros. D: Andrew Solt.
Documentary.

607a *John and Yoko: A Love Story* (1985). 160 min. Carson Production Group. D: Sandor Stern.
Lennon: Mark McGann
Yoko Ono: Kim Miyori
Supporting cast: Peter Capaldi, Richard Morant, Kenneth Price, Philip Walsh

SEE ALSO: **Beatles, The.**

Leonski, Edward J., 1917–1942. (World War II American soldier stationed in Australia convicted of strangling three women in 1942)

607b *Death of a Soldier* (1986). 93 min. Scotti Brothers Pictures. D: Phillipe Mora.
Leonski: Reb Brown
Supporting cast: James Coburn, Belinda Davey, Max Fairchild, Maurie Fields, Bill Hunter

Leonowens, Anna Harriette, 1834–1914. (British teacher and governess at the court of King Mongkut of Siam)

608. *Anna and the King of Siam* (1946). 128 min. 20th Century-Fox. D: John Cromwell.
Leonowens: Irene Dunne
Mongkut: Rex Harrison
Supporting cast: Lee J. Cobb, Linda Darnell, Mikhail Rasumny, Gale Sondergaard

609. *The King and I* (1956). 133 min. 20th Century-Fox. D: Walter Lang.
Leonowens: Deborah Kerr
Mongkut: Yul Brynner
Supporting cast: Martin Benson, Rita Moreno, Terry Saunders

Leopold, Nathan, 1906–1971. (American murderer who, with Richard Loeb, committed the thrill murder of 14-year-old Robert Franks)

610. *Compulsion* (1959). 103 min. 20th Century-Fox. D: Richard Fleischer.
Leopold: Dean Stockwell
Richard Loeb: Bradford Dillman
Clarence Darrow: Orson Welles
Supporting cast: E.G. Marshall, Martin Milner, Diane Varsi

Lepke, Louis, 1897–1944. (American gangster and top executive in Murder, Inc.)

611. *Lepke* (1975). 110 min. Warner Bros. D: Menahem Golan.
Lepke: Tony Curtis
J. Edgar Hoover: Erwin Fuller
Supporting cast: Milton Berle, Anjanette Comer, Vic Tayback

612. *Murder Inc.* (1960). 103 min. 20th Century-Fox. D: Burt Balaban.
Lepke: David J. Stewart
Supporting cast: May Britt, Peter Falk, Stuart Whitman

SEE ALSO: **Hoover, J. Edgar.**

Leslie-Melville, Betty, 1929– (British naturalist)

613. *The Last Giraffe* (1979). 100 min. Westfall Prod. D: Jack Couffer.
Leslie-Melville: Susan Anspach
Jock Leslie-Melville: Simon Ward
Supporting cast: Gordon Jackson, Saeed Jaffrey, Don Warrington

Leslie-Melville, Jock, 1933–1984
See **Leslie-Melville, Betty.**

Lesser, Anna Maria, d. 1935. (German physician)

614. *Fraulein Doktor* (1969). 102 min. Paramount Pictures. D: Alberto Lattuada.
Lesser: Suzy Kendall
Supporting cast: James Booth, Capucine, Kenneth More

Levant, Oscar, 1906–1972
See **Gershwin, George.**

Levi, Carlo, 1902–1975. (Italian painter and writer)

615. *Eboli* (1979). 120 min. Franklin Media. D: Francesco Rosi.
Levi: Gian Maria Volonte
Supporting cast: Paolo Bonicelli, Alain Cluny, Lea Massari, Irene Papas

Lewis, C.S., 1898–1963. (British writer, medievalist, Christian apologist best known for *The screwtape letters* and his science fiction works)

616. *Shadowlands* (1985). 90 min. Gateways Films. D: Norman Stone.
Lewis: Joss Ackland
Joy Davidman: Claire Bloom
Supporting cast: Rupert Baderman, Rhys Hopkins, David Waller

Lewis, Jerry Lee, 1935– (American singer best known for his frenzied attacks on the piano and his renditions of *Great balls of fire* and *Whole lotta shakin' going on*)

616a *Great Balls of Fire* (1989). 102 min. Orion Pictures. D: Jim McBride.
Lewis: Dennis Quaid
Myra Gale Lewis: Winona Ryder
Jimmy Swaggart: Alec Baldwin
Supporting cast: Steve Allen, Lisa Blount, John Doe, Trey Wilson

Lewis, Joe E., 1901–1971. (American nightclub comic)

617. *The Joker Is Wild* (1957). 123 min. Paramount Pictures. D: Charles Vidor.
Lewis: Frank Sinatra
Supporting cast: Eddie Albert, Jeanne Crain, Mitzi Gaynor

Lewis, Meriwether, 1774–1809. (Leader of the expedition to explore the Louisiana Purchase)

618. *The Far Horizons* (1955). 108 min. Paramount Pictures. D: Rudolph Mate.
Lewis: Charlton Heston
William Clark: Fred MacMurray
Supporting cast: William Demarest, Barbara Hale, Donna Reed

Lewis, Myra Gale, 1944?–
See **Lewis, Jerry Lee.**

Leybourne, George, 1842?–1884. (British actor)

619. *Champagne Charlie* (1944). 107 min. Ealing Studios. D: Alberto Cavalcanti.
Leybourne: Tommy Trinder
Supporting cast: Stanley Holloway, Jean Kent, Guy Middleton, Austin Trevor, Betty Warren

Liddell, Eric, 1902–1945. (Scottish missionary and Olympic runner)

620. *Chariots of Fire* (1981). 123 min. Warner Bros. D: Hugh Hudson.
Liddell: Ian Charleson
Harold Abrahams: Ben Cross
Supporting cast: Nicholas Farrell, Daniel Gerroll, Nigel Havers

Liddy, G. Gordon, 1930– (American Watergate conspirator)

621. *Will, G. Gordon Liddy* (1982). 100 min. Shane Company Prod. D: Robert Lieberman.
Liddy (as an adult): Robert Conrad
Liddy (as a child): Danny Lloyd
John Dean: Peter Ratray
Jeb Magruder: Gary Bayer
John Mitchell: Maurice Copland
Supporting cast: Katherine Cannon, James Rebhorn, Red West, Maurice Woods

SEE ALSO: **Leary, Timothy.**

Lightner, Candy, 1946– (American anti-drunk driving activist and founder of M.A.D.D.)

622. *M.A.D.D.: Mothers Against Drunk Drivers* (1983). 100 min. Universal Television. D: William A. Graham.
Lightner: Mariette Hartley
Supporting cast: Paula Prentiss, Bert Remsen, John Rubinstein

Lincoln, Abraham, 1809–1865. (Sixteenth American president; assassinated)

623. *Abe Lincoln in Illinois* (1940). 110 min. RKO. D: John Cromwell.
Lincoln: Raymond Massey
Supporting cast: Ruth Gordon, Mary Howard, Gene Lockhart, Dorothy Tree

624. *Abraham Lincoln* (1930). 97 min. United Artists. D: D.W. Griffith.
Lincoln: Walter Huston
Supporting cast: Hobart Bosworth, Kay Hammond, Otto Hoffman, Ian Keith, Una Merkel

624a *Gore Vidal's Lincoln* (1988). 192 min. Chris/Rose Productions, Inc. D: Lamont Johnson.
Lincoln: Sam Waterston
Mary Lincoln: Mary Tyler Moore
Supporting cast: Ruby Dee, John Houseman, John McMartin, Richard Mulligan

625. *The Great Man's Whiskers* (1971). 96 min. Universal Television. D: Philip Leacock.
Lincoln: Dennis Weaver
Supporting cast: Cindy Eilbacher, Dean Jones, John McGiver, Ann Sothern

626. *Young Mr. Lincoln* (1939). 100 min. 20th Century-Fox. D: John Ford.
Lincoln: Henry Fonda
Supporting cast: Alice Brady, Richard Cromwell, Donald Meek, Marjorie Weaver

SEE ALSO: **Fremont, John Charles.**

Lincoln, Mary Todd, 1818–1882. (Wife of the sixteenth American president)

626a *The Last of Mrs. Lincoln* (1984). 117 min. Community Television of Southern California. D: George Schaefer.
Lincoln: Julie Harris
Supporting cast: Robby Benson, Michael Cristofer, Patrick Duffy, Denver Pyle

SEE ALSO: **Lincoln, Abraham.**

Lind, Jenny, 1820–1887. (Swedish opera singer, known as the "Swedish Nightingale")

627. *A Lady's Morals* (1930). 75 min. MGM. D: Sidney Franklin.
Lind: Grace Moore
P.T. Barnum: Wallace Beery
Supporting cast: Jobyna Howland, Giovanni Martino, Frank Reicher

SEE ALSO: **Barnum, P.T. (Phineas Taylor).**

Lindbergh, Anne Morrow, 1906–
See **Lindbergh, Charles.**

Lindbergh, Charles, 1902–1974. (American pilot who made the first solo nonstop transatlantic flight)

628. *The Lindbergh Kidnapping Case* (1976). 150 min. Columbia Pictures. D: Buzz Kulik.
Lindbergh: Cliff De Young
Bruno Hauptmann: Anthony Hopkins
Anne Morrow Lindbergh: Sian Barbara Allen
Supporting cast: Denise Alexander, Joseph Cotten, Peter Donat, John Fink

629. *The Spirit of St. Louis* (1957). 138 min. Warner Bros. D: Billy Wilder.
Lindbergh: James Stewart
Supporting cast: Marc Connelly, Murray Hamilton, Patricia Smith

Linder, Max, 1883–1925. (French comic whose silent film work was a major influence on American silent film comedy)

629a *The Man in the Silk Hat* (1983). 96 min. Kino International Corporation. D: Maud Linder.
Documentary.

Liston, Sonny, 1934–
See **Ali, Muhammad.**

Liszt, Franz, 1811–1886. (Hungarian composer and pianist best known as the creator of the symphonic poem and an innovative genius of modern piano technique)

630. *Lisztomania* (1975). 105 min. Warner Bros. D: Ken Russell.
Liszt: Roger Daltrey
Richard Wagner: Paul Nicholas
Supporting cast: Sara Kestelman, Fiona Lewis, Veronica Quilligan

631. *Song Without End* (1960). 141 min. Columbia Pictures. D: Charles Vidor, George Cukor.
Liszt: Dirk Bogarde
Frederic Chopin: Alexander Davion
Supporting cast: Capucine, Patricia Morison, Genevieve Page

SEE ALSO: **Chopin, Frederic; Grieg, Edvard; Montes, Lola; Schumann, Clara; Wagner, Richard.**

Livingstone, David, 1813–1873
See **Stanley, Henry M.**

Lodge, Henry Cabot, 1850–1924
See **Wilson, Woodrow.**

Loeb, Richard, 1907–1936
See **Leopold, Nathan.**

Lombard, Carole, 1908–1942
See **Gable, Clark.**

London, Arthur, 1915–1986. (Czechoslovakian Communist tried for treason in 1951)

632. *The Confession* (1970). 138 min. Paramount Pictures. D: Constantine Costa-Gavras
London: Yves Montand

Supporting cast: Gabriele Ferzetti, Simone Signoret, Michel Vitold

London, Jack, 1876–1916. (American novelist famous for his adventure tales of the sea and the Klondike)

633. *Jack London* (1943). 94 min. United Artists. D: Alfred Santell.
London: Michael O'Shea
Supporting cast: Frank Craven, Harry Davenport, Susan Hayward, Osa Massen

Long, Earl Kemp, 1895–1960. (American politician, lieutenant governor of Louisiana, 1936–1938 and three-time governor of Louisiana)

633a *Blaze* (1989). 119 min. Touchstone Pictures. D: Ron Shelton.
Long: Paul Newman
Blaze Starr: Lolita Davidovich
Supporting cast: Garland Bunting, Jeffrey DeMunn, Jerry Hardin, Gailard Sartain

Long, Huey, 1893–1935. (Politician who was governor of Louisiana, 1928–1931 and a U.S. senator, 1931–1935; assassinated)

634. *All the King's Men* (1949). 109 min. Columbia Pictures. D: Robert Rossen.
Long/Stark: Broderick Crawford
Supporting cast: John Derek, Joanne Dru, John Ireland, Mercedes McCambridge

635. *Huey Long* (1985). 88 min. RKP Prod./Florentine Films. D: Ken Burns.
Documentary.

636. *The Life and Assassination of the Kingfish* (1977). 100 min. NBC-TV. D: Robert Collins.
Long: Edward Asner
Supporting cast: Fred Cook, Diane Kagan, Nicholas Pryor

637. *A Lion in the Streets* (1953). 88 min. Warner Bros. D: Raoul Walsh.
Long: James Cagney
Supporting cast: Warner Anderson, Anne Francis, Barbara Hale

Longabaugh, Harry "The Sundance Kid," 1869?–1908?
See **Cassidy, Robert Parker ("Butch").**

Loren, Sophia, 1934– (Oscar-winning Italian film actress)

638. *Sophia Loren: Her Own Story* (1980). 150 min. EMI Television. D: Mel Stuart.
Loren (as an adult): Sophia Loren
Loren (as a child): Ritza Brown, Chiara Ferraro
Cary Grant: John Gavin
Carlo Ponti: Rip Torn
Supporting cast: Armand Assante, Edmund Purdom, Theresa Saldana, Veronica Wells

Lorraine, Lillian, 1892?–1955
See **Ziegfeld, Florenz.**

Louis II, King of Bavaria, 1845–1886
See **Ludwig II,** King of Bavaria.

Louis XI, King of France, 1423–1483
See **Villon, Francois.**

Louis XIII, King of France, 1601–1643
See **Richelieu, Armand.**

Louis XV, King of France, 1710–1774
See **Dubarry, Marie; Marie Antoinette,** Queen of France.

Louis XVI, King of France, 1754–1793
　　See **Marie Antoinette,** Queen of France.

Louis, Joe, 1914–1981. (African-American heavyweight boxer and world champion from 1936 to 1948, known as the "Brown Bomber")

639. *The Joe Louis Story* (1953). 88 min. United Artists. D: Robert Gordon.
　　Louis: Coley Wallace
　　Supporting cast: James Edwards, John Marley, Hilda Simms, Paul Stewart

640. *Ring of Passion* (1978). 100 min. 20th Century-Fox. D: Robert Michael Lewis.
　　Louis: Bernie Casey
　　Max Schmeling: Stephen Macht
　　Supporting cast: Joseph Campanella, Allen Garfield, Percy Rodrigues

Love, Mike, 1941–
　　See **Beach Boys.**

Lucan, George Charles Bingham, 1800–1888
　　See **Cardigan, James Thomas Brudenell.**

Luciano, Charles "Lucky," 1897–1962. (American gangster and king of the New York rackets in the 1930's)

641. *Lucky Luciano* (1974). 110 min. Avco Embassy. D: Francesco Rosi.
　　Luciano: Gian Maria Volonte
　　Supporting cast: Charles Cioffi, Vincent Gardenia, Edmond O'Brien, Rod Steiger

　　SEE ALSO: **Siegel, Benjamin ("Bugsy").**

Ludwig II, King of Bavaria, 1845–1886.

642. *Ludwig* (1972). 173 min. MGM. D: Luchino Visconti.
Ludwig: Helmut Berger
Richard Wagner: Trevor Howard
Supporting cast: Gert Frobe, Helmut Grien, John Moulder-Brown

Luhan, Mabel Dodge, 1879–1962
See **Lawrence, D.H.**

Lund, Doris, 1919– (American writer)

643. *Eric* (1975). 120 min. Lorimar Prod. D: James Goldstone.
Lund/Swenson: Patricia Neal
Eric Lund/Swenson: John Savage
Supporting cast: Claude Akins, Sian Barbara Allen, Mark Hamill

Lund, Eric, 1951?–1972
See **Lund, Doris.**

Luther, Martin, 1483–1546. (German leader of the Protestant Reformation)

644. *Luther* (1974). 112 min. AFT. D: Guy Green.
Luther: Stacy Keach
Supporting cast: Hugh Griffith, Patrick Magee, Robert Stephens

645. *Martin Luther* (1953). 105 min. Lutheran Church Prod. D: Irving Pichel
Luther: Niall MacGinnis
Supporting cast: David Horne, Pierre Lefevre, John Ruddock, Guy Verney

Luxemburg, Rosa, 1871–1919. (Murdered German socialist revolutionary and co-founder of the Spartakusbund)

645a *Rosa Luxemburg* (1987). 122 min. New Yorker Films. D: Margarethe von Trotta.
Luxemburg: Barbara Sukowa
Leo Jogiches: Daniel Olbrychski
Supporting cast: Adelheid Arndt, Jurgen Holtz, Doris Schade, Otto Sander

Lyne, Phil, 1947?–
See **Mahan, Larry.**

Lynn, Loretta, 1935– (American country-western singer)

646. *Coal Miner's Daughter* (1980). 125 min. Universal Pictures. D: Michael Apted.
Lynn: Sissy Spacek
Oliver "Moody" Lynn: Tommy Lee Jones
Supporting cast: Phyllis Boyens, Beverly D'Angelo, Levon Helm

Lynn, Oliver "Moody"
See **Lynn, Loretta.**

M

MacArthur, Douglas,1880–1964. (American general who led the World War II Allied forces in the Pacific)

647. *Collision Course* (1975). 100 min. N/A. D: Anthony Page.
MacArthur: Henry Fonda.
Harry S Truman: E.G. Marshall
Supporting cast: Lucille Benson, Lloyd Bochner, Ward Costello

648. *MacArthur* (1977). 130 min. Universal Pictures. D: Joseph Sargent.
MacArthur: Gregory Peck
Harry S Truman: Ed Flanders
Supporting cast: Ivan Bonar, Ward Costello, Dan O'Herlihy

MacCracken, Mary, 1926– (American special-education teacher)

649. *Circle of Children* (1977). 100 min. 20th Century-Fox. D: Don Taylor.
MacCracken: Jane Alexander
Supporting cast: Matthew Laborteaux, Nan Martin, Rachel Roberts, David Ogden Stiers

650. *Lovey: A Circle Of Children, Part II* (1978). 100 min. Time-Life Television. D: Jud Taylor.
MacCracken: Jane Alexander
Supporting cast: Ronny Cox, Jeff Lynas, Kris McKean

MacDonald, Jeffrey, 1944– (Green Beret officer and physician convicted of murdering his wife and children)

651. *Fatal Vision* (1984). 200 min. National Broadcasting Company, Inc. D: David Greene.
MacDonald: Gary Cole
Freddy Kassab: Karl Malden
Supporting cast: Andy Griffith, Barry Newman, Mitchell Ryan, Eva Marie Saint

Maclean, Donald, 1913–1983
See **Blunt, Anthony.**

MacLeod, Margaret Zelle "Mata Hari," 1876–1917. (World War I German spy executed by the French)

652. *Mata Hari* (1932). 90 min. MGM. D: George Fitzmaurice.
MacLeod: Greta Garbo
Supporting cast: Lionel Barrymore, Karen Morley, Ramon Novarro, Lewis Stone

652a *Mata Hari* (1985). 108 min. Cannon Productions. D: Curtis Harrington.
MacLeod: Sylvia Kristel
Supporting cast: Gaye Brown, Gottfried Brown, Christopher Cazenove, Oliver Tobias

Macy, John, 1877–1932
See **Keller, Helen.**

Madison, Dolley, 1768–1849. (Fourth American First Lady)

653. *Magnificent Doll* (1946). 95 min. Hallmark Prod. D: Frank Borzage.
Madison: Ginger Rogers
Aaron Burr: David Niven
James Madison: Burgess Meredith
Supporting cast: Stephen McNally, Peggy Wood

Madison, James, 1751–1836
See **Madison, Dolley; Washington, George.**

Madonna, 1959– (American singer, songwriter and actress best known for her erotic image)

653a *Madonna: Truth Or Dare* (1991). 118 min. Miramax Films. D: Alek Keshishian.
Documentary.

Magruder, Jeb Stuart, 1934-
See **Dean, John; Liddy, G. Gordon.**

Mahan, Larry, 1943– (American rodeo star and six-time all-around champion)

654. *The Great American Cowboy* (1974). 90 min. Sun International. D: Keith Merrill.
Documentary.

Mahdi, 1843–1885
  See **Gordon, Charles.**

Maher, John, 1940– (American founder of Delancey Street Foundation)

655. *Delancey Street: The Crisis Within* (1975). 90 min. Paramount Pictures. D: James Frawley.
  Maher/McCann: Walter McGinn
  Supporting cast: Carmine Caridi, Michael Conrad, Lou Gossett

Mahler, Gustav, 1860–1911. (Austrian composer, conductor and artistic director of the Vienna State Opera House, 1897–1907)

656. *Mahler* (1974). 115 min. Goodtime Enterprises. D: Ken Russell.
  Mahler: Robert Powell
  Supporting cast: Rosalie Crutchley, Georgina Hale, Lee Montague, Richard Morant

Maida, Tami, 1965?– (Canadian high school student who, while living in Oregon, played quarterback for the varsity football team)

657. *Quarterback Princess* (1983). 100 min. CBS Entertainment. D: Noel Black.
  Maida: Helen Hunt
  Supporting cast: Barbara Babcock, Dana Elcar, Don Murray, John Stockwell

Malcolm X, 1925–1965. (African-American civil rights activist; assassinated)

658. *Malcolm X* (1972). 92 min. Warner Bros. D: Perl Worth, Marvin Worth.
  Documentary.

Malle, Louis, 1932– (French "new wave" film director)

658a *Au Revoir Les Enfants* (1987). 103 min. Orion Pictures. D: Louis Malle.
   Malle/Julien Quentin: Gaspard Manesse
   Supporting cast: Raphael Fejto, Philippe Morier-Genoud, Francois Negret, Francine Racette

Mancini, Ray, 1961– (American lightweight boxing champion)

659. *Heart of a Champion: The Ray Mancini Story* (1985). 100 min. Rare Titles Production. D: Richard Michaels.
   Mancini: Doug McKeon
   Supporting cast: Robert Blake, Tony Burton, James Callahan, Mariclare Costello

Mandela, Nelson, 1918– (South African lawyer and anti- apartheid activist who was imprisoned by the South African government for twenty-seven years)

659a *Mandela* (1987). 135 min. HBO Pictures. D: Philip Saville.
   Mandela: Danny Glover
   Winnie Mandela: Alfre Woodard
   Supporting cast: Warren Clarke, Allan Corduner, Julian Glover, John Matshikiza

Mandela, Winnie, 1936–
   See **Mandela, Nelson.**

Mansfield, Jayne, 1933–1967. (American film actress and blonde sex symbol of the 1950's)

660. *The Jayne Mansfield Story* (1980). 100 min. Alan Landsburg Prod. D: Dick Lowry.
   Mansfield: Loni Anderson
   Mickey Hargitay: Arnold Schwarzenegger
   Supporting cast: Raymond Buktenica, Kathleen Lloyd, G.D. Spradlin

Manson, Charles, 1934– (American cult leader whose followers were responsible for the murder of six people in 1969)

661. *Helter Skelter* (1976). 194 min. Lorimar Prod. D: Tom Gries.
Manson: Steve Railsback
Vincent Bugliosi: George DiCenzo
Supporting cast: Marilyn Burns, Christina Hart, Nancy Wolfe

Marc Anthony, 83?–30 B.C.
See **Caesar, Julius,** Emperor of Rome; **Cleopatra,** Queen of Egypt.

Marciano, Rocco Francis "Rocky," 1924–1969. (American heavyweight boxing champion who retired from the ring undefeated)

662. *Marciano* (1979). 100 min. ABC Circle Films. D: Bernard L. Kowalski.
Marciano: Tony Lo Bianco
Supporting cast: Vincent Gardenia, Richard Herd, Belinda J. Montgomery

Marcucci, Robert, 1930– (American producer and songwriter who guided Frankie Avalon and Fabian to stardom in the 1950's)

663. *The Idolmaker* (1980). 119 min. United Artists. D: Taylor Hackford.
Marcucci: Ray Sharkey
Frankie Avalon: Paul Land
Fabian: Peter Gallagher
Supporting cast: John Aprea, Tovah Feldshuh, Maureen McCormick, Joe Pantoliano

Marcus, David "Mickey," 1901–1949. (American World War II colonel who commanded Jewish forces during the 1940's Palestinian conflict)

664. *Cast a Giant Shadow* (1966). 138 min. United Artists. D: Melville Shavelson.
Marcus: Kirk Douglas
Supporting cast: Senta Berger, Angie Dickinson, James Donald, Frank Sinatra

Marie Antoinette, Queen of France, 1755–1793.

665. *Marie Antoinette* (1938). 149 min. MGM. D: W.S. Van Dyke.
Marie Antoinette: Norma Shearer
Louis XV: John Barrymore
Louis XVI: Robert Morley
Supporting cast: Gladys George, Anita Louise, Tyrone Power

666. *Marie Antoinette* (1955). 108 min. Les Film Gibe. D: Jean Delannoy.
Marie Antoinette: Michele Morgan
Supporting cast: Jean Morel, Richard Todd

Markham, Beryl, 1902–1986. (British pilot who was the first person to fly solo from England to North America)

666a *Beryl Markham: A Shadow on the Sun* (1988). 192 min. New World Television. D: Tony Richardson.
Markham: Stefanie Powers
Supporting cast: Claire Bloom, Peter Bowles, Brian Cox, Frederic Forrest

Marshall, Penny, 1942–
See **Reiner, Rob.**

Marshall, Peter, 1903?–1949. (Scottish-American minister and U.S. Senate chaplain)

667. *A Man Called Peter* (1955). 119 min. 20th Century-Fox. D: Henry Koster.
Marshall: Richard Todd
Supporting cast: Doris Lloyd, Jean Peters, Marjorie Rambeau

Marshall, Thurgood, 1908–1993 (African-American lawyer and Supreme Court Justice, 1967–1991)

667a *Separate But Equal* (1991). 193 min. Republic Pictures. D: George Stevens, Jr.
Marshall: Sidney Poitier
John W. Davis: Burt Lancaster
Earl Warren: Richard Kiley
Supporting cast: Graham Beckel, Ed Hall, John McMartin, Lynne Thigpen

Martin, Ellen
See **Walker, William.**

Martinez, Ramiero, 1937?–
See **Whitman, Charles.**

Marto, Francisco, 1908–1919
See **Dos Santos, Lucia.**

Marto, Jacinta, 1910–1920
See **Dos Santos, Lucia.**

Marx, Julius H. "Groucho," 1891–1977. (American comic, actor and televison game host who started in vaudeville as one of the five Marx Brothers)

667b *Gabe Kaplan as Groucho* (1982). 90 min. Tomorrow Entertainment, Inc. D: John Bowab.
Marx: Gabe Kaplan
Supporting cast: Connie Danese, Michael Tucci

Mary, 20 B.C.?– (Hebrew maiden and mother of Jesus Christ)

668. *Mary and Joseph: A Story of Faith* (1979). 100 min. Astral Films. D: Eric Till.
Mary: Blanche Baker
Joseph: Jeff East
Supporting cast: Lloyd Bochner, Colleen Dewhurst, Stephen McHattie

669. *The Nativity* (1978). 100 min. 20th Century-Fox. D: Bernard L. Kowalski.
Mary: Madeline Stowe
Joseph: John Shea
Supporting cast: Leo McKern, Paul Stewart, Audrey Totter, Jane Wyatt

SEE ALSO: **Jesus Christ.**

Mary, Queen, consort of George V, King of Great Britain, 1867–1953
See **Simpson, Wallis Warfield.**

Mary Stuart, Queen of Scotland, 1542–1587.

670. *Mary of Scotland* (1936). 123 min. RKO. D: John Ford.
Mary Stuart: Katharine Hepburn
Elizabeth I: Florence Eldridge
James Hepburn, Earl of Bothwell: Fredric March
Supporting cast: Robert Barrat, John Carradine, Ian Keith, Gavin Muir

671. *Mary, Queen of Scots* (1971). 128 min. Universal Pictures. D: Charles Jarrott.
Mary Stuart: Vanessa Redgrave
Elizabeth I: Glenda Jackson
Supporting cast: Timothy Dalton, Nigel Davenport, Patrick McGoohan

Mason, Marsha, 1942–
 See **Simon, Neil.**

Masters, Hope, 1942– (American socialite and crime victim)

672. *A Death in California* (1985). 200 min. Lorimar Prod. D:
 Delbert Mann.
 Masters: Cheryl Ladd
 Supporting cast: Barry Corbin, Kerrie Keane, Alexis Smith,
 Fritz Weaver

Masterson, William Barclay "Bat," 1853–1921. (American lawman and sports writer for the *New York Morning Telegraph,*
 1902–1921)

673. *Gunfight at Dodge City* (1959). 81 min. United Artists. D:
 Joseph M. Newman.
 Masterson: Joel McCrea
 Supporting cast: Julie Adams, Richard Anderson, Nancy
 Gates, John McIntire

674. *Masterson of Kansas* (1954). 73 min. Columbia Pictures. D:
 William Castle.
 Masterson: George Montgomery
 Wyatt Earp: Bruce Cowling
 John H. Holliday: James Griffith
 Supporting cast: David Bruce, Nancy Gates, Benny Rubin,
 Jean Willes

675. *The Woman of the Town* (1943). 90 min. United Artists. D:
 George Archainbaud.
 Masterson: Albert Dekker
 Supporting cast: Henry Hull, Marion Martin, Barry Sulli-
 van, Claire Trevor

Mata Hari, 1876–1917
 See **MacLeod, Margaret Zelle "Mata Hari."**

Mathias, Robert, 1930– (American two-time Olympic gold medal winner for the decathlon)

676. *The Bob Mathias Story* (1954). 80 min. Allied Artists. D: Francis Lyon.
Mathias: Bob Mathias
Supporting cast: Ward Bond, Ann Doran, Diane Jergens, Melba Mathias

Mathis, June, 1892–1927
See **Valentino, Rudolph.**

Matlovich, Leonard, 1944–1988. (U.S. Air Force sergeant who sued the service for discharging him because of his sexual orientation)

677. *Sergeant Matlovich Vs. the U.S. Air Force* (1978). 100 min. Tomorrow Entertainment. D: Paul Leaf.
Matlovich: Brad Dourif
Supporting cast: Frank Converse, William Daniels, Stephen Elliott

Maugham, W. Somerset, 1874–1965
See **Gauguin, Paul.**

Maxim, Hiram Stephen, 1840–1916. (American inventor best known for the Maxim gun)

678. *So Goes My Love* (1946). 88 min. Universal Pictures. D: Frank Ryan.
Maxim: Don Ameche
Supporting cast: Bobby Driscoll, Richard Gaines, Myrna Loy

Maximilian, Emperor of Mexico, 1832–1867
See **Carlotta,** Empress of Mexico; **Juarez, Benito.**

Mayer, Louis B., 1885–1957
See **Parsons, Louella; Selznick, David O.**

McCarthy, Joseph, 1909–1957. (U.S. senator from Wisconsin who instigated the Communist witch-hunt of the 1950's)

679. *Tail Gunner Joe* (1977). 144 min. Universal Pictures Television. D: Jud Taylor.
McCarthy: Peter Boyle
Supporting cast: John Forsythe, Heather Menzies, Burgess Meredith

SEE ALSO: **Cohn, Roy; Kennedy, Robert F.**

McCartney, Paul, 1942–
See **Beatles, The.**

McConnell, Joseph, 1922–1954. (America's first triple-jet ace pilot in the Korean War)

680. *The McConnell Story* (1955). 107 min. Warner Bros. D: Gordon Douglas.
McConnell: Alan Ladd
Pearl "Butch" McConnell: June Allyson
Supporting cast: Robert Ellis, Frank Faylen, Gregory Walcott, James Whitmore

McConnell, Pearl "Butch"
See **McConnell, Joseph.**

McDonald, Anne, 1961– (Australian victim of cerebral palsy)

681. *A Test of Love* (1984). 93 min. Universal Pictures. D: Gil Brealey.
McDonald: Tina Arhondis
Rosemary Crossley: Angela Punch McGregor
Supporting cast: Simon Chilvers, Liddy Clark, Wallas Eaton, Drew Forsythe

McKenna, George, 1943?– (African-American high-school principal best known for his work in south Los Angeles inner-city schools)

681a *The George McKenna Story* (1986). 104 min. The Landsburg Co. D: Eric Laneuville.
McKenna: Denzel Washington
Supporting cast: Akousa Busia, Virginia Capers, Richard Masur, Lynn Whitfield

McPherson, Aimee Semple, 1890–1944. (American evangelist, faith healer and founder of the Angelus Temple)

682. *The Disappearance of Aimee* (1976). 100 min. Tomorrow Entertainment. D: Anthony Harvey.
McPherson: Faye Dunaway
Supporting cast: Bette Davis, John Lehne, James Sloyan, James Woods

McVicar, John, 1940– (British criminal)

683. *McVicar* (1980). 111 min. Crown International. D: Tom Clegg.
McVicar: Roger Daltrey
Supporting cast: Cheryl Campbell, Adam Faith, Brian Hall, Anthony Trent

Meir, Golda, 1898–1978. (Israeli prime minister, 1969–1974)

684. *A Woman Called Golda* (1982). 200 min. Paramount Pictures Television. D: Alan Gibson.
Meir: Ingrid Bergman
Meir (as a young woman): Judy Davis
Anwar Sadat: Robert Loggia
Supporting cast: Ned Beatty, Barry Foster, Anne Jackson, Leonard Nimoy

Melba, Nellie, 1861–1931. (Australian opera singer and most famous soprano of her time)

685. *Melba* (1953). 113 min. United Artists. D: Lewis Milestone.
Melba: Patrice Munsel
Supporting cast: Martita Hunt, John McCallum, Robert Morley, Sybil Thorndike

Mencken, H.L., 1880–1956
See **Darrow, Clarence.**

Mendoza, Ana de, 1540–1592. (Spanish noblewoman involved in the political intrigues of Philip II's court)

686. *That Lady* (1955). 100 min. 20th Century-Fox. D: Terence Young.
Mendoza: Olivia de Havilland
Philip II: Paul Scofield
Supporting cast: Dennis Price, Gilbert Roland, Francoise Rosay

Mercader, Ramon, 1914–1978
See **Trotsky, Leon.**

Mermelstein, Mel, 1926– (Czech-American concentration camp survivor who sued the Institute for Historical Review to claim a reward for proving that the Holocaust actually happened)

686a *Never Forget* (1991). 100 min. Turner Pictures, Inc. D: Joseph Sargent.
Mermelstein: Leonard Nimoy
Supporting cast: Dabney Coleman, Blythe Danner, Paul Hampton, Jason Presson

Merrick, John, 1862–1890. (British victim of craniodiaphyseal dysplasia)

687. *The Elephant Man* (1980). 125 min. Paramount Pictures. D: David Lynch.
Merrick: John Hurt

Supporting cast: Anne Bancroft, John Gielgud, Wendy Hiller, Anthony Hopkins

Mesta, Perle, 1891–1975. (U.S. envoy to Luxembourg and popular Washington, D.C., hostess in the 1940's and 1950's)

688. *Call Me Madam* (1953). 117 min. 20th Century-Fox. D: Walter Lang.
Mesta/Adams: Ethel Merman
Supporting cast: Billy De Wolfe, Donald O'Connor, George Sanders, Vera-Ellen

Methot, Mayo, 1903–1951
See **Bogart, Humphrey.**

Michelangelo
See **Buonarroti, Michelangelo.**

Milk, Harvey, 1930–1978. (Gay San Francisco supervisor; assassinated)

689. *The Times of Harvey Milk* (1984). 87 min. Black Sands. D: Robert Epstein.
Documentary.

Miller, Arthur, 1915–
See **Monroe, Marilyn.**

Miller, Barbara, 1940–
See **Miller, Kathy.**

Miller, Glenn, 1904–1944. (American bandleader of the 1930's and 1940's)

690. *The Glenn Miller Story* (1954). 116 min. Universal Pictures.
D: Anthony Mann.
Miller: James Stewart
Helen Burger Miller: June Allyson
Supporting cast: Irving Bacon, Charles Drake, Henry Morgan, George Tobias

Miller, Helen Burger, 1902?–1966
See **Miller, Glenn.**

Miller, Kathy, 1962– (American automobile accident victim)

691. *The Miracle of Kathy Miller* (1981). 100 min. Universal
Television. D: Robert Michael Lewis.
Miller: Helen Hunt
Barbara Miller: Sharon Gless
Larry Miller: Frank Converse
Supporting cast: Bill Beyers, John DeLancie, Bill Forsythe,
Michele Greene

Miller, Larry
See **Miller, Kathy.**

Miller, Marilyn, 1898–1938. (American stage actress, singer and
Ziegfeld star of the 1920's)

692. *Look for the Silver Lining* (1948). 100 min. Warner Bros. D:
David Butler.
Miller: June Haver
Jack Donahue: Ray Bolger
Supporting cast: Rosemary de Camp, Gordon MacRae,
Charlie Ruggles

SEE ALSO: **Ziegfeld, Florenz.**

Miller, Vernon C. "Vern," d. 1933. (American gangster and
former lawman who was responsible for the infamous
Kansas City massacre)

692a *Verne Miller* (1988). 95 min. Three Aces. D: Rod Hewitt.
   Miller: Scott Glenn
   Alphonse Capone: Thomas G. Waites
   Charles "Pretty Boy" Floyd: Andrew Robinson
   Supporting cast: Sonny Carl Davis, Lucinda Jenney, Ed
      O'Ross, Barbara Stock

Mills, Billy, 1938– (Native American Olympic gold medal
   runner)

693. *Running Brave* (1983). 105 min. Buena Vista. D: D.S.
   Everett.
   Mills: Robby Benson
   Supporting cast: Claudia Cron, Pat Hingle, Jeff McCraken,
      August Schellenberg

Mindszenty, Jozsef, 1892–1975. (Hungarian cardinal tried for
   treason in 1949 because of his opposition to the Communist
   regime)

694. *Guilty of Treason* (1949). 86 min. Eagle-Lion Prod. D: Felix E.
   Feist.
   Mindszenty: Charles Bickford
   Supporting cast: Richard Derr, Bonita Granville, Paul
      Kelly, Barry Kroeger

Miner, William, 1847–1913. (Canadian train robber in the late
   1800's)

695. *The Grey Fox* (1982). 92 min. MGM-United Artists. D: Philip
   Boros.
   Miner: Richard Farnsworth
   Supporting cast: Jackie Burroughs, Ken Pogue, Wayne
      Robson

Mishima, Yukio, 1925–1970. (Japanese novelist who committed
   hara-kiri)

696. *Mishima* (1985). 120 min. M Film Co. D: Paul Schrader.
Mishima: Ken Ogata
This is a one-man show.

Mitchell, Billy, 1879–1936. (American World War I pilot and general who was court-martialed in 1925 for his negative public pronouncements on the U.S. military's lack of interest in building up air power)

697. *The Court-Martial of Billy Mitchell* (1955). 100 min. Warner Bros. D: Otto Preminger.
Mitchell: Gary Cooper
Guthrie: Charles Bickford
Supporting cast: Ralph Bellamy, Fred Clark, Elizabeth Montgomery, Rod Steiger

Mitchell, Cathy
See **Mitchell, Dave.**

Mitchell, Dave. (Pulitzer Prize-winning American newspaper publisher who helped expose the workings of the controversial Synanon organization)

697a *Attack on Fear* (1984). 100 min. Tomorrow Entertainment Inc. D: Mel Damski.
Mitchell: Paul Michael Glaser
Cathy Mitchell: Linda Kelsey
Richard Ofshe: Kevin Conway
Supporting cast: Barbara Babcock, Alan Fudge, John Harkins, Tom Villard

Mitchell, John, 1913–1988
See **Dean, John; Liddy, G. Gordon.**

Mitchell, Reginald Joseph, 1895–1937. (British designer of the World War II Spitfire fighter plane)

698. *Spitfire* (1943). 90 min. RKO. D: Leslie Howard.
    Mitchell: Leslie Howard
    Supporting cast: Roland Culver, Rosamund John, David
    Niven

Modigliani, Amedeo, 1884–1920. (Italian painter, sculptor, and
    leader of modernism in art)

699. *The Lovers of Montparnasse* (1957). 103 min. 20th Century-
    Fox. D: Jacques Becker.
    Modigliani: Gerard Philipe
    Beatrice Hastings: Lilli Palmer
    Supporting cast: Anouk Aimee, Lea Padovani, Gerard
    Sety, Lino Ventura

Mohammad, 570–632. (Arabian founder of Islam)

700. *Mohammad, Messenger of God* (1977). 180 min. Filmco Inter-
    national. D: Moustapha Akkad.
    Mohammad: The person of Mohammad is never shown, as
    it is forbidden by Islamic law.
    Supporting cast: Michael Ansara, Irene Papas, Anthony
    Quinn

Mollison, Amy Johnson, 1903–1941
    See **Johnson, Amy.**

Mollison, Jim, 1905–1959
    See **Johnson, Amy.**

Mongkut, King of Siam, 1804–1868
    See **Leonowens, Anna Harriette.**

Monk, Thelonious, 1920–1982. (African-American jazz pianist
    and composer best known for his eccentric behavior and
    innovative music)

700a *Thelonious Monk: Straight No Chaser* (1989). 90 min. Warner Bros. D: Charlotte Zwerin.
Documentary.

Monroe, James, 1758–1831
See **Washington, George.**

Monroe, Marilyn, 1926–1962. (American film actress and blonde sex symbol of the 1950's)

701. *Goodbye, Norma Jean* (1976). 95 min. Filmways, Inc. D: Larry Buchanan.
Monroe: Misty Rowe
Supporting cast: Preston Hanson, Terence Locke, Patch Mackenzie, Marty Zago

701a *Goodnight, Sweet Marilyn* (1989). 93 min. Studio Entertainment. D: Larry Buchanan.
Monroe: Paula Lane
Supporting cast: Phyllis Coates, Stuart Lancaster, Misty Rowe, Jeremy Slate

702. *Marilyn* (1963). 83 min. 20th Century-Fox. D: N/A.
Documentary.

703. *Marilyn: The Untold Story* (1980). 150 min. Lawrence Schiller Prod. D: Jack Arnold, John Flynn, Lawrence Schiller.
Monroe: Catherine Hicks
Joe DiMaggio: Frank Converse
Arthur Miller: Jason Miller
Supporting cast: Richard Basehart, Kevin Geer, John Ireland, Viveca Lindfors, Sheree North

704. *The Sex Symbol* (1974). 90 min. Screen Gems. D: David Lowell Rich.
Monroe/Williams: Connie Stevens
Supporting cast: Jack Carter, William Castle, Shelley Winters

705. *This Year's Blonde* (1980). 100 min. Warner Bros. Television.
  D: John Erman.
  Monroe: Constance Forslund
  Supporting cast: Lloyd Bridges, Norman Fell, Michael
    Lerner, John Marley, Vic Tayback

Montes, Lola, 1818–1861. (Spanish dancer and mistress of Franz
  Liszt and King Ludwig of Bavaria)

706. *Lola Montes* (1955). 110 min. Gamma. D: Max Ophuls.
  Montes: Martine Carol
  Franz Liszt: Will Quadflieg
  Supporting cast: Ivan Desny, Peter Ustinov, Anton Wal-
    brook, Oskar Werner

  SEE ALSO: **Liszt, Franz.**

Montez, Lola, 1818–1861
  See **Montes, Lola.**

Monti, Carlotta
  See **Fields, W.C.**

Moon, Keith, 1946–1978
  See **Who, The.**

Moore, Grace, 1901–1947. (American lyric soprano)

707. *So This Is Love* (1953). 101 min. Warner Bros. D: Gordon
  Douglas.
  Moore: Kathryn Grayson
  Supporting cast: Douglas Dick, Merv Griffin, Joan Weldon

Morant, Harry, 1865–1902. (Australian soldier court-martialed
  and executed during the Boer War for murdering civilians)

708. *Breaker Morant* (1979). 107 min. New World Pictures. D:
Bruce Beresford.
Morant: Edward Woodward
Supporting cast: Bryan Brown, Lewis Fitz-Gerald, Jack
Thompson, John Waters

More, Thomas, 1478–1535. (English statesman executed by
Henry VIII for high treason for refusing to take an oath
renouncing jurisdiction of the pope over the church)

709. *A Man for All Seasons* (1966). 120 min. Columbia Pictures. D:
Fred Zinnemann.
More: Paul Scofield
Henry VIII: Robert Shaw
Supporting cast: Wendy Hiller, Leo McKern, Orson Welles

Morgan, Daniel, 1830–1865. (Legendary Australian outlaw)

710. *Mad Dog Morgan* (1976). 102 min. Jeremy Thomas Prod. D:
Philippe Mora.
Morgan: Dennis Hopper
Supporting cast: David Gulpilil, Jack Thompson, Frank
Thring

Morgan, Helen, 1900–1941. (American torch singer popular in
the 1920's and early 1930's)

711. *The Helen Morgan Story* (1957). 118 min. Warner Bros. D:
Michael Curtiz.
Morgan: Ann Blyth
Supporting cast: Richard Carlson, Gene Evans, Paul New-
man

Morgan, Henry, 1635–1688. (Reformed Welsh pirate who became lieutenant governor of Jamaica)

712. *The Black Swan* (1942). 85 min. 20th Century-Fox. D: Henry
King.
Morgan: Laird Cregar

Supporting cast: Maureen O'Hara, Tyrone Power, George Sanders

713. *Morgan the Pirate* (1961). 95 min. MGM. D: Andre de Toth.
Morgan: Steve Reeves
Supporting cast: Lydia Alfonsi, Chelo Alonso, Valerie Lagrange

Moro, Aldo, 1916–1978. (Italian president assassinated by the terrorist group Red Brigades)

713a *The Moro Affair* (1986). 110 min. Columbia Pictures. D: Giuseppe Ferrara.
Moro: Gian Maria Volonte
Supporting cast: Daniele Dublino, Margarita Lozano, Umberto Raho, Mattia Sbragia

Morris, Frank, 1927?– (American criminal who led the only successful escape from Alcatraz prison)

714. *Escape From Alcatraz* (1979). 112 min. Paramount Pictures.
D: Don Siegel.
Morris: Clint Eastwood
Clarence Anglin: Jack Thibeau
John Anglin: Fred Ward
Supporting cast: Bruce Fischer, Larry Hankin, Patrick McGoohan

Morris, Kathy, 1953–1983. (American music student and singer who suffered seizures caused by brain tumors)

715. *Seizure: The Story of Kathy Morris* (1980). 103 min. Jozak Co.
D: Gerald I. Isenberg.
Morris: Penelope Milford
Supporting cast: Christopher Allport, Fredric Lehne, Linda G. Miller, Leonard Nimoy

Morrison, Jim, 1943–1971. (American rock musician and lead singer for the rock group The Doors)

715a *The Doors* (1991). 135 min. Carolco Pictures Inc. D: Oliver Stone.
Morrison: Val Kilmer
Supporting cast: Kevin Dillon, Kyle MacLachlan, Meg Ryan, Frank Whaley

Morros, Boris, 1895–1963. (Soviet-American counterespionage agent for the FBI against the Soviet Union)

716. *Man on a String* (1960). 92 min. Clumbia Pictures. D: Andre de Toth.
Morros: Ernest Borgnine
Supporting cast: Colleen Dewhurst, Kerwin Mathews, Alexander Scourby

Morrow, Barry
See **Sackter, Bill.**

Morton, William Thomas Green, 1819–1868. (American dentist who pioneered the use of ether as an anesthetic)

717. *The Great Moment* (1944). 83 min. Paramount Pictures. D: Preston Sturges.
Morton: Joel McCrea
Supporting cast: Harry Carey, William Demarest, Betty Field

Moscone, George, 1929?–1978
See **Milk, Harvey.**

Moses, c. 13th century B.C. (Hebrew leader and lawgiver who freed the Jewish people from Egyptian bondage)

718. *Moses* (1975). 141 min. RAI Television. D: Gianfranco Del Bosio.
Moses: Burt Lancaster
Supporting cast: Irene Papas, Anthony Quayle, Ingrid Thulin

719. *The Ten Commandments* (1956). 220 min. Paramount Pictures. D: Cecil B. De Mille.
Moses: Charlton Heston
Supporting cast: Yul Brynner, Yvonne De Carlo, John Derek, Edward G. Robinson

Mowat, Farley, 1921– (Canadian writer who spent a year living with wolves in the Arctic wilderness)

720. *Never Cry Wolf* (1983). 105 min. Walt Disney Prod. D: Carroll Ballard.
Mowat: Charles Martin Smith
Supporting cast: Brian Dennehy, Zachary Ittimangnaq, Samson Jorah

Moylan, Mary Ellen, 1926–
See **Balanchine, George.**

Mozart, Wolfgang Amadeus, 1756–1791. (Austrian composer and one of the chief exponents of the Viennese school)

721. *Amadeus* (1984). 158 min. Orion Pictures. D: Milos Forman.
Mozart: Tom Hulce
Joseph II: Jeffrey Jones
Antonio Salieri: F. Murray Abraham
Supporting cast: Elizabeth Berridge, Simon Callow, Roy Dotrice, Christine Ebersole

722. *Eternal Melodies* (1948). 93 min. E.N.I.C. D: Carmine Gallone.
Mozart (as a child): Carlo Barbetti
Mozart (as an adult): Gino Cervi
Supporting cast: Luisella Beghi, Maria Jacobini, Conchita Montenegro, Luigi Pavese

Mudd, Samuel, 1833–1883. (American physician sent to prison for setting John Wilkes Booth's fractured leg)

723. *The Ordeal of Dr. Mudd* (1980). 143 min. Marble Arch Prod.
  D: Paul Wendkos.
  Mudd: Dennis Weaver
  John Wilkes Booth: Bill Grimble
  Supporting cast: Richard Dysart, Michael McGuire, Susan
    Sullivan

724. *The Prisoner of Shark Island* (1936). 94 min. 20th Century-Fox.
  D: John Ford.
  Mudd: Warner Baxter
  Supporting cast: Arthur Byron, Claude Gillingwater, Glo-
    ria Stuart

Mukhtar, Omar, 1860–1931. (Libyan guerrilla leader who fought
  against the Italians in Libya, 1911–1931)

725. *Lion of the Desert* (1981). 162 min. United Film. D: Mousta-
  pha Akkad.
  Mukhtar: Anthony Quinn
  Rodolfo Graziani: Oliver Reed
  Benito Mussolini: Rod Steiger
  Supporting cast: John Gielgud, Gastone Moschin, Irene
    Papas, Raf Vallone

Muldowney, Shirley, 1940– (American two-time world champion drag racer)

726. *Heart Like a Wheel* (1983). 113 min. 20th Century-Fox. D:
  Jonathan Kaplan.
  Muldowney: Bonnie Bedelia
  Connie Kalitta: Beau Bridges
  Supporting cast: Hoyt Axton, Bill McKinney, Leo Rossi

Mullen, Peg. (American anti-Vietnam War activist)

727. *Friendly Fire* (1979). 150 min. Marble Arch Prod. D: David
  Greene.
  Mullen: Carol Burnett
  Supporting cast: Ned Beatty, Dennis Erdman, Timothy
    Hutton, Sam Waterston

Munch, Edvard, 1863–1944. (Norwegian artist, pioneer of modern art and one of the most influential figures in European Expressionism)

728. *Edvard Munch* (1976). 167 min. Norsk Rikstringkasting. D: Peter Watkins.
Munch (as an adult): Geir Westby
Munch (age 5): Erik Allum
Munch (age 14): Amund Berge
Supporting cast: Gro Fraas, Johan Halsbog, Gro Jarlo, Lotte Teig

Murcia, Andy
See **Jillian, Ann.**

Murieta, Joaquin, 1828–1853. (Legendary Mexican bandit)

729. *The Desperate Mission* (1971). 120 min. 20th Century-Fox. D: Earl Bellamy.
Murieta: Ricardo Montalban
Supporting cast: Ina Balin, Rosey Grier, Slim Pickens

730. *Murieta* (1965). 108 min. Warner Bros. D: George Sherman.
Murieta: Jeffrey Hunter
Supporting cast: Roberto Camardiel, Arthur Kennedy, Sara Lezana, Diana Lorys

731. *The Robin Hood of El Dorado* (1936). 86 min. MGM. D: William Wellman.
Murieta: Warner Baxter
Supporting cast: Bruce Cabot, Eric Linden, Margo

Murphy, Audie, 1924–1971. (Film actor and America's most decorated World War II soldier)

732. *To Hell and Back* (1955). 106 min. Universal Pictures. D: Jesse Hibbs.
Murphy: Audie Murphy
Supporting cast: Charles Drake, Gregg Palmer, Marshall Thompson

Murrow, Edward R., 1908–1965. (American radio and television commentator for CBS in the 1930's, 1940's and 1950's)

733. *Murrow* (1986). 114 min. TVS, Ltd. D: Jack Gold.
    Murrow: Daniel J. Travanti
    Fred Friendly: Edward Herrmann
    William S. Paley: Dabney Coleman
    Frank Stanton: John McMartin
    Supporting cast: Kathryn Leigh Scott, Robert Sherman, David Suchet, Robert Vaughn

Mussolini, Benito, 1883–1945. (Italian dictator, 1922–1943)

734. *Mussolini: The Decline and Fall of Il Duce* (1985). 192 min.
    HBO Premiere Films. D: Alberto Negrin.
    Mussolini: Bob Hoskins
    Edda Mussolini Ciano: Susan Sarandon
    Galeazzo Ciano: Anthony Hopkins
    Adolf Hitler: Kurt Raab
    Rachele Mussolini: Annie Girardot
    Claretta Petacci: Barbara De Rossi
    Supporting cast: Vittorio Mezzogiorno, Francesca Rinaldi, Fabio Testi, Dietlinde Turban

734a *Mussolini: The Untold Story* (1985). 360 min. Trian Productions. D: William A. Graham.
    Mussolini: George C. Scott
    Edda Mussolini Ciano: Mary Elizabeth Mastrantonio
    Galeazzo Ciano: Raul Julia
    Adolf Hitler: Gunnar Moeller
    Rachele Mussolini: Lee Grant
    Claretta Petacci: Virginia Madsen
    Supporting cast: Gabriel Byrne, Kenneth Colley, Robert Downey, Godfrey James

SEE ALSO: **Hitler, Adolf; Mukhtar, Omar.**

Mussolini, Rachele, 1892–
    See **Mussolini, Benito.**

Myers, Lowell, 1929–
See **Lang, Donald.**

N

Napoleon Bonaparte, Emperor of France, 1769–1821.

735. *Conquest* (1937). 112 min. MGM. D: Clarence Brown.
Napoleon: Charles Boyer
Maria Walewska: Greta Garbo
Supporting cast: Alan Marshal, Reginald Owen, Henry Stephenson

736. *Desiree* (1954). 110 min. 20th Century-Fox. D: Henry Koster.
Napoleon: Marlon Brando
Desideria/Desiree: Jean Simmons
Josephine: Merle Oberon
Supporting cast: Cameron Mitchell, Michael Rennie, Elizabeth Sellars

737. *Eagle in a Cage* (1971). 98 min. Group W Prod. D: Fielder Cook.
Napoleon: Kenneth Haigh
Supporting cast: John Gielgud, Ralph Richardson, Billie Whitelaw

738. *Waterloo* (1971). 123 min. Paramount Pictures. D: Sergei Bondarchuk
Napoleon: Rod Steiger
Arthur Wellington: Christopher Plummer
Supporting cast: Jack Hawkins, Dan O'Herlihy, Orson Welles

SEE ALSO: **Bonaparte, Paolina.**

Nasser, Gamal Abdel, 1918–1970
See **Sadat, Anwar.**

Neal, Patricia, 1926– (American Oscar-winning film actress)

739. *The Patricia Neal Story* (1981). 100 min. Lawrence Schiller Prod. D: Anthony Harvey, Anthony Page.
Neal: Glenda Jackson
Roald Dahl: Dirk Bogarde
Mildred Dunnock: Mildred Dunnock
Supporting cast: Ken Kercheval, Jane Merrow, Jane Reilly

Nelson, George "Baby Face," 1908–1934. (American Depression era gangster)

740. *Baby Face Nelson* (1957). 85 min. United Artists. D: Don Siegel.
Nelson: Mickey Rooney
Supporting cast: Ted De Corsia, Jack Elam, Cedric Hardwicke, Carolyn Jones

Nelson, Horatio, 1758–1805. (British admiral and naval hero of the Napoleonic wars)

741. *The Nelson Affair* (1973). 118 min. Universal Pictures. D: James Cellan Jones.
Nelson: Peter Finch
Emma Hamilton: Glenda Jackson
Supporting cast: Michael Jayston, Margaret Leighton, Anthony Quayle

SEE ALSO: **Hamilton, Emma.**

Nesbit, Evelyn, 1885–1967. (American showgirl who was involved in a love triangle that led to the murder of Stanford White in 1906 by Nesbit's husband, Harry Thaw)

742. *The Girl in the Red Velvet Swing* (1955). 109 min. 20th Century-Fox. D: Richard Fleischer.
Nesbit: Joan Collins
Harry Thaw: Farley Granger
Stanford White: Ray Milland

Supporting cast: Luther Adler, Glenda Farrell, Cornelia Otis Skinner

Ness, Eliot, 1903–1957. (American F.B.I. agent credited with bringing Alphonse Capone to justice)

742a *The Untouchables* (1987). 120 min. Paramount Pictures. D: Brian DePalma.
Ness: Kevin Costner
Alphonse Capone: Robert DeNiro
Supporting cast: Richard Bradford, Sean Connery, Andy Garcia, Charles Martin Smith

Niccacci, Rufino. (Italian monk who assisted Jewish refugees to escape from German persecution during World War II)

742b *The Assisi Underground* (1984). 115 min. MGM. D: Alexander Ramati.
Rufino: Ben Cross
Supporting cast: James Mason, Irene Papas, Edmund Purdom, Maximilian Schell

Nicholas II, Emperor of Russia, 1868–1918.

743. *Nicholas and Alexandra* (1971). 183 min. Columbia Pictures. D: Franklin Schaffner.
Nicholas: Michael Jayston
Alexandra: Janet Suzman
Supporting cast: Harry Andrews, Tom Baker, Jack Hawkins

SEE ALSO: **Anderson, Anna; Rasputin, Grigori Efimovich.**

Nichols, Ernest Loring "Red," 1905–1965. (American jazz trumpeter of the 1920's and 1930's)

744. *Five Pennies* (1959). 117 min. Paramount Pictures. D: Melville Shavelson.
    Nichols: Danny Kaye
    Supporting cast: Louis Armstrong, Barbara Bel Geddes, Bob Crosby, Harry Guardino

Nightingale, Florence, 1820–1910. (British nurse and hospital reformer, considered the founder of the modern nursing profession)

745. *Florence Nightingale* (1985). 150 min. Cypress Point Productions. D: Daryl Duke.
    Nightingale: Jaclyn Smith
    Supporting cast: Claire Bloom, Timothy Dalton, Peter McEnery, Timothy West

746. *The Lady With a Lamp* (1951). 112 min. Wilcox-Neagle Prod. D: Herbert Wilcox.
    Nightingale: Anna Neagle
    Supporting cast: Felix Aylmer, Maureen Pryor, Michael Wilding

747. *The White Angel* (1936). 91 min. Warner Bros. D: William Dieterle.
    Nightingale: Kay Francis
    Supporting cast: Nigel Bruce, Ian Hunter, Donald Woods

Nijinsky, Waslaw, 1890–1950. (Legendary Russian ballet dancer of the early 1900's)

748. *Nijinsky* (1980). 125 min. Paramount Pictures. D: Herbert Ross.
    Nijinsky: George de la Pena
    Serge Diaghilev: Alan Bates
    Supporting cast: Alan Badel, Leslie Browne, Ronald Pickup

Nitti, Francesco Saverio, 1868–1953. (American gangster who become the new head of the Capone gang after Alphonse Capone was sent to Alcatraz Prison)

748a *Nitti: The Enforcer* (1988). 100 min. Academy Entertainment.
D: Michael Switzer.
Nitti: Anthony LaPaglia
Alphonse Capone: Vincent Guastaferro
Hugh Kelly: Michael Moriarty
Supporting cast: Trini Alvarado, Bruce Kirby, Clayton Landey, Michael Russo

Nixon, Richard M., 1913– (Thirty-seventh American president and the only one to resign from office)

749. *Secret Honor* (1984). 90 min. Sandcastle. D: Robert Altman.
Nixon: Philip Baker Hall
This was a one-man show.

SEE ALSO: **Colson, Charles; Dean, John; Hoover, J. Edgar.**

Nizer, Louis, 1902–
See **Faulk, John Henry.**

Nobile, Umberto, 1885–1978
See **Amundsen, Roald.**

Nordraak, Rikard, 1842–1866
See **Grieg, Edvard.**

Norton, Ken, 1945–
See **Ali, Muhammad.**

Norworth, Jack, 1879–1959
See **Baynes, Nora.**

Nureyev, Rudolf, 1938–1993 (Russian-born ballet dancer and one of the greatest male dancers of the 1960's and 1970's)

750. *I Am a Dancer* (1973). 93 min. EMI Film Prod. D: Pierre Jourdan, Bryan Forbes.
Documentary

O

Oakley, Annie, 1859–1926. (American sharpshooter and star of Buffalo Bill's Wild West Show for seventeen years)

751. *Annie Get Your Gun* (1950). 107 min. MGM. D: George Sidney.
Oakley: Betty Hutton
Supporting cast: Edward Arnold, Louis Calhern, Howard Keel, J. Carrol Naish

752. *Annie Oakley* (1935). 90 min. RKO. D: George Stevens.
Oakley: Barbara Stanwyck
Supporting cast: Andy Clyde, Melvyn Douglas, Preston Foster, Pert Kelton

O'Casey, Sean, 1880–1964. (Irish playwright best known for his plays about the Irish working class)

753. *Young Cassidy* (1965). 110 min. MGM. D: Jack Cardiff, John Ford.
O'Casey/Cassidy: Rod Taylor
William Butler Yeats: Michael Redgrave
Supporting cast: Julie Christie, Flora Robson, Maggie Smith

O'Donnell, Hugh Roe, 1571?–1602. (Irish nobleman who fought against the English in the late 1500's)

754. *The Fighting Prince of Donegal* (1966). 112 min. Walt Disney Prod. D: Michael O'Herlihy.
O'Donnell: Peter McEnery
Supporting cast: Tom Adams, Susan Hampshire, Gordon Jackson

O'Donnell, Lawrence, Jr., 1951–
  See **O'Donnell, Lawrence, Sr.**

O'Donnell, Lawrence, Sr. (American lawyer who sued the Boston Police Department for the unnecessary use of deadly force in 1975)

754a *A Case of Deadly Force* (1986). 100 min. Telecom Entertainment Inc. D: Michael Miller.
  O'Donnell: Richard Crenna
  Lawrence O'Donnell, Jr.: Tate Donovan
  Supporting cast: Tom Isbell, Frank McCarthy, Michael O'Hare, Lorraine Toussaint

O'Flaherty, Hugh, 1898–1963. (American cardinal who aided resistance to the Germans in World War II Rome)

755. *The Scarlet and the Black* (1983). 155 min. ITC Prod. D: Jerry London.
  O'Flaherty: Gregory Peck
  Herbert Kappler: Christopher Plummer
  Pius XII: John Gielgud
  Supporting cast: Barbara Bouchet, Kenneth Colley, Walter Gottell, Raf Vallone

Ofshe, Richard, 1941–
  See **Mitchell, Dave.**

Olcott, Chauncey, 1860–1932. (Irish-American songwriter and stage actor best known as star of Irish musical dramas)

756. *My Wild Irish Rose* (1947). 101 min. Warner Bros. D: David Butler.
  Olcott: Dennis Morgan
  Lillian Russell: Andrea King
  Supporting cast: Ben Blue, Arlene Dahl, George O'Brien

Omar Khayyam, 1048–1123. (Persian astronomer and poet best known for the *Rubaiyat*)

757. *Omar Khayyam* (1957). 101 min. Paramount Pictures. D: William Dieterle.
Omar: Cornel Wilde
Supporting cast: Raymond Massey, Debra Paget, Michael Rennie

Onassis, Jacqueline Kennedy, 1929–
See **Kennedy, Jacqueline Bouvier.**

O'Neil, Kitty, 1946– (American film stuntwoman and holder of the women's world land-speed record in a rocket-powered racing car)

758. *Silent Victory: The Kitty O'Neil Story* (1979). 120 min. Channing-Debin-Locke Co. D: Lou Antonio.
O'Neil (as an adult): Stockard Channing
O'Neil (age 2–4): Angelique Antonio
O'Neil (age 8–10): Elkin Antonio
Supporting cast: Edward Albert, Colleen Dewhurst, James Farentino

O'Neill, Eugene, 1888–1953
See **Reed, John.**

Ono, Yoko, 1933–
See **Lennon, John.**

Oppenheimer, J. Robert, 1904–1967. (American nuclear physicist who headed the team that created the first atomic bomb)

759. *The Day After Trinity: J. Robert Oppenheimer and the Atomic Bomb* (1981). 88 min. Pyramid Films. D: Jon Else.
Documentary.

759a *Day One* (1989). 150 min. CBS Television. D: Joseph Sargent.
Oppenheimer: David Strathairn
Leslie Groves: Brian Dennehy
Leo Szilard: Michael Tucker
Supporting cast: Hume Cronyn, Richard Dysart, Hal Holbrook, Barnard Hughes

759b *Fat Man and Little Boy* (1988). 126 min. Paramount Pictures. D: Roland Joffre.
Oppenheimer: Dwight Schultz
Leslie Groves: Paul Newman
Supporting cast: Bonnie Bedelia, John Cusack, Gerald Hiken, Jean Tatlock

O'Reilly, Beatrice, 1906?– (American activist who founded the first Los Angeles recovery house for female alcoholics)

760. *Life of the Party: The Story of Beatrice* (1982). 100 min. Columbia Pictures Television. D: Lamont Johnson.
O'Reilly: Carol Burnett
Johnny O'Reilly: Lloyd Bridges
Supporting cast: Geoffrey Lewis, Marian Mercer

O'Reilly, Johnny
See **O'Reilly, Beatrice.**

Orton, Joe, 1933–1967. (Murdered British playwright best known for the ''sick'' humor in his plays)

760a *Prick Up Your Ears* (1987). 111 min. Civilhand Zenith. D: Stephen Frears.
Orton: Gary Oldman
Kenneth Halliwell: Alfred Molina
John Lahr: Wallace Shawn
Peggy Ramsay: Vanessa Redgrave
Supporting cast: Janet Dale, Lindsay Duncan, James Grant, Julie Walters

Osmond, George
    See **Osmond, Olive.**

Osmond, Olive. (American Mormon and mother of the Osmond
    Family singers)

761. *Side by Side: The True Story of the Osmond Family* (1982). 100
    min. Osmond Television Prod. D: Russ Mayberry.
    Osmond: Marie Osmond
    George Osmond: Joseph Bottoms
    Supporting cast: Shane Chournos, Todd Dutson, David
    Eaves, Shane Wallace

Oswald, Lee Harvey, 1939–1963. (American assassin of Presi-
    dent John F. Kennedy)

762. *The Trial of Lee Harvey Oswald* (1977). 210 min. Charles Fries
    Prod. D: David Greene.
    Oswald: John Pleshette
    Supporting cast: Ben Gazzara, Lorne Greene, Frances Lee
    McCain

    SEE ALSO: **Ruby, Jack.**

Oswald, Russell
    See **Wicker, Tom.**

Owens, Jesse, 1913–1980. (African-American world-record- set-
    ting track-and-field star who won four gold medals at the
    1936 Olympic Games)

763. *The Jesse Owens Story* (1984). 200 min. Paramount Pictures.
    D: Richard Irving.
    Owens: Dorian Harewood
    Supporting cast: Tom Bosley, Georg Stanford Brown,
    LeVar Burton, Debbi Morgan

Ozu, Yasuiro, 1903–1963. (Japanese film director best known for portraying the lives of ordinary people and the relationship between generations in his films)

763a *I Lived, But . . .* (1986). 118 min. Shochiku Company Ltd. D: Kazuo Inoue
Documentary

P

Paganini, Nicolo, 1782–1840. (Legendary Italian violinist who revolutionized violin technique)

764. *The Magic Bow* (1947). 105 min. Universal-International. D: Bernard Knowles.
Paganini: Stewart Granger
Supporting cast: Phyllis Calvert, Cecil Parker, Dennis Price

Pagano, Bernard. (American priest mistakenly arrested as a stickup man)

765. *The Gentleman Bandit* (1981). 100 min. Highgate Pictures. D: Jonathan Kaplan.
Pagano: Ralph Waite
Supporting cast: Julie Bovasso, Joe Grifasi, Estelle Parsons, Jerry Zaks

Paige, Leroy "Satchel," 1906–1982. (African-American baseball player who broke into the majors at the age of forty-three as a pitcher for the Cleveland Indians)

766. *Don't Look Back: The Story Of Leroy "Satchel" Paige* (1981). 98 min. TBA Productions. D: Richard A. Colla.
Paige: Louis Gossett, Jr.
Supporting cast: Ernie Barnes, Clifton David, Cleavon Little, Beverly Todd

Painter, Hal W., 1931?– (American author and defendant in custody battle for his son Mark)

767. *Mark, I Love You* (1980). 96 min. Aubrey Company. D: Gunnar Hellstrom.
Painter: Kevin Dobson
Mark Painter: Justin Dana
Supporting cast: Dana Elcar, James Whitmore, Cassie Yates

Painter, Mark, 1959?–
See **Painter, Hal W.**

Paley, William S., 1901–1990
See **Murrow, Edward R.**

Palmer, Carl, 1948–
See **Emerson, Lake & Palmer.**

Parker, Bonnie, 1911–1934. (American Depression era gangster)

768. *Bonnie and Clyde* (1967). 111 min. Warner Bros.-7 Arts. D: Arthur Penn.
Parker: Faye Dunaway
Clyde Barrow: Warren Beatty
Supporting cast: Gene Hackman, Estelle Parsons, Michael J. Pollard, Dub Taylor

769. *The Bonnie Parker Story* (1958). 81 min. American International. D: William Witney.
Parker: Dorothy Provine
Clyde Barrow/Darrow: Jack Hogan
Supporting cast: Richard Bakalyan, Ken Lynch, William Stevens, Joseph Turkel

Parker, Charlie "Bird," 1920–1955. (African-American jazz alto saxophonist best known as the bebop style leader)

769a *Bird* (1988). 163 min. Warner Bros. D: Clint Eastood.
Parker (as an adult): Forest Whitaker
Parker (as a teenager): Damon Whitaker
Dizzy Gillespie: Samuel E. Wright
Supporting cast: Keith David, Michael McGuire, Diane Venora, Michael Zelniker

Parker, Dorothy, 1893–1967. (American writer best known for her satiric humor)

769b *Dorothy and Alan at Norma Place* (1987). 120 min. EZTV. D: John Dorr.
Parker: Strawn Bovee
Alan Campbell: George Lafleur
This was a two-person show.

SEE ALSO: **Hellman, Lillian.**

Parnell, Charles, 1846–1891. (Irish Nationalist leader whose political career was ruined when he was named corespondent in a divorce case)

770. *Parnell* (1937). 119 min. MGM. D: John M. Stahl.
Parnell: Clark Gable
Supporting cast: Myrna Loy, Alan Marshal, Edna May Oliver

Parr, Catherine, 1512–1548
See **Henry VIII,** King of England.

Parsons, Louella, 1881–1972. (Legendary American gossip columnist during Hollywood's golden era)

771. *Malice in Wonderland* (1985). 100 min. ITC Production. D: Gus Trikonis.
Parsons: Elizabeth Taylor
Hedda Hopper: Jane Alexander
Louis B. Mayer: Richard Dysart
Supporting cast: Leslie Ackerman, Thomas Byrd, Jon Cypher, Joyce Van Patten

Pasteur, Louis, 1822–1895. (French chemist who developed the process for pasteurization of milk and vaccines for anthrax and rabies)

772. *The Story of Louis Pasteur* (1936). 87 min. Warner Bros. D: William Dieterle.
Pasteur: Paul Muni
Supporting cast: Josephine Hutchinson, Anita Louise, Donald Woods

Patton, George, 1885–1945. (World War II general who commanded the U.S. 3rd Army in Western Europe)

773. *The Last Days of Patton* (1986). 146 min. Entertainment Partners. D: Delbert Mann.
Patton: George C. Scott
Dwight D. Eisenhower: Richard Dysart
Supporting cast: Murray Hamilton, Ed Lauter, Eva Marie Saint, Kathryn Leigh Scott

773a *Patton* (1970). 170 min. 20th Century-Fox. D: Franklin J. Schaffner.
Patton: George C. Scott
Omar Bradley: Karl Malden
Supporting cast: Cary Loftin, Michael Strong, Stephen Young

Paul, Saint, d. A.D. 67.
See **Peter,** Saint.

Pavarotti, Luciano, 1935– (Italian opera singer known as the "King of the High C's" and the most idolized tenor since Enrico Caruso)

773b *Distant Harmony: Pavarotti in China* (1987). 85 min. Luchina Ltd. Partnership Film. D: Dewitt Sage.
Documentary

Peale, Norman Vincent, 1898– (American minister whose writings emphasized the power of positive thinking)

774. *One Man's Way* (1964). 105 min. United Artists. D: Denis Sanders.
Peale: Don Murray
Supporting cast: Virginia Christine, Diana Hyland, William Windom

Peary, Robert Edwin, 1856–1920
See **Cook, Frederick Albert.**

Pelosi, James. (West Point cadet who was ostracized by his classmates after being accused of cheating)

775. *The Silence* (1975). 78 min. Palomar Pictures. D: Joseph Hardy.
Pelosi: Richard Thomas
Stanley Greenberg: Cliff Gorman
Supporting cast: Percy Granger, George Hearn, James Mitchell

Penn, Edward Lyle. (Australian showman who brought motion pictures to the Outback)

776. *The Picture Show Man* (1977). 99 min. Limelight. D: John Power.
Penn/Pop: John Meillon
Supporting cast: Patrick Cargill, John Ewart, Harold Hopkins, Rod Taylor

Penn, William, 1644–1718. (British Quaker and founder of the Pennsylvania colony)

777. *Courageous Mr. Penn* (1941). 79 min. J.H. Hoffberg. D: Lance Comfort.
Penn: Clifford Evans
Charles II: Dennis Arundell
Supporting cast: O.B. Clarence, Deborah Kerr, Aubrey Mallalieu, D.J. Williams

Pepys, Samuel, 1633–1703
See **Gwyn, Nell.**

Peron, Evita, 1919–1952. (Argentina's First Lady, 1946–1952)

778. *Evita Peron* (1981). 200 min. Hartwest Productions. D: Marvin Chomsky.
Peron: Faye Dunaway
Juan Peron: James Farentino
Supporting cast: Pedro Armendariz, Jr., Michael Constantine, Jose Ferrer, Rita Moreno

Peron, Juan, 1895–1974
See **Peron, Evita.**

Perot, H. Ross, 1930– (American businessman and presidential hopeful who arranged the rescue of two employees from Iran)

778a *On Wings of Eagles* (1986). 250 min. Taft Entertainment Television. D: Andrew V. McLaglen.
Perot: Richard Crenna
Arthur E. Simons: Burt Lancaster
Supporting cast: Paul LeMat, Jim Metzler, Lawrence Pressman, James Sutorius

Petacci, Claretta, d.1943
See **Mussolini, Benito.**

Peter I, "the Great," Emperor of Russia, 1672–1725.

778b *Peter the Great* (1986). 480 min. PTG Productions. D: Marvin J. Chomsky, Lawrence Schiller
Peter (as an adult): Maximilian Schell
Peter (as an old man): Denis DeMarne
Peter (as a young man): Jan Niklas
Peter (as a child): Graham McGrath
Alexis (as an adult): Boris Plotnikov

Alexis (as a child): Tolly Thwaites
Empress Catherine: Hanna Schygulla
Charles XII: Christoph Eichhorn
Eudoxia: Natalya Andreichenko
Patrick Gordon: Jeremy Kemp
Sophia: Vanessa Redgrave
Supporting cast: Helmut Griem, Trevor Howard, Laurence
Olivier, Omar Sharif

Peter III, Emperor of Russia, 1728–1762
See **Catherine II,** "the Great," Empress of Russia.

Peter, Saint, d. A.D. 64? (Hebrew fisherman, one of the Twelve
Apostles and the Roman Catholic Church's first pope)

779. *The Big Fisherman* (1959). 180 min. Buena Vista. D: Frank
Borzage.
Peter: Howard Keel
Supporting cast: Martha Hyer, Susan Kohner, Herbert
Lom, John Saxon, Ray Stricklyn

780. *Peter and Paul* (1981). 200 min. Universal Pictures Televi-
sion. D: Robert Day.
Peter: Robert Foxworth
Saint Paul: Anthony Hopkins
Supporting cast: Eddie Albert, Raymond Burr, Jose Ferrer

Petrofsky, Jerrold, 1948– (American bioengineer who developed computer electrodes to stimulate the muscles of
paraplegics, often allowing them to walk)

781. *First Steps* (1985). 100 min. CBS Entertainment. D: Sheldon
Larry.
Petrofsky: Judd Hirsch
Nan Davis: Amy Steel
Supporting cast: Kim Darby, Frances Lee McCain, John
Pankow, James B. Sikking

Phagan, Mary, 1900?–1913
See **Frank, Leo.**

Philip, Prince, 1921–
See **Charles,** Prince of Wales.

Philip II, King of Spain, 1527–1598
See **Mendoza, Ana de.**

Piaf, Edith, 1915–1963. (French music hall and cabaret singer best known for the life-at-street-level subject matter of her songs)

782. *Edith and Marcel* (1983). 104 min. Miramax Films. D: Claude Lelouch.
Piaf: Evelyne Bouix
Marcel Cerdan: Marcel Cerdan, Jr.
Supporting cast: Jean-Claude Brialy, Francis Huster, Jacques Villeret

783. *Piaf—The Early Years* (1982). 104 min. 20th Century-Fox. D: Guy Casaril.
Piaf: Brigitte Ariel
Supporting cast: Pascale Christophe, Guy Trejan, Pierre Vernier

Picasso, Pablo, 1881–1973. (Spanish artist who was the dominating figure of early-twentieth-century French art and a pioneer of cubism)

784. *The Mystery of Picasso* (1956). 77 min. United Artists. D: Henri-Georges Clouzet.
Documentary

Piccolo, Brian, 1943–1970. (American football player, Chicago Bears running back, and cancer victim)

785. *Brian's Song* (1970). 73 min. Screen Gems. D: Buzz Kulik.
   Piccolo: James Caan
   Gale Sayers: Billy Dee Williams
   Supporting cast: Shelley Fabares, Bud Furillo, Judy Pace, Jack Warden

Piersall, James Anthony "Jimmy," 1929– (American baseball player who suffered a nervous breakdown)

786. *Fear Strikes Out* (1957). 100 min. Paramount Pictures. D: Robert Mulligan.
   Piersall: Anthony Perkins
   Supporting cast: Karl Malden, Norma Moore, Adam Williams, Perry Wilson

Pierson, Harold
   See **Pierson, Louise Randall.**

Pierson, Louise Randall, 1890– (American writer best known for her autobiographical work)

787. *Roughly Speaking* (1945). 117 min. Warner Bros. D: Michael Curtiz.
   Pierson (as an adult): Rosalind Russell
   Pierson (as a child): Ann Todd
   Harold Pierson: Jack Carson
   Supporting cast: Alan Hale, Robert Hutton, Andrea King

Pirtle, Sue, 1952– (American world-champion rodeo star)

788. *Rodeo Girl* (1980). 100 min. Marble Arch Productions. D: Jackie Cooper.
   Pirtle/Garrett: Katharine Ross
   Supporting cast: Wilford Brimley, Jacqueline Brookes, Candy Clark, Bo Hopkins

Pitt, William, 1759–1806. (British prime minister during the Napoleonic wars, 1783–1801 and 1804–1805)

789. *Young Mr. Pitt* (1942). 118 min. 20th Century-Fox. D: Carol Reed.
    Pitt: Robert Donat
    George III, King of England: Raymond Lovell
    Supporting cast: Max Adrian, Phyllis Calvert, John Mills, Robert Morley

Pius XII, Pope, 1876–1958
    See **O'Flaherty, Hugh.**

Pizarro, Francisco, c. 1475–1541. (Spanish explorer and conqueror of Peru)

790. *The Royal Hunt of the Sun* (1969). 121 min. Security Pictures. D: Irving Lerner.
    Pizarro: Robert Shaw
    Atahualpa: Christopher Plummer
    Hernando De Soto: Nigel Davenport
    Supporting cast: Michael Craig, James Donald, Andrew Keir, Leonard Whiting

Place, Etta, 1880?–1911? (American teacher and criminal accomplice to Butch Cassidy and the Sundance Kid)

791. *Mrs. Sundance* (1974). 78 min. 20th Century-Fox. D: Marvin Chomsky.
    Place: Elizabeth Montgomery
    Supporting cast: Robert Foxworth, Arthur Hunnicutt, L.Q. Jones

    SEE ALSO: **Cassidy, Robert Parker** ("Butch").

Plath, Sylvia, 1932–1963. (American poet best known for her poems that explore the feminine identity, suffering, and death)

792. *The Bell Jar* (1979). 107 min. MGM. D: Larry Peerce.
    Plath/Esther: Marilyn Hassett
    Supporting cast: Barbara Barrie, Julie Harris, Anne Jackson, Robert Klein

Plimpton, George, 1927– (American journalist who joined the Detroit Lions to write a piece on football)

793. *Paper Lion* (1968). 107 min. United Artists. D: Alex March.
Plimpton: Alan Alda
Supporting cast: David Doyle, Lauren Hutton, Alex Karras

Pocahontas, d. 1617
See **Smith, John.**

Poe, Edgar Allan, 1809–1849. (American poet and short-story writer best known for his mystery stories and macabre tales of the supernatural)

794. *The Loves of Edgar Allan Poe* (1942) 67 min. 20th Century-Fox. D: Harry Lachman.
Poe (as an adult): John Shepperd
Poe (age 3): Skippy Wanders
Poe (age 12): Freddie Mercer
Supporting cast: Linda Darnell, Jane Darwell, Virginia Gilmore

Polidori, John, 1795–1821
See **Shelley, Percy Bysshe.**

Polo, Marco, 1254–1323? (Italian explorer who traveled to China and entered the diplomatic service of Kublai Khan, 1275–1292)

795. *The Adventures of Marco Polo* (1938). 100 min. United Artists. D: Archie Mayo.
Polo: Gary Cooper
Kublai Khan: George Barbier
Supporting cast: Binnie Barnes, Sigrid Gurie, Alan Hale, Basil Rathbone

796. *Marco* (1973). 109 min. Tomorrow Entertainment. D: Seymour Robbie.
Polo: Desi Arnaz, Jr.

Kublai Khan: Zero Mostel
Supporting cast: Aimee Eccles, Fred Sadoff, Jack Weston

797. *Marco Polo* (1962). 90 min. American International. D: Hugo
Fregonese.
Polo: Rory Calhoun
Kublai Khan: Camillo Pilotto
Supporting cast: Michael Chow, Pierre Cressoy, Robert
Hundar, Yoko Tani

797a *Marco Polo* (1982). 600 min. Cristaldi-Labella Productions.
D: Giuliano Montaldo.
Polo: Ken Marshall
Kublai Khan: Ying Ruocheng
Supporting cast: Anne Bancroft, Denholm Elliott, John
Gielgud, Tony Vogel

798. *Marco the Magnificent* (1966). 100 min. MGM. D: Denys De
La Patelliere.
Polo: Horst Buchholz
Kublai Khan: Anthony Quinn
Supporting cast: Elsa Martinelli, Omar Sharif, Akim Ta-
miroff, Orson Welles

Ponti, Carlo, 1913–
See **Loren, Sophia.**

Pontius Pilate, 1st century. (Roman governor of Judea who
ordered Jesus Christ's crucifixion)

799. *Pontius Pilate* (1966). 100 min. Glomer-Lux. D: Irving Rap-
per.
Pilate: Jean Marais
Jesus Christ: John Drew Barrymore
Supporting cast: Jeanne Crain, Basil Rathbone, Leticia
Roman, Massimo Serato

Porter, Cole, 1892–1964. (American songwriter known for his
witty lyrics and hit Broadway shows)

800. *Night and Day* (1946). 128 min. Warner Bros. D: Michael
Curtiz.
Porter: Cary Grant
Linda Lee: Alexis Smith
Monty Woolley: Monty Woolley
Supporting cast: Mary Martin, Ginny Simms, Jane Wyman

Porter, Edwin S., 1869–1941. (American inventor who collabo-
rated with Edison on the motion picture camera)

801. *Before the Nickelodeon: The Early Cinema of Edwin S. Porter*
(1983). 60 min. Film For Thought. D: Charles Musser.
Documentary

Porter, Linda Lee, d. 1954
See **Porter, Cole.**

Potts, Lamar, 1901?–
See **Wallace, John.**

Powell, John Wesley, 1834–1902. (American geologist and explorer of the Green and Colorado rivers)

802. *Ten Who Dared* (1960). 92 min. Walt Disney Prod. D:
William Beaudine.
Powell: John Beal
Supporting cast: R.G. Armstrong, James Drury, Brian
Keith

Powers, Francis Gary, 1929–1977. (CIA spy pilot shot down over
the Soviet Union in 1960)

803. *Francis Gary Powers: The True Story of the U-2 Spy Incident*
(1976). 100 min. NBC-Television. D: Delbert Mann.
Powers: Lee Majors
Supporting cast: Lew Ayres, Noah Beery, Jr., Brooke
Bundy, Nehemiah Persoff

Pran, Dith, 1942–
    See **Schanberg, Sydney.**

Presley, Elvis, 1935–1977. (American singer known as the ''King of Rock 'n' Roll'')

804. *Elvis* (1979). 150 min. Dick Clark Productions. D: John Carpenter.
    Presley: Kurt Russell
    Priscilla Presley: Season Hubley
    Supporting cast: Pat Hingle, Bing Russell, Shelley Winters

805. *Elvis on Tour* (1972). 99 min. MGM. D: Pierre Adidge, Robert Abel.
    Documentary

806. *Elvis That's The Way It Is* (1970). 106 min. MGM. D: Denis Sanders
    Documentary

807. *This Is Elvis* (1981). 101 min. Warner Bros. D: Malcolm Leo, Andrew Solt
    Presley (age 10): Paul Boensch
    Presley (age 18): David Scott
    Presley (age 35): Dana MacKay
    Presley (age 42): Johnny Harra
    Priscilla Presley: Rhonda Lynn
    Supporting cast: Debbie Edge, Lawrence Koller, Furry Lewis, Larry Rasperry

    SEE ALSO: **Presley, Priscilla.**

Presley, Priscilla, 1946– (American actress best known as Elvis Presley's child bride)

807a *Elvis and Me* (1987). 187 min. New World Television. D: Larry Peerce.
    Presley: Susan Walters
    Elvis Presley: Dale Midkiff
    Supporting cast: Jon Cypher, Billy Greenbush, Linda Miller, Marshall Teague

    SEE ALSO: **Presley, Elvis.**

Prinze, Freddie, 1954–1977. (American television comic of the 1970's)

808. *Can You Hear the Laughter? The Story of Freddie Prinze* (1979). 100 min. EMI Television. D: Burt Brinckerhoff.
Prinze: Ira Angustain
Supporting cast: Julie Carmen, Devon Ericson, Randee Heller, Kevin Hooks

Profumo, John D., 1915–
See **Keeler, Christine.**

Proust, Marcel, 1871–1922. (French novelist who introduced exhaustive psychological analysis as an element in fiction)

809. *Celeste* (1981). 107 min. Pelemele Film. D: Percy Adlon.
Proust: Jurgen Arndt
Celeste Albaret: Eva Mattes
Supporting cast: Wolf Euba, Joseph Manoth, Norbert Wartha

Pryor, Richard, 1940– (African-American comic and actor best known for his raunchy nightclub act)

809a *Jo Jo Dancer, Your Life is Calling* (1986). 97 min. Columbia Pictures. D: Richard Pryor.
Dancer/Pryor: Richard Pryor
Supporting cast: Debbie Allen, Art Evans, Fay Hauser, Paula Kelly

Pu Yi, 1906–1967. (Chinese emperor who ascended the royal throne at age three and was forced to abdicate in 1912 by the revolutionary government)

809b *The Last Emperor* (1987). 166 min. Columbia Pictures. D: Bernardo Bertolucci.
Pu Yi (as an adult): John Lone
Pu Yi (at age three): Richard Vuu
Pu Yi (at age eight): Tijger Tsou

Pu Yi (at age fifteen): Wu Tao
Reginald Johnston: Peter O'Toole
Wan-jung: Joan Chen
Wen Hsiu: Wu Jun Mei
Supporting cast: Dennis Dun, Ying Ruocheng, Ryuichi
    Sakamoto, Victor Wong

Pudaite, Rochunga, 1927?– (Indian scholar who translated the
    Bible into the Hmar language)

809c *Beyond the Next Mountain* (1984). 98 min. Inspirational Films
    Inc. D: Rolf Forsberg, James F. Collier
    Pudaite: Alberto Isaac
    Supporting cast: Barry Foster, Saeed Jaffrey, Richard Line-
    back

Pugachev, Emelyan Ivanovich, 1744?–1775. (Russian soldier
    who proclaimed himself Peter III and led a rebellion against
    Catherine II)

810. *Tempest* (1959). 125 min. Paramount Pictures. D: Alberto
    Lattuada.
    Pugachev: Van Heflin
    Catherine II: Viveca Lindfors
    Supporting cast: Helmut Dantine, Geoffrey Horne, Silvana
    Mangano

Pulitzer, Herbert Peter, 1930?–
    See **Pulitzer, Roxanne.**

Pulitzer, Roxanne, 1951– (American businesswoman best
    known for her messy divorce from the heir to the Pulitzer
    fortune)

810a *Roxanne: The Prize Pulitzer* (1989). 100 min. Quintex Enter-
    tainment. D: Richard Colla.
    Pulitzer: Chynna Phillips
    Herbert Pulitzer: Perry King
    Supporting cast: Amy Adams, Caitlin Brown, Courteney
    Cox, Betsy Russell

Purvis, Melvin, 1903–1960. (Leading Depression era FBI agent)

811. *The Kansas City Massacre* (1975). 120 min. ABC Circle Films.
D: Dan Curtis.
Purvis: Dale Robertson
Charles Floyd: Bo Hopkins
Alvin Karpis: Morgan Paull
Supporting cast: Scott Brady, Robert Walden, Mills Watson

812. *Melvin Purvis—G Man* (1974). 78 min. American International. D: Dan Curtis.
Purvis: Dale Robertson
George R. Kelly: Harris Yulin
Supporting cast: Margaret Blye, Matt Clark, Elliott Street

Pusser, Buford, 1937–1974. (Tennessee sheriff who waged a one-man war against local corruption)

813. *Final Chapter, Walking Tall* (1977) 112 min. American International Pictures. D: Jack Starrett.
Pusser: Bo Svenson
Supporting cast: Margaret Blye, Forrest Tucker, Lurene Tuttle, Morgan Woodward

814. *A Real American Hero* (1978). 100 min. Bing Crosby Productions. D: Lou Antonio.
Pusser: Brian Dennehy
Supporting cast: Ken Howard, Brian Kerwin, Forrest Tucker

815. *Walking Tall* (1973). 125 min. Cinerama BCP Prod. D: Phil Karlson.
Pusser: Joe Don Baker
Supporting cast: Noah Beery, Gene Evans, Elizabeth Hartman, Rosemary Murphy

816. *Walking Tall, Part 2* (1975). 109 min. American International Pictures. D: Earl Bellamy.
Pusser: Bo Svenson
Supporting cast: Luke Askew, Noah Beery, John Chandler, Richard Jaeckel

Pyle, Ernie, 1900–1945. (American World War II correspondent best known for his frontline reporting)

817. *The Story Of G.I. Joe* (1945). 108 min. United Artists. D: William A. Wellman.
Pyle: Burgess Meredith
Supporting cast: Wally Cassell, Jimmy Lloyd, Robert Mitchum, Freddie Steele

Q

Quinlan, Joe
See **Quinlan, Karen Ann.**

Quinlan, Julie
See **Quinlan, Karen Ann.**

Quinlan, Karen Ann, 1954–1985. (American accident victim whose parents petitioned to have her disconnected from a life-support system)

818. *In the Matter of Karen Ann Quinlan* (1977). 120 min. Warren V. Bush Prod. D: Hal Jordan.
Quinlan: Mary Anne Grayson
Joe Quinlan: Brian Keith
Julie Quinlan: Piper Laurie
Supporting cast: David Huffman, Biff McGuire, Stephanie Zimbalist

R

Radisson, Pierre Esprit, c. 1636–1710. (French explorer and fur trader who inspired organization of Hudson's Bay Company)

819. *Hudson's Bay* (1940). 95 min. 20th Century-Fox. D: Irving Pichel.

Radisson: Paul Muni
Charles II: Vincent Price
Supporting cast: Laird Cregar, John Sutton, Gene Tierney

Raft, George, 1895–1980. (American film actor best known for his gangster roles)

820. *The George Raft Story* (1961). 105 min. Allied Artists. D: Joseph M. Newman.
Raft: Ray Danton
Al Capone: Neville Brand
Supporting cast: Barrie Chase, Julie London, Jayne Mansfield, Barbara Nichols

Ragghianti, Marie, 1943– (Tennessee state employee who blew the whistle on government corruption)

821. *Marie* (1985). 108 min. MGM/United Artists. D: Roger Donaldson.
Ragghianti: Sissy Spacek
Supporting cast: Jeff Daniels, Morgan Freeman, Don Hood, Keith Szarabajka

Raglan, Fitzroy James Henry Somerset, Baron, 1788–1855
See **Cardigan, James Thomas Brudenell.**

Rainier III, Prince of Monaco, 1923–
See **Kelly, Grace.**

Raleigh, Walter, 1552–1618
See **Elizabeth I,** Queen of England.

Ramsay, Peggy
See **Orton, Joe.**

Rasputin, Grigori Efimovich, 1871–1916. (Russian monk and faith healer who wielded influence at the court of Nicholas II; assassinated)

822. *Nights of Rasputin* (1960). 95 min. N/A. D: Pierre Chenal.
Rasputin: Edmund Purdom
Supporting cast: John Drew Barrymore, Gianna Maria Canale, Jany Clair

823. *Rasputin* (1975). 107 min. Mosfilm Studios. D: Elem Klimov.
Rasputin: Alexei Petrenko
Supporting cast: Alice Freindlikh, Velta Linne, Anatoly Romanshin

823a *Rasputin and the Empress* (1932). 123 min. MGM. D: Richard Boleslawski.
Rasputin: Lionel Barrymore
Alexandra: Ethel Barrymore
Nicholas II: Ralph Morgan
Supporting cast: Tad Alexander, John Barrymore, Diana Wynyard

824. *Rasputin—The Mad Monk* (1966). 92 min. 20th Century-Fox.
D: Don Sharp.
Rasputin: Christopher Lee
Supporting cast: Francis Matthews, Richard Pasco, Barbara Shelley

SEE ALSO: **Youssoupoff, Felix.**

Ravel, Maurice, 1875–1937. (French composer who defied the established rules of harmony in his compositions and has become best known for his work *Bolero*)

824a *Ravel* (1988). 105 min. Rhombus Media Inc. D: Larry Weinstein.
Documentary

Rawlings, Marjorie Kinnan, 1896–1953. (American novelist best known for her stories of backwoods Florida)

825. *Cross Creek* (1983). 122 min. Universal Pictures. D: Martin Ritt.
   Rawlings: Mary Steenburgen
   Supporting cast: Peter Coyote, Dana Hill, Rip Torn

Rayburn, Sam, 1882–1961
   See **Johnson, Lyndon Baines.**

Raynor, Charles. (American physician convicted of plotting to murder his wife)

825a *Deadly Intentions* (1985). 120 min. Green-Epstein Prod. D: Noel Black.
   Raynor: Michael Biehn
   Katherine Raynor: Madolyn Smith
   Supporting cast: Cliff DeYoung, Morgana King, Jack Kruschen, Kevin McCarthy

Raynor, Katherine
   See **Raynor, Charles.**

Reagan, Ronald, 1911–
   See **Brady, James S.**

Redl, Alfred, 1864–1913. (Austrian intelligence officer guilty of betraying the Austro-Hungarian Empire to Russia)

826. *Colonel Redl* (1985). 149 min. Mafilm Studio. D: Istvan Szabo.
   Redl: Klaus Maria Brandauer
   Supporting cast: Hans Christian Blech, Gudrun Landgrebe, Armin Muller-Stahl, Jan Niklas

Reed, John, 1887–1920. (American writer and hero of the 1917 Russian Revolution)

827. *Reds* (1981). 196 min. Paramount Pictures. D: Warren Beatty.
Reed: Warren Beatty
Louise Bryant: Diane Keaton
Emma Goldman: Maureen Stapleton
Eugene O'Neill: Jack Nicholson
Supporting cast: Edward Herrmann, Jerzy Kosinski, Paul Sorvino

Reilly, Peter, 1955– (American teenager accused of murdering his mother)

828. *A Death in Canaan* (1978). 150 min. Warner Bros. Television. D: Tony Richardson.
Reilly: Paul Clemens
Joan Barthel: Stefanie Powers
Supporting cast: Tom Atkins, Jacqueline Brookes, Brian Dennehy, James Sutorious

Reiner, Rob, 1945– (American television and film actor and director)

829. *More Than Friends* (1978). 100 min. Columbia Pictures. D: Jim Burrows.
Reiner/Corkus: Rob Reiner
Penny Marshall/Pearlman: Penny Marshall
Supporting cast: Phillip R. Allen, Dabney Coleman, Kay Medford

Rembrandt Harmenszoon van Rijn, 1609–1669. (Leading representative of the Dutch school of painting and a master of light and shadow)

830. *Rembrandt* (1937). 85 min. London Films. D: Alexander Korda.
Rembrandt: Charles Laughton
Supporting cast: Edward Chapman, Elsa Lanchester, Gertrude Lawrence

Renoir, Jean, 1894–1979. (French film director best known for anti-war masterpiece *La Grande Illusion*)

830a *Jean Renoir, The Boss* (1967). 60 min. Zanzibar Productions. D: Jacques Rivette, Andre S. Labarthe
Documentary

Reuter, Julius, 1816–1899. (German founder of Reuter's News Agency)

831. *Dispatch From Reuters* (1940). 90 min. Warner Bros. D: William Dieterle.
Reuter: Edward G. Robinson
Supporting cast: Eddie Albert, Albert Basserman, Edna Best, Nigel Bruce

Reynolds, Andre, 1961?–
See **Butsicaris, Jimmy.**

Rhodes, Cecil, 1853–1902. (British expatriate to South Africa who became Prime Minister of Cape Colony, 1890–1896 and founder of Rhodesia)

831a *Rhodes* (1936). 91 min. Gaumont. D: Berthold Viertel.
Rhodes: Walter Huston
Paul Kruger: Oscar Homolka
Supporting cast: Peggy Ashcroft, Frank Cellier, Renee De Vaux, Basil Sydney

Rice-Davies, Mandy, 1944–
See **Keeler, Christine.**

Richard I, King of England, 1157–1199.

832. *The Crusades* (1935). 123 min. Paramount Pictures. D: Cecil B. De Mille.
Richard: Henry Wilcoxon
Saladin: Ian Keith

Supporting cast: C. Henry Gordon, C. Aubrey Smith, Loretta Young

833. *King Richard and the Crusades* (1954). 114 min. Warner Bros. D: David Butler.
Richard: George Sanders
Saladin: Rex Harrison
Supporting cast: Robert Douglas, Virginia Mayo, Michael Pate

Richard III, King of England, 1452–1485.

834. *Richard III* (1956). 138 min. Loppert/Korda. D: Laurence Olivier.
Richard: Laurence Olivier
Supporting cast: John Gielgud, Cedric Hardwicke, Ralph Richardson

835. *Tower of London* (1939). 92 min. Universal Pictures. D: Rowland V. Lee.
Richard: Basil Rathbone
Edward IV: Ian Hunter
Supporting cast: Boris Karloff, Barbara O'Neil, Vincent Price

Richards, Renee, 1935?– (American transvestite who had a sex change operation and later joined the professional women's tennis tour)

835a *Second Serve* (1986). 120 min. Linda Yellen Productions. D: Anthony Page.
Richards: Vanessa Redgrave
Supporting cast: Martin Balsam, Kerrie Keane, Alice Krige, William Russ

Richardson, J.P. "Big Bopper," 1932?–1959
See **Valens, Richie.**

Richardson, Robert. (American reporter best known for his reporting of the 1965 Watts riots in Los Angeles)

835b *Heat Wave* (1990). 94 min. Turner Pictures Inc. D: Kevin Hooks.
Richardson: Blair Underwood
Supporting cast: Margaret Avery, James Earl Jones, Sally Kirkland, Cicely Tyson

Richelieu, Armand, 1585–1642. (French cardinal and chief minister of Louis XIII, 1624–1642)

836. *Cardinal Richelieu* (1935). 80 min. United Artists. D: Rowland V. Lee.
Richelieu: George Arliss
Louis XIII: Edward Arnold
Supporting cast: Francis Lister, Maureen O'Sullivan, Cesar Romero

837. *Under the Red Robe* (1937). 80 min. 20th Century-Fox. D: Victor Seastrom.
Richelieu: Raymond Massey
Supporting cast: Annabella, Romney Brent, Conrad Veidt

SEE ALSO: **Dubarry, Marie.**

Richthofen, Manfred von, 1882–1918. (German World War I pilot and leading air ace, with eighty kills)

838. *Von Richthofen and Brown* (1971). 97 min. United Artists. D: Roger Corman.
Richthofen: John Phillip Law
Roy Brown: Don Stroud
Supporting cast: Hurd Hatfield, Karen Huston, Barry Primus, Corin Redgrave

Rickenbacker, Eddie, 1890–1973. (American World War I pilot, awarded the Congressional Medal of Honor)

839. *Captain Eddie* (1945). 107 min. 20th Century-Fox. D: Lloyd Bacon.
Rickenbacker: Fred MacMurray
Supporting cast: Lynn Bari, Charles Bickford, Thomas Mitchell, Lloyd Nolan

Rideout, Greta, 1955– (American litigant in landmark rape case)

840. *Rape and Marriage: The Rideout Case* (1980). 100 min. Lorimar Productions. D: Peter Levin.
Rideout: Linda Hamilton
John Rideout: Mickey Rourke
Supporting cast: Conchata Ferrell, Eugene Roche, Gail Strickland, Rip Torn

Rideout, John, 1957–
See **Rideout, Greta.**

Rimsky-Korsakov, Nikolai, 1844–1908. (Russian composer best known for his operas based on Russian legends)

841. *Song of Scheherezade* (1947). 107 min. Universal- International. D: Walter Reisch.
Rimsky-Korsakov: Jean-Pierre Aumont
Supporting cast: Eve Arden, Yvonne De Carlo, Brian Donlevy, Philip Reed

Rivera, Diego, 1886–1957
See **Kohlo, Frida.**

Robespierre, Maximilien de, 1758–1794
See **Danton, Georges.**

Robinson, Eddie, 1919–
See **Gregory, Jim.**

Robinson, Jackie, 1919–1972. (First African-American baseball player in the major leagues)

842. *The Jackie Robinson Story* (1950). 76 min. Eagle-Lion. D: Alfred E. Green.
Robinson: Jackie Robinson
Supporting cast: Louise Beavers, Ruby Dee, Minor Watson

Robinson, Ray, 1921–
See **La Motta, Jake.**

Rockne, Knute, 1888–1931. (Legendary Norwegian-American collegiate football coach at the University of Notre Dame, 1918–1931)

843. *Knute Rockne—All American* (1940) 84 min. Warner Bros. D: Lloyd Bacon.
Rockne: Pat O'Brien
Supporting cast: Donald Crisp, Gale Page, Ronald Reagan

Rodgers, Richard, 1902–1979. (American composer best known for his Broadway musicals created first with Lorenz Hart and later with Oscar Hammerstein)

844. *Words and Music* (1948). 119 min.
Rodgers: Tom Drake
Lorenz Hart: Mickey Rooney
Supporting cast: June Allyson, Judy Garland, Gene Kelly, Ann Sothern

Rodin, Auguste, 1840–1917
See **Claudel, Camille.**

Rodriguez, Alberto. (American police officer who ran three hundred miles in five days as an act of faith)

845. *Three Hundred Miles for Stephanie* (1981). 100 min. Yellow Ribbon Productions. D: Clyde Ware.

Rodriguez: Tony Orlando
Supporting cast: Julie Carmen, Peter Graves, Edward James Olmos, Pepe Serna

Rogers, Betty, 1881?–1944
See **Rogers, Will.**

Rogers, Will, 1879–1935. (American film actor, lecturer and humorist popular in the early 1900's)

846. *The Story of Will Rogers* (1952). 109 min. Warner Bros. D: Michael Curtiz.
Rogers: Will Rogers, Jr.
Betty Rogers: Jane Wyman
Supporting cast: James Gleason, Eve Miller, Carl Benton Reid

Rollins, Betty, 1936– (Correspondent for NBC News and breast cancer victim)

847. *First, You Cry* (1978). 100 min. MTM Productions. D: George Schaefer.
Rollins: Mary Tyler Moore
Supporting cast: Richard Crenna, Florence Eldridge, Anthony Perkins, Jennifer Warren

Romberg, Sigmund, 1887–1951. (Hungarian composer best known for his light operas written the 1920's and 1930's)

848. *Deep in My Heart* (1954). 132 min. MGM. D: Stanley Donen.
Romberg: Jose Ferrer
Supporting cast: Doe Avedon, Merle Oberon, Walter Pidgeon, Helen Traubel

Romero, Oscar Arnulfo, 1917–1980. (Salvadorian Archbishop who was assassinated because of his role as a political activist in defense of his people and the church)

848a *Romero.* (1989). 105 min. Four Seasons Entertainment. D: John Duigan.
Romero: Raul Julia
Supporting cast: Ana Alicia, Alejandro Bracho, Richard Jordan, Eddie Velez

Rommel, Erwin, 1891–1944. (General who commanded German forces in Africa, 1941–1943)

849. *The Desert Fox* (1951). 88 min. 20th Century-Fox. D: Henry Hathaway.
Rommel: James Mason
Supporting cast: Luther Adler, Cedric Hardwicke, Jessica Tandy

850. *The Desert Rats* (1953). 88 min. 20th Century-Fox. D: Robert Wise.
Rommel: James Mason
Supporting cast: Richard Burton, Robert Douglas, Robert Newton, Chips Rafferty

Roncalli, Angelo Giuseppe, 1881–1963
See **John XXIII,** Pope.

Rooney, Mickey, 1920–
See **Garland, Judy.**

Roosevelt, Eleanor, 1884–1962. (Wife of the thirty-second American president and United States representative to the United Nations, 1946–1952)

851. *Eleanor, First Lady of the World* (1982). 100 min. Embassy Television. D: John Erman.
Roosevelt: Jean Stapleton
Supporting cast: Coral Browne, E.G. Marshall, Joyce Van Patten

852. *The Eleanor Roosevelt Story* (1965). 87 min. Glazier Productions. D: Richard Kaplan.
Documentary

SEE ALSO: **Roosevelt, Franklin Delano.**

Roosevelt, Franklin Delano, 1882–1945. (Thirty-second American president and the only man elected president four times)

853. *Eleanor and Franklin* (1976). 208 min. Talent Associates. D: Daniel Petrie.
Roosevelt: Edward Herrmann
Eleanor Roosevelt: Jane Alexander
Sara Delano Roosevelt: Rosemary Murphy
Supporting cast: Ed Flanders, Pamela Franklin, Linda Kelsey

854. *Eleanor and Franklin: The White House Years* (1977). 152 min. Talent Associates. D: Daniel Petrie.
Roosevelt: Edward Herrmann
Eleanor Roosevelt: Jane Alexander
Sara Delano Roosevelt: Rosemary Murphy
Supporting cast: Blair Brown, Walter McGinn, Peggy McKay

855. *FDR: The Last Year* (1980). 180 min. Titus Productions. D: Anthony Page.
Roosevelt: Jason Robards
Eleanor Roosevelt: Eileen Heckart
Supporting cast: Edward Binns, Augusta Dabney, Larry Gates, Michael Gross

856. *Sunrise at Campobello* (1960). 143 min. Warner Bros. D: Vincent J. Donehue.
Roosevelt: Ralph Bellamy
Eleanor Roosevelt: Greer Garson
Sara Delano Roosevelt: Ann Shoemaker
Supporting cast: Alan Bunce, Hume Cronyn, Lyle Talbot

Roosevelt, Sara Delano, 1854–1941
    See **Roosevelt, Franklin Delano.**

Rose, Billy, 1899–1966
    See **Brice, Fanny.**

Rose, Mason
    See **Carney, Bill.**

Rosenberg, Jerry, 1938?– (American convict sentenced to life in Sing Sing Prison who is considered the "dean" of America's jailhouse lawyers)

856a *Doing Life* (1986). 104 min. Phoenix Entertainment Group.
    D: Gene Reynolds
    Rosenberg: Tony Danza
    Supporting cast: Jon DeVries, Alvin Epstein, Mitchell Jason, Lisa Langlois

Ross, Barney, 1909–1967. (American lightweight and welterweight boxing champion, World War II Silver Star recipient and recovered drug addict)

857. *A Monkey on My Back* (1957). 93 min. United Artists. D: Andre de Toth.
    Ross: Cameron Mitchell
    Supporting cast: Jack Albertson, Dianne Foster, Paul Richards

Roth, Lillian, 1910–1980. (American singer, film actress of the 1920's and recovered alcoholic)

858. *I'll Cry Tomorrow* (1955). 117 min. MGM. D: Daniel Mann.
    Roth: Susan Hayward
    Supporting cast: Eddie Albert, Richard Conte, Don Taylor

Rothschild, Nathan, 1777–1836. (German-born British financier who opened the first Rothschild Bank branch in London)

859. *The House of Rothschild* (1934). 88 min. United Artists. D: Alfred L. Werker.
Rothschild: George Arliss
Supporting cast: Boris Karloff, Loretta Young, Robert Young

Rothstein, Arnold, 1882–1928. (American gangster known as "Mr. Big" in 1920's New York, reputed to be able to "fix" anything)

860. *King of the Roaring 20's—The Story of Arnold Rothstein* (1961). 106 min. Allied Artists. D: Joseph M. Newman.
Rothstein: David Janssen
Supporting cast: Jack Carson, Diana Dors, Dianne Foster

Rousseau, Jean-Jacques, 1712–1778. (French philosopher, political theorist and novelist whose writings had a profound effect on the French Revolution)

861. *The Roads of Exile* (1981). 169 min. Corinth Films. D: Claude Goretta
Rousseau: Francois Simon.
Supporting cast: Roland Bertin, Dominique Labourier, David Markham, John Sharp

Rowe, Gary Thomas, Jr. (American Ku Klux Klan member who worked undercover in the Klan for the F.B.I. during the 1960's and was later convicted of murdering a Freedom Rider)

861a *Undercover with the KKK* (1979). 120 min. Columbia Pictures Television. D: Barry Shear.
Rowe: Don Meredith
Supporting cast: Michele Carey, Clifton James, Ed Lauter, Albert Salmi

Roy, Julie, 1938– (American patient who sued her psychiatrist for malpractice)

862. *Betrayal* (1978). 100 min. EMI Television. D: Paul Wendkos.
Roy: Lesley Ann Warren
Supporting cast: Richard Masur, Ron Silver, Rip Torn

Rubin, Jerry, 1938?–
See **Ginsberg, Allen.**

Ruby, Harry, 1895–1974
See **Kalmar, Bert.**

Ruby, Jack, 1911–1967. (American killer of Lee Harvey Oswald)

863. *Ruby and Oswald* (1978). 133 min. Alan Landsburg Productions. D: Mel Stuart.
Ruby: Michael Lerner
Lee Harvey Oswald: Frederic Forrest
Supporting cast: Bruce French, Lou Frizzell, Doris Roberts

Rudolph, Crown Prince of Austria, 1858–1889.

864. *Mayerling* (1936). 91 min. Nero Films. D: Anatole Litvak.
Rudolph: Charles Boyer
Maria Vetsera: Danielle Darrieux
Supporting cast: Jean Dax, Jean Debucourt, Gabrielle Dorziat, Suzy Prim

865. *Mayerling* (1969). 140 min. MGM. D: Terence Young.
Rudolph: Omar Sharif
Maria Vetsera: Catherine Deneuve
Supporting cast: Ava Gardner, James Robertson Justice, James Mason

Rudolph, Wilma, 1940– (African-American Olympic gold medal runner)

866. *Wilma* (1977). 100 min. Cappy Productions, Inc. D: Bud Greenspan.
Rudolph: Shirley Jo Finney
Supporting cast: Jason Bernard, Joe Seneca, Cicely Tyson, Denzel Washington

Russell, Lillian, 1868–1922. (American singer and musical star of the Gay Nineties)

867. *Lillian Russell* (1940). 127 min. 20th Century-Fox. D: Irving Cummings.
Russell: Alice Faye
James Brady: Edward Arnold
Supporting cast: Don Ameche, Henry Fonda, Warren William

SEE ALSO: **Brady, James ("Diamond Jim"); Olcott, Chauncey.**

Ruth, c. 11th century B.C. (Moabite maiden and ancestress of King David).

868. *The Story of Ruth* (1960). 132 min. 20th Century-Fox. D: Henry Koster.
Ruth: Elana Eden
Boaz: Stuart Whitman
Supporting cast: Viveca Lindfors, Tom Tryon, Peggy Wood

Ruth, George Herman "Babe," 1895–1948. (American baseball player and home-run king of the New York Yankees)

869. *The Babe Ruth Story* (1948). 107 min. Allied Artists. D: Roy Del Ruth.
Ruth: William Bendix
Supporting cast: Charles Bickford, William Frawley, Sam Levene, Claire Trevor

Ryan, Cornelius, 1920–1974. (American writer best known for his meticulous accounts of World War II battles)

870. *A Private Battle* (1980). 100 min. Procter & Gamble Productions. D: Robert Lewis.
Ryan: Jack Warden
Kathryn Ryan: Anne Jackson
Geoffrey Ryan: David Stockton
Supporting cast: Walter Cronkite, Rachel Kelly, Rebecca Schull

Ryan, Geoffrey
See **Ryan, Cornelius.**

Ryan, Kathryn Morgan, 1925–
See **Ryan, Cornelius.**

Ryan, Leo J., 1925–1978
See **Jones, Jim.**

S

Sacco, Nicola, 1891–1927. (Italian-American anarchist convicted and executed for a payroll murder even though another man confessed to the crime)

871. *Sacco and Vanzetti* (1971). 120 min. Jolly-Undis-Theatre Le Rex. D: Giuliano Montaldo.
Sacco: Riccardo Cucciolla
Bartolomeo Vanzetti: Gian Maria Volonte
Supporting cast: Cyril Cusack, Geoffrey Keen, Milo O'Shea, William Prince

Sacks, Oliver, 1933– (American physician who used an experimental drug treatment on victims of paralysis agitans)

872. *Awakenings* (1990). 120 min. Columbia Pictures. D: Penny Marshall.
Sacks: Robin Williams
Supporting cast: Robert De Niro, John Heard, Julie Kavner, Ruth Nelson

Sackter, Bill, 1913?–1983. (American who spent forty-three years as a mental institution patient)

872a *Bill* (1981). 100 min. Alan Landsburg Productions. D: Anthony Page.
Sackter: Mickey Rooney
Barry Morrow: Dennis Quaid
Supporting cast: Harry Goz, Anna Maria Horsford, Largo Woodruff

872b *Bill: On His Own* (1983). 100 min. Alan Landsburg Productions. D: Anthony Page.
Sackter: Mickey Rooney
Supporting cast: Helen Hunt, Dennis Quaid, Teresa Wright

Sadat, Anwar, 1918–1981. (Egyptian president, 1970–1981; assassinated)

873. *Sadat* (1983). 200 min. Blatt/Singer Productions. D: Richard Michaels.
Sadat: Louis Gossett, Jr.
Jihan Sadat: Madolyn Smith
Gamal Abdel Nassar: John Rhys-Davies
Supporting cast: Anne Heywood, Jeremy Kemp, Paul L. Smith, Jeffrey Tambor

SEE ALSO: **Meir, Golda.**

Sadat, Jihan, 1933–
See **Sadat, Anwar.**

Sage, Anna, 1889?–1947. (American madam who betrayed John Dillinger to the FBI)

874. *The Lady in Red* (1979). 93 min. New World Pictures. D: Lewis Teague.
Sage: Louise Fletcher
Polly Hamilton/Franklin: Pamela Sue Martin
John Dillinger: Robert Conrad

Supporting cast: Rod Gist, Laurie Heinemann, Robert Hogan, Glenn Withrow

Sakharov, Andrei, 1921–1989. (Soviet physicist and political dissident)

875. *Sakharov* (1984). 120 min. Titus Productions. D: Jack Gold.
Sakharov: Jason Robards
Elena Bonner: Glenda Jackson
Supporting cast: Michael Bryant, Frank Finlay, Paul Freeman, Nicol Williamson

Saladin, Sultan of Egypt and Syria, 1137–1193
See **Richard I,** King of England.

Saldana, Theresa, 1955– (American film actress and founder of a support group for victims of violent crimes)

876. *Victims for Victims: The Theresa Saldana Story* (1984). 100 min.
Orion Television. D: Karen Arthur.
Saldana: Theresa Saldana
Supporting cast: Linda Carlson, Lelia Goldoni, Lawrence Pressman, Adrian Zmed

Salieri, Antonio, 1750–1825
See **Mozart, Wolfgang Amadeus.**

Salome, b. c. A.D. 14. (Daughter of Herodias who demanded the head of John the Baptist as a reward for her dancing)

877. *Salome* (1953). 103 min. Columbia Pictures. D: William Dieterle.
Salome: Rita Hayworth
John the Baptist: Alan Badel
Supporting cast: Judith Anderson, Stewart Granger, Charles Laughton

Samson, c. 12th cent. B.C. (Legendary Biblical strongman who destroyed the Philistines)

877a *Samson and Delilah* (1949). 128 min. Paramount Pictures. D: Cecil B. De Mille.
Samson: Victor Mature
Delilah: Hedy Lamarr
Supporting cast: Olive Deering, Angela Lansbury, George Sanders, Henry Wilcoxon

877b *Samson and Delilah* (1984). 120 min. Comworld Productions. D: Lee Philips.
Samson: Antony Hamilton
Delilah: Belinda Bauer
Supporting cast: Stephen Macht, Clive Revill, Daniel Stern, Max von Sydow

Sand, George, 1804–1876. (French writer best known for her liaisons with famous men)

877c *Impromptu* (1990). 109 min. Sovereign Pictures Ltd. D: James Lapine.
Sand: Judy Davis
Frederic Chopin: Hugh Grant
Supporting cast: Mandy Patinkin, Bernadette Peters, Julian Sands, Emma Thompson

SEE ALSO **Chopin, Frederic.**

Sanger, Margaret, 1879–1966. (Early-twentieth-century American activist for legalized birth control)

878. *Portrait of a Rebel: The Remarkable Mrs. Sanger* (1980). 96 min. Marvin Minoff Productions. D: Virgil W. Vogel.
Sanger: Bonnie Franklin
Supporting cast: David Dukes, Richard Johnson, Frances Lee McCain, Milo O'Shea

Santa Ana, Antonio Lopez De, 1794?–1876
See **Bowie, Jim; Houston, Sam.**

Sayers, Gale, 1943–
   See **Piccolo, Brian.**

Schanberg, Sydney, 1933– (American Pulitzer Prize-winning journalist and *New York Times* correspondent in Cambodia, 1972–1975)

879. *The Killing Fields* (1984). 139 min. Warner Bros. D: Roland Joffe.
   Schanberg: Sam Waterston
   Dith Pran: Haing S. Ngor
   Supporting cast: Spalding Gray, John Malkovich, Craig T. Nelson, Julian Sands

Schmeling, Max, 1905–
   See **Louis, Joe.**

Schmid, Albert Andrew, 1921?– (U.S. Marine and World War II hero blinded in a Japanese attack)

880. *Pride of the Marines* (1945). 119 min. Warner Bros. D: Delmer Daves.
   Schmid: John Garfield
   Supporting cast: Dane Clark, Rosemary de Camp, Eleanor Parker, John Ridgely

Scholl, Hans, 1918–1943. (Executed German political activist and founder of the anti-Nazi White Rose Society)

880a *The White Rose* (1982). 108 min. TeleCulture Films. D: Michael Verhoeven.
   Scholl: Wulf Kessler
   Sophie Scholl: Lena Stolze
   Supporting cast: Martin Benrath, Oliver Siebert, Werner Stocker, Ulrich Tucker

Scholl, Sophie, 1921–1943
   See **Scholl, Hans.**

Schubert, Franz, 1797–1828. (Austrian composer considered the originator and greatest exponent of lieder)

881. *New Wine* (1941). 89 min. United Artists. D: Reinhold Schunzel.
Schubert: Alan Curtis
Ludwig van Beethoven: Albert Basserman
Supporting cast: Binnie Barnes, Sterling Holloway, Ilona Massey

Schultz, Arthur "Dutch," 1902–1935
See **Coll, Vincent "Mad Dog."**

Schumann, Clara, 1819–1896. (German pianist, composer and principal pianoforte teacher at Frankfurt-am-Main conservatory, 1878–1892)

882. *Song of Love* (1947). 119 min. MGM. D: Clarence Brown.
Schumann: Katharine Hepburn
Johannes Brahms: Robert Walker
Franz Liszt: Henry Daniell
Robert Schumann: Paul Henreid
Supporting cast: Leo G. Carroll, Else Janssen, Gigi Perreau, Henry Stephenson

882a *Spring Symphony* (1984). 102 min. Greentree Productions Ltd. D: Peter Schamoni.
Schumann (as an adult): Nastassia Kinski
Schumann (as a child): Anja-Christine Preussler
Robert Schumann: Herbert Gronemeyer
Supporting cast: Andre Heller, Rolf Hoppe, Gidon Kremer, Edda Sieppel

Schumann, Robert, 1810–1856
See **Schumann, Clara.**

Scopes, John T., 1901–1970
See **Darrow, Clarence.**

Scott, Robert Falcon, 1868–1912. (British explorer beaten to the South Pole by Roald Amundsen)

883. *Scott of the Antarctic* (1948). 111 min. Ealing Studios. D: Charles Frend.
Scott: John Mills
Supporting cast: Derek Bond, James Robertson Justice, Kenneth More

Scott, Robert Lee, 1908– (American World War II pilot with the Flying Tigers)

884. *God Is My Co-Pilot* (1945) 90 min. Warner Bros. D: Robert Florey.
Scott: Dennis Morgan
Claire Lee Chennault: Raymond Massey
Supporting cast: Dane Clark, Alan Hale, Andrea King, Craig Stevens

Scott, Wendell, 1923– (First African-American champion stock-car racer)

885. *Greased Lightning* (1977). 94 min. Warner Bros. D: Michael Schultz.
Scott: Richard Pryor
Supporting cast: Beau Bridges, Vincent Gardenia, Pam Grier, Cleavon Little

Scruggs, Jan C., 1950?– (American Vietnam War veteran who started the campaign to build the Vietnam War Memorial)

885a *To Heal a Nation* (1987). 100 min. Orion Pictures Television. D: Michael Pressman.
Scruggs: Eric Roberts
Supporting cast: Marshall Colt, Glynnis O'Connor, Scott Paulin, Lee Purcell

Sedgwick, Edie, 1943–1972. (American film actress best known for her work in Andy Warhol films)

886. *Ciao! Manhattan* (1973). 90 min. Maron Films. D: John Palmer, David Weisman.
Sedgwick/Susan: Edie Sedgwick
Supporting cast: Geoffrey Briggs, Wesley Hayes, Isabel Jewell

Seeger, Pete, 1919–
See **Weavers, The.**

Seeley, Blossom, 1892?–1974. (American song-and-dance headliner in burlesque and vaudeville in the early 1900's)

887. *Somebody Loves Me* (1952). 97 min. Paramount Pictures. D: Irving S. Brecher.
Seeley: Betty Hutton
Benny Fields: Ralph Meeker
Supporting cast: Billie Bird, Adele Jergens, Robert Keith

Selznick, David O., 1902–1965. (American film producer whose most famous work is *Gone with the Wind*)

888. *The Scarlet O'Hara War* (1980). 105 min. Warner Bros. Television. D: John Erman.
Selznick: Tony Curtis
Louis B. Mayer: Harold Gould
Myron Selznick: Bill Macy
Supporting cast: George Furth, Sharon Gless, Edward Winter, Barrie Youngfellow

Selznick, Myron, 1898–1944
See **Selznick, David O.**

Senesh, Hanna, 1921–1944. (Hungarian World War II freedom fighter executed by the Germans)

888a *Hanna's War* (1988). 150 min. Cannon Group. D: Menahem Golan
Senesh: Maruschka Detmers.

Supporting cast: Anthony Andrews, Ellen Burstyn, Donald Pleasence, David Warner

Serpico, Frank, 1936– (American police officer who blew the whistle on New York City police corruption)

889. *Serpico* (1973). 130 min. Paramount Pictures. D: Sidney Lumet.
Serpico: Al Pacino
Supporting cast: Biff McGuire, Cornelia Sharpe, Barbara Young

890. *Serpico: The Deadly Game* (1976). 100 min. Paramount Pictures Television. D: Robert Collins.
Serpico: David Birney
Supporting cast: Lane Bradbury, Allen Garfield, Burt Young

Seton, Elizabeth Bayley, 1774–1821. (Nun and first nativeborn American saint)

891. *A Time for Miracles* (1980). 100 min. ABC Circle Films. D: Michael O'Herlihy.
Seton: Kate Mulgrew
Supporting cast: Jean-Pierre Aumont, Rossano Brazzi, John Forsythe, Lorne Greene

Seymour, Jane, 1541–1561
See **Henry VIII,** King of England.

Shaw, Robert Gould, 1837–1863. (American Civil War soldier who commanded the all-Black 54th Regiment Massachusetts Infantry)

891a *Glory* (1988). 122 min. Tri-Star Pictures. D: Edward Zwick.
Shaw: Matthew Broderick
Supporting cast: Cary Elwes, Morgan Freeman, Jihmi Kennedy, Denzel Washington

Sheehy, Gail, 1937– (American writer best known for her work *Passages*)

892. *Hustling* (1975). 120 min. Filmways. D: Joseph Sargent.
Sheehy/Morrison: Lee Remick
Supporting cast: Jill Clayburgh, Monte Markham, Alex Rocco

Shelley, Mary Wollstonecraft, 1797–1851
See **Shelley, Percy Bysshe.**

Shelley, Percy Bysshe, 1792–1822. (British poet whose anti-establishment views are reflected in his poetry, especially in *Prometheus unbound*)

892a *Haunted Summer* (1989). 115 min. Cannon Group. D: Ivan Passer.
Shelley: Eric Stoltz
George Byron: Philip Anglim
Clara Clairmont: Laura Dern
John Polidori: Alex Winter
Mary Shelley: Alice Krige
Supporting cast: Don Hodson, Giusto Lo Pipero, Terry Richards

Sheppard, Jack, 1702–1721. (British thief and four-time prison escapee who became a celebrity in eighteenth-century London)

893. *Where's Jack?* (1969). 119 min. Paramount Pictures. D: James Clavell.
Sheppard: Tommy Steele
Supporting cast: Alan Badel, Stanley Baker, Dudley Foster, Fiona Lewis

Sheppard, Sam, 1923–1970. (American physician acquitted of his wife's murder after serving twelve years in prison)

894. *Guilty or Innocent: The Sam Sheppard Murder Case* (1975). 150 min. Universal Pictures. D: Robert Michael Lewis.
Sheppard: George Peppard

F. Lee Bailey: Walter McGinn
Supporting cast: Paul Fix, Barnard Hughes, Nina Van Pallandt, William Windom

Sieber, Al, 1844–1907
See **Horn, Tom.**

Siegel, Benjamin "Bugsy", 1906–1947. (American gangster who established the rackets on the West Coast for the crime syndicate)

894a *Bugsy* (1991). 136 min. Columbia Pictures. D: Barry Levinson.
Siegel: Warren Beatty
Virginia Hill: Annette Bening
Meyer Lansky: Ben Kingsley
Charles Luciano: Bill Graham
Supporting cast: Elliott Gould, Harvey Keitel, Joe Mantegna, Bebe Neuwirth

SEE ALSO: **Hill, Virginia.**

Silkwood, Karen, 1946–1974. (American nuclear-parts factory worker who died in a mysterious car accident while trying to expose occupational hazards)

895. *Silkwood* (1983). 131 min. 20th Century-Fox. D: Mike Nichols.
Silkwood: Meryl Streep
Supporting cast: Cher, Craig T. Nelson, Kurt Russell

Silva, Chica da, d.1796. (Black Brazilian slave who became the unofficial empress of Brazil in the late eighteenth century)

895a *Xica* (1976). 107 min. New Yorker Films. D: Carlos Diegues.
Silva: ZeZe Motta
Supporting cast: Walmor Chagas, Altair Lima, Marcus Vinicius, Jose Wilker

Simon, Neil, 1927– (Leading American Broadway playwright from the 1960's through the 1980's)

896. *Chapter Two* (1979). 124 min. Columbia Pictures. D: Robert Moore.
Simon/Schneider: James Caan
Marsha Mason/MacLaine: Marsha Mason
Supporting cast: Joseph Bologna, Valerie Harper

Simons, Arthur E. "Bull," 1928?–
See **Perot, H. Ross.**

Simpson, Wallis Warfield, 1896–1986. (American divorcee who King Edward VIII abdicated from the throne of England to wed)

896a *The Woman He Loved* (1988). 96 min. New World Entertainment. D: Charles Jarrott.
Simpson: Jane Seymour
Winston Churchill: Robert Hardy
Edward VIII: Anthony Andrews
Queen Mary: Phyllis Calvert
Supporting cast: Olivia de Havilland, Lucy Gutteridge, Julie Harris, David Waller

Sinclair, John
See **Ginsberg, Allen.**

Sirisomphene, Keo
See **Everingham, John.**

Sitting Bull, 1835–1890. (Sioux chief who planned the attack against General Custer)

897. *Sitting Bull* (1954). 105 min. United Artists. D: Sidney Salkow.
Sitting Bull: J. Carrol Naish
Crazy Horse: Iron Eyes Cody

Supporting cast: Douglas Kennedy, John Litel, Mary Murphy, Dale Robertson

Skinner, Cornelia Otis, 1901–1979. (American stage actress, playwright and author of several autobiographical works)

898. *Our Hearts Were Growing Up* (1946) 83 min. Paramount Pictures. D: William D. Russell.
Skinner: Gail Russell
Emily Kimborough: Diana Lynn
Supporting cast: James Brown, Brian Donlevy, Bill Edwards

899. *Our Hearts Were Young and Gay* (1944) 83 min. Paramount Pictures. D: Lewis Allen.
Skinner: Gail Russell
Emily Kimborough: Diana Lynn
Supporting cast: James Brown, Dorothy Gish, Charlie Ruggles

Slaton, John Marshall, 1866–1955
See **Frank, Leo.**

Slaton, Lewis
See **Williams, Wayne Bertram.**

Slovik, Eddie, 1920–1945. (American World War II soldier executed for desertion)

900. *The Execution of Private Slovik* (1974). 120 min. Universal Pictures Television. D: Lamont Johnson.
Slovik: Martin Sheen
Supporting cast: Ned Beatty, Gary Busey, Mariclare Costello, Warren Kemmerling

Slovo, Shawn, 1950?–
See **First, Ruth.**

Smith, Florence Margaret "Stevie," 1902–1971. (British poet whose work often dealt with loneliness)

901. *Stevie* (1978). 102 min. First Artists. D: Robert Enders.
Smith (as an adult): Glenda Jackson
Smith (as a child): Emma Louise Fox
Supporting cast: Trevor Howard, Alec McCowen, Mona Washbourne

Smith, James, 1737–1812. (American lawyer and legislator)

902. *Allegheny Uprising* (1939). 81 min. RKO. D: William Seiter.
Smith: John Wayne
Supporting cast: Brian Donlevy, Wilfrid Lawson, George Sanders, Claire Trevor

Smith, John, 1580–1631. (British explorer who helped colonize Virginia)

903. *Captain John Smith and Pocahontas* (1953). 76 min. United Artists. D: Lew Landers.
Smith: Anthony Dexter
Pocahontas: Jody Lawrence
Supporting cast: Robert Clarke, Douglass Dumbrille, Alan Hale, Jr., James Seay

Smith, Joseph, 1805–1844
See **Young, Brigham.**

Smith, Madeleine, 1835–1928. (Scottish woman who was acquitted of poisoning her lower-class lover in a sensational murder trial)

903a *Madeleine* (1949). 101 min. Universal Pictures. D: David Lean.
Smith: Ann Todd
Supporting cast: Leslie Banks, Edward Chapman, Ivan Desny, Norman Wooland

Smith, Perry, 1928–1965. (American vagrant who murdered a Kansas farm family for no apparent reason)

904. *In Cold Blood* (1967). 134 min. Columbia Pictures. D: Richard Brooks.
Smith: Robert Blake
Richard Hickock: Scott Wilson
Supporting cast: Jeff Corey, John Forsythe, Charles McGraw, Paul Stewart

Snider, Paul, d. 1980
See **Stratten, Dorothy.**

Snyder, Martin
See **Etting, Ruth.**

Snyder, Mitch, 1944–1990. (American social activist who crusaded to obtain government assistance for the homeless)

904a *Samaritan: The Mitch Snyder Story* (1986). 150 min. LeVine-Robins Productions Ltd. D: Richard T. Heffron.
Snyder: Martin Sheen
Supporting cast: Roxanne Hart, Joe Seneca, Stan Shaw, Cicely Tyson

Soffel, Kate, d. 1909. (American prison warden's wife who assisted two prisoners in an attempt to escape to Canada)

905. *Mrs. Soffel* (1984). 110 min. MGM/United Artists. D: Gillian Armstrong.
Soffel: Diane Keaton
Ed Biddle: Mel Gibson
Supporting cast: Trini Alvarado, Jennie Dundas, Edward Herrmann, Matthew Modine

Sofia Alekseevna, Regent of Russia, 1657–1704
See **Peter I,** Emperor of Russia.

Somoza, Anastasio, 1925–1980
See **Cox, Jack.**

Sousa, John Philip, 1854–1932. (American composer and band-master whose best-known compositions are his marches)

906. *Stars and Stripes Forever* (1952). 89 min. 20th Century-Fox. D: Henry Koster.
Sousa: Clifton Webb
Supporting cast: Ruth Hussey, Debra Paget, Robert Wagner

Soyer, David, 1923–
See **Guarneri String Quartet.**

Spartacus, d. 71 B.C. (Thracian slave and gladiator who led a revolt against the Roman Empire)

907. *Spartacus* (1960). 196 min. Universal Pictures. D: Stanley Kubrick.
Spartacus: Kirk Douglas
Supporting cast: Tony Curtis, Laurence Olivier, Jean Simmons

Speer, Albert, 1905–1981. (Leading architect of Adolf Hitler's Third Reich)

908. *Inside the Third Reich* (1982). 250 min. ABC Circle Films. D: Marvin J. Chomsky.
Speer: Rutger Hauer
Adolf Hitler: Derek Jacobi
Supporting cast: Blythe Danner, John Gielgud, Maria Schell

Speke, John Hanning, 1827–1864
See **Burton, Richard.**

Spencer, Diana, 1961–
    See **Charles,** Prince of Wales.

Spungen, Nancy, d. 1979
    See **Vicious, Sid.**

Stalin, Joseph, 1879–1953
    See **Davies, Joseph E.**

Stallings, James O., 1938–
    See **Harmon, Leola Mae.**

Stanford, Sally, 1903–1982. (American madam of the 1930's who
    became the mayor of Sausalito, California, in 1976)

909. *Lady of the House* (1978). 100 min. Metromedia Prod. D:
    Ralph Nelson, Vincent Sherman.
    Stanford: Dyan Cannon
    Supporting cast: Armand Assante, Zohra Lampert, Susan
    Tyrrell

Stanley, Henry M., 1841–1904. (Britishborn American journalist
    who led an expedition to Africa in 1871 to find Dr.
    Livingstone)

910. *Stanley and Livingstone* (1939). 101 min. 20th Century-Fox.
    D: Henry King.
    Stanley: Spencer Tracy
    David Livingstone: Cedric Hardwicke
    Supporting cast: Walter Brennan, Richard Greene, Nancy
    Kelly

Stanton, Frank, 1908–
    See **Murrow, Edward R.**

Starkweather, Charles, 1940–1959. (American murderer who went on a killing spree across the Plains states in January 1958)

911. *Badlands* (1974). 95 min. Warner Bros. D: Terrence Malik.
Starkweather/Carruthers: Martin Sheen
Caril Ann Fugate/Sargis: Sissy Spacek
Supporting cast: Ramon Bieri, Warren Oates, Alan Vint

Starr, Belle, 1848–1889. (American outlaw and horse thief who led a gang of rustlers in Oklahoma, 1875–1880)

912. *Belle Starr* (1941). 87 min. 20th Century-Fox. D: Irving Cummings.
Starr: Gene Tierney
Supporting cast: Dana Andrews, Louise Beavers, Randolph Scott, Chill Wills

913. *Belle Starr* (1980). 97 min. Hanna-Barbera Productions. D: John A. Alonzo.
Starr: Elizabeth Montgomery
Jesse James: Michael Cavanaugh
Cole Younger: Cliff Potts
Supporting cast: Gary Combs, Alan Vint, Jesse Vint, Fred Ward

914. *Montana Belle* (1952). 81 min. RKO. D: Allan Dwan.
Starr: Jane Russell
Supporting cast: Scott Brady, George Brent, Andy Devine

Starr, Blaze, 1935?–
See **Long, Earl.**

Starr, Ringo, 1940–
See **Beatles, The.**

Stavisky, Serge Alexandre, 1886–1934. (Russian-French swindler whose exposure revealed widespread corruption in the government and caused the downfall of two ministries)

914a *Stavisky* (1974). 117 min. Cinemation. D: Alain Resnais.
    Stavisky: Jean-Paul Belmondo
    Supporting cast: Charles Boyer, Anny Duprey, Michael
    Lonsdale, Francois Perier

Stein, Gertrude, 1874–1946
    See **Toklas, Alice B.**

Steinem, Gloria, 1934– (Leading American feminist and foun-
    der of *Ms.* magazine)

914b *A Bunny's Tale* (1985). 104 min. ABC Circle Films. D: Karen
    Arthur.
    Steinem: Kirstie Alley
    Supporting cast: Joanna Kerns, Lisa Pelikan, Cotter Smith,
    Deborah Van Valkenburgh

Steinhardt, Arnold, 1937–
    See **Guarneri String Quartet.**

Stern, Isaac, 1920– (Renowned Russian-American violinist)

915. *From Mao to Mozart: Isaac Stern in China* (1980). 84 min. N/A.
    D: Murray Lerner.
    Documentary

Stevens, George, 1904–1975. (American film director best
    known for his work in the late 1930's and the 1940's)

916. *George Stevens: A Filmmaker's Journey* (1984). 110 min.
    George Stevens, Jr. D: George Stevens, Jr.
    Documentary

Stokes, Maurice, 1933–1970. (African-American basketball
    player whose career was cut short by a stroke)

917. *Maurie* (1973). 113 min. National General. D: Daniel Mann.
     Stokes: Bernie Casey
     Jack Twyman: Bo Svenson
     Supporting cast: Stephanie Edwards, Janet MacLachlan,
       Paulene Myers

Stone, I.F., 1907–1989. (American journalist and radical pamphleteer)

918. *I.F. Stone's Weekly* (1973). 62 min. N/A. D: Jerry Bruck, Jr.
     Documentary

Stratten, Dorothy, 1960–1980. (Canadian film actress and *Playboy* Playmate of the Year)

919. *Death of a Centerfold: The Dorothy Stratten Story* (1981). 100
     min. MGM Television. D: Gabrielle Beaumont.
     Stratten: Jamie Lee Curtis
     Hugh Hefner: Mitchell Ryan
     Paul Snider: Bruce Weitz
     Supporting cast: Bibi Besch, Robert Reed, Tracy Reed

920. *Star 80* (1983). 102 min. Warner Bros. D: Bob Fosse.
     Stratten: Mariel Hemingway
     Hugh Hefner: Cliff Robertson
     Paul Snider: Eric Roberts
     Supporting cast: Carroll Baker, David Clennon, Roger Rees

Stratton, Ethel
     See **Stratton, Monty.**

Stratton, Monty, 1912–1982. (Chicago White Sox pitcher whose
     career in the major leagues was curtailed by the loss of a leg
     in a hunting accident)

921. *The Stratton Story* (1949). 106 min. MGM. D: Sam Wood.
     Stratton: James Stewart
     Ethel Stratton: June Allyson
     Supporting cast: Bruce Cowling, Agnes Moorehead, Frank
       Morgan, Bill Williams

Strauss, Johann, Jr., 1825–1899. (Austrian violinist, conductor and composer best known for his more than four hundred waltzes)

922. *The Great Waltz* (1934). 80 min. Gaumont. D: Alfred Hitchcock.
Strauss: Esmond Knight
Supporting cast: Fay Compton, Edmund Gwenn, Jessie Matthews, Frank Vosper

923. *The Great Waltz* (1938). 103 min. MGM. D: Julien Duvier.
Strauss: Fernand Gravet
Supporting cast: Lionel Atwill, Hugh Herbert, Milza Korjus, Louise Rainer

924. *The Great Waltz* (1972). 135 min. MGM. D: Andrew L. Stone.
Strauss: Horst Buchholz
Supporting cast: Rossano Brazzi, Mary Costa, Yvonne Mitchell, Nigel Patrick

925. *The Waltz King* (1960). 95 min. Walt Disney Studios. D: Steve Previn.
Strauss: Kerwin Mathews
Supporting cast: Brian Aherne, Senta Berger, Peter Kraus

Strindberg, August, 1849–1912
See **Gauguin, Paul.**

Strindberg, Nils, 1854–1897
See **Andree, Salomon August.**

Stroud, Robert, 1887–1963. (American murderer who became interested in ornithology while serving a life sentence in prison)

926. *Birdman of Alcatraz* (1962). 147 min. United Artists. D: John Frankenheimer.
Stroud: Burt Lancaster

Supporting cast: Neville Brand, Betty Field, Karl Malden, Thelma Ritter

SEE ALSO: **Carnes, Clarence.**

Stuart, Charles, 1720–1788. (British prince who led the 1745 Jacobite rebellion in Scotland against George II)

927. *Bonnie Prince Charlie* (1947). 100 min. British-Lion. D: Anthony Kimmins.
Stuart: David Niven
Supporting cast: Judy Campbell, Morland Graham, Jack Hawkins, Margaret Leighton

Stuart, Charles Edward, 1959–1990. (American businessman who murdered his pregnant wife for money)

927a *Good Night, Sweet Wife: A Murder in Boston* (1990). 96 min. CBS Entertainment Productions. D: Jerrold Freedman.
Stuart: Ken Olin
Carol Stuart: Annabella Price
Supporting cast: Margaret Colin, Michael C. Gwynne, James Handy, Bruce McGill

Stuart, Leslie, 1864–1928. (British songwriter best known for his music hall songs)

928. *You Will Remember* (1941). 74 min. British-Lion. D: Jack Raymond.
Stuart: Robert Morley
Supporting cast: Tom E. Finglass, Dorothy Hyson, Emlyn Williams

Sullavan, Margaret, 1911–1960
See **Hayward, Leland.**

Sullivan, Albert, d. 1942. (American World War II sailor killed with his four brothers on U.S.S. *Juneau*)

929. *The Sullivans* (1944). 112 min. 20th Century-Fox. D: Lloyd Bacon.
    Sullivan (as a child): Bobby Driscoll
    Sullivan (as an adult): Edward Ryan
    Frank Sullivan (as a child): Marvin Davis
    Frank Sullivan (as an adult): John Campbell
    George Sullivan (as a child): Buddy Swan
    George Sullivan (as an adult): James Cardwell
    Joe Sullivan (as a child): Johnny Calkins
    Joe Sullivan (as an adult): George Offerman, Jr.
    Matt Sullivan (as a child): Billy Cummings
    Matt Sullivan (as an adult): John Alvin
    Supporting cast: Anne Baxter, Thomas Mitchell, Roy Roberts, Selena Royle

Sullivan, Anne, 1886–1936
    See **Keller, Helen.**

Sullivan, Arthur, 1842–1900
    See **Gilbert, W.S.**

Sullivan, Francis "Frank," d. 1942
    See **Sullivan, Albert.**

Sullivan, George, d. 1942
    See **Sullivan, Albert.**

Sullivan, Joseph "Joe," d. 1942
    See **Sullivan, Albert.**

Sullivan, John L., 1858–1918. (American heavyweight boxing champion 1882–1892)

930. *The Great John L.* (1945). 98 min. United Artists. D: Frank Tuttle.
    Sullivan: Greg McClure
    James Corbett: Rory Calhoun

Supporting cast: Barbara Britton, Linda Darnell, Otto Kruger, Lee Sullivan

SEE ALSO: **Corbett, James** ("Gentleman Jim").

Sullivan, Madison "Matt," d. 1942
See **Sullivan, Albert.**

Sullivan, Tom, 1947– (American film actor)

931. *If You Could See What I Hear* (1982). 103 min. Cypress Grove Films. D: Eric Till.
Sullivan: Marc Singer
Supporting cast: Shari Belafonte Harper, R.H. Thompson, Sarah Torgov

Summersby, Kay, 1908–1975
See **Eisenhower, Dwight** ("Ike").

Sundance Kid, d. 1908
See **Cassidy, Robert Parker** ("Butch").

Sutter, Johan, 1803–1880. (German-American pioneer on whose property gold was discovered in 1848, instigating the 1849 California gold rush)

932. *Sutter's Gold* (1936). 94 min. Universal-International. D: James Cruze.
Sutter: Edward Arnold
Supporting cast: Katherine Alexander, Binnie Barnes, Lee Tracy

Swaggart, Jimmy, 1933?–
See **Lewis, Jerry Lee.**

Szabo, Violette, 1918–1945. (British World War II spy executed by the Germans)

933. *Carve Her Name With Pride* (1958). 119 min. United Artists. D: Lewis Gilbert.
Szabo: Virginia McKenna
Supporting cast: Denise Gray, Paul Scofield, Sidney Tafler, Jack Warner

T

Tabor, H.A.W., 1830–1899. (Businessman, silver king, lieutenant governor of Colorado, 1879–1883, and U.S. senator, 1883, whose investments in Denver helped transform it from a town into a city)

934. *Silver Dollar* (1932). 84 min. Warner Bros. D: Alfred E. Green.
Tabor/Martin: Edward G. Robinson
Supporting cast: Bebe Daniels, Jobyna Howland, Aline MacMahon

Tallchief, Maria, 1925–
See **Balanchine, George.**

Tanguay, Eva, 1878–1948. (American singer who was the highest paid vaudeville performer of her time)

935. *The I Don't Care Girl* (1953). 78 min. 20th Century-Fox. D: Lloyd Bacon.
Tanguay: Mitzi Gaynor
Supporting cast: Bob Graham, Oscar Levant, David Wayne

Tarkovsky, Andrei, 1932–1986. (Russian film director in whose works memory is shown as the great shaping force of the psyche)

935a *Directed By Andrei Tarkovsky* (1989). 101 min. Swedish Film Institute. D: Michal Leszcylowski.
Documentary

Taylor, Estelle, 1899–1958
See **Dempsey, Jack.**

Taylor, Kenneth, 1934– (Canadian ambassador to Iran who helped six American embassy workers escape capture by Iranian radicals)

936. *Escape From Iran: The Canadian Caper* (1981). 100 min. Canamedia Productions. D: Lamont Johnson.
Taylor: Gordon Pinsent
Supporting cast: Diana Barrington, James B. Douglas, Robert Joy, Chris Wiggins

Taylor, Leslie "Squizzy." (Australian gangster who was prominent in 1920's Melbourne)

936a *Squizzy Taylor* (1984). 89 min. Satori Entertainment. D: Kevin Dobson.
Taylor: David Atkins
Supporting cast: Alan Cassell, Kim Lewis, Michael Long, Jacki Weaver

Tchaikovsky, Modeste, 1850–1916
See **Tchaikovsky, Peter.**

Tchaikovsky, Nina Milyukova, d. 1917
See **Tchaikovsky, Peter.**

Tchaikovsky, Peter, 1840–1893. (Russian composer best known for his ballets, *Sleeping Beauty* and *Swan Lake*)

937. *The Music Lovers* (1971). 122 min. United Artists. D: Ken Russell.

Tchaikovsky: Richard Chamberlain
Modeste Tchaikovsky: Kenneth Colley
Nina Milyukova Tchaikovsky: Glenda Jackson
Supporting cast: Max Adrian, Christopher Gable, Maureen Pryor, Izabella Telezynska

938. *Song of My Heart* (1948). 84 min. Monogram Prod. D: Benjamin Glazer.
Tchaikovsky: Frank Sundstrom
Supporting cast: Cedric Hardwicke, Audrey Long, Mikhail Rasumny, Gale Sherwood

Teach, Edward "Blackbeard," 1680–1718. (British pirate who terrorized the Caribbean)

939. *Blackbeard the Pirate* (1952). 99 min. RKO. D: Raoul Walsh.
Teach: Robert Newton
Supporting cast: William Bendix, Linda Darnell, Richard Egan

SEE ALSO: **Bonney, Anne.**

Terasaki, Gwen, 1908– (American wife of a World War II Japanese diplomat)

940. *Bridge to the Sun* (1961). 112 min. MGM. D: Etienne Perier.
Terasaki: Carroll Baker
Hidenari Terasaki: James Shigeta
Supporting cast: Sean Garrison, Tetzuro Tamba, Hiroshi Tomono, James Yagi

Terasaki, Hidenari, 1900–1950?
See **Terasaki, Gwen.**

Teresa, Mother, 1910– (Nobel Prize-winning Albanian-Indian nun who founded the Missionaries of Charity to work with the very poorest)

940a *Mother Teresa* (1986). 81 min. Petrie Productions. D: Ann Petrie, Jeanette Petrie.
Documentary

Thaw, Evelyn Nesbit, 1885–1967
See **Nesbit, Evelyn.**

Thaw, Harry, 1872–1947
See **Nesbit, Evelyn.**

Theotokopoulos, Domenico, 1541–1614
See **Greco, El.**

Therese of Lisieux, Saint, 1873–1897. (French Carmelite nun best known for her "little way" philosophy which contends that ordinary persons can obtain sainthood)

940b *Therese* (1986). 96 min. Circle Films. D: Alain Cavalier.
Therese: Catherine Mouchet
Supporting cast: Helene Alexandridis, Sylvie Habault, Clemence Massart, Aurore Prieto

Thompson, Hunter S., 1939– (American journalist, national affairs editor for *Rolling Stone* magazine, 1970–1976)

941. *Where the Buffalo Roam* (1980). 96 min. Universal Pictures. D: Art Linson.
Thompson: Bill Murray
Supporting cast: Rene Auberjonois, Peter Boyle, Bruno Kirby

Thornwell, James, 1938–1984. (American soldier on whom the U.S. Army used LSD during an interrogation and whose story was reported originally on "60 Minutes")

942. *Thornwell* (1981). 100 min. MTM Enterprises. D: Harry Moses.

Thornwell: Glynn Turman
Supporting cast: Vincent Gardenia, Julius Harris, Todd Susman, Craig Wasson

Thorpe, Jim, 1888–1953. (Native-American Olympic athlete who was stripped of his medals after it was discovered that he had played semiprofessional baseball)

943. *Jim Thorpe—All American* (1951). 107 min. Warner Bros. D: Michael Curtiz.
Thorpe: Burt Lancaster
Supporting cast: Charles Bickford, Jack Big Head, Phyllis Thaxter

Thorson, Ralph, 1926– (American bounty hunter)

944. *The Hunter* (1980). 97 min. Paramount Pictures. D: Buzz Kulik.
Thorson: Steve McQueen
Supporting cast: LeVar Burton, Kathryn Harrold, Eli Wallach

Thrash, George, 1938?–
See **Yann, Linn.**

Thrash, Prissy, 1939?–
See **Yann, Linn.**

Thum, Jack, d. 1980. (American clown who was foster parent to thirty-seven children)

945. *Leave 'Em Laughing* (1981). 100 min. Charles Fries Prod. D: Jackie Cooper.
Thum: Mickey Rooney
Shirlee Thum: Anne Jackson
Supporting cast: Red Buttons, Elisha Cook, Allen Goorwitz, William Windom

Thum, Shirlee
    See **Thum, Jack.**

Tibbets, Paul, 1915– (American World War II pilot who led the forces that dropped atomic bombs on Japan)

946. *Above and Beyond* (1952). 122 min. MGM. D: Melvin Frank.
    Tibbets: Robert Taylor
    Supporting cast: Larry Gates, Larry Keating, Eleanor Parker, James Whitmore

947. *Enola Gay: The Men, the Mission, the Atomic Bomb* (1980). 150 min. The Production Co. D: David Lowell Rich.
    Tibbets: Patrick Duffy
    Supporting cast: Billy Crystal, Kim Darby, Gary Frank, Gregory Harrison

Tilley, Vesta, 1864–1952. (British singer and music hall star famous for her male impersonations)

948. *After the Ball* (1957). 89 min. Romulus Films. D: Compton Bennett.
    Tilley (as an adult): Pat Kirkwood
    Tilley (as a child): Margaret Sawyer
    Walter de Frece: Laurence Harvey
    Supporting cast: June Clyde, Clive Morton, Marjorie Rhodes, Jerry Verno

Timerman, Jacobo, 1923– (Argentinian newspaper publisher who was imprisoned and tortured for his antigovernment writings)

949. *Jacobo Timerman: Prisoner Without a Name, Cell Without a Number* (1983). 100 min. Chrysalis-Yellen Prod. D: Linda Yellen.
    Timerman: Roy Scheider
    Risha Timerman: Liv Ullmann
    Supporting cast: David Cryer, Zach Galligan, Michael Pearlman, Sam Robards

Timerman, Risha
   See **Timerman, Jacobo.**

Tisdale, Betty
   See **Balin, Ina.**

Toklas, Alice B., 1877–1967. (American secretary and constant companion to Gertrude Stein, 1907–1946)

949a *Waiting for the Moon* (1987). 88 min. American Playhouse Theatrical Films. D: Jill Godmilow.
   Toklas: Linda Hunt
   Gertrude Stein: Linda Bassett
   Supporting cast: Jacques Boudet, Bernadette Lafont, Andrew McCarthy, Bruce McGill

Toma, David, 1934– (American police officer who was a master of disguise)

950. *Toma* (1972). 74 min. Universal Pictures Television. D: Richard Heffron.
   Toma: Tony Musante
   Supporting cast: Nicholas Colasanto, Simon Oakland, Susan Strasberg

Torrance, Dean, 1940–
   See **Barry, Jan.**

Torres, Martha, 1941?– (U.S. Drug Enforcement Agency undercover agent)

951. *Courage* (1986). 150 min. New World Television. D: Jeremy Kagan.
   Torres/Miraldo: Sophia Loren
   Supporting cast: Hector Elizondo, Michael Galardi, Dan Hedaya, Billy Dee Williams

Touhy, Roger, 1898–1959. (American gangster and bootlegger who resisted Capone's efforts to move into Chicago's northwest suburbs)

952. *Roger Touhy—Gangster* (1944). 73 min. 20th Century-Fox. D: Robert Florey.
Touhy: Preston Foster
Supporting cast: Lois Andrews, Victor McLaglen, Anthony Quinn, Kent Taylor

Toulouse-Lautrec, Henri de, 1864–1901. (French painter and lithographer best known for his works depicting life in Montmartre)

953. *Moulin Rouge* (1952). 123 min. United Artists. D: John Huston.
Toulouse-Lautrec: Jose Ferrer
Supporting cast: Suzanne Flon, Zsa Zsa Gabor, Eric Pohlmann

Townshend, Pete, 1945–
See **Who, The.**

Trapp, Georg
See **Trapp, Maria.**

Trapp, Maria, 1905– (World War II Austrian refugee and head of the Trapp Family Singers)

954. *The Sound of Music* (1965). 176 min. 20th Century-Fox. D: Robert Wise.
Trapp: Julie Andrews
Georg Trapp: Christopher Plummer
Supporting cast: Charmian Carr, Richard Haydn, Eleanor Parker, Peggy Wood

955. *The Trapp Family* (1961). 104 min. 20th Century-Fox. D: Wolfgang Liebeneiner.
Trapp: Ruth Leuwerik

Georg Trapp: Hans Holt
Supporting cast: Friedrich Domin, Maria Holst, Josef
Meinrad, Hilde von Stolz

Travis, William, 1809–1836
See **Bowie, Jim.**

Tree, Michael, 1934–
See **Guarneri String Quartet.**

Trotsky, Leon, 1877–1940. (Russian who organized the October
Revolution with Lenin and was ousted from power by
Stalin; assassinated in exile)

956. *The Assassination of Trotsky* (1972). 103 min. Valoria Films.
D: Joseph Losey.
Trotsky: Richard Burton
Ramon Mercader/Jacson: Alain Delon
Supporting cast: Valentina Cortese, Enrico Maria Salerno,
Romy Schneider, Luigi Vannucchi

SEE ALSO: **Kohlo, Frida.**

Truman, Harry S, 1884–1972. (Thirty-third American president,
who made the decision to use the atomic bomb against
Japan)

957. *Give 'Em Hell, Harry!* (1975). 102 min. Theater Television
Corp. D: Steve Binder.
Truman: James Whitmore
This was a one-man show.

SEE ALSO: **MacArthur, Douglas.**

Tubman, Harriet, 1815–1913. (African-American abolitionist
who founded the Underground Railroad)

958. *A Woman Called Moses* (1978). 200 min. Henry Jaffe Enterprises. D: Paul Wendkos.
Tubman: Cicely Tyson
Supporting cast: Will Geer, Robert Hooks, James Wainwright, Dick Anthony Williams

Tucker, Preston, 1901–1956. (American businessman who tried to build the car of the future in the 1940's)

958a *Tucker: The Man and His Dream* (1988). 105 min. Paramount Pictures. D: Francis Ford Coppola.
Tucker: Jeff Bridges
Supporting cast: Joan Allen, Frederic Forrest, Martin Landau, Christian Slater

Tudor, Mary, 1496–1533. (English princess, sister of Henry VIII and wife of Louis XII of France)

959. *The Sword and the Rose* (1953). 93 min. Disney Productions. D: Ken Annakin.
Tudor: Glynis Johns
Henry VIII: James Robertson Justice
Supporting cast: Jane Barrett, Michael Gough, Richard Todd

Twain, Mark, 1835–1910. (American novelist best known for his depiction of life on the Mississippi River)

960. *The Adventures of Mark Twain* (1944). 130 min. Warner Bros. D: Irving Rapper.
Twain (as an adult): Fredric March
Twain (age 12): Dickie Jones
Twain (age 15): Jackie Brown
Olivia Langdon Clemens: Alexis Smith
Bret Harte: John Carradine
Supporting cast: Donald Crisp, Alan Hale, William Henry, C. Aubrey Smith

Tweed, George R., 1903?–1989. (World War II U.S. Navy radioman who eluded capture by the Japanese on Guam for thirty-one months)

961. *No Man Is an Island* (1962). 114 min. Universal Pictures. D: John Monks, Jr.
Tweed: Jeffrey Hunter
Supporting cast: Paul Edwards, Jr., Barbara Perez, Ronald Remy, Marshall Thompson

Twyman, Jack, 1934–
See **Stokes, Maurice.**

U

Ufema, Joy, 1943– (American nurse working with the terminally ill)

962. *A Matter of Life And Death* (1981). 98 min. Lorimar Productions. D: Russ Mayberry.
Ufema: Linda Lavin
Supporting cast: Ramon Bieri, Tyne Daly, Salome Jens, Gail Strickland

V

Valachi, Joseph, 1904–1971. (American gangster who turned informer on the Cosa Nostra in 1959)

963. *The Valachi Papers* (1972). 125 min. Columbia Pictures. D: Terence Young.
Valachi: Charles Bronson
Supporting cast: Walter Chiari, Jill Ireland, Gerald S. O'Loughlin, Lino Ventura

Valens, Richie, 1941–1959. (Mexican-American singer who became a rock 'n' roll sensation at seventeen and was killed in an air plane accident with Buddy Holly and the Big Bopper)

963a *La Bamba* (1987). 106 min. Columbia Pictures. D: Luis Valdez.
Valens: Lou Diamond Phillips
Big Bopper: Stephen Lee
Alan Freed: Alan Chandler
Buddy Holly: Marshall Crenshaw
Supporting cast: Rosana De Soto, Esai Morales, Elizabeth Pena, Danielle Von Zerneck

Valentino, Rudolph, 1895–1926. (American film actor considered the major male sex symbol of the 1920's)

964. *The Legend of Valentino* (1962). 72 min. Embassy Home Entertainment. D: N/A.
Documentary

965. *The Legend of Valentino* (1975). 100 min. Spelling/Goldberg Prod.. D: Melville Shavelson.
Valentino: Franco Nero
June Mathis: Suzanne Pleshette
Supporting cast: Milton Berle, Judd Hirsch, Lesley Warren

966. *Valentino* (1951). 102 min. Columbia Pictures. D: Lewis Allen.
Valentino: Anthony Dexter
Supporting cast: Joseph Calleia, Richard Carlson, Patricia Medina, Eleanor Parker

967. *Valentino* (1977). 127 min. United Artists. D: Ken Russell.
Valentino: Rudolf Nureyev
June Mathis: Felicity Kendall
Supporting cast: June Bolton, Leslie Caron, Leland Palmer, Michelle Phillips

Van Gogh, Theo, 1857–1891
See **Van Gogh, Vincent.**

Van Gogh, Vincent, 1853–1890. (Dutch Postimpressionist painter and a pioneer of Expressionism)

968. *Lust for Life* (1956). 122 min. MGM. D: Vincente Minnelli.
Van Gogh: Kirk Douglas
Paul Gauguin: Anthony Quinn
Supporting cast: Pamela Brown, James Donald, Everett Sloane

968a *Van Gogh* (1991). 159 min. Artificial Eye. D: Maurice Pialat.
Van Gogh: Jacques Dutronc
Theo Van Gogh: Bernard Le Coq
Supporting cast: Corinne Bourdon, Alexandra Loudon, Gerard Sety, Jacques Vidal

968b *Vincent* (1987). 99 min. Roxie Video. D: Paul Cox.
Documentary

968c *Vincent & Theo* (1990). 138 min. Hemdale Film Corporation. D: Robert Altman.
Van Gogh: Tim Roth
Theo Van Gogh: Paul Rhys
Supporting cast: Anne Canovas, Jean Pierre Cassel, Johanna Ter Steege, Wladimir Yordanoff

SEE ALSO: **Gauguin, Paul.**

Vanderbilt, Alice Claypool, 1845?–1934
See **Vanderbilt, Gloria.**

Vanderbilt, Cornelius, 1794–1877
See **Fisk, James.**

Vanderbilt, Gloria, 1924– (American heiress who was the center of a custody battle between her mother and aunt in the 1930's)

969. *Little Gloria . . . Happy at Last* (1982). 200 min. Cine-Gloria Prod. D: Waris Hussein.
Vanderbilt: Jennifer Dundas
Alice Claypool Vanderbilt: Bette Davis
Gloria Morgan Vanderbilt: Lucy Gutteridge
Gertrude Vanderbilt Whitney: Angela Lansbury

Supporting cast: Martin Balsam, John Hillerman, Barnard Hughes, Glynis Johns

Vanderbilt, Gloria Morgan, 1905?–1965
See **Vanderbilt, Gloria.**

Vanzetti, Bartolomeo, 1888–1927
See **Sacco, Nicola.**

Vetsera, Marie, 1871–1889
See **Rudolph,** Crown Prince of Austria.

Vicious, Sid, d. 1979. (British singer and member of the punk rock group The Sex Pistols)

969a *Sid and Nancy* (1986). 111 min. Zenith Productions. D: Alex Cox.
Vicious: Gary Oldman
Nancy Spungen: Chloe Webb
Supporting cast: Debby Bishop, David Hayman, Tony London, Drew Schofield

Victoria, Queen of England, 1819–1901.

970. *Sixty Glorious Years* (1938). 90 min. RKO. D: Herbert Wilcox.
Victoria: Anna Neagle
Albert: Anton Walbrook
Benjamin Disraeli: Derrick de Marney
William Ewart Gladstone: Malcolm Keen
Supporting cast: Felix Aylmer, Charles Carson, Walter Rilla, C. Aubrey Smith

971. *Victoria the Great* (1937). 112 min. RKO. D: Herbert Wilcox.
Victoria: Anna Neagle
Albert: Anton Walbrook
Benjamin Disraeli (as a young man): Derrick de Marney
Benjamin Disraeli (as an older man): Hugh Miller
William Ewart Gladstone: Arthur Young

Supporting cast: Felix Aylmer, Mary Morris, Walter Rilla, H.B. Warner

SEE ALSO: **Disraeli, Benjamin.**

Villa, Pancho, 1878–1923. (Mexican revolutionary leader and bandit; assassinated)

972. *Pancho Villa* (1972). 92 min. Scotia International. D: Eugenio Martin.
Villa: Telly Savalas
Supporting cast: Chuck Connors, Angel Del Pozo, Anne Francis, Clint Walker

973. *Villa* (1958). 72 min. 20th Century-Fox. D: James B. Clark.
Villa: Rodolfo Hoyos
Supporting cast: Margia Dean, Brian Keith, Rosenda Monteros, Cesar Romero

974. *Villa Rides* (1968). 125 min. Paramount Pictures. D: Buzz Kulik.
Villa: Yul Brynner
Supporting cast: Charles Bronson, Herbert Lom, Robert Mitchum, Robert Viharo

975. *Viva Villa* (1934). 115 min. MGM. D: Howard Hawks, Jack Conway.
Villa (as an adult): Wallace Beery
Villa (as a boy): Phillip Cooper
Supporting cast: Leo Carrillo, Stuart Erwin, H.B. Warner, Fay Wray

SEE ALSO: **Zapata, Emiliano.**

Villani, Romilda, 1915–
See **Loren, Sophia.**

Villon, Francois, 1431–? (One of France's greatest poets, whose career was hampered by his involvement in criminal activities)

976. *The Beloved Rogue* (1927). 99 min. Paramount Pictures. D: Ludwig Berger.
Villon: John Barrymore
Louis XI: Conrad Veidt
Supporting cast: Lawson Butt, Marceline Day, Henry Victor

977. *If I Were King* (1938). 101 min. Paramount Pictures. D: Frank Lloyd.
Villon: Ronald Colman
Louis XI: Basil Rathbone
Supporting cast: France Dee, Ellen Drew, Ralph Forbes

978. *The Vagabond King* (1930). 90 min. Paramount Pictures. D: Ludwig Berger.
Villon: Dennis King
Louis XI: Warner Oland
Supporting cast: O.P. Heggie, Jeanette MacDonald, Lillian Roth

979. *The Vagabond King* (1956). 86 min. Paramount Pictures. D: Michael Curtiz.
Villon: Oreste
Louis XI: Walter Hampden
Supporting cast: Kathryn Grayson, Rita Moreno, Leslie Nielsen

Voltaire, Francois, 1694–1778. (French satirist and novelist considered the embodiment of the eighteenth-century Enlightenment)

980. *Voltaire* (1933). 72 min. Warner Bros. D: John Adolfi.
Voltaire: George Arliss
Supporting cast: Doris Kenyon, Margaret Lindsay, Theodore Newton

Von Braun, Werner, 1912–1977. (German World War II rocket engineer who later worked on the U.S. space program)

981. *I Aim at the Stars* (1960). 107 min. Columbia Pictures. D: J. Lee Thompson.

Von Braun: Curt Jurgens
Supporting cast: Herbert Lom, Gia Scala, Victoria Shaw

Von Bulow, Claus, 1926– (Danish-American aristocrat tried twice for the attempted murder of his wife)

981a *Reversal of Fortune* (1990). 109 min. Reversal Films Inc. D: Barbet Schroeder
Von Bulow: Jeremy Irons
Alan M. Dershowitz: Ron Silver
Martha "Sunny" Crawford Von Bulow: Glenn Close
Supporting cast: Uta Hagen, Jack Gilpin, Annabella Sciorra, Fisher Stevens

Von Bulow, Martha "Sunny" Crawford, 1931–
See **Von Bulow, Claus.**

W

Wagner, Cosima, 1837–1930
See **Wagner, Richard.**

Wagner, Richard, 1813–1883. (German composer who is credited with reforming the structure of opera)

982. *Magic Fire* (1956). 95 min. Republic Pictures. D: William Dieterle.
Wagner: Alan Badel
Franz Liszt: Carlos Thompson
Cosima Wagner: Rita Gam
Supporting cast: Valentina Cortese, Peter Cushing, Yvonne De Carlo, Frederick Valk

983. *Wagner* (1983). 540 min. Alan Landsburg Prod. D: Tony Palmer.
Wagner: Richard Burton
Franz Liszt: Ekkerhard Schall
Cosima Wagner: Vanessa Redgrave

Supporting cast: Gemma Craven, Laszlo Galffi, John Gielgud, Ralph Richardson

SEE ALSO: **Liszt, Franz; Ludwig II,** King of Bavaria.

Wakatuski, Jeanne, 1934–
See **Houston, Jeanne Wakatuski.**

Walewska, Maria, 1789–1817
See **Napoleon Bonaparte,** Emperor of France.

Walker, James, 1881–1946. (American politician and mayor of New York, 1926–1932)

984. *Beau James* (1957). 105 min. Paramount Pictures. D: Melville Shavelson.
Walker: Bob Hope
Supporting cast: Paul Douglas, Darren McGavin, Vera Miles, Alexis Smith

Walker, William, 1824–1860. (American adventurer who invaded Nicaragua in 1855, was elected President, and later was expelled from the country)

984a *Walker* (1988). 90 min. Universal Pictures. D: Alex Cox.
Walker: Ed Harris
Ellen Martin: Marlee Matlin
Supporting cast: Rene Auberjonois, Richard Masur, Sy Richardson, Keith Szarabajka

Wallace, John, d. 1950. (American murderer)

985. *Murder in Coweta County* (1983). 100 min. Telecom Entertainment. D: Gary Nelson.
Wallace: Andy Griffith
Lamar Potts: Johnny Cash
Supporting cast: June Carter Cash, Earl Hindman, Cindi Knight, Ed Van Nuys

Wallenberg, Raoul, 1912–? (Swedish diplomat who helped more than ten thousand Hungarian Jews escape the Holocaust)

986. *Raoul Wallenberg: Between the Lines* (1984). 85 min. Jethro Films. D: Karin Altmann.
Documentary

986a *Wallenberg: A Hero's Story* (1985). 200 min. Paramount Pictures Television. D: Lamont Johnson.
Wallenberg: Richard Chamberlain
Adolph Eichmann: Kenneth Colley
Supporting cast: Bibi Andersson, Alice Krige, Melanie Mayron, Stuart Wilson

Wallenda, Karl, 1905–1978. (Legendary American circus aerialist)

987. *The Great Wallendas* (1978). 100 min. Daniel Wilson Productions. D: Larry Elikann.
Wallenda: Lloyd Bridges
Supporting cast: Britt Ekland, Taina Elg, Cathy Rigby

Wallis, Barnes, 1887–1979
See **Gibson, Guy.**

Wallis, Hal B., 1898–
See **Flynn, Errol.**

Walsh, Adam, 1975?–1981. (American kidnap and murder victim whose parents' crusade after his death led to the passage of the Missing Children's Bill)

988. *Adam* (1983). 100 min. Alan Landsburg Prod. D: Michael Tuchner.
Walsh: John Boston
John Walsh: Daniel J. Travanti
Reve Walsh: JoBeth Williams
Supporting cast: Mason Adams, Richard Masur, Paul Regina, Martha Scott

Walsh, John, 1941?– (American businessman and television personality who led the crusade for the passage of the Missing Children's Bill after his son was kidnapped and murdered)

988a *Adam: His Song Continues* (1986). 104 min. Landsburg Company. D: Robert Markowitz.
Walsh: Daniel J. Travanti
Reve Walsh: JoBeth Williams
Supporting cast: Lindsey Amelio, Richard Masur, Paul Regina, Martha Scott

SEE ALSO: **Walsh, Adam.**

Walsh, Raoul, 1887–
See **Flynn, Errol.**

Walsh, Reve
See **Walsh, Adam; Walsh, John.**

Ward, Stephen Thomas, 1912–1963
See **Keeler, Christine.**

Warhol, Andy, 1928–1987. (American artist best known for pop art works)

988b *Andy Warhol* (1987). 53 min. Michael Blackwood Prod. D: Lana Jokel.
Documentary

988c *Superstar: The Life and Times of Andy Warhol* (1991). 87 min. Marilyn Lewis Entertainment Ltd. D: Chuck Workman.
Documentary

Warner, Jack, 1894–
    See **Flynn, Errol.**

Warren, Earl, 1891–1974
    See **Marshall, Thurgood.**

Washington, George, 1732–1799 (First American president and commander of the Continental armies during the American Revolution)

988d *George Washington* (1984). 480 min. MGM Television. D: Buzz Kulik.
    Washington (as an adult): Barry Bostwick
    Washington (at age 11): Gavin Pearce
    Alexander Hamilton: Robert Schenkkan
    Marquis de Lafayette: Philip Casnoff
    Martha Washington: Patty Duke Astin
    Supporting cast: Lloyd Bridges, David Dukes, Jose Ferrer, Jaclyn Smith

988e *George Washington II: The Forging of a Nation* (1986). 240 min. MGM/UA Television. D: William A. Graham.
    Washington: Barry Bostwick
    John Adams: Paul Collins
    Thomas Jefferson: Jeffrey Jones
    Alexander Hamilton: Richard Bekins
    James Madison: Guy Paul
    James Monroe: Robert Kelly
    Martha Washington: Patty Duke
    Supporting cast: Penny Fuller, Lise Hilboldt, Haviland Morris, Norman Snow

    SEE ALSO: **Hamilton, Alexander; Lafayette, Marie Joseph Paul Yves Roch Gilbert du Motier,** Marquis de.

Washington, Martha, 1732–1802
    See **Washington, George.**

Wassell, Corydon McAlmont, 1884– (World War II U.S. Navy physician who helped twelve wounded sailors on Java elude capture by the Japanese)

989. *The Story of Dr. Wassell* (1944). 140 min. Paramount Pictures. D: Cecil B. De Mille.
Wassell: Gary Cooper
Supporting cast: Laraine Day, Signe Hasso, Dennis O'Keefe

Wasson, William, 1923– (American priest, founder and director of a home for Mexican orphans)

990. *A Home of Our Own* (1975). 120 min. Quinn Martin Prod. D: Robert Day.
Wasson: Jason Miller
Supporting cast: Pancho Cordova, Enrique Nori, Guillermo San Juan, Carmen Zapata

Watson, James D., 1928–
See **Crick, Francis.**

Wead, Frank, 1895–1947. (U.S. Navy pilot)

991. *The Wings of Eagles* (1957). 110 min. MGM. D: John Ford.
Wead: John Wayne
Supporting cast: Ward Bond, Ken Curtis, Dan Dailey, Maureen O'Hara

Weaver, Harriet Shaw, 1876–1961
See **Joyce, James.**

Weavers, The. (American folksinging group)

992. *Wasn't That a Time* (1982). 78 min. United Artists. D: Jim Brown.
Documentary.

Webster, Billie
    See **Webster, Randy.**

Webster, John
    See **Webster, Randy.**

Webster, Randy, d. 1977. (American youth whose death at the hands of the Houston police was investigated by his parents, who found that the police had planted a gun on their son)

993. *The Killing of Randy Webster* (1981). 100 min. EMI TV. D: Sam Wanamaker.
    Webster: Gary McCleery
    Billie Webster: Dixie Carter
    John Webster: Hal Holbrook
    Supporting cast: Jennifer Jason-Leigh, Nancy Malone, Sean Penn, James Whitmore, Jr.

Weisman, Mary-Lou, 1937– (American writer whose son was a victim of muscular dystrophy)

994. *A Time to Live* (1985). 100 min. ITC Prod. D: Rick Wallace.
    Weisman: Liza Minnelli
    Supporting cast: Jeffrey DeMunn, Corey Haim, Swoosie Kurtz, Scott Schwartz

Welles, Orson, 1915–1985
    See **Hayworth, Rita.**

Wellington, Arthur, 1769–1852
    See **Napoleon Bonaparte**, Emperor of France.

Wells, H.G., 1866–1946
    See **Jack the Ripper.**

West, Mae, 1892–1980. (American stage and film actress best known for her risque sense of humor)

995. *Mae West* (1982). 100 min. Hill/Mandelker Prod. D: Lee Philips.
West: Ann Jillian
W.C. Fields: Chuck McCann
Supporting cast: James Brolin, Piper Laurie, Roddy McDowall

White, Daniel James, 1946?–
See **Milk, Harvey.**

White, Marian Rose. (American woman who was, at age nine, committed by her mother to the mental institution where she remained for thirty years)

996. *Marian Rose White* (1982). 100 min. Cypress Point Prod. D: Robert Day.
White: Nancy Cartwright
Supporting cast: Charles Aidman, Louis Giambalvo, Valerie Perrine, Katharine Ross

White, Mary, 1904–1921. (Victim of a horseback-riding accident who was immortalized by her father, Pulitzer Prize- winning journalist William Allen White, in an editorial in the *Emporia* (Kansas) *Gazette*)

997. *Mary White* (1977). 100 min. Radnitz/Mattel Prod. D: Jud Taylor.
White: Kathleen Beller
William Allen White: Ed Flanders
Supporting cast: Fionnula Flanagan, Tim Matheson, Donald Moffat

White, Pearl, 1889–1938. (American silent-film actress best known for the constant peril to which she was subjected in her films)

998. *The Perils Of Pauline* (1947). 96 min. Paramount Pictures. D: George Marshall.
White: Betty Hutton
Supporting cast: Constance Collier, Billy DeWolfe, William Demarest, John Lund

White, Stanford, 1853–1906
See **Nesbit, Evelyn.**

White, William Allen, 1868–1944
See **White, Mary.**

Whitman, Charles, 1941–1966. (American who, on August 4, 1966, shot forty-seven people, killing thirteen, on the University of Texas campus)

999. *The Deadly Tower* (1975). 100 min. MGM D: Jerry Jameson.
Whitman: Kurt Russell
Ramiero Martinez: Richard Yniguez
Supporting cast: Ned Beatty, John Forsythe, Pernell Roberts, Pepe Serna

Whitney, Gertrude Vanderbilt, 1877–1942
See **Vanderbilt, Gloria.**

Who, The. (British rock group who helped popularize the concept of rock opera with *Tommy*)

1000. *The Kids Are Alright* (1979). 108 min. Who Films Ltd. D: Jeff Stein.
Documentary.

Wicker, Tom, 1926– (American writer and columnist for the *New York Times* who was an observer at Attica Prison during the 1971 riot)

1000a *Attica* (1980). 100 min. ABC Circle Films. D: Marvin J. Chomsky
Wicker: George Grizzard

Russell Oswald: Charles Durning
Supporting cast: Henry Darrow, Joel Fabiani, Morgan Freeman, David Harris

Wiesenthal, Simon, 1908– (Polish concentration camp survivor who became the leading investigator of Nazi war crimes)

1000b *Murderers Among Us: The Simon Wiesenthal Story* (1987). 157 min. HBO Pictures. D: Brian Gibson.
Wiesenthal: Ben Kingsley
Supporting cast: Louisa Haigh, Craig T. Nelson, Jack Shepherd, Renee Soutendijk

Wilde, Oscar, 1854–1900. (Irish poet, wit and dramatist best known for his penetrating commentaries on society)

1000c *Oscar Wilde* (1960). 96 min. Films Around the World. D: Gregory Ratoff.
Wilde: Robert Morley
Supporting cast: Phyllis Calvert, John Neville, Ralph Richardson

1000d *The Trials of Oscar Wilde* (1960). 123 min. Warwick Pictures. D: Ken Hughes.
Wilde: Peter Finch
Supporting cast: John Fraser, Lionel Jeffries, Yvonne Mitchell, Nigel Patrick

Wilder, Laura Ingalls 1867–1957. (American writer)

1001. *Little House on the Prairie* (1974). 120 min. NBC Prod. D: Michael Landon.
Ingalls: Melissa Gilbert
Supporting cast: Victor French, Karen Grassle, Michael Landon

Wilkins, Maurice Hugh, 1916–
See **Crick, Francis.**

Williams, Audrey, 1923–
See **Williams, Hank; Williams, Hank, Jr.**

Williams, Hank, 1923–1953. (American country-western singer)

1002. *Your Cheatin' Heart* (1964). 99 min. MGM. D: Gene Nelson.
Williams (as an adult): George Hamilton
Williams (age 14): Donald Losby
Audrey Williams: Susan Oliver
Supporting cast: Red Buttons, Chris Crosby, Rex Ingram,
Shary Marshall, Arthur O'Connell

Williams, Hank, Jr. 1949– (American country-western singer)

1003. *Living Proof: The Hank Williams, Jr., Story* (1983). 100 min.
Telecom, Inc. D: Dick Lowry.
Williams: Richard Thomas
Audrey Williams: Allyn Ann McLerie
Supporting cast: Ann Gillespie, Clu Gulager, Liane Lan-
gland, Leora May

Williams, Wayne Bertram, 1958– (Murderer who was held
responsible for the death of twenty-seven persons during
the 1970's in Atlanta)

1003a *The Atlanta Child Murders* (1985). 245 min. Abby Mann
Productions. D: John Erman.
Williams: Calvin Levels
Alvin Binder: Jason Robards
Lewis Slaton: Rip Torn
Supporting cast: Morgan Freeman, James Earl Jones,
Lynne Moody, Martin Sheen

Wills, William John, 1834–1861
See **Burke, Robert O'Hara.**

Wilson, Brian, 1942–
  See **Beach Boys.**

Wilson, Carl, 1946–
  See **Beach Boys.**

Wilson, Dennis, 1944–1983
  See **Beach Boys.**

Wilson, Edith, 1872–1961
  See **Wilson, Woodrow.**

Wilson, Ellen, 1860–1914
  See **Wilson, Woodrow.**

Wilson, Woodrow, 1856–1924. (Twenty-eighth American president, awarded Nobel Peace Prize in 1919 for his work in ending World War I and for laying the foundation of the League of Nations)

1004. *Wilson* (1944). 154 min. 20th Century-Fox. D: Henry King.
  Wilson: Alexander Knox
  Henry Cabot Lodge: Cedric Hardwicke
  Edith Wilson: Geraldine Fitzgerald
  Ellen Wilson: Ruth Nelson
  Supporting cast: Charles Coburn, William Eythe, Thomas Mitchell, Vincent Price

Winchell, Walter, 1897–1972
  See **Cohn, Roy.**

Windsor, Edward, 1894–1972. (British king who resigned his position to marry a divorcee, Wallis Simpson)

1005. *A King's Story* (1967). 100 min. Continental. D: Harry Booth.
Documentary.

SEE ALSO: **Simpson, Wallis Warfield.**

Windsor, Wallis Simpson, 1896–1986
See **Simpson, Wallis Warfield.**

Woffington, Peg, 1720–1760. (Irish stage actress best known for her comic roles)

1006. *Peg of Old Drury* (1935). 84 min. Herbert Wilcox. D: Herbert Wilcox.
Woffington: Anna Neagle
David Garrick: Cedric Hardwicke
Supporting cast: Jack Hawkins, Maire O'Neill, Hay Petrie, Margaretta Scott

Wojtyla, Karol, 1920–
See **John Paul II,** Pope.

Woods, Donald, 1933–
See **Biko, Steve.**

Woods, Wendy
See **Biko, Steve.**

Woodward, Bob, 1943– (American journalist on the *Washington Post* who broke the Watergate scandal)

1007. *All the President's Men* (1976). 136 min. Warner Bros. D: Alan J. Pakula.
Woodward: Robert Redford
Carl Bernstein: Dustin Hoffman
Ben Bradlee: Jason Robards

Supporting cast: Jane Alexander, Martin Balsam, Hal Holbrook, Jack Warden

Woolley, Monty, 1888–1963
See **Porter, Cole.**

Worker, Dwight, 1946– (American escapee from a Mexican prison where he had been sent for drug smuggling)

1008. *Escape* (1980). 100 min. Henry Jaffe Enterprises. D: Robert Michael Lewis.
Worker: Timothy Bottoms
Supporting cast: Colleen Dewhurst, Antonio Fargas, Kay Lenz, Allan Miller

Wright, Orville, 1871–1948. (American inventor of the first successful motor-driven airplane)

1009. *The Winds of Kitty Hawk* (1978). 100 min. Charles Fries Prod. D: E.W. Swackhamer.
Wright: David Huffman
Wilbur Wright: Michael Moriarty
Supporting cast: Tom Bower, Robin Gammell, Scott Hylands

Wright, Wilbur, 1867–1912
See **Wright, Orville.**

Wycliffe, John, 1329?–1384. (British reformer who attacked the manifest abuses of the Catholic Church and is best known for translating the Bible into English)

1009a *John Wycliffe: The Morning Star* (1983). 75 min. Vision Video. D: Tony Teu.
Wycliffe: Peter Howell
John of Gaunt: Keith Buckley
Supporting cast: Michael Burtenshaw, Barrie Cookson, Noel Howlet, Jeremy Robert

Wynette, Tammy, 1942– (American country-western singer)

1010. *Stand by Your Man* (1981). 100 min. Robert Papazian Prod.
  D: Jerry Jameson.
  Wynette: Annette O'Toole
  George Jones: Tim McIntire
  Supporting cast: Helen Page Camp, James Hampton,
    Cooper Huckabee

Y

Yablonski, Joseph A. "Jock," 1910–1969. (American labor leader
  who was murdered after challenging the corrupt leader-
  ship of the United Mine Workers in 1969)

1011. *Act of Vengeance* (1986). 95 min. Lorimar-Telepictures
  Prod. D: John Mackenzie.
  Yablonski: Charles Bronson
  William Anthony "Tony" Boyle: Wilford Brimley
  Margaret Yablonski: Ellen Burstyn
  Supporting cast: Hoyt Axton, Ellen Barkin, Maury
    Chaykin, Robert Schenkkan

Yablonski, Margaret, d. 1969
  See **Yablonski, Joseph A. ("Jock")**

Yann, Linn, 1970?– (Cambodian refugee who arrived in America unable to speak English but became four years later a
  National Spelling Champion)

1011a *The Girl Who Spelled Freedom* (1986). 120 min. Walt Disney
  Pictures. D: Simon Wincer.
  Yann: Jade Chinn
  George Thrash: Wayne Rogers
  Prissy Thrash: Mary Kay Place
  Supporting cast: Kieu Chinh, Margot Pinvidic, Kathleen
    Sisk, Susan Walden

Yeats, William Butler, 1865–1939
    See **O'Casey, Sean.**

York, Alvin, 1887–1964. (American World War I soldier who captured 132 German soldiers at Argonne after losing most of his detachment)

1011b *Sergeant York* (1941). 134 min. Warner Bros. D: Howard Hawks.
    York: Gary Cooper
    Supporting cast: Walter Brennan, Joan Leslie, Stanley Ridges

Young, Brigham, 1801–1877. (Mormon who directed the mass migration to the Great Salt Lake Valley in Utah)

1012. *Brigham Young—Frontiersman* (1940). 112 min. 20th Century-Fox. D: Henry Hathaway.
    Young: Dean Jagger
    Joseph Smith: Vincent Price
    Supporting cast: Linda Darnell, Brian Donlevy, Tyrone Power

Younger, Cole, 1844–1916. (American outlaw who rode with Quantrill's raiders during the Civil War and who, with his brothers, was a member of the James gang)

1013. *Bad Men of Missouri* (1941). 77 min. Warner Bros. D: Ray Enright.
    Younger: Dennis Morgan
    James Younger: Arthur Kennedy
    Robert Younger: Wayne Morris
    Supporting cast: Alan Baxter, Walter Catlett, Victor Jory, Jane Wyman

1014. *Cole Younger, Gunfighter* (1958). 78 min. Allied Artists. D: R.G. Springsteen.
    Younger: Frank Lovejoy
    Supporting cast: James Best, Abby Dalton, Jan Merlin

1015. *The Younger Brothers* (1949). 74 min. Warner Bros. D: Ray Enright.
Younger: Wayne Morris
James Younger: Bruce Bennett
John Younger: Robert Hutton
Robert Younger: James Brown
Supporting cast: Geraldine Brooks, Fred Clark, Alan Hale, Janis Paige

SEE ALSO: **James, Jesse; Starr, Belle.**

Younger, James, 1850–1902
See **Younger, Cole.**

Younger, John, 1846–1874
See **Younger, Cole.**

Younger, Robert, 1853–1889
See **Younger, Cole.**

Youssoupoff, Felix, 1887–1967. (Russian soldier who was responsible for the assassination of Rasputin)

1015a *I Killed Rasputin* (1969). 95 min. Ben Barry & Associates. D: Robert Hossein.
Youssoupoff: Gert Frobe
Grigori Rasputin: Peter McEnery
Supporting cast: Geraldine Chaplin, Ivan Desny, Ira Furstenberg, Robert Hossein

Z

Zaharias, Babe Didrickson, 1911–1956. (American Olympic gold medalist in track and field and world-champion golfer)

1016. *Babe* (1975). 100 min. MGM. D: Buzz Kulik.
Zaharias: Susan Clark

George Zaharias: Alex Karras
Supporting cast: Ellen Geer, Jeanette Nolan, Slim Pickens, Ford Rainey

Zaharias, George, 1908–1984
See **Zaharias, Babe Didrickson.**

Zapata, Emiliano, 1877–1919. (Mexican revolutionary and champion of agrarianism)

1017. *Viva Zapata!* (1952). 112 min. 20th Century-Fox. D: Elia Kazan.
Zapata: Marlon Brando
Pancho Villa: Alan Reed
Supporting cast: Arnold Moss, Jean Peters, Anthony Quinn, Joseph Wiseman

Ziegfeld, Florenz, 1869–1932. (American theatrical producer best known for the Ziegfeld Follies, 1907–1932)

1018. *The Great Ziegfeld* (1936). 184 min. MGM. D: Robert Z. Leonard.
Ziegfeld: William Powell
Billie Burke: Myrna Loy
Anna Held: Luise Rainer
Supporting cast: Virginia Bruce, Frank Morgan, Reginald Owen, Nat Pendleton

1019. *Ziegfeld: The Man and His Women* (1978). 150 min. Columbia Pictures. D: Buzz Kulik.
Ziegfeld: Paul Shenar
Billie Burke: Samantha Eggar
Anna Held: Barbara Parkins
Lillian Lorraine: Valerie Perrine
Marilyn Miller: Pamela Peadon
Supporting cast: Ron Hussman, David Opatoshu, Nehemiah Persoff, Inga Swenson

SEE ALSO: **Brice, Fanny; Cantor, Eddie.**

Zigo, Ed. (American police officer responsible for the capture of "Son of Sam")

1020. *Out of the Darkness* (1985). 100 min. Centerpoint Productions. D: Jud Taylor.
Zigo: Martin Sheen
David Berkowitz: Robert Trebor
Supporting cast: Matt Clark, Hector Elizondo, Jennifer Salt, Ann Talman

Zola, Emile, 1840–1902. (French novelist whose works championed social reform)

1021. *The Life of Emile Zola* (1937). 116 min. Warner Bros. D: William Dieterle.
Zola: Paul Muni
Alfred Dreyfus: Joseph Schildkraut
Supporting cast: Donald Crisp, Gloria Holden, Gale Sondergaard

SEE ALSO: **Dreyfus, Alfred.**

Zumwalt, Elmo, 1920–   (American admiral and Secretary of the Navy who ordered the use of Agent Orange in Vietnam)

1022. *My Father, My Son* (1988). 100 min. Fred Weintraub Productions. D: Jeff Bleckner.
Zumwalt: Karl Malden
Elmo Zumwalt III: Keith Carradine
Supporting cast: Dirk Blocker, Michael Horton, Jenny Lewis, Billy Sullivan

Zumwalt, Elmo, III, 1946–1988
See **Zumwalt, Elmo.**

SELECTED BIBLIOGRAPHY

Adams, Les, and Rainey Adams. *Shoot-em-ups: The Complete Reference Guide to Westerns of the Sound Era*. New Rochelle, N.Y.: Arlington House, 1978.

Bergan, Ronald. *The United Artists Story*. New York: Crown Publishers, 1986.

Eames, John Douglas. *The MGM Story: The Complete History of Fifty Roaring Years*. London: Octopus Books, 1975.

———. *The Paramount Story*. 1st ed. New York: Crown Publishers, 1985.

Fernett, Gene. *Poverty Row*. Satellite Beach, Fla.: Coral Reef Publishers, 1973.

Film Review Annual. 4 vols. Englewood, N.J.: Jerome S. Ozer, 1983–1986.

Halliwell, Leslie. *The Filmgoer's Companion*. 6th ed. New York: Hill and Wang, 1977.

———. *Halliwell's Film Guide*. 3rd ed. New York: Scribner's, 1981.

Hirschhorn, Clive. *The Universal Story*. New York: Crown Publishers, 1983.

———. *The Warner Bros. Story*. New York: Crown Publishers, 1979.

Hollywood and History: Costume Design in Film. New York: Thames and Hudson, 1987.

Jewell, Richard B. *The RKO Story*. New York: Arlington House, 1982.

Maltin, Leonard. *The Disney Films*. New York: Crown Publishers, 1973.

———. *Leonard Maltin's TV Movies*. 1988 ed. New York: New American Library, 1987.

Marill, Alvin H. *Movies Made for Television: The Telefeature and the Mini-Series, 1964–1979*. Westport, Conn.: Arlington House, 1980.

The Motion Picture Guide. 12 vols. Chicago: Cinebooks, 1985.

Nash, Jay Robert. *Bloodletters and Badmen: A Narrative Encyclope-*

dia of American Criminals from the Pilgrims to the Present. New York: M. Evans and Co., 1973.

Ottoson, Robert. *American International Pictures: A Filmography.* New York: Garland, 1985.

Pickard, Roy. *Who Played Who in the Movies.* New York: Schocken Books, 1981.

Thomas, Tony. *Cads and Cavaliers: The Gentlemen Adventurers of the Movies.* New York: A.S. Barnes and Co., 1973.

———, and Aubrey Solomon. *The Films of 20th Century-Fox: A Pictorial History.* Secaucus, N.J.: The Citadel Press, 1979.

TV Feature Film Source Book. 2 vols. New York: Broadcast Information Bureau, 1978.

PERFORMER INDEX

Abbott, Bruce 412
Abraham, F. Murray 336a, 721
Abrikossov, A.L. 7a
Ackerman, Leslie 365b, 771
Ackland, Joss 302a, 367c, 443, 616
Ackroyd, David 293
Adamira, Jiri 238
Adams, Amy 810a
Adams, Brooke 269a
Adams, Casey 550
Adams, Julia 408
Adams, Julie 673
Adams, Mason 988
Adams, Maud 310
Adams, Michael 550
Adams, Nick 246
Adams, Tom 754
Adamson, George 4
Adamson, Terence 4
Addie, Robert 99
Adjani, Isabelle 92, 164b, 492
Adler, Luther 290, 742, 849
Adrian, Max 789, 937
Aherne, Brian 349, 546, 925
Aidman, Charles 66, 996
Aiello, Danny 569
Aimee, Anouk 51d, 699
Ainley, Richard 127
Ajoret, Daniele 49
Akersten, Donna 379b
Akins, Claude 186, 213a, 218, 643
Alari, Nadine 49

Albert, Eddie 314, 617, 780, 831, 858
Albert, Edward 569, 758,
Albertson, Jack 857
Alda, Alan 154,793
Alda, Robert 358
Alda, Rutanya 199
Alderton, John 439
Aleandro, Norma 90a, 311a
Alexander, Denise 628
Alexander, Jane 114, 310, 394, 534, 649, 650, 771, 853, 854, 1007
Alexander, Katherine 32, 932
Alexander, Tad 823a
Alexandridis, Helene 940b
Alexandrov, Constantin 322a
Alfonsi, Lydia 713
Ali, Muhammad 12
Alicia, Ana 124, 848a
Allan, Elizabeth 405
Allegret, Catherine 581a
Allen, Debbie 809a
Allen, Joan 85a, 958a
Allen, Jonelle 323
Allen, Phillip R. 829
Allen, Sian Barbara 628, 643
Allen, Steve 371
Alley, Kirstie 914b
Allgood, Sara 403, 500
Allister, Claude 433
Allport, Christopher 715
Allum, Erik 728
Allyson, June 680, 690, 844, 921

Almaz, Noam 120b
Alonso, Chelo 713
Altman, John 42
Alvarado, Trini 748a, 905
Alvaro, Anne 216
Alvin, John 929
Ameche, Don 48, 325, 678, 867
Amelio, Lindsey 988a
Ames, Leon 138
Amos, John 112
Anders, Merry 515
Anderson, Carl 522
Anderson, Cheryl 172
Anderson, Donna 218
Anderson, Evert 454
Anderson, Herbert 456
Anderson, John 207
Anderson, Judith 877
Anderson, Loni 660
Anderson, Mary 591
Anderson, Melody 583
Anderson, Richard 673
Anderson, Stanley 208a
Anderson, Warner 637
Andersson, Bibi 986
Ando, Eiko 415
Andor, Paul 370
Andreichenko, Natalya 778b
Andrews, Anthony 888a, 896a
Andrews, Dana 125, 183, 207, 292, 353b, 566, 912
Andrews, Harry 98, 121, 505a, 743
Andrews, Julie 601, 954
Andrews, Lois 952
Angel, Heather 73
Anglim, Philip 892a
Angustain, Ira 808
Ann-Margret 334
Annabella 227, 837
Annis, Francesca 436

Ansara, Michael 169, 408, 700
Anspach, Susan 613
Antonio, Angelique 758
Antonio, Elkin, 758
Antonio, Jim 33a, 491
Antony, Scott 351
Aprea, John 663
Archer, John 234
Arden, Eve 841
Arhondis, Tina 681
Ariel, Brigitte 783
Arkin, Alan 586
Arlen, Richard 178, 511
Arliss, Dimitra 455
Arliss, Florence 247
Arliss, George 247, 401, 836, 859, 980
Armendariz, Pedro 80, 329, 574, 778
Armstrong, Bess 605
Armstrong, Louis 744
Armstrong, R.G. 509, 802
Armstrong, Robert 191
Arnaz, Desi, Jr. 796
Arndt, Adelheid 645a
Arndt, Jurgen 809
Arner, Gwen 51a
Arness, James 81a
Arno, Sig 156
Arnold, Edward 85, 313, 751, 836, 867, 932
Arnoux, Robert 49
Arquette, Rosanna 208a, 366
Arruza, Carlos 22, 81
Arthur, Jean 85, 447
Arundell, Dennis 777
Ashcroft, Peggy 831a
Ashcroft, Ray 42
Asher, Jane 409a, 432
Asherson, Renee 431
Ashley, Jennifer 539
Ashley, John 246
Askew, Luke 509, 816

Asner, Edward 194, 581, 636
Assante, Armand 412, 499a, 638, 909
Astaire, Fred 133, 548
Astin, Patty Duke 556, 988d
Astor, Mary 252
Ates, Roscoe 63
Atkins, David 936a
Atkins, Tom 828
Attenborough, Richard 158
Atwill, Lionel 122, 923
Auberjonois, Rene 66a, 941, 984a
Aumont, Jean Pierre 471, 541, 841, 891
Aumont, Tina 130
Avalon, Frankie 81
Avedon, Doe 848
Avery, Margaret 20, 305a, 835b
Axton, Hoyt 358a, 726, 1011
Aylmer, Felix 526, 746, 970–971
Ayres, Leah 269b
Ayres, Lew 803

Babcock, Barbara 657, 697a
Babochkin, Boris 145a
Bacall, Lauren 47
Bacon, Irving 690
Badel, Alan 748, 877, 893, 982
Baderman, Rupert 616
Baggetta, Vincent 124
Bailey, G.W. 379c
Bailey, Pearl 406
Baines, Christopher 151
Bainter, Fay 283, 505
Baker, Blanche 28a, 668
Baker, Carroll 410, 920, 940
Baker, Diane 428
Baker, Joby 101
Baker, Joe Don 180b, 468, 815
Baker, Kathy 28a

Baker, Ray 28a
Baker, Stanley 893
Baker, Tom 743
Bakewell, William 203
Baldwin, Alec 81a
Balin, Ina 27, 729
Ball, Suzan 200
Balsam, Martin 249, 409, 414, 835a, 969, 1007
Balsam, Talia, 128a, 185
Baltz, Kirk 407a
Bancroft, Anne 162, 406a, 523, 555, 687, 797a
Bancroft, George 283
Bankhead, Tallulah 136
Banks, Ernie 577
Banks, Jonathan 185
Banks, Leslie 431, 903a
Banner, John 291
Barbeau, Adrienne 483
Barbetti, Carlo 722
Barbier, George 795
Bari, Lynn 125, 324, 839
Barkin, Ellen 1011
Barnes, Binnie 85, 251, 275, 433, 795, 881, 932
Barnes, Ernie 766
Barnett, Vince 140
Barrat, Robert 670
Barrett, Jane 959
Barrie, Barbara 102, 584, 792
Barrie, Wendy 433
Barrington, Diana 936
Barry, Gene 58, 539
Barry, Patricia 59
Barry, Raymond J. 583a
Barrymore, Ethel 823a
Barrymore, John 252, 665, 823a, 976
Barrymore, John Drew 552, 799, 822
Barrymore, Lionel 281, 532, 652, 823a

Barth, Eddie 101
Barton, James 198
Barty, Billy 311
Basaraba, Gary 170, 524a
Basehart, Richard 460, 703
Basserman, Albert 831, 881
Bassett, Linda 949a
Bastien, Fanny 353a
Bat-Adam, Michal 180a
Bateman, Justine 505b
Bates, Alan 99a, 748
Battaglia, Rick 105, 303
Battista, Lloyd 197
Bauer, Belinda 877b
Bauer, Richard 367c
Baur, Harry 45b
Bavier, Frances 501
Baxter, Alan 1013
Baxter, Anne 136, 186, 469, 929
Baxter, Jane 259
Baxter, Warner 724, 731
Baye, Nathalie 45cb
Bayer, Gary 621
Bazinet, Brenda 231b
Beach, Michael 162a
Beal, John 594, 802
Beale, Edie 38
Beale, Edith Bouvier 38
Bean, Sean 120b
Beatty, Ned 540, 569a, 684, 727, 900, 999
Beatty, Robert 338
Beatty, Warren, 768, 827, 894a
Beaven, Ellen 285a
Beavers, Louise 842, 912
Beck, Michael 123, 486a
Beck, Stanley 95
Beckel, Graham 667a
Becker, Harmut 21a
Bedelia, Bonnie 52, 231b, 726, 759b

Beddoe, Don 75
Beecher, Janet 31
Beer, Ulrich 45c
Beery, Noah, Jr. 202, 803, 815–816
Beery, Wallace 31, 63, 627, 975
Beggs, Hagan 581
Beghi, Luisella 722
Begley, Ed, Jr. 26
Bekassy, Stephen 156
Bekins, Richard 988e
Bel Geddes, Barbara 744
Belack, Doris 423
Belafonte, Harry 384
Bellamy, Ralph 7, 332, 468, 565, 697, 856
Bellaver, Harry 304
Beller, Kathleen 997
Bellwood, Pamela 34
Belmondo, Jean-Paul 914a
Belmore, Lionel 401
Beltran, Robert 90a
Belushi, James 84
Bendix, William 869, 939
Bening, Annette 894a
Benjamin, Paul 19, 126, 604, 606
Bennett, Bruce 74, 419, 508, 1015
Bennett, Constance 140, 451
Bennett, Jill 121
Bennett, Joan 247
Bennett, Joe 185
Bennett, Tony 577
Benrath, Martin 880a
Benson, Lucille 647
Benson, Martin 609
Benson, Robby 243, 394, 626a, 693
Benton, Suzanne 316
Berenger, Tom 131

Berenstein, Daniel Emilfork 130

Berge, Amund 728

Bergen, Candice 33a

Berger, Senta 228, 664, 925

Berggren, Thommy 454

Bergin, Patrick 100a

Bergman, Ingrid 24, 525, 684

Bergner, Elisabeth 134

Berle, Milton 611, 965

Bernard, Jason 866

Bernardi, Herschel 505a

Berridge, Elizabeth 721

Berry, Chuck 336

Berti, Marina 79

Bertin, Roland 92, 861

Bertinelli, Valerie 29a, 365b

Bertish, Jane 298

Besch, Bibi 919

Best, Edna 831

Best, James 1014

Betz, Carl 505

Bevans, Clem 201

Bey, Turhan 129

Beyers, Bill 691

Beymer, Richard 330, 428

Bickford, Allen 560

Bickford, Charles 50, 76, 447, 694, 697, 839, 869, 943

Biehn, Michael 825a

Bieri, Ramon 111, 911, 962

Big Head, Jack 943

Bikel, Theodore 566

Bingham, Bob 522

Binns, Edward 855

Bird, Billie 887

Birkin, Jane 45c

Birman, Serafina 497–498

Birney, David 417, 890

Birtwell, Celia 467

Bishop, Debby 969a

Bishop, Kristen 30

Bisset, Jacqueline 39

Black, Karen 144, 468, 479

Blades, Ruben 311a

Blair, Janet 256

Blaisdell, Nesbitt 564a

Blake, Robert 569, 659, 904

Blakely, Colin 10, 439, 517

Blakely, Ronee 476

Blakely, Susan 118, 308, 459, 560a

Blanc, Dominique 599a

Blanche, Ronald 216

Blech, Hans Christian 826

Blessed, Brian 431a

Blinov, Boris 145a

Bliss, Caroline 150

Blocker, Dirk 90, 1022

Bloom, Claire 8, 16a, 35a, 590, 616, 666a, 745

Bloom, Verna 287, 524a

Blore, Eric 85

Blue, Ben 756

Blue, Simone 185

Blye, Margaret 812–813

Blyth, Ann 128, 149, 551a, 711

Bochner, Hart 420

Bochner, Lloyd 647, 668

Boehm, Karl 46, 333, 389

Boensch, Paul 807

Bogarde, Dirk 195, 631, 739

Bolger, Ray 15, 692

Bologna, Joseph 180b, 416a, 896

Bolton, June 967

Bonar, Ivan 648

Bond, Derek 883

Bond, Ward 190, 451, 461, 508, 525, 676, 991

Bondi, Beulah 571

Bonicelli, Paolo 615

Booke, Sorrell 491

Boone, Richard 81

Boorman, Katrine 164b

Booth, James 614
Boothe, Powers 540
Borgnine, Ernest 12, 239, 523, 716
Bos, Jenny 432
Bosley, Tom 763
Boston, John 988
Bostwick, Barry 347, 988d-988e
Bosworth, Hobart 263, 624
Bottoms, Joseph 761
Bottoms, Timothy 26, 223, 332, 580, 1008
Bouchet, Barbara 755
Boudet, Jacques 949a
Bouix, Evelyne 782
Bourdon, Corinne 968a
Bourke, Anthony 4
Bovasso, Julie 416a, 765
Bovee, Strawn 769b
Bowens, Mallick 56
Bower, Tom 192, 1009
Bowker, Judi 328
Bowles, Peter 121, 666a
Boxleitner, Bruce 274
Boyd, Guy 327a
Boyd, Stephen 61, 575
Boyden, Peter 564a
Boyens, Phyllis 646
Boyer, Charles 735, 864, 914a
Boyle, Peter 345, 404, 679, 941
Bracho, Alejandro 848a
Bradbury, Lane 890
Bradford, Richard 120a, 742a
Bradley, David 106
Brady, Alice 626
Brady, Scott 68, 811, 914
Braga, Sonia 99c
Branagh, Kenneth 431a
Brand, Neville 820, 926
Brandauer, Klaus Maria 56, 826

Brandet, Alicia 552
Brando, Marlon 55, 107, 736, 1017
Brandon, Michael 229
Brasselle, Keefe 116
Brauner, Asher 568
Brazzi, Rossano 184a, 891, 924
Brega, Mario 176
Bremer, Lucille 129, 572
Brennan, Eileen 243
Brennan, Walter 40, 133, 279, 441, 910, 1011b
Brent, Evelyn 122
Brent, George 914
Brent, Romney 837
Bressart, Felix 325
Brialy, Jean-Claude 782
Brian, David 234, 557
Bridges, Beau 85a, 425, 536, 579, 726, 885
Bridges, Jeff 958a
Bridges, Lloyd 115, 426a, 559, 760, 987, 988d
Briggs, Geoffrey 886
Brimley, Wilford 66a, 788, 1011
Britt, May 612
Brittany, Morgan 535a
Britton, Barbara 321, 576, 930
Broderick, Matthew 891a
Brolin, James 342, 995
Bromberg, J. Edward 227, 321
Bron, Eleanor 362a
Bronson, Charles 450, 530, 558, 963, 974, 1011
Brook, Claudio 547
Brooke, Bunney 333a
Brookes, Jacqueline 788, 828
Brooks, Geraldine 1015
Brown, Blair 293, 564a, 854
Brown, Bryan 322a, 708
Brown, Caitlin 810a

Brown, Carlos 536
Brown, Charles 564a
Brown, Gaye 652a
Brown, Georg Stanford 763
Brown, Georgia 503
Brown, Gottfried 652a
Brown, Jackie 960
Brown, James 898–899, 1015
Brown, John Mack 63
Brown, Pamela 168, 968
Brown, Reb 607b
Brown, Ritza 638
Brown, Roger Aaron 323, 434
Brown, Tom 446
Browne, Cicely 130
Browne, Coral 99a, 200b,
    409a, 851
Browne, Leslie 748
Browne, Roscoe Lee 305a,
    577
Bruce, David 75, 674
Bruce, Ed 512
Bruce, Nigel 747, 831
Bruce, Virginia 31, 1018
Bruhl, Linda 387
Brunkhorst, Natja 306
Brunoy, Blanchette 49
Bryant, Michael 875
Brynner, Yul 590, 609, 719,
    974
Buchanan, Edgar 280
Buchholz, Horst 142, 798, 924
Buckingham, Yvonne 552
Buckley, Betty 124
Buckley, Keith 1009a
Buetel, Jack 70
Buggy, Niall 222
Bujold, Genevieve 60
Buke, Donald 291
Buktenica, Raymond 58, 660
Bunce, Alan 856
Bundy, Brooke 803
Bunel, Marie 599a

Bunting, Garland 633a
Burge, James 564a
Burke, Alfred 409
Burnett, Carol 727, 760
Burnette, Smiley 65
Burns, Bart 307
Burns, Catherine 272
Burns, Carol 379b
Burns, Marilyn 661
Burr, Raymond 78, 169, 780
Burroughs, Jackie 469a, 695
Burroughs, William S. 100
Burstyn, Ellen 414, 888a, 1011
Burtenshaw, Michael 1009a
Burton, LeVar 598, 606, 763,
    944
Burton, Norman 269b
Burton, Richard 8, 45, 60, 76,
    168, 850, 959, 983
Burton, Tony 659
Busey, Gary 97, 474, 900
Bushnell, Anthony 247
Busia, Akousa 681a
Bustamonte, Sergio 311a
Butler, Paul 598
Butt, Lawson 976
Buttons, Red 20, 410, 945,
    1002
Byrd, Richard 103
Byrd, Thomas 771
Byrne, Gabriel 184a, 734a
Byrne, Patsy 1a
Byrnes, Edward 217
Byron, Arthur 724
Bythe, William 136

Caan, James 87, 785, 896
Cabot, Bruce 155, 451, 731
Cabot, Susan 558
Cage, Nicolas 406b
Cagney, James 145, 180, 304,
    400, 637
Caine, Michael 499a

Caldicott, Helen 109
Calhern, Louis 107, 281, 475, 751
Calhoun, Rory 340, 797, 930
Calkins, Johnny 929
Callahan, James 490, 659
Callan, Michael 231a, 320a
Calleia, Joseph 83, 546, 966
Callow, Simon 721
Calvert, Phyllis 764, 789, 896a, 1000c
Calvet, Corinne 596
Camardiel, Roberto 730
Cambridge, Godfrey 543
Cameron, Rod 582
Cammarata, Pietro 367b
Camp, Helen Page 1010
Campanella, Joseph 640
Campbell, Cheryl 683
Campbell, John 929
Campbell, Judy 927
Campbell, Louise 286
Campbell, Nicholas 605a
Campbell, William 153
Campo, Wally 558
Canale, Gianna Maria 822
Cannon, Dyan 456, 909
Cannon, J.D. 58, 292
Cannon, Katherine 621
Canovas, Anne 968c
Capaldi, Peter 607
Capers, Virginia 681a
Capucine 614, 631
Cara, Irene 305a, 540
Cardinale, Claudia 14
Cardwell, James 929
Carey, Harry 278, 717
Carey, Macdonald 78, 82, 508, 541
Carey, Michele 861a
Carey, Philip 113, 210
Cargill, Patrick 776
Cargol, Jean-Pierre 496

Caridi, Carmine 655
Carlo, Johann 185
Carlson, Karen 536
Carlson, Linda 876
Carlson, Richard 711, 966
Carmen, Julie 66a, 197, 808, 845
Carmichael, Hoagy 47
Carney, Art 52, 123, 399
Carol, Martine 80, 706
Caron, Leslie 967
Carpenter, Frank 446
Carr, Charmian 954
Carr, Darleen 568
Carr, Marian 153
Carra, Raffaella 105
Carradine, David 352, 395, 479, 513
Carradine, John 275, 442, 576, 604a, 670, 960
Carradine, Keith 120a, 379c, 513, 1022
Carradine, Robert 513
Carrez, Florence 526a
Carriere, Mathieu 45c
Carrillo, Elpedia 84
Carrillo, Leo 975
Carroll, Beeson 258, 453
Carroll, Diahann 19
Carroll, Leo G. 882
Carroll, Matthew 298
Carson, Charles 531, 970
Carson, Jack 36, 787, 860
Carter, Dixie 993
Carter, Jack 207, 704
Carter, Helena Bonham 385
Carter, Lynda 421
Cartwright, Nancy 996
Cartwright, Veronica 540, 569a
Caruso, Barbara 151
Caruso, Margherita 518
Casados, Eloy Phil 495

Casey, Bernie 225, 640, 917
Cash, Johnny 512, 985
Cash, June Carter 512, 519, 985
Cash, Rosalind 540
Casnoff, Philip 988d
Cason, Barbara 44a
Cassavetes, John 118
Cassel, Jean Pierre 968c
Cassell, Alan 936a
Cassell, Wally 817
Cassidy, Jack 311
Castang, Veronica 564a
Castelli, Ralph 41
Castle, John 165
Castle, William 704
Catlett, Walter 1013
Cavanagh, Paul 68
Cavanaugh, Michael 913
Cazenove, Christopher 528, 652a
Cegani, Elisa 188
Celi, Adolfo 98, 463
Cellier, Frank 831a
Cerdan, Marcel, Jr. 782
Cervi, Gino 722
Chagas, Walmor 895a
Chamberlain, Richard 108, 189, 315, 336a, 592, 937, 986
Chandler, Alan 963a
Chandler, Chick 325
Chandler, Jeff 23, 173, 270
Chandler, John 181, 816
Chaney, Lon 74
Channing, Stockard 302, 758
Chao, Rosalind 326
Chaplin, Geraldine 177, 1015a
Chapman, Edward 531, 830, 903a
Chapman, Lonny 231a, 577
Charleson, Ian 620

Charney, Jordan 583
Chase, Barrie 820
Chase, Guy 445
Chater, Geoffrey 57
Chaykin, Maury 1011
Chen, Joan 809b
Chen, Moira 305
Cher 235, 895
Chereau, Patrice 216
Cherkasov, Nikolai 497, 498
Chew, Sam, Jr. 568
Chiari, Walter 963
Chiklis, Michael 48a
Chilvers, Simon 681
Chinh, Kieu 1011a
Chinn, Jade 1011a
Choreau, Etchika 217
Chournos, Shane 761
Chris, Marilyn 44a
Christie, Julie 753
Christine, Virginia 774
Christophe, Pascale 783
Christopher, Dennis 434
Churn, Iris 327b
Ciannelli, Eduardo 273
Cicero, Fernando 367b
Cilento, Diane 98, 463
Cioffi, Charles 7, 478, 504, 641
Clair, Jany 822
Clanton, Rony 126
Clapp, Gordon 258a
Clapton, Eric 163
Clarence, O.B. 777
Clark, Bryan 85a
Clark, Candy 229, 788
Clark, Dane 229, 880, 884
Clark, Dick 34
Clark, Ellen 544
Clark, Fred 697, 1015
Clark, Liddy 681
Clark, Matt 102, 389a, 812, 1020

Clark, Ossie 467
Clark, Susan 101, 272, 1016
Clarke, Angela 257, 327, 484
Clarke, Caitlin 33a
Clarke, Robert 903
Clarke, Warren 528, 659a
Clay, Nicholas 219
Clayburgh, Jill 342, 372, 892
Clemens, Paul 828
Clennon, David 170, 478, 920
Clevenot, Philippe 164b
Clift, Montgomery 337
Clive, Colin 171
Cloak, Theodore 106
Close, Glenn 981a
Cluny, Alain 615
Cluzet, Francois 599a
Clyde, Andy 752
Clyde, June 948
Coates, Phyllis 701a
Cobb, Lee J. 193, 608
Coburn, Charles 48, 136, 282, 541, 1004
Coburn, James 72, 607b
Coco, James 331
Cody, Iron Eyes 897
Coe, George 320a
Colasanto, Nicholas 950
Colbert, Claudette 167, 553
Cole, Gary 208a, 651
Cole, George 168
Cole, Nat King 406
Coleman, Dabney 358a, 686a, 733, 829
Coleman, Nancy 93
Colicos, John 60
Colin, Margaret 927a
Collet, Christopher 505b
Colley, Kenneth 734a, 755, 937, 986
Collier, Constance 998
Collins, Denver John 473
Collins, Joan 296, 303, 742

Collins, Paul 988e
Collins, Phil 285a
Colman, Ronald 171, 977
Colt, Marshall 885a
Combs, Gary 913
Comer, Anjanette 611
Compton, Faye 248, 922
Connelly, Marc 629
Connery, Sean 14, 742a
Connolly, Walter 435
Connors, Chuck 357, 972
Connors, Michael 410
Conrad, Michael 655
Conrad, Robert 246, 621, 874
Conrad, William 162a, 196
Conried, Hans 203
Conroy, Kevin 564a
Considine, John 421
Constantine, Michael 128a, 778
Conte, Richard 858
Conti, Tom 581a
Converse, Frank 677, 691, 703
Conway, Kevin 564, 697a
Cook, Elisha, Jr. 99c, 244, 480, 945
Cook, Fred 636
Cooke, Wendy J. 331a
Cookson, Barrie 1009a
Cooper, Gary 40, 355, 447, 697, 795, 989, 1011b
Cooper, Garry 120b
Cooper, Gladys 403
Cooper, Jackie 506
Cooper, Philip 975
Copland, Maurice 621
Corbett, Glenn 155
Corbin, Barry 327a, 399, 484a, 535a, 672
Corby, Ellen 320
Cordova, Pancho 990
Corduner, Allan 659a

Corey, Jeff 131–132, 904
Corey, Wendell 508
Corfman, Caris 409a
Corkill, Danny 231b
Cornwell, Charlotte 583b
Corrigan, Douglas 191
Cortes, Lolita 547
Cortese, Valentina 328, 523, 956, 982
Cosell, Howard 52
Costa, Mary 924
Costello, Mariclare 659, 900
Costello, Ward 647–648
Costner, Kevin 742a
Cotten, Joseph 539, 628
Cotterill, Ralph 99b
Coulouris, George 156
Court, Hazel 285
Cowling, Bruce 674, 921
Cowper, Nicola 409a
Cox, Brian 666a
Cox, Courteney 810a
Cox, Ronny 123, 236, 440, 650
Coyote, Peter 414, 825
Craig, Michael 790, 601
Craig, Yvonne 585
Crain, Jeanne 617, 799
Cranham, Kenneth 1a
Craven, Frank 633
Craven, Gemma 983
Crawford, Broderick 6, 476, 634
Crawford, Joan 281
Crawford, John 174
Creaghan, Dennis 560a
Cregar, Laird 500, 712, 819
Crenna, Richard 124, 231, 601, 754a, 778a, 847
Crenshaw, Marshall 963a
Crews, Laura Hope 127, 286
Crewson, Wendy 603b
Crisp, Donald 289, 295, 546, 843, 960, 1021

Cristofer, Michael 626a
Crompton, Michael 529
Cromwell, Richard 626
Cron, Claudia 693
Cronkite, Walter 870
Cronyn, Hume 168, 187, 425, 759a, 856
Crosby, Bing 286, 300, 744 BoB
Crosby, Chris 1002
Crosby, Mary 197
Croset, Paule 147
Cross, Ben 198a, 436, 620, 742b
Crowden, Graham 159
Cruise, Tom 583a
Crutchley, Rosalie 311b, 656
Cryer, David 949
Crystal, Billy 947
Cuka, Frances 362a, 432
Culbertson, Rod 42
Culp, Robert 567
Culver, Roland 698
Cummings, Billy 929
Cupito, Suzanne 397
Currie, Finlay 329
Curtis, Alan 442, 881
Curtis, Jamie Lee 919
Curtis, Ken 991
Curtis, Tony 228a, 232, 359, 419, 484, 511, 611, 888, 907
Cusack, Cyril 94a, 159, 871
Cusack, John 759b
Cushing, Peter 554, 982
Cuthbertson, Iain 322a
Cypher, Jon 771, 807a

Dabney, Augusta 855
Dafoe, Willem 21a, 524a, 583a
Dahl, Arlene 548, 756
Dailey, Dan 231, 239, 476, 991
Dale, Cynthia 406b
Dale, Janet 760a

Dalton, Abby 448, 1014
Dalton, Timothy 144, 157,
   204, 430, 671, 745
Daltrey, Roger 630, 683
Daly, Tyne 962
Damon, Cathryn 334
Dana, Justin 767
Dance, Charles 302a
Dane, Karl 63
Dane, Lawrence 196
Danese, Connie 667b
D'Angelo, Beverly 128a, 646
Daniell, Henry 147, 882
Daniels, Bebe 934
Daniels, Jeff 302, 821
Daniels, William 2, 215, 231a,
   677
Danner, Blythe 315, 354, 554,
   686a, 908
Dano, Royal 308
Danson, Ted 440
Dantine, Helmut 810
Danton, Ray 35, 200, 241, 820
Danza, Tony 856a
D'Aquila, Diane 469a, 524b
D'Arbanville, Patti 48a
Darby, Kim 320, 781, 947
Darnell, Linda 148, 175, 279,
   608, 794, 930, 939, 1012
Darren, James 585
Darrieux, Danielle 8, 37, 597,
   864
Darrow, Henry 287, 1000a
Darwell, Jane 794
Da Silva, Howard 2
Daste, Jean 496
Dater, Alan 519
Davenport, Doris 40
Davenport, Harry 633
Davenport, Nigel 5, 398, 671,
   790
Davey, Belinda 607b
David, Clifford 231a

David, Clifton 766
David, Eleanor 22a, 406a
David, Michael 24
Davidovich, Lolita 633a
Davidson, Davey 350a
Davion, Alexander 631
Davis, Bette 295–296, 541,
   546, 682, 969
Davis, Brad 120a, 162a, 418,
   569a
Davis, Clifton 543
Davis, Daniel 198a
Davis, Judy 684, 877c
Davis, Marvin 929
Davis, Ossie 577
Davis, Sonny Carl 692a
Davison, Bruce 34
Dawson, Anthony 260
Dawson, Paddy 545b
Dax, Jean 864
Day, Dennis 198
Day, Doris 9, 47, 113, 304,
   547a
Day, Laraine 989
Day, Marceline 976
Day-Lewis, Daniel 94a
Dayan, Assaf 350
Days, Gabrielle 158
De Baer, Jean 406a
De Carlo, Yvonne 115, 539,
   719, 841, 982
De Cordova, Arturo 129
De Corsia, Ted 740
De Havilland, Olivia 16a, 93,
   151, 209, 295, 686, 896a
De Hetre, Katherine 271
De Lint, Derek 1a
De Louvres, Shane 5
De Marney, Derrick 970–971
De Niro, Robert 593
De Rossi, Barbara 734
De Sica, Vittorio 588
De Vaux, Renee 831a

De Vries, Jon 379a, 856a
De Witt, Jacqueline 234
De Wolfe, Billy 300, 688, 998
De Young, Cliff 628
Deacon, Brian 521
Dean, Margia 973
Debucourt, Jean 864
DeCamp, Rosemary 180, 692, 880
Dee, Frances 977
Dee, Ruby 19, 111, 406, 624a, 842
Deering, Olive 877a
Degischer, Vilma 333
Dehner, John 69, 591
DeHaven, Gloria 548
Dekker, Albert 67, 78, 675
Del Pozo, Angel 972
Del Rio, Dolores 264
DeLancie, John 691
Delon, Alain 164b, 956
Demarest, William 537–538, 618, 717, 998
DeMarne, Denis 778b
Dempsey, Martin 545b
Dempsey, Patrick 128a
DeMunn, Jeffrey 274, 307, 484a, 633a, 994
Dench, Judi 406a
Deneuve, Catherine 865
Denham, Maurice 406a
Dennehy, Brian 120a, 131, 569, 598, 720, 759a, 814, 828
Dennen, Barry 522
Denner, Charles 597
Depardieu, Gerard 164b, 216, 390
Derek, John 76, 634, 719
Dern, Laura 235, 892a
Derr, Richard 694
Desiderio, Robert 198a
Desmond, Florence 553

Desny, Ivan 46, 706, 903a, 1015a
DeSoto, Rosana 302b, 963a
Detmers, Maruschka 888a
Deuel, Geoffrey 155
Devane, William 309, 565
Devine, Andy 914
Dewhurst, Colleen 505a, 668, 716, 758, 1008
Dexter, Anthony 71, 903, 966
Dey, Susan 332
Dibbs, Kem 74
Dicenzo, George 661
Dick, Douglas 707
Dickinson, Angie 530, 664
Diedrich, John 333a
Dietrich, Marlene 137
Diffring, Anton 443
Dignam, Basil 260
Dillman, Bradford 329, 448, 539, 610
Dillon, Kevin 715a
Dionne Quintuplets 212–213
Dix, Richard 280, 444, 487
Dix, Robert 515
Dobie, Alan 302a
Dobson, Kevin 767
Doe, John 616a
Dolenz, George 466
Domin, Friedrich 955
Donald, James 96, 664, 790, 968
Donaldson, Lesleh 269a
Donat, Peter 628
Donat, Robert 24, 338, 433, 789
Donath, Ludwig 466, 537
Donlevy, Brian 64, 413, 441, 511, 841, 898, 902, 1012
Donnadieu, Bernard-Pierre 390
Donovan, Tate 754a
Doran, Ann 116, 676

Dorey, Reubin 492
Dors, Diana 860
Dorsey, Jimmy 256
Dorsey, Tommy 256
Dorziat, Gabrielle 864
Dotrice, Roy 484a, 721
Douglas, James B. 936
Douglas, Kirk 47, 276, 664, 907, 968
Douglas, Melvyn 281, 752
Douglas, Paul 984
Douglas, Robert 21, 253, 833, 850
Dourif, Brad 162a, 677
Downey, Robert 734a
Downs, Cathy 279
Doyle, David 793
Drake, Charles 82, 690, 732
Drake, Tom 844
Drescher, Fran 335
Dresser, Louise 137
Drew, Ellen 202, 505, 508, 977
Drier, Moosie 348
Driscoll, Bobby 21, 678, 929
Dru, Joanne 231, 267, 284, 634
Drury, James 802
Dublino, Daniele 713a
Ducaux, Annie 45b
Duff, Howard 115
Duffy, Patrick 626a, 947
Duggan, Andrew 475a
Duke, Patty 416a, 556, 988e
Dukes, David 878, 988d
Dullea, Keir 164, 228
DuMaurier, Gerald 134
Dumbrille, Douglas 903
Dun, Dennis 809b
Dunaway, Faye 184a, 199, 473, 682, 768, 778
Duncan, Lindsay 760a
Dundas, Jennie 905
Dundas, Jennifer 969

Dunne, Irene 226, 608
Dunnock, Mildred 739
Duperey, Anny 914a
Durning, Charles 99c, 489, 1000a
Dusenberry, Anne 573
Dutronc, Jacques 968a
Dutson, Todd 761
Duvall, Robert 12, 287, 292, 326, 509
Dvorak, Ann 594
Dyall, Franklyn 433
Dysart, Richard 59, 83a, 235, 399, 414, 723, 759a, 771, 773

Eareckson, Joni 271
East, Jeff 668
Eastwood, Clint 714
Eaton, Wallas 681
Eaves, David 761
Ebersole, Christine 721
Ebsen, Buddy 201, 203
Eccles, Aimee 796
Eden, Elana 868
Edge, Debbie 807
Edwards, Anthony 533
Edwards, Bill 898
Edwards, Bruce 138, 461
Edwards, Edward 421
Edwards, James 639
Edwards, Paul, Jr. 961
Edwards, Stephanie 917
Edwards, Vince 153
Egan, Eddie 287
Egan, Richard 303, 939
Eggar, Samantha 200b, 1019
Eichhorn, Christoph 778b
Eilbacher, Cindy 625
Eilbacher, Lisa 422, 584
Ekland, Britt 552a, 987
Elam, Jack 740

Elcar, Dana 509, 565, 657, 767
Eldridge, Florence 184, 218, 670, 847
Elfstrom, Robert 519
Elg, Taina 987
Elian, Yona 505a
Elizondo, Hector 951, 1020
Elliman, Yvonne 522
Elliott, Denholm 1a, 388, 797a
Elliott, Sam 235, 455, 486a, 545
Elliott, Stephen 422, 550, 561, 568, 677
Ellis, Edward 487
Ellis, Mirco 176
Ellis, Robert 680
Ellison, James 447
Elwes, Cary 891a
Emerson, Keith 299
Emo, Maria 460
Enriquez, Rene 336a
Epstein, Alvin 856a
Erdman, Dennis 727
Ericson, Devon 486a, 495, 808
Ericson, John 319
Erskine, Marilyn 116
Erwin, Stuart 975
Estevez, Emilio 72a
Euba, Wolf 809
Evans, Art 809a
Evans, Clifford 777
Evans, Gene 81a, 711, 815
Evans, Judi 312a
Evans, Linda 480
Evans, Maurice 363
Evans, Richard 66
Everett, Rupert 99, 298
Evers, Herb 319
Ewart, John 776
Eythe, William 50, 136, 1004

Fabares, Shelley 785
Fabiani, Joel 1000a
Fairbanks, Douglas, Jr. 134, 147, 251
Fairchild, Max 607b
Faith, Adam 683
Falk, Peter 612
Fantoni, Sergio 303
Farber, Arlene 288
Farentino, James 550, 758, 778
Fargas, Antonio 1008
Farger, Matthew 99b
Farmer, Frances 313, 444
Farnsworth, Richard 480, 695
Farnum, William 263
Farr, Felicia 486
Farrell, Glenda 742
Farrell, Mike 215, 254
Farrell, Nicholas 620
Farrell, Sharon 214
Faulkner, Graham 328
Fawcett, Farrah 258a, 455, 490, 581a
Faye, Alice 88, 341, 867
Faylen, Frank 680
Fejto, Raphael 658a
Feldshuh, Tovah 491, 663
Fell, Norman 705
Ferguson, Karen 327b
Ferraro, Chiara 638
Ferrell, Conchata 185, 604a, 840
Ferrer, Jose 142, 262, 362, 476, 484a, 525, 778, 780, 848, 953, 988d
Ferrer, Mel 381
Ferzetti, Gabriele 61, 407, 632
Field, Betty 717, 926
Field, Sally 90
Fields, Lew 133
Fields, Maurie 607b
Finch, Jon 592

Finch, Peter 14, 159, 284, 599, 741, 1000d
Finglass, Tom E. 928
Fink, John 628
Finlay, Frank 204, 875
Finney, Albert 529
Finney, Shirley Jo 866
Firth, Colin 99
Fischer, Bruce 714
Fisher, Carrie 35a
Fisher, Frances 422a
Fitz-Gerald, Lewis 142b, 708
Fitzgerald, Geraldine 564a, 1004
Fitzpatrick, Neil 142b
Fix, Paul 894
Flanagan, Fionnula 77, 379c, 545b, 997
Flanders, Ed 51a, 77, 231a, 491, 648, 853, 997
Fleetwood, Susan 302a, 583b
Fleischer, Charles 243
Fleming, Rhonda 169, 276, 449, 551a
Flemyng, Robert 219
Fletcher, Dexter 120b
Fletcher, Louise 475a, 874
Flon, Suzanne 953
Fluellen, Joel 534
Flynn, Errol 35, 190, 209, 253, 284, 295
Flynn, Steven 85a
Foch, Nina 156
Fonda, Bridget 552a
Fonda, Henry 48, 228a, 279, 362, 506, 510, 626, 647, 867
Fonda, Jane 426
Fontaine, Joan 487
Forbes, John 446
Forbes, Ralph 32, 73, 977
Ford, Glenn 413, 469, 602
Ford, Ruth 416
Ford, Wallace 486, 507

Forrest, Frederic 97a, 114, 180b, 334, 404, 505b, 666a, 863, 958a
Forrest, Steve 199
Forrest, William 116
Forslund, Constance 26, 705
Forsythe, Bill 691
Forsythe, Drew 681
Forsythe, Henderson 489
Forsythe, John 272, 679, 891, 904, 999
Forsythe, William 422a
Forte, Fabian 318
Fossey, Brigitte 144
Foster, Barry 684, 809c
Foster, Dianne 206, 857, 860
Foster, Dudley 893
Foster, Julia 316
Foster, Meg 229, 427
Foster, Preston 141, 321, 594, 752, 952
Foster, Susanna 435
Fourneau, Jean-Claude 526a
Fox, Colin 472
Fox, Edward 53
Fox, Emma Louise 901
Fox, James 269
Fox, Kerry 327b
Foxworth, Robert 549, 780, 791
Fraas, Gro 728
Francen, Victor 93, 205
Franciosa, Anthony 376
Francis, Anne 21, 86, 183, 549, 637, 972
Francis, Jan 143
Francis, Kay 747
Franciscus, James 419, 516, 561
Frank, Charles 535a
Frank, Gary 947
Frankel, Mark 137a
Franklin, Bonnie 878

Franklin, Pamela 398, 853
Franz, Eduard 329, 353b, 475
Fraser, John 503, 1000d
Fraser, Ronald 398
Frawley, William 88, 190, 869
Frederick, Lynne 432
Freed, Alan 336
Freed, Bert 582
Freindlikh, Alice 823
Freeman, Kathleen 128a
Freeman, Morgan 164a, 182, 821, 891a, 1000a, 1003a
Freeman, Paul 311b, 875
French, Bruce 863
French, Victor 1001
Fricker, Brenda 94a
Frisch, Max 339
Frizzell, Lou 863
Frobe, Gert 146, 642, 1015a
Fryer, Eric 326
Fudge, Alan 27, 697a
Fugard, Athol 394a
Fuller, Erwin 611
Fuller, Penny 988e
Furillo, Bud 785
Furneaux, Yvonne 284
Furstenberg, Ira 1015a
Furth, George 132, 888

Gaal, Franciska 589
Gable, Christopher 937
Gable, Clark 54, 770
Gabor, Zsa Zsa 953
Gaby, Sasson 180a
Gaines, Richard 678
Galffi, Laszlo 983
Gallagher, Peter 331a, 409a, 663
Galligan, Zach 949
Gam, Rita 23, 407, 982
Gammell, Robin 1009
Gammon, James 192

Garbo, Greta 160, 652, 735
Garcia, Andy 302b, 742a
Gardenia, Vincent 181, 564a, 641, 662, 885, 942
Gardiner, Reginald 250, 488
Gardner, Ava 39, 600, 865
Gardner, David 51c, 603b
Gardner, Joan 134, 251
Garfield, Allen 456, 640, 890
Garfield, John 880
Garland, Judy 844
Garner, James 217, 277, 603b
Garrison, Sean 940
Garson, Greer 107, 205, 368, 856
Gates, Larry 164, 855, 946
Gates, Nancy 673–674
Gauthier, Vincent 581a
Gavin, John 638
Gaynor, Mitzi 198, 617, 935
Gazelle, Wendy 21a
Gazzara, Ben 118, 243, 762
Geer, Ellen 1016
Geer, Kevin 703
Geer, Will 82, 173, 958
Geeson, Judy 158
Genn, Leo 262, 431
George, Christopher 155
George, Gladys 665
George, Joseph 22a
George, Lynda Day 516
George, Susan 499a
Gere, Richard 222
Gerroll, Daniel 620
Getty, Estelle 235
Giambalvo, Louis 996
Gibb, Donald 269b
Gibson, Mel 53, 905
Gielgud, John 33, 45, 107, 108, 110, 121, 248, 526, 600, 687, 725, 737, 755, 797a, 834, 908, 983
Gierasch, Stefan 320a

Gifford, Frances 280
Gift, Roland 552a
Gilbert, Henry 386
Gilbert, John 160
Gilbert, Lou 534
Gilbert, Melissa 254, 331, 556, 1001
Gilchrist, Connie 558
Gilford, Jack 15
Gillespie, Ann 1003
Gilliam, Stu 225
Gillibert, Jean 526a
Gillingwater, Claude 724
Gilmore, Virginia 794
Gilmour, Geoff 560
Gilpin, Jack 981a
Girafi, Chaim 180a
Girardot, Annie 734
Girardot, Etienne 133
Girotti, Massimo 14, 61
Gish, Dorothy 899
Gist, Rod 874
Glaser, Paul Michael 483, 697a
Gleason, James 846
Glen, Iain 100a
Glenn, Grosvenor 106
Glenn, Scott 692a
Gless, Sharon 691, 888
Glover, Danny 400a, 659a
Glover, John 426, 583
Glover, Julian 10, 505a, 659a
Goddard, Paulette 78
Gold, Tracey 334
Goldberg, David 521
Goldblatt, Harold 545a
Goldblum, Jeff 200a, 583
Goldoni, Lelia 194, 876
Goldwyn, Tony 90a
Gomez, Paulina 90a
Gomez, Thomas 62
Gonzalez, Erando 469a
Good, Constance 19

Goodwin, Bill 538
Goorwitz, Allen 945
Gordon, C. Henry 832
Gordon, Don 126, 152
Gordon, Ruth 289, 483, 623
Goring, Marius 161
Gorman, Cliff 322, 459, 775
Gossett, Louis, Jr. 111, 367, 655, 766, 873
Gottell, Walter 755
Gough, Michael 56, 959
Gould, Elliott 894a
Gould, Harold 249, 888
Goz, Harry 872a
Grable, Betty 250
Graboel, Sofie 353a
Graham, Bill 894a
Graham, Bob 935
Graham, Morland 927
Grahame, Margot 589
Grandy, Fred 231a
Granger, Farley 16, 742
Granger, Percy 775
Granger, Stewart 96, 151, 166, 297, 764, 877
Grant, Cary 313, 800
Grant, David Marshall 180b, 400a
Grant, Hugh 877c
Grant, James 760a
Grant, Kathryn 153
Grant, Lee 180b, 308, 734a
Grant, Richard E. 100a
Granville, Bonita 694
Grapewin, Charles 209
Grassle, Karen 1001
Graves, Peter 285, 845
Gravet, Fernand 923
Gray, Charles 150
Gray, Denise 933
Gray, Linda 420
Gray, Spalding 879
Grayson, Kathryn 707, 979

Grayson, Mary Anne 818
Green, Kerri 484a
Greenburg, Dan 473
Greenbush, Billy 807a
Greene, Lorne 81a, 762, 891
Greene, Michele 691
Greene, Richard 148, 285, 341, 910
Greenwood, Charlotte 312
Greenwood, Joan 104
Greer, Jane 145
Gregg, Everley 433
Gregorio, Rose 598
Gregory, Celia 157
Gregory, James 117, 266, 567
Gregory, Pascal 92
Gregson, John 599
Grevill, Laurent 164b
Grey, Joel 177
Grey, Virginia 482
Griem, Helmut 337a, 642, 778b
Grier, Pam 885
Grier, Rosey 729
Grifasi, Joe 765
Griffin, Merv 707
Griffith, Andy 455, 985
Griffith, Hugh 55, 644
Griffith, James 674
Grimble, Bill 723
Grizzard, George 97a, 569a, 1000a
Gronemeyer, Herbert 882a
Groom, Sam 569
Groomes, Gary 48a
Gross, Michael 189, 855
Guardino, Harry 118, 744
Guastaferro, Vincent 748a
Guest, Christopher 231a, 420
Guffey, Cary 97
Guillaume, Robert 164a, 566
Guinness, Alec 204, 328, 463, 603

Gulager, Clu 1003
Gulpilil, David 710
Gurie, Sigrid 795
Gurrola, Juan Jose 547
Guttenberg, Steve 94, 584
Gutteridge, Lucy 896a, 969
Gwenn, Edmund 226, 922
Gwynne, Michael C. 131, 320a, 486a, 927a

Habault, Sylvie 940b
Hackett, Buddy 1
Hackett, Gillian 240
Hackman, Gene 288, 400a, 768
Haddrick, Ron 333a
Hadley, Reed 321
Hafner, Ingrid 596
Hageman, Richard 128
Hagen, Uta 981a
Haigh, Kenneth 737
Haigh, Louisa 1000b
Haim, Corey 994
Hale, Alan 190, 253, 295, 514, 787, 797a, 884, 960, 1015
Hale, Alan, Jr. 68, 903
Hale, Barbara 537, 618, 637
Hale, Georgina 656
Hale, Jean 119
Hall, Brian 683
Hall, Ed 667a
Hall, Jon 125
Hall, Philip Baker 749
Hall, Porter 447
Hallaren, Jane 421
Hallwachs, Hans Peter 337a
Halsbog, Johan 728
Hamill, Mark 643
Hamilton, Antony 877b
Hamilton, George 416, 582, 1002
Hamilton, Linda 840
Hamilton, Margaret 15

Hamilton, Murray 629, 773
Hammond, Kay 624
Hampden, Walter 37, 979
Hampshire, Susan 5, 223, 754
Hampton, James 491, 1010
Hampton, Paul 686a
Handy, James 927a
Hankin, Larry 714
Hanno, Eva von 17
Hansen, John 544
Hanson, Preston 701
Harari, Clement 17
Hardie, Kate 51e
Hardin, Jerry 633a
Hardin, Ty 567
Harding, Ann 224, 475
Harding, Jeff 560a
Hardwicke, Cedric 396, 740, 834, 849, 910, 938, 1004, 1006
Hardy, Mashaune 182
Hardy, Robert 896a
Harewood, Dorian 323, 358a, 763
Harkins, John 697a
Harmon, Deborah 320a
Harmon, Joy 181
Harmon, Mark 97a
Harper, Robert 475a
Harper, Shari Belafonte 931
Harper, Valerie 896
Harra, Johnny 807
Harris, Cynthia 29a
Harris, David 1000a
Harris, Ed 170, 984a
Harris, Julie 91, 322a, 626a, 792, 896a
Harris, Julius 942
Harris, Richard 55, 204
Harris, Rosemary 96
Harrison, George 43–44
Harrison, Gregory 947

Harrison, Rex 98, 168, 608, 833
Harrold, Kathryn 59, 550, 944
Harrow, Lisa 438–439, 528
Hart, Christina 661
Hart, Dolores 329
Hart, Dorothy 115, 210
Hart, Mary 65
Hart, Roxanne 162a, 904a
Hartley, Mariette 622
Hartman, Elizabeth 815
Harvey, Joan 319
Harvey, Laurence 81, 389, 948
Haskell, David 422
Hasse, O.E. 112a
Hassett, Marilyn 579, 580, 792
Hasso, Signe 989
Hatch, Richard 34
Hatfield, Hurd 69, 411, 524, 838
Hatton, Raymond 278
Haudepin, Didier 350
Hauer, Rutger 144, 908
Hauff, Thomas 524b
Haupt, Ulrich 263
Hauser, Fay 809a
Haustein, Thomas 306
Haver, June 28, 250, 312, 488, 692
Havers, Nigel 42, 99b, 620
Havoc, June 353b, 469
Hawkins, Jack 135, 588, 603, 738, 743, 927, 1006
Hawthorne, Nigel 529
Hayakawa, Sessue 553
Hayden, Sterling 482
Haydn, Richard 55, 954
Hayes, Alan 595
Hayes, George 452
Hayes, Wesley 886
Hayman, David 969a

Haymes, Dick 28
Haynes, George 179
Haynes, Michael 318
Hays, Lee 992
Hayward, Brooke 181
Hayward, Louis 267
Hayward, Susan 220, 340, 378, 505, 574, 633, 858
Haywood, Chris 99b
Hayworth, Rita 261, 877
Healy, David 543, 560a
Heard, John 308, 573, 872
Hearn, George 775
Heartfield, John 424
Heckart, Eileen 855
Hedaya, Dan 951
Heflin, Van 532, 572, 810
Heggie, O.P. 978
Heinemann, Laurie 874
Heinrich, Mimi 552
Held, Martin 112a
Heller, Andre 882a
Heller, Randee 808
Hellerman, Fred 992
Helm, Levon 646
Helmond, Katherine 77, 258
Hemingway, Mariel 920
Hemmings, David 10, 114, 121
Hendrix, Jimi 429
Hendrix, Wanda 79
Henner, Marilu 404
Henreid, Paul 93, 591, 882
Henry, Gregg 598
Henry, William 960
Hepburn, Katharine 430, 670, 882
Hepton, Bernard 1a
Herbert, Hugh 923
Herd, Richard 52, 662
Herlie, Eileen 337
Hernandez, Juano 47

Hernandez, Maria 581
Herrmann, Edward 354, 733, 827, 853, 854, 905
Hershey, Barbara 311b, 320a, 524a
Hersholt, Jean 211, 212, 213
Heston, Charlton 98, 106, 108, 165, 242, 373, 449, 505, 520, 590, 618, 719
Heyman, Burton 51a
Heywood, Anne 873
Hicks, Catherine 703
Higby, Mary Jane 44a
Higgins, Brendan 142b
Higgins, Michael 30
Hiken, Gerald 759b
Hilboldt, Lise 988e
Hill, Arthur 332, 394, 481
Hill, Bernard 53
Hill, Dana 825
Hiller, Wendy 687, 709
Hillerman, John 154, 969
Hills, Denis 13
Hilton, Edward 221
Hindle, Art 475a
Hindman, Earl 985
Hines, John W. 544
Hingle, Pat 29, 83a, 180b, 213a, 535a, 693, 804
Hirsch, Elroy 457
Hirsch, Judd 309, 781, 965
Hobart, Rose 78
Hobbs, Peter 128a
Hobel, Mara 199
Hockney, David 467
Hodiak, John 174
Hodson, Don 892a
Hoffman, Dustin 95, 152, 157, 1007
Hoffman, Otto 624
Hogan, Bosco 240
Hogan, Jack 769
Hogan, Robert 566, 874

Holbrook, Hal 236, 426, 759a, 993, 1007
Holden, Gloria 1021
Holder, Ram John 126
Holiday, Kene 536
Hollander, Xaviera 472
Holloway, Stanley 619
Holloway, Sterling 881
Holm, Ian 298, 409a, 431a
Holm, Sonia 104
Holst, Maria 955
Holt, Hans 955
Holt, Jany 45b
Holt, Jennifer 178
Holtz, Jurgen 645a
Homolka, Oscar 831a
Hong, James 51c
Honorat, Roger 526a
Hood, Don 821
Hooks, Kevin 808
Hooks, Robert 958
Hoover, Elva Mai 326
Hope, Bob 327, 984
Hopkins, Anthony 53, 57, 311a, 406a, 430, 438, 459, 628, 687, 734, 780
Hopkins, Bo 418, 486a, 788, 811
Hopkins, Harold 776
Hopkins, Miriam 127
Hopkins, Rhys 616
Hoppe, Rolf 882a
Hopper, Dennis 710
Hopton, Russell 278
Horne, David 645
Horne, Geoffrey 810
Horsford, Anna Maria 872a
Horton, Michael 1022
Hoskins, Bob 734
Hossein, Robert 1015a
Houghton, Barrie 352
Houseman, John 309, 624a
Houser, Jerry 94

Houston, Donald 503
Houston, George 445
Hoven, Adrian 112a
Howard, Alan 200a
Howard, Clint 243
Howard, Ken 2, 215, 814
Howard, Leslie 698
Howard, Mary 64, 623
Howard, Ron 399
Howard, Trevor 55, 121, 146, 161, 642, 778b, 901
Howell, Peter 1009a
Howland, Jobyna 627, 934
Howlet, Noel 1009a
Hoyos, Rodolfo 973
Huber, Harold 125
Hubley, Season 804
Huckabee, Cooper 271, 1010
Hudson, Rochelle 31, 213
Hudson, Rock 408
Huffman, David 197, 315, 440, 1009
Hughes, Barnard 453, 759a, 894, 969
Hulce, Tom 721
Hull, Dianne 420
Hull, Henry 317, 506, 510, 590, 675
Hundar, Robert 402, 797
Hunnicutt, Arthur 791
Hunt, Helen 254, 657, 691, 872b
Hunt, Linda 949a
Hunt, Martita 45, 685
Hunter, Bill 607b
Hunter, Ian 64, 599, 747, 835
Hunter, Jeffrey 18, 206, 208, 514, 524, 730, 961
Huppert, Isabelle 92, 599a
Hurt, John 143, 158, 302a, 398, 552a, 687
Hussey, Ruth 532, 906
Hussman, Ron 1019

Huster, Francis 782
Huston, John 228
Huston, Karen 838
Huston, Walter 70, 180, 224, 278, 624, 831a
Hutchinson, Josephine 772
Hutton, Betty 392, 751, 887, 998
Hutton, Lauren 793
Hutton, Robert 787, 1015
Hutton, Timothy 83a, 727
Hyde-White, Wilfrid 215
Hyer, Martha 779
Hyland, Diana 774
Hylands, Scott 196, 1009
Hylton, Richard 231
Hyson, Dorothy 928

Ihnat, Steve 277
Ingham, Barrie 320a
Ingram, Rex 1002
Irazoque, Enrique 518
Ireland, Jill 963
Ireland, John 276, 321, 634, 703
Irizarry, Vince 327a
Irons, Jeremy 981a
Irving, Amy 16a
Isaac, Alberto 809c
Isbell, Tom 754a
Ittimangnaq, Zachary 720

Jack, Wolfman 34
Jackson, Anne 595, 684, 792, 870, 945
Jackson, Glenda 51, 671, 739, 741, 875, 901, 937
Jackson, Gordon 613, 754
Jackson, Sherry 257
Jacobi, Derek 431a, 908
Jacobi, Lou 330
Jacobini, Maria 722
Jacobs, Lisa 362a

Jaeckel, Richard 72, 400, 816
Jaeger, Frederick 386
Jaffe, Sam 137, 415
Jaffrey, Saeed 613, 809c
Jagger, Dean 420, 482, 571, 1012
Jagger, Mick 560
James, Clifton 861a
James, Gennie 231b
James, Godfrey 734a
James, Ron 269a
Jameson, Brian 42
Janssen, David 860
Janssen, Else 882
Jarlo, Gro 728
Jarman, Claude, Jr. 18
Jarrett, Renne 236
Jarvis, Graham 231a
Jarvis, Martin 459
Jason, Mitchell 856a
Jason-Leigh, Jennifer 993
Jayston, Michael 741, 743
Jeanmaire 16
Jeans, Ursula 285
Jeffreys, Anne 244
Jeffries, Lionel 1000d
Jenn, Michael 99
Jenner, Bruce 384
Jenney, Lucinda 48a, 692a
Jens, Salome 962
Jergens, Adele 887
Jergens, Diane 676
Jewel, Jimmy 583b
Jewell, Isabel 886
Jillian, Ann 397, 524b, 995
Jinnette, Betty 128a
Johann, Zita 141
John, Rosamund 698
John, Shannon 489
Johns, Glynis 959, 969
Johnson, Arte 1

Johnson, Ben 143, 155, 245, 336a
Johnson, Kay 63
Johnson, Richard 108, 402, 420, 878
Johnson, Rita 282
Johnson, Van 255
Johnston, Amy 474
Johnston, John Dennis 320a
Johnston, Margaret 338
Jolson, Al 88, 325
Jones, Allan 435
Jones, Carolyn 740
Jones, Dean 183, 625
Jones, Dickie 960
Jones, Freddie 165, 438
Jones, Gordon 594
Jones, Henry 132
Jones, James Earl 453, 523, 534, 835b, 1003a
Jones, Jeffrey 721, 988e
Jones, Jennifer 33, 50
Jones, L.Q. 791
Jones, Shirley 27, 258
Jones, Tommy Lee 366, 491, 646
Jonfield, Peter 502
Jorah, Samson 720
Jordan, Richard 51a, 331a, 459, 586, 848a
Jordan, William 577
Jory, Victor 152, 264, 280, 555, 1013
Jourdan, Louis 62, 142
Joy, Robert 936
Joyce, Brenda 341
Judd, Edward 5
Julia, Raul 81a, 734a, 848a
Jurado, Katy 72
Jurgens, Curt 24, 981
Justice, James Robertson 184, 200b, 220, 865, 883, 959

Kadochnikev, Piotr 498
Kagan, Diane 636
Kaplan, Gabe 667b
Karlen, John 172
Karlin, Miriam 362a
Karloff, Boris 835, 859
Karlsen, Jim 130
Karras, Alex 101, 123, 793, 1016
Kasatu, Clyde 485
Kashfi, Anna 413
Katt, William 131
Kaufman, Christine 188
Kava, Caroline 583a
Kavner, Julie 872
Kaye, Danny 16, 744
Keach, James 513
Keach, Stacy 473, 513, 644
Keane, Kerrie 196, 672, 835a
Keating, Larry 946
Keaton, Diane 827, 905
Keel, Howard 113, 751, 779
Keen, Geoffrey 3, 5, 13, 871
Keen, Malcolm 405, 970
Kehoe, Jack 268
Keir, Andrew 790
Keitel, Harvey 456, 524a, 894a
Keith, Brian 81a, 425, 802, 818, 973
Keith, Ian 160, 167, 624, 670, 832
Keith, Penelope 600
Keith, Robert 304, 887
Kellaway, Cecil 297, 329, 602
Keller, Marthe 137a
Kellerman, Sally 233
Kellin, Mike 228a
Kelly, Gene 218, 844
Kelly, James F. 475a, 535a, 566
Kelly, Joseph 269a
Kelly, Nancy 275, 510, 910

Kelly, Paul 191, 694
Kelly, Paula 809a
Kelly, Rachel 870
Kelly, Robert 988e
Kelsey, Linda 120, 697a, 853
Kelton, Pert 752
Kemmerling, Warren 900
Kemp, Gary 583b
Kemp, Jeremy 873, 778b
Kemp, Martin 583b
Kemp-Welch, Joan 531
Kempson, Rachel 56
Kendall, Felicity 967
Kendall, Suzy 614
Kennedy, Arthur 93, 209, 730, 1013
Kennedy, Douglas 897
Kennedy, George 35a, 228a, 425
Kennedy, Jihmi 891a
Kent, Jean 596, 619
Kenyon, Doris 401, 980
Keogh, Alexia 327b
Kercheval, Ken 114, 481, 739
Kerlow, Max 547
Kerns, Joanna 914b
Kerr, Deborah 107, 297, 314, 609, 777
Kerslake, Rosie 57
Kerwin, Brian 814
Kerwin, Shane 568
Kessler, Wulf 880a
Kestelman, Sara 630
Keyes, Evelyn 538
Kikumura, Akemi 485
Kiley, Richard 667a
Kilmer, Val 66a, 99c, 715a
King, Andrea 756, 787, 884
King, Dennis 978
King, Morgana 825a
King, Perry 323, 554, 810a
Kingsford, Walter 273

Kingsley, Ben 346, 894a, 1000b
Kinnear, Roy 404
Kinski, Nastassia 882a
Kippen, Manart 224
Kirby, Bruce 748a
Kirby, Bruno 941
Kirby, Max 405
Kirk, Phyllis 83
Kirkland, Sally 835b
Kirkwood, Pat 948
Kirsten, Dorothy 128
Kitt, Eartha 406
Klein, Robert 792
Klemperer, Werner 291
Kline, Kevin 51e
Klugman, Jack 416
Kmit, Leonid 145a
Knell, David 399
Knight, Cindi 985
Knight, Esmond 431, 922
Knight, Shirley 7, 310, 586
Knowles, Patric 553
Knox, Alexander 25, 554, 571, 1004
Kohner, Susan 337, 585, 779
Kolb, Clarence 313
Koller, Lawrence 807
Kopecky, Milos 238
Korhel, Erna 45c
Korjus, Milza 923
Korman, Harvey 1
Kortner, Willy 466
Kosinski, Jerzy 827
Kosleck, Martin 460, 462
Kremer, Gidon 882a
Krige, Alice 222, 336a, 835a, 892a, 986
Kristel, Sylvia 652a
Kristofferson, Kris 72, 512
Krabbe, Jeroen 311b
Kraus, Peter 925
Krause, Willy 464

Kroeger, Berry 353b, 694
Kronos 221
Kruger, Hardy 14
Kruger, Otto 289, 930
Kruschen, Jack 825a
Kukura, Juraj 238
Kuphal, Jens 306
Kurtz, Swoosie 605, 994

Laborteaux, Matthew 649
Labourier, Dominique 861
Ladd, Alan 83, 680
Ladd, Cheryl 559, 672
Ladd, Diane 559
Ladengast, Walter 416b
Lafleur, George 769b
Lafon, Yoland 45b
Lafont, Bernadette 949a
Lagrange, Valerie 713
Lake, Greg 299
Lamarr, Hedy 877a
Lamb, Larry 285a
Lambert, Christopher 367c
Lamour, Dorothy 300
Lampe, Jutta 301
Lampert, Zohra 909
Lancaster, Burt 30, 177, 276,
    667a, 718, 778a, 926, 943
Lancaster, Stuart 701a
Lanchester, Elsa 433, 830
Land, Paul 663
Landau, Martin 958a
Landey, Clayton 748a
Landgrebe, Gudrun 826
Landis, Carole 261
Landon, Michael 305, 595,
    1001
Lane, Diane 112
Lane, Jocelyn 318
Lane, Paula 701a
Lang, June 211
Lang, Matheson 259
Lange, Hope 514, 517

Lange, Jessica 170, 307, 322
Langella, Frank 35a
Langland, Liane 1003
Langlois, Lisa 856a
Langton, David 150
Lansbury, Angela 877a, 969
Lanza, Mario 128
LaPaglia, Anthony 748a
Larkin, Byran 583a
Larsen, Keith 200
Larsson, Lotta 17
Laughton, Charles 32, 54,
    297, 433, 576, 830, 877
Laurie, Piper 389a, 459, 818,
    995
Lauter, Ed 530, 773, 861a
Lavin, Linda 962
Law, John Phillip 838
Lawford, Peter 410
Lawrence, Gertrude 830
Lawrence, Jody 903
Lawrence, Muriel 324
Lawrence, Stephanie 285a
Lawson, Leigh 328
Lawson, Richard 361a
Lawson, Wilfrid 405, 902
Le Coq, Bernard 968a
Le Mesurier, John 499
Le Royer, Michel 588
Leachman, Cloris 245, 583
Leake, Cynthia 97
Learned, Michael 112, 186
Lebrun, Danielle 164b
Leduc, Valentina 547
Lee, Anna 441
Lee, Belinda 188
Lee, Christopher 150, 824
Lee, Kaaren 604a
Lee, Larry 519
Lee, Michele 1
Lee, Ruta 291
Lee, Stephen 963a
Leeds, Andrea 325

Leeds, Elissa 320a
Leeds, Thelma 313
Lefevre, Pierre 645
Lehne, Frederic 102, 715
Lehne, John 335, 361a, 682
Leibman, Ron 383
Leigh, Janet 481
Leigh, Spencer 120b
Leigh, Vivien 166, 294, 403
Leigh-Hunt, Barbara 432
Leighton, Margaret 592, 741, 927
Leipnitz, Harald 402
LeMat, Paul 268, 490, 778a
Lemmon, Jack 331a, 413, 478
Lennon, John 43–44
Leno, Jay 335
Lenz, Kay 549, 1008
Leon, David 41
Leonard, David 305
Lerner, Michael 316, 421, 705, 863
Leroux, Maxime 164b
Leslie, Joan 180, 1011b
Leuwerik, Ruth 955
Levant, Oscar 358, 935
Levels, Calvin 1003a
Levene, Sam 416, 869
Levin, Rachel 90a
Lewis, Fiona 630, 893
Lewis, Furry 807
Lewis, Geoffrey 29a, 760
Lewis, Jenny 1022
Lewis, Kim 936a
Lezana, Sara 730
Licht, Jeremy 124
Ligon, Tom 316
Lill, Dennis 379b
Lima, Altair 895a
Linden, Eric 731
Linden, Hal 320a
Lindfors, Viveca 253, 262, 524b, 703, 810, 868

Lindsay, Margaret 980
Lineback, Richard 809c
Linne, Velta 823
Linton, John 379a
Lisi, Virna 184a
Lister, Francis 171, 184, 836
Litel, John 897
Little Richard 336
Little, Cleavon 885
Little, Clifton 766
Liu, Harrison 51d
Lloyd, Danny 621
Lloyd, Doris 667
Lloyd, Jimmy 817
Lloyd, Kathleen 660
Lo Pipero, Giusto 892a
LoBianco, Tony 44a, 288, 505a, 524a, 662
Locke, Sondra 172
Locke, Terence 701
Lockhart, Gene 270, 282, 623
Lockwood, Gary 549
Lodge, John 137
Lofton, Cary 773a
Logan, Gwendolin 401
Loggia, Robert 21a, 90a, 520, 684
Lollobrigida, Gina 61, 142
Lom, Herbert 779, 974, 981
London, Julie 820
London, Tony 969a
Lone, John 809b
Long, Audrey 938
Long, Jodi 422a
Long, Michael 936a
Long, Richard 511
Lonsdale, Michael 914a
Lopez, Sylvia 437
Loren, Sophia 242, 638, 951
Lorimer, Louise 457
Lorre, Peter 551a
Lorys, Diana 730
Loudon, Alexandra 968a

Louis, Willard 252
Louise, Anita 264, 665, 772
Love, Montagu 401
Love, Victor 358a
Lovejoy, Frank 9, 210, 547a, 1002, 1014
Lovell, Raymond 789
Lowe, Edmund 244
Loy, Myrna 364, 365, 678, 770, 1018
Lozano, Margarita 713a
Lu, Lisa 434
Lucci, Susan 16a, 359
Luisi, James 606
Lukoye, Peter 3, 5
Lund, John 78, 998
Lundigan, William 169, 256
Lupino, Ida 93
Lupo, Alberto 98, 437
LuPone, Patti 535a
Lupton, John 18
Lydon, James 226
Lynas, Jeff 120, 650
Lynch, Alfred 195
Lynch, Ken 769
Lynch, Kenneth 472
Lynley, Carol 411
Lynn, Diana 898, 899
Lynn, Rhonda 807
Lyon, Sue 582
Lyons, Robert F. 94
Lyons, Tony 545b

MacBride, Donald 191
MacDonald, Jeanette 978
MacGinnis, Niall 645
Macht, Stephen 272, 640, 877b
Mackay, Dana 807
Mackay-Payne, Bronwyn 333a
Mackenzie, Patch 701
MacLachlan, Janet 20, 917

MacLachlan, Kyle 715a
MacMahon, Aline 116, 934
MacMurray, Fred 273, 341, 618, 839
MacRae, Gordon 239, 692
Macready, Susan 219
Macy, Bill 888
Madden, Donald 2
Madsen, Virginia 423, 734a
Magee, Patrick 92, 644
Mahan, Larry 654
Maher, Joseph 308
Majors, Lee 803
Makepeace, Chris 326
Mako 236
Maksimovic, Dragan 394a
Malave, Kelvin 454
Malden, Karl 94, 651, 773a, 786, 926, 1022
Malkovich, John 343, 879
Mallalieu, Aubrey 777
Malone, Dorothy 35, 145
Malone, Nancy 51a, 993
Mancuso, Nick 409
Mander, Miles 433
Manesse, Gaspard 658a
Mangano, Silvana 810
Mann, Margaret 247
Manning, Irene 36, 180
Manoth, Joseph 809
Mansfield, Jayne 820
Manson, Alan 604
Mantegna, Joe 894a
Marais, Jean 799
March, Fredric 8, 32, 140, 184, 218, 589, 670, 960
March, Hal 116
Margo 731
Marion, Beth 445
Markham, David 861
Markham, Monte 892
Marley, John 12, 311, 639, 705
Marotte, Carl 603b

Marriott, Sylvia 492
Mars, Kenneth 566
Marsh, Joan 141
Marshal, Alan 735, 770
Marshall, E.G. 564a, 610, 647, 851
Marshall, Herbert 62, 273, 296, 353
Marshall, Ken 797a
Marshall, Penny 829
Marshall, Shary 1002
Martin, Marion 675
Martin, Mary 435, 800
Martin, Nan 579–580, 649
Martin, Pamela Sue 874
Martin, Ross 274
Martin, Strother 132
Martinelli, Elsa 798
Martino, Giovanni 627
Marvin, Lee 530
Mason, James 37, 107, 502, 575, 742b, 849, 850, 865
Mason, Madison 407a
Mason, Marsha 360, 896
Mason, Tom 605
Massari, Lea 615
Massart, Clemence 940b
Massen, Osa 633
Massey, Anna 99, 228
Massey, Daniel 51, 552a, 601
Massey, Ilona 881
Massey, Raymond 76, 220, 294, 623, 757, 837, 884
Masters, Ben 97a
Mastrantonio, Mary Elizabeth 734a
Masur, Richard 302, 479, 490, 605, 681a, 862, 984a, 988, 988a
Matheson, Tim 997
Mathews, Kerwin 716, 925
Mathias, Bob 676

Mathias, Melba 676
Matlin, Marlee 984a
Matshikiza, John 51e, 659a
Mattes, Eva 809
Matthews, Francis 824
Matthews, Jessie 922
Mature, Victor 200, 261, 279, 407, 557, 877a
Maursted, Torval 386
Maxey, Paul 572
May, Donald 59
May, Jodhi 311b
May, Leora 1003
Mayer, Ray 594
Maynard, Bill 439
Mayo, Virginia 83, 833
Mayron, Melanie 308, 478, 986
Mazman, Melanie 231b
McAleer, Des 240
McAnally, Ray 94a, 499a
McArdle, Andrea 348
McArdle, Kip 44a
McCain, Frances Lee 762, 781, 878
McCallum, John 685
McCambridge, Mercedes 634
McCann, Chuck 995
McCarey, Rod 350a
McCarthy, Andrew 949a
McCarthy, Frank 754a
McCarthy, Kevin 177, 535a, 825a
McCarthy, Nobu 485
McCartney, Paul 43–44
McCleery, Garry 993
McClure, Greg 930
McCormick, Maureen 663
McCowen, Alec 431a, 901
McCraken, Jeff 693
McCrea, Joel 175, 486, 673, 717
McDermott, Mo 467

McDowall, Betty 499
McDowall, Roddy 87, 995
McDowell, Malcolm 110, 504
McEnery, Peter 745, 754, 1015a
McGann, Mark 607
McGavin, Darren 292, 320a, 984
McGee, Vonetta 225
McGill, Bruce 192, 927a, 949a
McGinn, Walter 154, 655, 854, 894
McGiver, John 625
McGoohan, Patrick 671, 714
McGrath, Graham 778b
McGraw, Charles 924
McGregor, Angela Punch 393, 681
McGuire, Biff 889
McGuire, Dorothy 520
McGuire, Michael 723, 769a
McHattie, Stephen 229, 668
McIntire, John 21, 673
McIntire, Tim 335, 1010
McKay, Peggy 854
McKay, Scott 255
McKean, Kris 650
McKellen, Ian 552a, 600
McKenna, Siobhan 524
McKenna, Stephen 42
McKenna, Virginia 3, 4, 33, 933
McKeon, Doug 659
McKeon, Nancy 327a
McKern, Leo 669, 709
McKinney, Bill 726
McLaglen, Victor 952
McLerie, Allyn Ann 26, 113, 1003
McLiam, John 417
McManus, Mark 560
McMartin, John 586, 624a, 667a, 733

McNally, Stephen 653
McNamara, Maggie 76
McNichol, Kristy 389a
McPeak, Sandy 604a
McPhatter, Clyde 336
McQueen, Steve 152, 480, 944
McShane, Ian 559
McStay, Michael 57
Medford, Kay 86, 829
Medina, Ofelia 547
Medina, Patricia 966
Meek, Donald 313, 626
Meeker, Ralph 119, 887
Mei, Wu Jun 809b
Meillon, John 776
Meinrad, Josef 955
Melton, Sid 470
Menjou, Adolphe 31
Menzies, Heather 679
Mercer, Freddie 794
Mercer, Marian 760
Mercier, Michele 402
Mercouri, Melina 350, 425
Meredith, Burgess 564, 653, 679, 817
Meredith, Don 861a
Merivale, Philip 571
Merkel, Una 624
Merlin, Jan 1014
Merman, Ethel 688
Merrill, Gary 232
Merrow, Jane 430, 739
Metzler, Jim 778a
Meyer, Emile 515
Mezzogiorno, Vittorio 734
Michael, Brian 42
Michael, Gertrude 167
Michell, Keith 223, 260, 505a, 517
Mickelbury, Denise 416a
Middleton, Charles 401
Middleton, Guy 619

Middleton, Ray 324
Midkiff, Dale 407a, 807a
Milan, Lita 69
Miles, Joanna 516
Miles, Sarah 302a, 592
Miles, Vera 293, 481, 554, 984
Milford, John 271
Milford, Penelope 172, 715
Miljan, John 452
Milland, Ray 151, 742
Miller, Allan 94, 1008
Miller, Dennis 142b
Miller, Eve 9, 846
Miller, Hugh 971
Miller, Jason 316, 703, 990
Miller, Kristine 75
Miller, Linda 807a
Miller, Linda G. 715
Miller, Rebecca 331a
Miller, Sidney 317
Millican, James 210
Mills, John 162, 402, 592, 789,
883
Milner, Martin 610
Milo, Sandra 437
Miluwi, John Omirah 322a
Mineo, Sal 585
Miner, Jan 95
Minn, Haunani 194
Minnelli, Liza 994
Mira, Brigitte 416b
Miracle, Irene 418
Mirren, Helen 51d, 110
Mitchell, Cameron 105, 304,
566, 736, 857
Mitchell, James 775
Mitchell, Thomas 175, 839,
929, 1004
Mitchell, Yvonne 51, 924,
1000d
Mitchum, Robert 423, 817,
974
Miyori, Kim 607

Mobley, Mary Ann 246
Modglin, Dara 416a
Modine, Matthew 905
Moeller, Gunnar 734a
Moffat, Donald 334, 486a, 997
Molina, Alfred 760a
Moody, Lynne 1003a
Monoson, Lawrence 90a
Montague, Lee 328, 656
Montalban, Ricardo 545a, 729
Montand, Yves 632
Montenegro, Conchita 722
Monteros, Rosenda 973
Montez, Maria 147
Montgomery, Belinda J. 579–
580, 662
Montgomery, Elizabeth 77,
697, 791, 913
Montgomery, George 202,
674
Montgomery, Julie 194
Mooney, Debra 379a
Moore, Grace 627
Moore, Mary Tyler 603b,
624a, 847
Moore, Norma 786
Moore, Pauline 179
Moore, Roger 602
Moorehead, Agnes 270, 514,
574, 921
Morales, Esai 963a
Morant, Richard 607, 656
Morante, Marcello 518
Morawski, Cezary 528
More, Kenneth 25, 614, 883
Morea, Valerie 353a
Moreau, Jeanne 135
Morel, Jean 666
Morell, Andre 158
Moreno, Rita 609, 778, 979
Morgan, Debbi 358a, 763
Morgan, Dennis 36, 756, 884,
1013

Morgan, Frank 140, 921, 1018
Morgan, Henry 690
Morgan, Michele 597, 666
Morgan, Ralph 442, 823a
Morgan, Wendy 42
Moriarty, Cathy 593
Moriarty, Michael 748a, 1009
Morier-Genoud, Philippe 658a
Morison, Patricia 442, 631
Morley, Karen 652
Morley, Robert 96, 204, 363, 398, 665, 685, 789, 928, 1000c
Morrill, Priscilla 414
Morris, Barboura 558
Morris, Haviland 988e
Morris, Mary 971
Morris, Wayne 1013, 1015
Morrow, Jeff 486
Morrow, Vic 266
Morse, David 365b
Morse, Helen 157
Morton, Clive 948
Morton, Gary 95
Moschin, Gastone 725
Mosley, Roger E. 12, 604
Moss, Arnold 1017
Mostel, Zero 135, 796
Motta, ZeZe 895a
Mouchet, Catherine 940b
Moulder-Brown, John 642
Mowbray, Alan 401, 403
Muir, Gavin 670
Muldaur, Diana 556
Mulgrew, Kate 891
Muller-Stahl, Armin 826
Mulligan, Richard 624a
Mulroney, Dermot 72a
Mundin, Herbert 54
Muni, Paul 156, 546, 772, 819, 1021
Munsel, Patrice 685

Murcelo, Karmin 505b
Murphy, Audie 67, 511, 732
Murphy, Ben 90
Murphy, Mary 897
Murphy, Michael 84
Murphy, Rosemary 426, 815, 853, 854
Murphy, Timothy Patrick 595
Murray, Bill 941
Murray, Don 164, 448, 657, 774
Murray, John T. 401
Murray, Stephen 248
Musante, Tony 950
Musaus, Hans 416b
Muse, Clarence 73
Myasnikova, Varvara 145a
Myers, Bruce 394a
Myers, Paulene 917

Nadhering, Ernst 46
Nagel, Conrad 122, 263
Naish, J. Carrol, 525, 751
Nares, Owen 248
Naughton, David 406b
Neagle, Anna 139, 161, 396, 531, 746, 970, 971, 1006
Neal, Patricia 365b, 643
Neal, Tom 507
Neeley, Ted 522
Neff, Hildegarde 597
Negret, Francois 658a
Neil, Hildegard 165
Neill, Sam 142b, 528
Nelligan, Kate 51c, 343
Nelson, Craig T. 231a, 455, 560a, 879, 895, 1000b
Nelson, Ruth 872, 1004
Nelson, Willie 436, 512
Nephew, Neil 181
Nero, Franco 137a, 965
Nettleton, Lois 213a, 290, 309
Neuwirth, Bebe 894a

Neville, John 503, 1000c
Nevins, Claudette 561
Newman, Barry 319, 651
Newman, Laraine 3
  35
Newman, Paul 39, 69, 132,
  177, 380, 428, 633a, 711,
  759b
Newmar, Julie 169
Newth, Jonathan 529
Newton, Robert 431, 531,
  850, 939
Newton, Theodore 980
Ngor, Haing S. 879
Nicholas, Paul 630
Nichols, Barbara 820
Nicholson, Jack 302, 827
Nielsen, Leslie 448, 979
Niklas, Jan 16a, 778b, 826
Nimoy, Leonard 684, 686a,
  715
Nitai, Niko 521
Niven, David 149, 653, 698,
  927
Noiman, Rivka 521
Nolan, Jeanette 1016
Nolan, Lloyd 457, 566, 839
Nolte, Nick 573
Noonan, Tommy 239
Nori, Enrique 990
North, Alan 164a
North, Sheree 239, 703
Northrop, Wayne 533
Norton, Edgar 263
Novak, Kim 265, 270,
  450
Novara, Medea 122
Novarro, Ramon 652
Novello, Jay 257
Novikov, Vassily 7a
Novotna, Jarmila 128
Nureyev, Rudolf 967
Nutter, Tarah 399

Oakie, Jack 313, 591
Oakland, Simon 568, 950
Oates, Warren 245, 911
Ober, Philip 314, 475
Oberon, Merle 156, 251, 433,
  500, 736, 848
O'Brian, Hugh 408
O'Brien, Edmond 107, 232,
  641
O'Brien, Erin 541
O'Brien, George 73, 756
O'Brien, Pat 138, 843
O'Connell, Arthur 232, 1002
O'Connor, Carroll 207
O'Connor, Donald 551a,
  688
O'Connor, Glynnis 97a, 186,
  412, 885a
O'Connor, Kevin 59
O'Conor, Hugh 94a
O'Dea, Denis 303
Offerman, George, Jr. 929
O'Flynn, Damian 75
Ogata, Ken 696
Ogg, Sammy 257
O'Grady, Timothy E. 545b
O'Hara, Maureen 82, 175,
  712, 991
O'Hare, Michael 754a
O'Herlihy, Dan 648, 738
O'Keefe, Dennis 469, 989
O'Keefe, Michael 120a
O'Keefe, Paul 15
Okhlopov, N.P. 7a
Oland, Warner 978
Olanick, Anita 469a
Olbrychski, Daniel 645a
Oldman, Gary 760a, 969a
Olek, Henry 550
Olin, Ken 927a
Olita, Joseph 13
Oliver, Edna May 133, 139,
  770

Oliver, Susan 272, 585, 1002

Olivier, Laurence 53, 294, 373, 403, 431, 778b, 834, 907

Olkewicz, Walter 114

Olmos, Edward James 21a, 192, 302b, 845

O'Loughlin, Gerald S. 120, 963

Olsen, Moroni 88

Olson, James 258

O'Neal, Ron 225

O'Neal, Ryan 258a

O'Neil, Barbara 835

O'Neill, Chris 545b

O'Neill, Dick 453

O'Neill, Maire 1006

Opatoshu, David 1019

O'Quinn, Terrance 505b

O'Quinn, Terry 208a

Orbach, Jerry 181, 336a

Oreste 979

Orlando, Tony 172, 845

Orlov, Dmitri 7a

Ormond, Julia 137a

O'Ross, Ed 312a, 692a

O'Shea, Michael 633

O'Shea, Milo 871, 878

Osmond, Marie 274, 761

O'Sullivan, Maureen 32, 267, 836

O'Toole, Annette 1010

O'Toole, Peter 45, 110, 135, 430, 603, 809b

Ousdal, Sverre Anker 17

Ovasapian, Samuel 582a

Overman, Lynne 282, 300

Owen, Reginald 264, 735, 1018

Oxenberg, Catherine 151

Pace, Diane 297

Pace, Judy 785

Pacino, Al 889

Padovani, Lea 545a, 699

Page, Gale 843

Page, Genevieve 242, 631

Page, Geraldine 120, 581a

Page, Joy 174

Paget, Debra 62, 173, 757, 906

Paige, Janis 1015

Palance, Jack 23, 214, 391, 501

Palette, Eugene 283

Palmer, Anthony 475a

Palmer, Byron 501

Palmer, Carl 299

Palmer, Gregg 732

Palmer, Leland 322, 967

Palmer, Lilli 228, 699

Pankow, John 781

Pantoliano, Joe 569a, 663

Papas, Irene 60, 615, 700, 718, 725, 742b

Parfrey, Woodrow 258

Paris, Virginia 302b

Park-Lincoln, Lar 605a

Parker, Cecil 166, 764

Parker, Eleanor 224, 602, 880, 946, 954, 966

Parker, Fess 18, 201, 203

Parker, Mary Louise 379a

Parker, Sarah Jessica 533

Parker, Willard 507, 515

Parkins, Barbara 568, 1019

Parks, Larry 337, 537, 538

Parks, Michael 320, 476

Parsons, Estelle 453, 765, 768

Pasco, Richard 824

Pasolini, Susanna 518

Pate, Michael 833

Patinkin, Mandy 877c

Patrick, Dorothy 572

Patrick, Gail 487

Patrick, Gil 178

Patrick, Nigel 924, 1000d
Patterson, Lee 499
Patterson, Neva 35
Paul, Guy 988e
Paul, Lee 27
Paulin, Scott 312a, 885a
Paull, Morgan 811
Pavan, Marisa 541
Pavese, Luigi 722
Pavlow, Muriel 25
Payer, Ivo 105, 221
Paymer, David 389a
Payne, John 250
Payton, Barbara 507
Peadon, Pamela 1019
Pearce, Gavin 988d
Pearce, John 509
Pearlman, Michael 949
Pearson, Richard 439
Peau, Stephane 390
Peck, Gregory 220, 314, 648, 755
Peeples, Cornelia 106
Pelikan, Lisa 914b
Pellegrin, Raymond 61
Pena, Elizabeth 963a
Pena, George de la 748
Pendleton, Nat 1018
Penn, Sean 83a, 993
Peppard, George 894
Percy, Esme 396
Perez, Barbara 961
Perier, Francois 914a
Perkins, Anthony 786, 847
Perkins, Emily 258a
Perkins, Millie 194, 330, 365b
Perkins, Osgood 264
Perreau, Gigi 882
Perrine, Valerie 95, 311, 996, 1019
Perry, John Bennett 274
Perschy, Maria 195

Persoff, Nehemiah 117, 803, 1019
Pesci, Joe 593
Peters, Bernadette 311, 877c
Peters, Jean 62, 193, 667, 1017
Peters, Roberta 493
Petrenko, Alexei 823
Petrie, Hay 1006
Pettet, Joanna 266
Pevtsov, Illarion 145a
Pfeiffer, Michelle 102
Philipe, Gerard 699
Phillips, Chynna 810a
Phillips, Leslie 552a
Phillips, Lou Diamond 72a, 302b, 963a
Phillips, Michelle 245, 967
Piazza, Ben 27
Pickens, Slim 729, 1016
Pickup, Ronald 362a, 748
Pidgeon, Walter 86, 205, 557, 848
Pigott-Smith, Tim 200a
Pilotto, Camillo 797
Pinsent, Gordon 936
Pinvidic, Margot 1011a
Pinza, Ezio 493
Pisier, Marie-France 92, 144
Pitts, Zasu 139, 226
Place, Mary Kay 1011a
Pleasence, Donald 200b, 432, 586, 888a
Pleshette, John 762
Pleshette, Suzanne 426a, 965
Plotnikov, Boris 778b
Plowright, Joan 331
Plummer, Christopher 137a, 146, 406b, 502, 738, 755, 790, 954
Pogue, Ken 695
Pohlmann, Eric 953
Poitier, Sidney 667a
Pollack, Cheryl 407a

Pollard, Michael J. 66, 768
Poole, Roy 2
Pope, Alexander 462
Porks, Gabriele 46
Porter, Eric 165
Post, Guy Bates 122
Poston, Tom 471
Potts, Annie 412
Potts, Cliff 214, 913
Powell, Robert 523, 656
Powell, Lovelady 471
Powell, William 226, 1018
Power, Tyrone 79, 88, 193,
    227, 265, 510, 665, 712,
    1012
Powers, Stefanie 666a, 828
Preiss, Wolfgang 112a, 588
Prentiss, Paula 622
Presle, Micheline 61
Presley, Priscilla 305
Press, Laura 30
Pressman, Lawrence 231a,
    290, 778a, 876
Presson, Jason 686a
Preussler, Anja-Christine
    882a
Price, Annabella 927a
Price, Dennis 104, 686,
    764
Price, Kenneth 607
Price, Vincent 50, 819, 835,
    1004, 1012
Prieto, Aurore 940b
Prim, Suzy 864
Primus, Barry 838
Prince, William 564, 871
Principal, Victoria 39
Prine, Andrew 555
Prinz, Dietmar 45c
Prochnow, Jurgen 305
Prosky, Robert 331a
Provine, Dorothy 769
Pryor, Maureen 746, 937

Pryor, Nicholas 636
Pryor, Richard 470, 809a,
    885
Pszoniak, Wojciech 216
Purcell, Lee 66, 320a, 491,
    885a
Purdom, Edmund 149, 437,
    638, 742b, 822
Purl, Linda 58
Pyle, Denver 626a

Quadfleig, Will 706
Quaid, Dennis 513, 872a-
    872b
Quaid, Randy 214, 418, 513,
    535a, 584
Quayle, Anthony 60, 223,
    599, 718, 741
Quillan, Eddie 54
Quilley, Denis 222
Quilligan, Veronica 630
Quinlan, Kathleen 382, 605a
Quinn, Anthony 28, 175, 603,
    700, 725, 798, 952, 968,
    1017
Quo, Beulah 27

Raab, Kurt 734
Racette, Francine 658a
Rafferty, Chips 850
Raffin, Deborah 112, 420
Raffoul, Francois 350
Raho, Umberto 713a
Railsback, Steve 661
Rainer, Luise 923, 1018
Raines, Cristina 112, 427
Rainey, Ford 1016
Rains, Claude 127, 166
Rambeau, Marjorie 145, 667
Ramer, Henry 472
Rampling, Charlotte 432
Ramsey, Logan 164
Ramus, Nick 545

Randell, Ron 524
Randolph, John 58, 231a
Randone, Salvo 367b
Ransome, Priscilla 10
Rasperry, Larry 807
Rasumny, Mikhail 608, 938
Rathbone, Basil 206, 795, 799, 835, 977
Ratray, Peter 621
Reagan, Ronald 9, 843
Rebhorn, James 621
Redeker, Quinn 544
Redford, Robert 56, 132, 1007
Redgrave, Corin 838
Redgrave, Lynn 471
Redgrave, Michael 361, 753
Redgrave, Vanessa 121, 137a, 157, 269, 310, 426, 671, 760a, 778b, 835a, 983
Reed, Alan 1017
Reed, Donna 618
Reed, Jerry 400a
Reed, Oliver 184a, 725
Reed, Pamela 268
Reed, Philip 202, 841
Reed, Robert 1, 601, 919
Reed, Tracy 919
Rees, Roger 920
Reeves, Steve 713
Regalbuto, Joe 426a
Regan, Mary 22a
Regas, George 73
Regehr, Duncan 66a, 320a
Regina, Paul 988, 988a
Reicher, Frank 627
Reichmann, Wolfgang 45c
Reid, Carl Benton 846
Reid, Elliott 218
Reilly, Jane 739
Reiner, Rob 829
Reinking, Ann 322
Remick, Lee 292, 420, 892
Remsen, Bert 271, 622

Remy, Ronald 961
Rendall, John 4
Rennie, Michael 37, 736, 757
Revere, Anne 508
Revill, Clive 877b
Rey, Alejandro 421, 559
Rey, Fernando 165, 288
Reynolds, Gene 191, 317
Reynolds, Marjorie 234, 300
Rhames, Ving 422a
Rhodes, Marjorie 948
Rhys, Paul 968c
Rhys-Davies, John 873
Ribeiro, Catherine 176
Richards, Paul 857
Richards, Terry 892a
Richards, Tom 333a
Richardson, Ian 57, 219
Richardson, James G. 293
Richardson, Miranda 298
Richardson, Ralph 737, 834, 983, 1000c
Richardson, Sy 984a
Richardson, William 422a
Richman, Peter Mark 233
Richwine, Maria 474
Ridgely, John 880
Ridgely, Robert 172
Ridges, Stanley 1011b
Rigby, Cathy 987
Rigg, Diana 108
Rilla, Walter 970–971
Rinaldi, Francesca 734
Rist, Robbie 249
Ritchie, Clint 119
Ritter, Thelma 340, 926
Rivera, Chita 33a
Rivero, Jorge 600
Robards, Jason 72, 108, 119, 268–269, 277, 416, 420, 426, 855, 875, 1003a, 1007
Robards, Jason, Sr. 122

Robards, Sam 949
Robb, David 150
Robbins, Gale 113
Roberts, Doris 331, 863
Roberts, Eric 885a, 920
Roberts, Pernell 999
Roberts, Rachel 649
Roberts, Roy 929
Robertson, Cliff 7, 312a, 509, 657, 920
Robertson, Dale 198, 214, 811, 812, 897
Robinson, Andrew 692a
Robinson, Bruce 492
Robinson, Edward G. 289, 719, 831, 934
Robinson, Jackie 842
Robinson, Jay 183, 296
Robson, Flora 134, 166, 294, 753
Robson, May 139
Robson, Wayne 695
Rocco, Alex 892
Roche, Eugene 840
Rodrigues, Percy 640
Rogers, Buddy 71
Rogers, Ginger 133, 653
Rogers, Paul 96, 159
Rogers, Roy 65, 179, 452
Rogers, Wayne 1011a
Rogers, Will, Jr. 846
Rohner, Clayton 400a
Roker, Ronny 225
Roland, Gilbert 257, 576, 686
Rolle, Esther 19
Rollins, Howard, Jr. 305a, 361a
Roman, Leticia 799
Roman, Susan 269a
Romanshin, Anatoly 823
Romero, Cesar 6, 85, 193, 212, 275, 836, 973
Romero, Ned 545

Roney, John 30
Rooney, Mickey 283, 317, 740, 844, 872a, 872b, 945
Rosay, Francoise 686
Roscoe, Frederick 106
Rose, Bianca 604a
Rose, George 499
Ross, Diana 470
Ross, Katherine 132, 455, 788, 996
Rossi, Leo 726
Rossi-Drago, Eleanora 221
Roth, Lillian 978
Roth, Tim 968c
Rourke, Mickey 840
Rowe, Misty 701, 701a
Roy, Rob 30
Royle, Selena 929
Rozemberg, Lucien 45b
Rubin, Benny 674
Rubinstein, John 622
Rudd, Paul 564
Ruddock, John 645
Rudley, Herbert 314, 358
Rudnick, Franz 301
Ruetting, Barbara 112a
Ruggles, Charlie 692, 899
Rumann, Sig 289
Running Fox, Joseph 495
Runyon, Jennifer 312a
Ruocheng, Ying 797a, 809b
Russ, William 835a
Russell, Betsy 810a
Russell, Bing 804
Russell, Gail 898, 899
Russell, Jane 70, 914
Russell, Kurt 804, 895, 999
Russell, Lisa Maria 198a
Russell, Rosalind 273, 571, 787
Russell, Theresa 231a

Russo, Michael 748a
Rutherford, Ann 444
Ruysdael, Basil 173, 203
Ryan, Edward 929
Ryan, Kathleen 184
Ryan, Meg 715a
Ryan, Mitchell 417, 569a, 651, 919
Ryan, Robert 138, 208, 277, 524
Ryder, Alfred 59

S, Bruno 416b
Saadetian, Onig 582a
Sacks, Michael 412
Sadoff, Fred 796
Saint, Eva Marie 236, 332, 651, 773
St. Jacques, Raymond 476
Saint James, Susan 434
St. John, Al 445
St. John, Betta 68
St. John, Howard 588
Sakall, S.Z. 36, 250, 312
Sakamoto, Ryuichi 809b
Saldana, Theresa 593, 638, 876
Salerno, Enrico Maria 956
Salinger, Matt 213a
Salmi, Albert 277, 861a
Salt, Jennifer 1020
Sampson, Will 123, 450
San Juan, Guillermo 990
Sanchez, Salvador 547
Sander, Otto 645a
Sanders, George 21, 139, 148, 149, 353, 500, 596, 688, 712, 833, 877a, 902
Sanders, Hugh 231
Sanderson, Martyn 379b
Sands, Julian 877c, 879
Sarandon, Chris 33a, 35a, 517
Sarandon, Susan 315, 734

Sartain, Gailard 633a
Saunders, Terry 609
Savage, John 84, 436, 440, 643
Savalas, Telly 123, 972
Savident, John 100a
Savoy, Teresa Ann 110
Sawyer, Joe 70
Sawyer, Margaret 948
Saxon, John 779
Sbragia, Mattia 713a
Scacchi, Greta 99b, 302a
Scala, Gia 981
Scarwid, Diana 199
Schade, Doris 301, 645a
Schall, Ekkerhard 983
Scheider, Roy 288, 322, 949
Schell, Maria 338, 908
Schell, Maximilian 137a, 290, 331, 426, 545a, 742b, 778b
Schellenberg, August 693
Schenkkan, Robert 988d, 1011
Schildkraut, Joseph 167, 227, 330, 1021
Schlesinger, Peter 467
Schmidinger, Walter 337a
Schmidt, Ania 454
Schnabel, Stefan 484
Schneider, Magda 333
Schneider, Romy 146, 333, 956
Schofield, Drew 969a
Schroder, Ricky 379a
Schuck, John 131
Schull, Rebecca 870
Schultz, Dwight 759b
Schwartz, Scott 994
Schwarzenegger, Arnold 660
Schygulla, Hanna 30, 778b
Sciorra, Annabella 981a
Scofield, Paul 362a, 686, 709, 933
Scott, David 807

Scott, George C. 309, 734a, 773–773a
Scott, Gordon 176
Scott, Kathryn Leigh 733, 773
Scott, Margaretta 1006
Scott, Martha 988, 988a
Scott, Randolph 275, 510, 576, 912
Scourby, Alexander 716
Seales, Franklyn 440
Seay, James 903
Seberg, Jean 526
Sedgewick, Kyra 99c, 583a
Sedgwick, Edie 886
Segal, George 119, 377
Seigner, Francoise 496
Selby, David 383
Sellars, Elizabeth 736
Selzer, Milton 581
Semmelrogge, Willy 416b
Seneca, Joe 866, 904a
Serato, Massimo 80, 188, 221, 799
Serna, Pepe 845, 999
Sety, Gerard 699, 968a
Seyler, Athene 259
Seymour, Anne 556
Seymour, Jane 223, 499a, 896a
Shankley, Amelia 409a
Shannon, Michael J. 560a
Sharif, Omar 16a, 86–87, 391, 575, 778b, 798, 865
Sharkey, Ray 48a, 124, 573, 663
Sharp, John 861
Sharpe, Cornelia 889
Shaver, Helen 51d
Shaw, Fiona 94a, 100a
Shaw, Martin 443
Shaw, Robert 162, 208, 709, 790
Shaw, Stan 904a

Shaw, Victoria 265, 981
Shawn, Wallace 760a
Shea, John 180a, 258a, 478, 564a, 669
Shearer, Norma 32, 665
Sheen, Charlie 72a
Sheen, Martin 231a, 254, 320, 350a, 564a, 565, 900, 904a, 911, 1003a, 1020
Shellen, Stephen 494a
Shelley, Barbara 824
Shenar, Paul 1019
Shepard, Sam 307
Shepherd, Jack 1000b
Shepley, Michael 405
Shepperd, John 794
Sheridan, Ann 36
Sheridan, Frank 141
Sherman, Kerry 550
Sherman, Robert 733
Sherwood, Gale 938
Sherwood, Madeleine 28a
Shigeta, James 940
Shiloah, Yossef 521
Shimoda, Yuki 485
Shire, Talia 154, 323
Shirley, Bill 324
Shoemaker, Ann 856
Shoop, Kimber 560a
Shumway, Lee 178
Siebert, Charles 556
Siebert, Oliver 880a
Sieppel, Edda 882a
Signoret, Simone 632
Sikking, James B. 781
Silva, Geno 495
Silva, Henry 448
Silver, Ron 862, 981a
Silvera, Frank 257
Simmons, Jean 297, 374, 736, 907
Simms, Ginny 800
Simms, Hilda 639

Simon, Francois 861
Simon, Josette 51e
Simpson, Russell, 278
Sinatra, Frank 617, 664
Sinclair, Madge 101, 187, 604, 606
Singer, Marc 120, 931
Singer, Raymond 426a
Sinjen, Sabine 337a
Sisk, Kathleen 1011a
Siyolwe, Wabei 51e
Skelton, Red 548
Skinner, Cornelia Otis 742
Skoda, Albin 464
Slate, Jeremy 701a
Slater, Christian 958a
Sloane, Everett 968
Sloyan, James 682
Slue, Errol 494a
Smith, Alexis 190, 482, 672, 800, 960, 984
Smith, C. Aubrey 137, 205, 832, 960, 970
Smith, Cathy 454
Smith, Charles Martin 474, 720, 742a
Smith, Constance 501
Smith, Cotter 569, 914b
Smith, Jaclyn 561, 745, 988d
Smith, Madolyn 583, 825a, 873
Smith, Maggie 753
Smith, Patricia 334, 629
Smith, Paul 519
Smith, Paul L. 873
Smith, Roger 145
Snow, Norman 988e
Socrate, Mario 518
Sokoloff, Vladimir 224
Solon, Ewen 499
Sommer, Josef 180b
Sondergaard, Gale 466, 546, 608, 1021

Sorenson, Linda 196
Sorvino, Paul 598, 827
Sothern, Ann 266, 625, 844
Sothern, Hugh 179, 589
Soutendijk, Renee 1000b
Spacek, Sissy 478, 573, 646, 821, 911
Spain, Fay 117
Sparks, Ned 286
Spillman, Harry 183
Spradlin, G.D. 293, 336a, 660
Stack, Robert 174, 444, 541
Stadlen, Lewis J. 481
Staley, James 170
Stallone, Sylvester 118
Stamp, Terence 367c, 394a
Stangertz, Goran 17
Stanley, Kim 307
Stanton, Harry Dean 97
Stanwyck, Barbara 752
Stapel, Huub 362a
Stapleton, Jean 249, 851
Stapleton, Maureen 302, 827
Starr, Ringo 43–44
Steel, Amy 781
Steele, Freddie 817
Steele, Karen 241
Steele, Tommy 893
Steenburgen, Mary 268, 362a, 504, 825
Steiger, Rod 117, 189, 311, 641, 697, 725, 738
Stephens, James 29a
Stephens, Robert 644
Stephenson, Henry 735, 882
Sterling, Jan 449, 536
Stern, Daniel 877b
Stern, Isaac 915
Stevens, Andrew 94, 530
Stevens, Connie 704
Stevens, Craig 884
Stevens, Fisher 981a

Stevens, Mark 312, 488, 590
Stevens, William 769
Stevenson, Juliet 200a
Stewart, David J. 612
Stewart, Elaine 241
Stewart, James 173, 281, 629, 690, 921
Stewart, Martha 488
Stewart, Paul 639, 669, 904
Stiers, David Ogden 81a, 194, 215, 475a, 649
Stirner, Brian 438
Stock, Barbara 692a
Stock, Nigel 195
Stocker, Werner 880a
Stockton, David 870
Stockwell, Dean 610
Stockwell, Guy 448
Stockwell, John 657
Stoler, Shirley 44a
Stoltz, Eric 235, 892a
Stone, Fred 40
Stone, Lewis 160, 652
Stone, Milburn 115
Storm, Gale 67
Storm, Roy 42
Stowe, Madeline 669
Straight, Beatrice 569a
Strasberg, Susan 950
Strathairn, David 85a, 208a, 759a
Strauss, Peter 568
Streep, Meryl 56, 142b, 302, 426, 895
Street, Elliott 812
Streisand, Barbra 86, 87
Strickland, Gail 840, 962
Stricklyn, Ray 515, 779
Strong, Michael 773a
Stroock, Gloria 568
Stroud, Don 29, 474, 838
Strudwick, Shepperd 67, 265
Struthers, Sally 483, 581

Stuart, Gloria 724
Suchet, David 83a, 311b, 733
Sukowa, Barbara 301, 645a
Sullivan, Barry 411, 675
Sullivan, Billy 1022
Sullivan, Francis L. 166, 184, 525
Sullivan, Lee 930
Sullivan, Sean 406b
Sullivan, Susan 34, 723
Summerville, Slim 211
Sundquist, Gerry 394a
Sundstrom, Frank 938
Surgere, Helen 92
Surovy, Nicolas 16a
Sus, Arthur 106
Susman, Todd 942
Sutherland, Donald 51c-51d, 130, 353a, 502
Sutherland, Kiefer 72a
Sutorious, James 778a, 828
Sutton, Dolores 316, 422
Sutton, John 129, 193, 261, 314, 819
Suzman, Janet 409, 600, 743
Svenson, Bo 813, 816, 917
Swan, Buddy 929
Sweet, Dolph 249, 577
Swenson, Inga 555, 1019
Swinburne, Nora 184, 531
Swinton, Tilda 120b
Swit, Loretta 312a
Sydney, Basil 831a
Szarabajka, Keith 821, 984a

Taegar, Ralph 6
Tafler, Sydney 25, 933
Takeshita, Oori 485
Talbot, Lyle 856
Talmadge, Norma 263
Talman, Ann 1020
Talun, Walter 220
Tamba, Tetzuro 940

Tambor, Jeffrey 569a, 873
Tamiroff, Akim 135, 545a, 589, 797a
Tamu 489
Tandy, Jessica 849
Tani, Yoko 797
Tanner, Clay 479
Tao, Wu 809b
Tasker, Harold 106
Tatlock, Jean 759b
Tavernier, Nils 599a
Tayback, Vic 611, 705
Taylor, Don 858
Taylor, Dub 768
Taylor, Elizabeth 96, 168, 226, 771
Taylor, Estelle 252
Taylor, Holland 151
Taylor, Kent 280, 952
Taylor, Mark L. 584
Taylor, Robert 6, 64, 281, 946
Taylor, Rod 150, 561, 776
Tchenko, Ivan 269
Tcherina, Ludmilla 23
Teague, Marshall 807a
Teasdale, Verree 264
Teeley, Tom 41
Teig, Lotte 728
Telezynska, Izabella 937
Tennant, Victoria 233
Ter Steege, Johanna 968c
Terry, Denine 350a
Terry, Nigel 22a, 120b
Tessier, Ventine 80
Testi, Fabio 734
Thatcher, Torin 484
Thaxter, Phyllis 255, 943
Thibeau, Jack 714
Thigpen, Lynne 164a, 667a
Thomas, Carmen 97
Thomas, Danny 547a
Thomas, Henry 494a
Thomas, Marlo 28a

Thomas, Richard 775, 1003
Thompson, Carlos 982
Thompson, Emma 431a, 877c
Thompson, Ernest 315
Thompson, Jack 99b, 379b, 708, 710
Thompson, Marshall 732, 961
Thompson, R.H. 931
Thomson, Kim 1a
Thorndike, Sybil 685
Thring, Frank 710
Thulin, Ingrid 718
Thundercloud, Chief 202, 356
Thwaites, Tolly 778b
Ticotin, Rachel 389a
Tierney, Gene 353b, 506, 819, 912
Tiller, Nadja 402
Tobey, Kenneth 201
Tobias, George 327, 690
Tobias, Oliver 652a
Tobisch, Lotte 464
Tocci, Bruno 105
Todd, Ann 285, 787, 903a
Todd, Beverly 164a, 766
Todd, Hallie 595
Todd, Richard 296, 361, 526, 666, 667, 959
Tomono, Hiroshi 940
Tompkins, Joan 544
Tone, Franchot 54, 281
Tonge, Philip 16
Toomey, Regis 532
Toone, Geoffrey 200b
Topol 344, 409
Torgov, Sarah 931
Torn, Rip 26, 213a, 231a, 336a, 475a, 476, 638, 825, 840, 862, 1003a
Torres, Fernanda 311a
Totter, Audrey 669
Touliatos, George 524b

Toumanova, Tamara 493
Toussaint, Cecilia 547
Toussaint, Lorraine 754a
Tracy, Lee 932
Tracy, Spencer 206, 218, 255, 282, 317, 910
Trantow, Cordula 460
Traubel, Helen 848
Travanti, Daniel J. 733, 988, 988a
Travers, Bill 3, 4, 33
Trebor, Robert 1020
Tree, Dorothy 461, 623
Treen, Mary 75
Trejan, Guy 783
Tremayne, Les 400
Trent, Anthony 683
Trevor, Austin 619
Trevor, Claire 212, 675, 869, 902
Trinder, Tommy 619
Tristan, Dorothy 309, 516
Trolley, Leonard 13
Truffaut, Francois 496
Tryon, Tom 868
Tselikovskaya, Ludmila 497
Tsou, Tijger 809b
Tucci, Michael 667b
Tucker, Forrest 40, 155, 449, 813–814
Tucker, Michael 759a
Tucker, Ulrich 880a
Tufts, Sonny 71
Turban, Dietlinde 734
Turco-Lyon, Kathleen 604a
Turkel, Joseph 769
Turman, Glynn 942
Turner, Barbara 291
Turonovova, Bozidara 238
Turturro, John 367c
Tutin, Dorothy 204, 351
Tuttle, Lurene 813
Twardowski, Hans V. 441

Tyrrell, Susan 909
Tyson, Cicely 182, 577, 835b, 866, 904a, 958
Tyzack, Margaret 150

Ullmann, Liv 90a, 159, 949
Underwood, Blair 835b
Ure, Mary 208
Urich, Robert 52
Ustinov, Peter 96, 161, 706

Vaccaro, Brenda 427
Valentine, Karen 369
Valk, Frederick 982
Vallone, Raf 184a, 242, 725, 755
Van Damme, Jean Claude 269b
Van Dyke, Jennifer 407a
Van Fleet, Jo 276
Van Nuys, Ed 985
Van Pallandt, Nina 894
Van Patten, Joyce 83a, 771, 851
Van Peebles, Mario 605a
Van Valkenburgh, Deborah 533, 914b
Vance, Vivian 483
Vannucchi, Luigi 956
Varconi, Victor 447, 462
Varsi, Diane 610
Vaughn, Robert 108, 733
Vega, Isela 81a
Veidt, Conrad 837, 976
Velez, Eddie 848a
Venora, Diane 189, 769a
Ventura, Lino 699, 963
Venture, Richard 564
Vera-Ellen 548, 688
Vereen, Ben 20, 87
Verney, Guy 645
Vernier, Claude 581a
Vernier, Pierre 783

Verno, Jerry 948
Vernon, John 456
Vestoff, Virginia 2
Victor, Henry 976
Vidal, Jacques 968a
Viharo, Robert 974
Villard, Tom 697a
Ville, Paul 496
Villeret, Jacques 782
Villiers, James 100a
Vincent, Frank 593
Vincent, Jan-Michael 197
Vinicius, Marcus 895a
Vinson, Helen 213
Vint, Alan 911, 913
Vint, Jesse 233, 913
Vitale, Milly 327, 407
Vitold, Michel 632
Vogel, Tony 797a
Vogelsang, Sybille 582a
Vogler, Rudiger 301
Vohs, Joan 457
Voight, Jon 187
Voldstedlund, Merete 353a
Volonte, Gian Maria 615, 641,
    713a, 871
Von Stolz, Hilde 955
Von Sydow, Max 17, 353a,
    520, 877b
Von Zerneck, Danielle 963a
Vosper, Frank 922
Vuu, Richard 809b
Vye, Murvyn 117, 239

Wade, Russell 138
Wagner, Lindsay 379
Wagner, Robert 340, 514, 906
Wainwright, James 90, 476,
    958
Waite, Ralph 765
Waites, Thomas G. 692a
Walbrook, Anton 262, 526,
    706, 970, 971

Walcott, Gregory 419, 680
Walden, Robert 811
Walden, Susan 1011a
Walker, Clint 972
Walker, Joyce 126
Walker, Kathryn 331a
Walker, Robert 255, 572, 882
Wallace, Coley 639
Wallace, Dee 417
Wallace, Morgan 65
Wallace, Shane 761
Wallach, Eli 180a, 194, 416,
    428, 575, 595, 944
Waller, David 616, 896a
Walsh, J.T. 48a
Walsh, Joey 16
Walsh, Philip 607
Walter, Robert 205
Walters, Julie 285a, 760a
Walters, Susan 807a
Wanamaker, Sam 603b
Wanders, Skippy 794
Ward, Fred 714, 913
Ward, Simon 162, 438, 463,
    613
Ward, Wally 605a
Warden, Jack 217, 450, 554,
    569a, 785, 870, 1007
Warner, Astrid 318
Warner, David 504, 888a
Warner, H.B. 971, 975
Warner, Jack 933
Warren, Betty 619
Warren, Jennifer 847
Warren, Lesley 965
Warren, Lesley-Ann 862
Warrick, Ruth 138
Warrington, Don 613
Wartha, Norbert 809
Washbourne, Mona 150, 901
Washington, Denzel 51e,
    681a, 866, 891a
Wass, Ted 29a

Wasson, Craig 412, 942
Waterman, Juanita 51e
Waters, John 708
Waterston, Sam 233, 624a, 727, 879
Watson, Bobby 461, 462
Watson, Mills 811
Watson, Minor 842
Wayborn, Kristina 347
Wayne, David 340, 493, 549, 935
Wayne, Ethan 81a
Wayne, John 81, 155, 415, 574, 902, 991
Wayne, Pat 81
Wayne, Patrick 72a
Weaver, Dennis 379a, 400, 422, 495, 533, 625, 723
Weaver, Fritz 336a, 423, 672
Weaver, Jacki 936a
Weaver, Marjorie 626
Weaver, Sigourney 322a
Webb, Chloe 969a
Webb, Clifton 364, 906
Wedgeworth, Ann 59, 170, 505b
Weidler, Virginia 283
Weissman, Mitch 41
Weitz, Bruce 426a, 919
Weld, Tuesday 316
Weldon, Joan 707
Welles, Mel 552
Welles, Orson 79, 221, 588, 610, 709, 738, 797a
Welling, Albert 57
Wells, Jacqueline 452
Wells, Veronica 638
Werner, Oskar 464, 706
West, Red 621
West, Timothy 745
Westby, Geir 728
Westcott, Helen 446
Westley, Helen 127

Weston, Jack 796
Whalen, Michael 211
Whaley, Frank 715a
Whalley-Kilmer, Joanne 552a
Wheaton, Wil 484a
Whitaker, Damon 769a
Whitaker, Forest 269b, 769a
White, Jesse 241
Whitelaw, Billie 583b, 737
Whiteman, Paul 256
Whitfield, Lynn 361a, 681a
Whiting, Leonard 790
Whitman, Stuart 217, 329, 539, 612, 868
Whitmore, James 265, 545, 680, 767, 946, 957
Whitmore, James, Jr. 417, 434, 993
Whitney, Mike 473
Whitney, Susan 257
Whitty, May 93
Wickes, Mary 547a
Widmark, Richard 81, 479, 526
Wiggins, Chris 936
Wilcox, Frank 67
Wilcox, Larry 214
Wilcoxon, Henry 167, 832, 877a
Wilde, Cornel 21, 148, 156, 188, 757
Wilder, James 494a
Wilding, Michael 21, 746
Wilker, Jose 895a
Wilkinson, David 42
Wilkinson, Tom 22a
Willes, Jean 674
William, Warren 167, 451, 867
Williams, Adam 786
Williams, Bill 921
Williams, Billy Dee 470, 543, 785, 951

Williams, D.J. 777
Williams, Dick Anthony 577, 958
Williams, Emlyn 262, 928
Williams, Esther 557
Williams, JoBeth 988, 988a
Williams, Kent 504, 573
Williams, Michael 57
Williams, Robin 872
Williams, Samm-Art 189
Williams, Treat 233, 475a
Williamson, Nicol 184a, 875
Willingham, Noble 102
Wills, Chill 912
Wilmer, Douglas 51
Wilms, Dominque 105
Wilson, K.J. 327b
Wilson, Perry 786
Wilson, Scott 904
Wilson, Stuart 986
Wilson, Trey 569a
Wilton, Penelope 51e
Wimberly, Roderick 182
Windom, William 90, 197, 566, 774, 894, 945
Windsor, Frank 436
Windsor, Marie 71
Winfield, Paul 111, 187, 305a, 577
Winningham, Mare 198a, 379a, 554, 604a
Winter, Alex 892a
Winter, Edward 888
Winters, Shelley 6, 29, 330, 704, 804
Wiseman, Joseph 1017
Withers, Mark 231b
Withrow, Glenn 874
Wolfe, Ian 475, 484
Wolfe, Nancy 661
Wolff, Frank 367b
Wolfit, Donald 45, 259
Wolk, Rainer 306

Wong, Victor 809b
Wood, Cindi 164
Wood, Natalie 397
Wood, Peggy 653, 868, 954
Woodard, Alfre 659a
Woodruff, Largo 872a
Woods, Donald 747, 772
Woods, James 84, 180b, 440, 682
Woods, Maurice 621
Woodward, Edward 143, 222, 305, 708
Woodward, Joanne 489
Woodward, Morgan 813
Wooland, Norman 903a
Woolley, Monty 28, 800
Worth, Irene 260
Woskanjan, Margarita 582a
Wray, Fay 140, 975
Wright, Samuel E. 769a
Wright, Teresa 355, 872b
Wyatt, Jane 669
Wyman, Jane 800, 846, 1013
Wynn, Ed 330
Wynter, Dana 151
Wynyard, Diana 248, 823a
Wyss, Amanda 327a

Yagi, James 940
Yamamura, Soh 415
Yates, Cassie 767
Yates, Curtis 101
Yniguez, Richard 486a, 999
Yordanoff, Wladimir 968c
York, Dick 218, 413
York, Jeff 18, 201
York, Michael 10
York, Susannah 337
Young, Arthur 971
Young, Barbara 889
Young, Burt 890
Young, Faron 74

Young, Loretta 48, 171, 832, 859
Young, Robert 859
Young, Stephen 773a
Young, William Allen 361a
Youngfellow, Barrie 888
Youngs, Gail 512
Yulin, Harris 214, 569a

Zabriskie, Grace 490
Zago, Marty 701

Zaks, Jerry 765
Zapata, Carmen 990
Zardi, Federico 367b
Zarragoza, Javier Torres 469a
Zelniker, Michael 769a
Zerbe, Anthony 336a
Zetterling, Mai 104
Zimbalist, Efrem, Jr. 35, 411
Zmed, Adrian 876

FILM TITLE INDEX

(Numbers refer to entries, not pages.)

Abdication, The 159
Abe Lincoln in Illinois 623
Above and Beyond 946
Abraham Lincoln 624
Act Of Vengeance 1011
Act One 416
Actress, The 374
Adam 988
Adam: His Song Continues 988a
Adventures of Casanova, The 129
Adventures of Marco Polo, The 795
Adventures of Mark Twain, The 960
Adventures of Nellie Bly, The 58
Affairs of Cellini, The 140
After the Ball 948
Agatha 157
Agony and the Ecstasy, The 98
AKA Cassius Clay 11
Al Capone 117
Alamo, The 81
Alamo: Thirteen Days To Glory, The 81a
Alcatrez: The Whole Shocking Story 123
Alex: The Life Of A Child 231b
Alexander Hamilton 401
Alexander Nevsky 7a
Alexander the Great 8
Alfred The Great 10
All Creatures Great and Small 438
All the King's Men 634
All the President's Men 1007
All That Jazz 322
All Things Bright and Beautiful 439
Allegheny Uprising 902

Amadeus 721
Amazing Howard Hughes, The 491
Amelia Earhart 272
American Hot Wax 335
Amin, the Rise and Fall 13
Anastasia: The Mystery of Anna 16a
Anatomy of an Illness 194
And I Alone Survived 293
Andy Warhol 988b
Angel at My Table, An 327b
Ann Jillian Story, The 524b
Anna and the King of Siam 608
Anne Devlin 240
Anne of the Indies 62
Anne of the Thousand Days 60
Annie Get Your Gun 751
Annie Oakley 752
Another Country 99
Antonia: A Portrait of the Woman 89
Antonio Gaudi 350b
Antony and Cleopatra 165
Arruza 22
Assassination of Trotsky, The 956
Assisi Underground, The 742b
Atlanta Child Murders, The 1003a
Attack On Fear 697a
Attic: The Hiding of Anne Frank, The 362a
Attica 1000a
Au Revoir Les Enfants 658a
Aunt Mary 249
Awakenings 872

Babe 1016
Babe Ruth Story, The 869
Baby Face Nelson 740
Bad Blood 379b
Bad Lord Byron 104
Bad Men of Missouri 1013
Badge 373 287
Badlands 911
Badlands of Dakota 444
Ballad of Gregorio Cortez, The 192
Barbarian and the Geisha, The 415

Barnum 30
Barretts of Wimpole Street, The 32, 33
Bat 21 400a
Battle of the River Plate, The 599
Beach Boys: An American Band, The 37a
Bear, The 97
Beatlemania 41
Beau Brummel 96
Beau James 984
Becket 45
Beethoven's Great Love 45b
Beethoven's Nephew 45c
Before the Nickelodeon: The Early Cinema of Edwin S. Porter
    801
Bell Jar, The 792
Belle Starr 912, 913
Belles on Their Toes 365
Beloved Infidel 314
Beloved Rogue, The 976
Benny Goodman Story, The 371
Bernadette of Lourdes 49
Beryl Markham: A Shadow On The Sun 666a
Best Things in Life Are Free, The 239
Bethune 51c
Bethune, The Making of A Hero 51d
Betrayal 862
Beyond The Next Mountain 809c
Big Fisherman, The 779
Bigger Splash, A 467
Bill 872a
Bill: On His Own 872b
Billy The Kid 63, 64
Billy The Kid Returns 65
Bird 769a
Birdman of Alcatraz 926
Birth of the Beatles, The 42
Bitter Harvest 399
Black Fox, The 458
Black Swan, The 712
Blackbeard the Pirate 939
Blaze 633a
Blind Ambition 231a
Blood Feud 569

Bloodsport 269b
Bloody Mama 29
Blossoms in the Dust 368
Bluebeard's Ten Honeymoons 596
Blunt 57
Bob Mathias Story, The 676
Bogie 59
Bonnie and Clyde 768
Bonnie Parker Story, The 769
Bonnie Prince Charlie 927
Born Again 183
Born Free 3
Born On The Fourth of July 583a
Boston Strangler, The 228a
Bound for Glory 395
Bounty, The 53
Boy In Blue, The 406b
Boys Town 317
Breaker Morant 708
Brian's Song 785
Bride of Vengeance 78
Bridge to the Sun 940
Bridger 90
Brigham Young—Frontiersman 1012
Broken Arrow 173
Bronte 91
Bronte Sisters, The 92
Brother Sun, Sister Moon 328
Brothers 225
Buccaneer, The 589, 590
Bud and Lou 1
Buddy Holly Story, The 474
Buffalo Bill 175, 176
Buffalo Bill and the Indians 177
Buffalo Bill Rides Again 178
Bugsy 894a
Bullet for Pretty Boy, A 318
Bunker, The 459
Bunny's Tale, A 914b
Burke & Wills 99b
Burning Bed, The 490
Burroughs 100
Buster 285a

Buster Keaton: A Hard Act To Follow 551
Buster Keaton Story, The 551a
Butch and Sundance: The Early Days 131
Butch Cassidy and the Sundance Kid 130

Caesar and Cleopatra 166
Calamity Jane 113, 114
Calamity Jane and Sam Bass 115
Caligula 110
Call Me Madam 688
Camille Claudel 164b
Can You Hear the Laughter? The Story of Freddie Prinze 808
Canaris, Master Spy 112a
Capone 118
Captain Eddie 839
Captain From Castile 193
Captain John Smith and Pocahontas 903
Captain Kidd 576
Caravaggio 120b
Cardinal Richelieu 836
Carve Her Name With Pride 933
Case of Deadly Force, A 754a
Case of the Legless Veteran, The 587
Caspar David Friedrich 337a
Cast a Giant Shadow 664
Catherine the Great 134
Celeste 809
Cell 2455, Death Row 153
Cervantes 142
Champagne Charlie 619
Champions 143
Champions Forever 11a
Chanel Solitaire 144
Chapayev 145a
Chapter Two 896
Charge of the Light Brigade, The 121
Chariots of Fire 620
Charles and Diana: A Royal Love Story 150
Che 391
Cheaper by the Dozen 364
Chief Crazy Horse 200
Children Nobody Wanted, The 102
Children of An Lac, The 27

Children of the Night 605a
Chisum 155
Choices of the Heart 254
Christian the Lion 4
Christiane F. 306
Christine Jorgensen Story, The 544
Christine Keeler Affair, The 552
Christopher Columbus 184, 184a
Chuck Berry Hail! Hail! Rock'N'Roll 51b
Ciao! Manhattan 886
Circle of Children 649
Citizen Cohn 180b
Cleopatra 167, 168
Clive of India 171
Coal Miner's Daughter 646
Cole Younger, Gunfighter 1014
Collision Course 647
Colonel Redl 826
Comanche Territory 82
Coming Out of the Ice 436
Compleat Beatles, The 43
Compulsion 610
Confession, The 632
Conqueror, The 574
Conquest 735
Conquest of Cochise 174
Conrack 187
Constantine and the Cross 188
Cook & Peary: The Race to the Pole 189
Country Doctor, The 211
Courage 951
Courageous Mr. Penn 777
Court-Martial of Billy Mitchell, The 697
Cowboy 413
Crazy Joe 345
Crazylegs 457
Crisis at Central High 489
Cromwell 204
Cross Creek 825
Crusades, The 832
Cry Freedom 51e
Cry In The Dark, A 142b
Custer of the West 208

Dam Busters, The 361
Damien, the Leper Priest 215
Dance With a Stranger 298
Dangerous Company 536
Daniel Boone 73
Daniel Boone, Trail Blazer 74
Danton 216
Darby's Rangers 217
Darwin Adventure, The 219
David and Bathsheba 220
David and Goliath 221
Davy Crockett and the River Pirates 201
Davy Crockett, Indian Scout 202
Davy Crockett, King of the Wild Frontier 203
Dawn 333a
Day After Trinity: J. Robert Oppenheimer and the Atomic Bomb, The 759
Day Christ Died, The 517
Day One 759a
Daydreamer, The 15
De Sade 228
Deadly Intentions 825a
Deadly Tower, The 999
Deadman's Curve 34
Death Be Not Proud 394
Death Hunt 530
Death in California, A 672
Death in Canaan, A 828
Death of a Centerfold: The Dorothy Stratten Story 919
Death of a Soldier 607b
Death of Richie, The 243
Deep in My Heart 848
Defection of Simas Kudirka, The 586
Delancey Street: The Crisis Within 655
Deliberate Stranger, The 97a
Dempsey 233
Desert Fox, The 849
Desert Rats, The 850
Desiree 736
Desperate Mission, The 729
Devotion 93
Diamond Jim 85

Diary of Anne Frank, The 330, 331
Dillinger 244, 245
Directed By Andrei Tarkovsky 935a
Dirty Little Billy 66
Disappearance of Aimee, The 682
Dispatch From Reuters 831
Disraeli 247
Distant Harmony: Pavarotti In China 773b
Divine Emma, The 238
Dixie 300
Doc 473
Doing Life 856a
Dolly Sisters, The 250
Don Juan 252
Don't Cry, It's Only Thunder 434
Don't Look Back: The Story of Leroy "Satchel" Paige 766
Doors, The 715a
Dorothy and Alan At Norma Place 769b
Double Helix, The 200a
Dr. Crippen 200b
Dr. Ehrlich's Magic Bullet 289
Drake of England 259
Dream West 336a
Dreamchild 409a
Dreams of Gold: The Mel Fisher Story 312a
Dubarry, Woman of Passion 263
Duffy of San Quentin 267
Dummy 598

Eagle in a Cage 737
Eboli 615
Eddie Cantor Story, The 116
Eddy Duchin Story, The 265
Edison, The Man 282
Edith and Marcel 782
Education of Sonny Carson, The 126
Edvard Munch 728
Eight Minutes to Midnight 109
84 Charing Cross Road 406a
El Cid 242
El Greco 381
Eleanor and Franklin 853
Eleanor and Franklin: The White House Years 854

Eleanor, the First Lady of The World 851
Eleanor Roosevelt Story, The 852
Eleni 343
Elephant Man, The 687
Elvis 804
Elvis and Me 807a
Elvis on Tour 805
Elvis That's the Way It Is 806
Emerson, Lake & Palmer in Concert 299
Enemy of Women 370
Englishman Abroad, An 99a
Enola Gay: The Men, the Mission, the Atomic Bomb 947
Eric 643
Eric Clapton and His Rolling Hotel 163
Ernie Kovacs: Between the Laughter 583
Escape 1008
Escape From Alcatraz 714
Escape From Iran: The Canadian Caper 935
Esther and the King 303
Eternal Melodies 722
Eternal Sea, The 482
Evel Knieval 582
Evita Peron 778
Execution of Private Slovik, The 900
Executioner's Song, The 366
Exile, The 147
Eye On The Sparrow 604a

FBI Story: The FBI Versus Alvin Karpis, The 549
F. Scott Fitzgerald and ''The Last of the Belles'' 315
F. Scott Fitzgerald in Hollywood 316
Fabulous Dorseys, The 256
Falcon and The Snowman, The 83a
Family Nobody Wanted, The 258
Far Horizons, The 618
Farewell to Manzanar 485
Fat Man and Little Boy 759b
Fatal Vision 651
FDR: The Last Year 855
Fear on Trial 309
Fear Strikes Out 786
Fellini's Casanova 130
Fighting Back 52

Fighting Prince of Donegal, The 754
Final Chapter, Walking Tall 813
Finest Hours, The 161a
Fire Over England 294
Firefighter 327a
First Steps 781
First Texan, The 486
First, You Cry 847
Five Fingers 37
Five of a Kind 212
Five of Me 417
Five Pennies 744
Flight for Freedom 273
Flight of the Eagle 17
Florence Nightingale 745
Flying Irishman 191
Follow the Sun 469
For Us The Living: The Medgar Evers Story 305a
Forever Amber 148
Forever My Love 333
Foster and Laurie 323
Four Days in November 562
Frances 307
Francis Gary Powers: The True Story of the U-2 Spy Incident 803
Francis of Assisi 329
Fraulein Doktor 614
French Connection, The 288
Freud 337
Frida: Naturaleza Vida 547
Friendly Fire 727
From a Far Country: Pope John Paul II 528
From Mao to Mozart: Isaac Stern in China 915
Frontier Marshal 275
Frontier Scout 445
Funny Girl 86
Funny Lady 87

Gabe Kaplan As Groucho 667b
Gable and Lombard 342
Gaby—a True Story 90a
Gaiety George 285
Gaily, Gaily 425
Galileo 344

Gallant Hours, The 400
Gandhi 346
Gauguin the Savage 352
Gene Krupa Story, The 585
General Idi Amin Dada 13a
Genghis Khan 575
Gentleman Bandit, The 765
Gentleman Jim 190
George McKenna Story, The 681a
George Raft Story, The 820
George Stevens: A Filmmaker's Journey 916
George Washington 988d
George Washington II: The Forging of a Nation 988e
Geronimo 356, 357
Gideon's Trumpet 362
Girl in the Red Velvet Swing, The 742
Girl Who Spelled Freedom, The 1011a
Give 'Em Hell, Harry! 957
Glenn Miller Story, The 690
Glory 891a
God Is My Co-Pilot 884
Going for the Gold: The Bill Johnson Story 533
Golden Girl 198
Good Night, Sweet Wife: A Murder In Boston 927a
Goodbye, Norma Jean 701
Goodnight, Sweet Marilyn 701a
Gore Vidal's Billy The Kid 66a
Gore Vidal's Lincoln 624a
Gorgeous Hussy, The 281
Gorillas In The Mist 322a
Gospel According to St. Matthew, The 518
Gospel Road 519
Grace Kelly 559
Grambling's White Tiger 384
Greased Lightning 885
Great American Cowboy, The 654
Great Balls of Fire 616a
Great Caruso, The 128
Great Catherine, The 135
Great Garrick, The 349
Great Gilbert and Sullivan, The 363
Great Houdinis, The 483
Great Imposter, The 232

Great Jesse James Raid, The 507
Great Jewel Robber, The 234
Great John L., The 930
Great Locomotive Chase, The 18
Great Man's Whiskers, The 625
Great Missouri Raid, The 508
Great Mr. Handel, The 405
Great Moment, The 717
Great Northfield Minnesota Raid, The 509
Great Victor Herbert, The 435
Great Wallendas, The 987
Great Waltz, The 922, 923, 924
Great White Hope, The 534
Great Ziegfeld, The 1018
Greatest, The 12
Greatest Story Ever Told, The 520
Grey Fox, The 695
Grey Gardens 38
Growing Up In America 367a
Guilty of Innocence: The Lenell Geter Story 358a
Guilty of Treason 694
Guilty or Innocent: The Sam Shepard Murder Case 894
Gunfight at Dodge City 673
Gunfight at the O.K. Corral 275
Guyana: Cult of the Damned 539
Guyana Tragedy: The Story of Jim Jones, The 540
Gypsy 397

Hammett 404
Hangmen Also Die 441
Hanna's War 888a
Hannibal 407
Hans Christian Andersen 15
Happy Hooker, The 471
Harlow 410, 411
Haunted Summer 892a
Haywire 420
He Makes Me Feel Like Dancin' 214a
Hearst and Davies Affair, The 423
Heart Beat 573
Heart Like a Wheel 726
Heart of a Champion: The Ray Mancini Story 659
Heartburn 302

Heartsounds 603b
Heat Wave 835b
Helen Keller: The Miracle Continues 554
Helen Morgan Story, The 711
Helter Skelter 661
Hemingway's Adventures of a Young Man 428
Henry V 431, 431a
Henry VIII and His Six Wives 432
Herod the Great 437
Hero's Journey: The World of Joseph Campbell, A 111a
Hey, I'm Alive 581
High Fidelity—The Adventures of The Guarneri String Quartet
    389b
Hitler 460
Hitler—Dead or Alive 461
Hitler Gang, The 462
Hitler: The Last Ten Days 463
Hitler's Hangman 442
Homage To Chagall—The Colours of Love 142a
Home of Our Own, A 990
Honeymoon Killers, The 44a
Hoodlum Priest, The 164
Hopper's Silence 477
Hotel Terminus: The Life and Times of Klaus Barbie 26b
Houdini 484
Hour of the Gun 277
House Is Not a Home, A 6
House of Rothschild, The 859
House on Garibaldi Street, The 409
Houston: The Legend of Texas 486a
Hoxsey: Quacks Who Cure Cancer 488a
Hudson's Bay 819
Huey Long 635
Hungry Feeling: The Life and Death of Brendan Behan 46a
Hunter, The 944
Hustling 892

I Accuse 262
I Aim at the Stars 981
I Am a Dancer 750
I Don't Care Girl, The 935
I Dream of Jeannie 324
I.F. Stone's Weekly 918

I Killed Rasputin 1015a
I Killed Wild Bill Hickok 446
I Know Why the Caged Bird Sings 19
I Lived, But… 763a
I Married Wyatt Earp 274
I Never Promised You a Rose Garden 382
I Shot Jesse James 321
I Want to Live 378, 379
I Was a Communist for the FBI 210
I Will Fight No More Forever 545
I Wonder Who's Kissing Her Now 488
I Would Be called John 526b
Idolmaker, The 663
If I Were King 977
If You Could See What I Hear 931
Ike: The War Years 292
I'll Cry Tomorrow 858
I'll See You in My Dreams 547a
I'm Dancing As Fast As I Can 372
Imagine: John Lennon 607
Imperial Venus 61
Impossible Spy, The 180a
Impromptu 877c
In Cold Blood 904
In Old New York 341
In the Matter of Karen Ann Quinlan 818
In The Mood 128a
Incendiary Blonde 392
Incredible Sarah, The 51
Inherit the Wind 218
Inn of the Sixth Happiness, The 24
Inside the Third Reich 908
Interrupted Melody 602
Irish Eyes Are Smiling 28
Iron Curtain 353b
Iron Major, The 138
Iron Mistress, The 83
Isadora 269
Ishi: The Last of His Tribe 495
Islands 160a
It's Good to Be Alive 111

Ivan the Terrible, Part 1 497
Ivan the Terrible, Part 2 498

J. Edgar Hoover 475a
Jack Johnson 535
Jack London 633
Jack the Ripper 499, 499a
Jackie Robinson Story, The 842
Jacobo Timerman: Prisoner Without a Name, Cell Without a
    Number 949
Jacqueline Bouvier Kennedy 561
James Dean 229
James Dean Story, The 230
James Joyce's Women 545b
Janis 542
Jayne Mansfield Story, The 660
Jean Renoir, The Boss 830a
Jeanne Eagels 270
Jesse James 510
Jesse Owens Story, The 763
Jesus 521
Jesus Christ Superstar 522
Jesus of Nazareth 523
Jim Thorpe—All American 943
Jimi Hendrix 429
Jimi Plays Monterey 429a
Jimmy B and Andre 101
Jo Jo Dancer, Your Life Is Calling 809a
Joan of Arc 525
Joe Hill 454
Joe Louis Story, The 639
John and Yoko: A Love Story 607a
John F. Kennedy: Years of Lightning, Days of Drums 563
John Heartfield, Photomontagist 424
John Huston and The Dubliners 493a
John Paul Jones 541
John Wycliffe: The Morning Star 1009a
Johnnie Mae Gibson: F.B.I. 361a
Johnny Cash! The Man, His World, His Music 130a
Johnny, We Hardly Knew Ye 564
Joker Is Wild, The 617
Jolson Sings Again 537

Jolson Story, The 53
Joni 271
Juarez 546
Judge Horton and the Scottsboro Boys 481
Julia 426
Julius Caesar 106, 107, 108

Kansas City Massacre, The 811
Kansas Raiders, The 511
Kennedy 564a
Kerouac 573a
Khartoum 373
Kid From Texas, The 67
Kids Are Alright, The 1000
Kill Me If You Can 154
Killing Fields, The 879
Killing of Randy Webster, The 993
King 577
King: A Filmed Record . . . Montgomery to Memphis 578
King and I, The 609
King David 222
King of Kings 524
King of the Roaring 20's—The Story of Arnold Rothstein 860
King Richard and the Crusades 833
King's Story, The 1005
King's Thief, The 149
Kit Carson 125
Knute Rockne—All American 843
Komitas 582a
Krays, The 583b

La Bamba 963a
Lady Caroline Lamb 592
Lady Hamilton 402
Lady in Red, The 874
Lady Jane 385
Lady of the House 909
Lady Sings the Blues 470
Lady With a Lamp, The 746
Lady With Red Hair, The 127
Lady's Morals, The 627
Lafayette 588
Landru 597

Last Days of Frank and Jesse James, The 512
Last Days of Patton, The 773
Last Emperor, The 809b
Last Giraffe, The 613
Last Hurrah, The 206, 207
Last of Mrs. Lincoln, The 626a
Last of the Buccaneers, The 591
Last Plane Out 197
Last Ride of the Dalton Gang, The 214
Last Temptation of Christ, The 524a
Last Ten Days, The 464
Law and Order 278
Law Vs. Billy the Kid, The 68
Lawless Breed, The 408
Lawrence of Arabia 603
LBJ: The Early Years 535a
Leadbelly 604
Lean On Me 164a
Leave 'Em Laughing 945
Left-Handed Gun, The 69
Legend of Lizzie Borden, The 77
Legend of Valentino, The 964, 965
Lenny 95
Leona Helmsley: The Queen of Mean 426a
Lepke 611
Let It Be 4
Liberty 35a
Life and Assassination of the Kingfish, The 636
Life and Times of Judge Roy Bean, The 39
Life of Emile Zola, The 1021
Life of the Party: The Story of Beatrice 760
Life With Father 226
Lillian Russell 867
Lindbergh Kidnapping Case, The 628
Lion in the Streets, A 637
Lion in Winter, The 430
Lion of the Desert 726
Listen Up: The Lives of Quincy Jones 541a
Lisztomania 630
Little Gloria . . . Happy at Last 969
Little House on the Prairie 1001
Little Mo 186
Living Free 5

Living Proof: The Hank Williams, Jr., Story 1003
Lodger, The 500
Lois Gibbs and the Love Canal 360
Lola Montes 706
Long Riders, The 513
Look for the Silver Lining 692
Looking For Langston 491a
Louis Armstrong, Chicago Style 20
Love Affair: The Eleanor and Lou Gehrig Story, A 354
Love Is Forever 305
Love Leads the Way 332
Love, Mary 389a
Love Me or Leave Me 304
Lovers of Montparnasse, The 700
Loves of Edgar Allan Poe, The 794
Lovey: A Circle of Children 650
Lucky Luciano 641
Lucretia Borgia 80
Ludwig 642
Lust for Life 968
Luther 644

M.A.D.D.: Mothers Against Drunk Drivers 622
MacArthur 648
Machine Gun Kelly 558
Mad Dog Coll 181
Mad Dog Morgan 710
Mad Empress, The 122
Madame Curie 205
Madame Dubarry 264
Madeleine 903a
Madonna: Truth Or Dare 653a
Mae West 995
Mafia Princess 359
Magic Bow, The 764
Magic Box, The 338
Magic Fire 982
Magnificent Rebel, The 46
Magnificent Yankee, The 475
Mahler 656
Malcolm X 658
Malice in Wonderland 771
Man Called Peter, A 667

Man for All Seasons, A 709
Man in the Glass Booth, The 290
Man In The Silk Hat, The 629a
Man Named John, A 527
Man of a Thousand Faces 145
Man of Conquest 487
Man on a String 716
Man Who Broke 1,000 Chains, The 99c
Man Who Dared, The 141
Mandela 659a
Manhunt For Claude Dallas 213a
Marciano 662
Marco 796
Marco Polo 797, 797a
Marco the Magnificent 798
Maria 110a
Marian Rose White 996
Marianne and Juliane 301
Marie 821
Marie Antoinette 665, 666
Marilyn 703
Marilyn: The Untold Story 704
Marjoe 375
Mark, I Love You 767
Marla Hanson Story, The 407a
Marlene 243a
Martin Luther 645
Marva Collins Story, The 182
Mary and Joseph: A Story of Faith 668
Mary of Scotland 670
Mary, Queen of Scots 671
Mary White 997
Mask 235
Masterson of Kansas 674
Mata Hari 652, 652a
Matter of Heart, A 546a
Matter of Life and Death, A 962
Maurie 917
Max Frisch: Journal I-III 339
Mayerling 864, 865
Mayflower Madam 33a
McConnell Story, The 680
McVicar 683

Meetings With Remarkable Men 394a
Melba 685
Melvin and Howard 268
Melvin Purvis—G Man 812
Midnight Express 418
Mighty Barnum, The 31
Million Dollar Mermaid, The 557
Miracle of Kathy Miller, The 692
Miracle of Our Lady of Fatima, The 257
Miracle on Ice 94
Miracle Worker, The 555, 556
Mishima 697
Missiles of October 565
Missing 478
Mission to Moscow 224
Mr. Horn 479
Mr. Rock and Roll 336
Mohammad, Messenger of God 700
Mommie Dearest 199
Monkey on My Back, A 857
Montana Belle 914
Moon and Sixpence, The 353
More Than Friends 829
Morgan the Pirate 713
Moro Affair, The 713a
Moses 718
Mother Teresa 940a
Moulin Rouge 953
Mountains of The Moon 100a
Mrs. Soffel 905
Mrs. Sundance 791
Muggable Mary, Street Cop 369
Murder by Decree 502
Murder in Coweta County 985
Murder in Texas 455
Murder Inc. 612
Murder of Fred Hampton, The 404a
Murder of Mary Phagan, The 331a
Murder One 494a
Murderers Among Us: The Simon Wiesenthal Story 1000b
Murieta 730
Murrow 733
Music Lovers, The 937

Mussolini: The Decline and Fall of Il Duce 734
Mussolini: The Untold Story 734a
Mutiny on the Bounty 54, 55
My Darling Clementine 279
My Father, My Son 1022
My Gal Sal 261
My Left Foot 94a
My Life For Zarah Leander 603a
My Pleasure Is My Business 472
My Wicked, Wicked Ways 320a
My Wild Irish Rose 756
Mystery of Kasper Hauser, The 416b
Mystery of Picasso, The 784

Nadia 185
Naked Maja, The 376
Nativity, The 669
Nazi Hunter: The Beate Klarsfeld Story 581a
Ned Kelly 560
Nell Gwyn 396
Nelson Affair, The 741
Never Cry Wolf 720
Never Forget 686a
New Wine 881
Nicholas and Alexandra 743
Night and Day 800
Night In Havana: Dizzy Gillespie In Cuba 365a
Nights of Rasputin 822
Nijinsky 748
Nitti: The Enforcer 748a
No Drums, No Bugles 350a
No Man Is an Island 961
Nobody's Child 28a
Nurse Edith Cavell 139

Odette 161
Oh You Beautiful Doll 312
Omar Khayyam 757
On Wings of Eagles 778a
One in a Million: The Ron LeFlore Story 606
One Man's War 311a
One Man's Way 774
Onion Field, The 440

Operation Daybreak 443
Operation Eichmann 291
Ordeal of Bill Carney, The 124
Ordeal of Dr. Mudd, The 723
Ordeal of Patty Hearst, The 422
Oscar Wilde 1000c
Other Side of the Mountain, The 579
Other Side of the Mountain, Part 2, The 580
Our Hearts Were Growing Up 898
Our Hearts Were Young and Gay 899
Our Hitler 465
Out of Africa 56
Out of The Darkness 1020
Outlaw, The 70
Outsider, The 419

Pacific Destiny 388
Pancho Barnes 29a
Pancho Villa 972
Papa's Delicate Condition 387
Paper Lion 793
Papillon 152
Parnell 770
Parson and the Outlaw, The 71
Password Is Courage, The 195
Pat Garrett and Billy the Kid 72
Patricia Neal Story, The 739
Patton 773a
Patty Hearst 422a
Peg of Old Drury 1006
People Vs. Jean Harris, The 414
Perils of Pauline, The 998
Peter and Paul 780
Peter The Great 778b
Piaf—The Early Years 783
Picture Show Man, The 776
Plainsman, The 447, 448
Playing for Time 310
Pontius Pilate 799
Pony Express 449
Pope John Paul II 529
Portrait of a Rebel: The Remarkable Mrs. Sanger 878
Power 468

President's Lady, The 505
Pretty Boy Floyd 319
Prick Up Your Ears 760a
Pride of St. Louis, The 231
Pride of the Marines 880
Pride of the Yankees, The 355
Priest of Love, The 600
Prime Minister, The 248
Prince Jack 566
Prince of Foxes 79
Prince of Players 76
Prisoner of Shark Island, The 725
Private Battle, A 870
Private Files of J. Edgar Hoover, The 476
Private Life of Don Juan, The 253
Private Life of Henry VIII, The 433
Private Lives of Elizabeth and Essex, The 295
Promise at Dawn 350
PT 109 567

Quarterback Princess 657
Queen Christina 160

Raging Bull 593
Rainbow 348
Rape and Marriage: The Rideout Case 840
Rasputin 823
Rasputin and the Empress 823a
Rasputin—The Mad Monk 824
Raoul Wallenberg: Between The Lines 986
Ravel 824a
Reach for the Sky 25
Real American Hero, A 814
Red Tent, The 14
Reds 827
Reluctant Saint, The 545a
Rembrandt 830
Return Engagement 603c
Return of Ruben Blades, The 51f
Return of Frank James, The 506
Return of Martin Guerre, The 390
Return to Earth 7
Reunion 213

Reversal of Fortune 981a
Rhapsody in Blue 358
Rhodes 831a
Richard III 834
Right to Kill? 505b
Ring of Passion 640
Rise and Fall of Legs Diamond, The 241
Rita Hayworth: The Love Goddess 421
Roads of Exile, The 861
Robert Kennedy and His Times 569a
Robin Hood of El Dorado, The 731
Rodeo Girl 788
Roger Touhy—Gangster 952
Romero 848a
Rosa Luxemburg 645a
Rose of Washington Square 88
Rosie: The Rosemary Clooney Story 172
Roughly Speaking 787
Roxanne: The Prize Pulitzer 810a
Royal Hunt of the Sun, The 790
Royal Romance of Charles and Diana, The 151
Royal Scandal, A 136
Ruby and Oswald 863
Rumor of War, A 120a
Running Brave 694

Sacco and Vanzetti 871
Sadat 873
Saint Joan 526
St. Louis Blues 406
St. Valentine's Day Massacre, The 119
Sakharov 875
Salome 877
Salvador 84
Salvatore Giuliano 367b
Samaritan: The Mitch Snyder Story 904a
Sam's Son 595
Samson and Delilah 877a-877b
Samuel Beckett: Silence To Silence 45a
Savage Messiah 351
Scandal 552a
Scarlet and the Black, The 755
Scarlet Coat, The 21

Scarlet Empress, The 137
Scarlett O'Hara War, The 888
Scott Joplin 543
Scott of the Antarctic 883
Second Serve 835a
Secret Honor 749
Secret Land, The 103
Seizure: The Story of Kathy Morris 716
Separate But Equal 667a
Sergeant Matlovich Vs. the U.S. Air Force 677
Sergeant York 1011b
Serpent of the Nile 169
Serpico 889
Serpico: The Deadly Game 890
Seven Little Foys, The 327
Seven Seas to Calais 260
1776 2
Sex Symbol, The 705
Shadowlands 616
Shattered Vows 365b
She Stood Alone 198a
Shine on Harvest Moon 36
Shining Season, A 26
Shocktrauma 196
Sicilian, The 367c
Sid and Nancy 969a
Side by Side: The True Story of the Osmond Family 761
Sign of the Pagan, The 23
Silence, The 775
Silent Lovers, The 347
Silent Victory: The Kitty O'Neil Story 758
Silkwood 895
Silver Dollar 934
Sinful Davy 398
Sister Kenny 571
Sitting Bull 897
Sixty Glorious Years 970
Small Sacrifices 258a
So Goes My Love 678
So This Is Love 708
Somebody Loves Me 887
Somebody Up There Like Me 380
Something for Joey 120

Son of The Morning Star 208a
Son Rise: A Miracle of Love 550
Song of Bernadette, The 50
Song of Love 882
Song of My Heart 938
Song of Norway 386
Song of Scheherezade 841
Song to Remember, A 156
Song Without End 631
Sophia Loren: Her Own Story 638
Sound of Music, The 954
Spartacus 907
Special People 269a
Spirit of St. Louis, The 629
Spitfire 699
Spring Symphony 882a
Squizzy Taylor 936a
Stand and Deliver 302b
Stand by Your Man 1010
Stanley and Livingstone 910
Star! 601
Star 80 920
Star Maker, The 286
Stars and Stripes Forever 906
Stavisky 914a
Stealing Heaven 1a
Stevie 901
Story of Adele H, The 492
Story of Alexander Graham Bell, The 48
Story of David, The 223
Story of Dr. Wassell, The 989
Story of G.I. Joe, The 817
Story of Jacob and Joseph, The 505a
Story of Louis Pasteur, The 772
Story of Pretty Boy Floyd, The 320
Story of Ruth, The 868
Story of Vernon and Irene Castle, The 133
Story of Will Rogers, The 846
Story of Women 599a
Strange Death of Adolf Hitler, The 466
Stratton Story, The 921
Study in Terror, A 503
Suez 227

Sullivans, The 929
Sunrise at Campobello 856
Sunshine 427
Super Cops, The 383
Superstar: The Life and Times of Andy Warhol 988c
Sutter's Gold 932
Swanee River 326
Sweet Dreams 170
Sword and the Rose, The 959
Sylvia 22a

Tail Gunner Joe 679
Ted Kennedy Jr. Story, The 560a
Tempest 810
Ten Commandents, The 720
10 Rillington Place 158
Ten Who Dared 802
Tennessee Johnson 532
Terry Fox Story, The 326
Test of Love, A 681
That Hamilton Woman 403
That Lady 686
Thelonious Monk: Straight No Chaser 700a
Therese 940b
They Died With Their Boots On 209
Thin Blue Line, The 2a
Thirty Seconds Over Tokyo 255
This Is Elvis 807
This Man Stands Alone 367
This Year's Blonde 706
Thornwell 942
Three Came Home 553
Three Hundred Miles for Stephanie 845
Three Little Words 548
Till the Clouds Roll By 572
Time After Time 504
Time for Miracles, A 891
Time to Live, A 994
Time to Triumph, A 416a
Times of Harvey Milk, The 690
To Heal a Nation 885a
To Hell and Back 732
To Race the Wind 584

Toast of New York, The 313
Tom Horn 480
Toma 950
Tombstone, the Town Too Tough to Die 280
Tonight We Sing 493
Too Much Too Soon 35
Too Young The Hero 379a
Touched by Love 112
Tower of London 835
Trackdown: Finding the Goodbar Killer 377
Trapp Family, The 955
Trial of the Catonsville Nine, The 51a
Trial of Chaplain Jensen, The 516
Trial of Joan of Arc, The 526a
Trial of Lee Harvey Oswald, The 762
Trials of Alger Hiss, The 457a
Trials of Oscar Wilde, The 1000d
Triple Cross 146
Triumph of The Spirit 21a
True Story of Jesse James, The 514
Tucker: The Man and His Dream 958a

UFO Incident, The 453
Under the Red Robe 837
Unfinished Journey of Robert Kennedy, The 570
Unforgettable Nat King Cole, The 180c
Untouchables, The 742a
Used Innocence 48b

Vagabond King, The 978, 979
Valachi Papers, The 963
Valentino 966, 967
Van Gogh 968a
Vengeance: The Story of Tony Cimo 162a
Verne Miller 692a
Victims for Victims: The Theresa Saldana Story 876
Victoria the Great 971
Villa 973
Villa Rides 974
Vincent 968b
Vincent & Theo 968c
Virgin Queen, The 296

Virginia Hill Story, The 456
Vision Shared: A Tribute To Woody Guthrie and Leadbelly, A 395a
Viva Villa 975
Viva Zapata! 1017
Vladmir Horowitz, The Last Romantic 480a
Voltaire 980
Von Richthofen and Brown 838

W.C. Fields and Me 311
Wagner 983
Waiting for the Moon 949a
Walker 984a
Walking Tall 815
Walking Tall, Part 2 816
Walking Through the Fire 605
Wallenberg: A Hero's Story 986a
Waltz King, The 925
Warriors, The 284
Wasn't That a Time! 992
Waterloo 738
We of the Never-Never 393
We Who Are About to Die 594
Weekend Nun, The 266
Westerner, The 40
What Happened to Kerouac? 573b
When Hell Was in Session 236
Where the Buffalo Roam 941
Where's Jack? 893
White Angel, The 747
White Buffalo, The 450
White Mischief 302a
White Rose, The 880a
Who Will Love My Children? 334
Why Me? 412
Wild Bill Hickok 451
Wild Child, The 496
Will, G. Gordon Liddy 621
Will There Really Be a Morning? 308
Wilma 866
Wilson 1004
Winds of Kitty Hawk, The 1009
Wings and the Woman 531

Wings of the Eagles, The 991
Winner Never Quits, A 379c
Winning Team, The 9
Winter Tan, A 469a
Wired 48a
With a Song In My Heart 340
Without Warning: The James Brady Story 85a
Wizard of Babylon, The 308a
Wolf At The Door 353a
Woman Called Golda, A 684
Woman Called Moses, A 958
Woman He Loved, The 896a
Woman of the Town, The 675
Wonderful World of the Brothers Grimm, The 389
Words and Music 844
World Apart, A 311b

Xica 895a

Yankee Doodle Dandy 180
You Will Remember 928
Young Bess 297
Young Bill Hickok 452
Young Buffalo Bill 179
Young Cassidy 753
Young Catherine 137a
Young Daniel Boone 75
Young Dillinger 246
Young Guns 72a
Young Harry Houdini 484a
Young Jesse James 515
Young Joe, the Forgotten Kennedy 568
Young Man With a Horn 47
Young Mr. Lincoln 626
Young Mr. Pitt 789
Young Tom Edison 283
Young Winston 162
Younger Brothers, The 1015
Your Cheatin' Heart 1002

Ziegfeld: The Man and His Women 1014

SUBJECT INDEX

Abolitionists
Tubman, Harriet

Accident survivors
Elder, Lauren
Froman, Jane
Klaben, Helen
Miller, Kathy

Acquitted murder suspects
Adams, Randall Dale
Borden, Lizzie
Broughton, Henry John
Evans, Timothy
Frank, Leo
Lamson, David
Sheppard, Sam
Smith, Madeleine
Von Bulow, Claus

Activists
See also Abolitionists; Anarchists; Civil rights activists; Conservationists; Revolutionaries
Abernathy, Ralph
Balter, Marie
Berrigan, Daniel
Biko, Ntsiki
Biko, Steve
Brady, James S.
Brady, Sarah
Butterfield, Tom
Caldicott, Helen

Cox, Don
Crandall, Prudence
Davis, Angela
Ensslin, Gudrun
Evers, Medgar Wiley
Filartiga, Joel
First, Ruth
Gatrell, Ashby
Gibb, Lois
Gies, Jan
Gies, Miep
Ginsberg, Allen
Giuliano, Salvatore
Gladney, Edna
Goldman, Emma
Halbert, Frederic
Halbert, Sandra
Hampton, Fred
Hill, Joe
Hoffman, Abbie
Jackson, George
Jogiches, Leo
Johnson, Deborah
Kovic, Ron
Kunstler, William
Leary, Timothy
Lightner, Candy
Luxemburg, Rosa
Maher, John
Mandela, Nelson
Mandela, Winnie
Mullen, Peg
Niccacci, Rufino
O'Reilly, Beatrice

Ragghianti, Marie
Romero, Oscar
Rubin, Jerry
Sakharov, Andrei
Sanger, Margaret
Scholl, Hans
Scholl, Sophie
Scruggs, Jan C.
Senesh, Hanna
Silkwood, Karen
Sinclair, John
Snyder, Mitch
Steinem, Gloria
Teresa, Mother
Tisdale, Betty
Walsh, John
Walsh, Reve
Wasson, William
Ufema, Joy

Actors and actresses
  See also Comedians; Show-
  men; Singers
Abbott, Bud
Adams, Edie
Ali, Muhammad
Avalon, Frankie
Aykroyd, Dan
Bacall, Lauren
Baker, Josephine
Balin, Ina
Ball, Ernest
Barrymore, Diana
Barrymore, John
Baynes, Nora
Belushi, John
Bernhardt, Sarah
Blades, Ruben
Bogart, Humphrey
Booth, Edwin
Booth, John Wilkes
Browne, Coral
Burke, Billie

Cantor, Eddie
Cash, Johnny
Chaney, Lon
Chaney, Lon, Jr.
Christy, Edwin P.
Clooney, Rosemary
Cohan, George M.
Costello, Lou
Coward, Noel
Crawford, Joan
Damita, Lily
Davies, Marion
Davis, Bette
De Havilland, Olivia
Dean, James
Dietrich, Marlene
Dunnock, Mildred
Eagels, Jeanne
Earp, Josephine
Egan, Eddie
Fabian
Farmer, Frances
Ferrer, Jose
Fields, W.C.
Flynn, Errol
Foy, Eddie
Gable, Clark
Garbo, Greta
Garland, Judy
Garrick, David
Gilbert, John
Gordon, Ruth
Gortner, Marjoe
Grant, Cary
Griffith, Corinne
Gwyn, Nell
Harlow, Jean
Havoc, June
Hayworth, Rita
Held, Anna
Hepburn, Katharine
Jillian, Ann
Jolson, Al

Kacew, Nina
Keaton, Joseph
Kelly, Grace
Kovacs, Ernie
Landon, Michael
Lawrence, Gertrude
Leander, Zarah
Levant, Oscar
Leybourne, George
Linder, Max
Lombard, Carole
Loren, Sophia
Madonna
Mansfield, Jayne
Marshall, Penny
Mason, Marsha
Marx, Julius H.
Methot, Mayo
Miller, Marilyn
Monroe, Marilyn
Monti, Carlota
Murphy, Audie
Neal, Patricia
Olcott, Chauncey
Presley, Elvis
Presley, Priscilla
Prinze, Freddie
Pryor, Richard
Raft, George
Reiner, Rob
Rogers, Will
Rooney, Mickey
Roth, Lillian
Saldana, Theresa
Sedgwick, Edie
Skinner, Cornelia Otis
Stratten, Dorothy
Sullavan, Margaret
Sullivan, Tom
Taylor, Estelle
Valentino, Rudolph
Welles, Orson
West, Mae

White, Pearl
Woffington, Peg
Woolley, Monty

Admirals
Byrd, Richard
Canaris, Wilhelm
Halsey, William F.
Hoskins, John
Nelson, Horatio
Zumwalt, Elmo

Adventurers
See also Astronauts; Daredevils; Explorers; Frontiersmen; Pioneers; Pirates; Safari guides; Scouts
Casanova, Giovanni
Walker, William

Addicts
See Alcoholics; Drug addicts

Aerialists
Wallenda, Karl

Air Force officers
See Astronauts; Pilots

Alcoholics
Barrymore, Diana
Bronte, Bramwell
O'Reilly, Beatrice
Roth, Lillian

Ambassadors
See also Envoys; Political figures
Davies, Joseph E.
Franklin, Benjamin
Harris, Townsend

Kennedy, Joseph P.
Taylor, Kenneth

Anarchists
See also Activists
Goldman, Emma
Sacco, Nicola
Vanzetti, Bartolomeo

Anti-war activists
See Activists

Archbishops
See Clergy

Architects
See also Artists
Gaudi, Antonio
Speer, Albert
White, Stanford

Armed Services
See Admirals; Generals; Pilots; Sailors; Soldiers

Army officers
See Generals; Soldiers

Artists
See also Architects; Photographers; Sculptors
Brown, Christy
Buonarroti, Michelangelo
Caravaggio, Michelangelo
Chagall, Marc
Christo
Eareckson, Joni
Elder, Lauren
Friedrich, Caspar David
Gauguin, Paul
Goya y Lucientes, Francisco
Greco, El
Heartfield, John

Hockney, David
Hopper, Edward
Kahlo, Frida
Levi, Carlo
Modigliani, Amedeo
Munch, Edvard
Picasso, Pablo
Rembrandt Harmenszoon van Rijn
Rivera, Diego
Toulouse-Lautrec, Henri de
Van Gogh, Vincent
Warhol, Andy

Assassins and murderers
See also Criminals; Outlaws
Barker, Arizona
Beck, Martha
Bembenek, Lawrencia
Berkowitz, David
Booth, John Wilkes
Brutus
Bundy, Theodore Robert
Chamberlin, Lindy
Christie, John
Coleman, Wayne Carl
Crippen, Hawley Harvey
Dallas, Claude
De Salvo, Albert
Downs, Elizabeth Diane
Dungee, George Elder
Ellis, Ruth
Fernandez, Ray
Gilmore, Gary
Graham, Barbara
Graham, Stan
Halliwell, Kenneth
Harris, Jean
Harris, David
Hauptmann, Bruno Richard
Hickock, Richard
Hill, John Robert
Hughes, Francine

Isaacs, Carl Junior
Isaacs, William Carroll
Jack the Ripper
Jahnke, Richard, Jr.
Landru, Henri-Desire
Lang, Donald
Leonski, Edward J.
Leopold, Nathan
Loeb, Richard
MacDonald, Jeffrey
Manson, Charles
Mercader, Ramon
Oswald, Lee Harvey
Reilly, Peter
Rowe, Gary Thomas
Ruby, Jack
Smith, Perry
Snider, Paul
Starkweather, Charles
Stuart, Charles Edward
Thaw, Harry
Vicious, Sid
White, Daniel
Whitman, Charles
Williams, Wayne Bertram
Youssoupoff, Felix

Astronauts
Aldrin, Edwin E.

Athletes
    See specific sport

Attorneys
    See Judges; Lawyers

Authors
See Journalists; Playwrights;
    Writers

Autistic persons
Kaufman, Raun

Automobile racers
Kalitta, Conrad
Muldowney, Shirley
O'Neil, Kitty
Scott, Wendell

Aviators
    See Astronauts; Pilots

Ballet dancers
    See Dancers

Bandits
See Assassins and murderers;
    Criminals; Outlaws

Bandleaders
    See Musicians

Bankers and banking
    See Business and financial
    figures

Baseball players
    See also Olympic athletes
Alexander, Grover Cleveland
Campanella, Roy
Dean, Jay "Dizzy"
Dean, Paul
DiMaggio, Joe
Gehrig, Lou
Gray, Pete
LeFlore, Ron
Paige, Leroy
Piersall, James "Jimmy"
Robinson, Jackie
Ruth, George "Babe"
Stratton, Monty

Basketball players
Stokes, Maurice
Twyman, Jack

Biblical figures
See also Saints
Ahasuerus
Bathsheba
Boaz
David
Delilah
Esau
Esther
Goliath
Jacob
Jesus Christ
John the Baptist
Joseph
Joseph, Saint
Mary
Moses
Ruth
Salome
Samson

Biologists
See Scientists

Bishops
See Clergy

Black activists
See Activists

Blind persons
See Handicapped
persons

Body builders
Hargitay, Mickey

Bootleggers
See Criminals

Bounty hunters
Horn, Tom
Thorson, Ralph

Boxers
Ali, Muhammad
Arouch, Salamo
Cerdan, Marcel
Corbett, James
Dempsey, Jack
Foreman, George
Frazier, Joe
Graziano, Rocky
Johnson, Jack
La Motta, Jake
Liston, Sonny
Louis, Joe
Mancini, Ray
Marciano, Rocky
Robinson, Ray
Ross, Barney
Schmeling, Max
Sullivan, John L.

Broadcasters
See also Disc jockeys
Faulk, John Henry
Murrow, Edward R.
Rollins, Betty
Walsh, John

Bullfighters
Arruza, Carlos

Burglars and robbers
See Criminals

Business and financial figures
Barnum, P.T.
Beach, Sylvia
Brady, James
Burns, Robert Elliot
Butsicaris, Jimmy
Day, Clarence
Dietrich, Noah
Doel, Frank

Drew, Daniel
Epstein, Brian
Fisher, Mel
Fisk, James
Frank, Leo
Helmsley, Harry
Helmsley, Leona
Horman, Edmund
Hughes, Howard
Kruger, Paul
Lahr, John
Mayer, Louis B.
Paley, William S.
Penn, Edward Lyle
Penn, William
Perot, H. Ross
Ponti, Carlo
Pulitzer, Herbert Peter
Pulitzer, Roxanne
Reuter, Julius
Rhodes, Cecil
Rothschild, Nathan
Stanton, Frank
Sutter, Johan
Tabor, H.A.W.
Thrash, George
Tucker, Preston
Van Gogh, Theo
Vanderbilt, Cornelius
Vanderbilt, Gloria
Warner, Jack

Cabinet members
See Political figures

Cardinals
See Clergy

Chaplains
See Clergy

Chemists
See Scientists

Child-welfare activists
See Activists

Children of prominent parents
Beethoven, Karl
Ciano, Edda Mussolini
Crawford, Christina
Giancana, Antoinette
Gunther, John, Jr.
Hargreaves, Alice Pleasance
Hayward, Bridget
Hayward, Brooke
Hayward, William
Hearst, Patty
Hugo, Adele
Painter, Mark
Ryan, Geoffrey
Slovo, Shawn
White, Mary
Williams, Hank, Jr.
Vanderbilt, Gloria

Choreographers
See also Dancers
Balanchine, George
Fosse, Bob

Civil rights activists
See also Activists
Abernathy, Ralph
Davis, Angela
Evers, Medgar Wiley
Gilmore, Thomas E.
King, Coretta Scott
King, Martin Luther, Jr.
Malcolm X

Clarinetists
See Musicians

Clergy
See also Evangelists; Mis-

sionaries; Popes; Religious
  leaders
Abelard, Peter
Becket, Thomas
Berrigan, Daniel
Clark, Charles Dismas
Doss, Carl
Duco, Joyce
Flanagan, Edward James
Gilligan, Mary
Jensen, Andrew
King, Martin Luther, Jr.
King, Martin Luther, Sr.
Komitas
Marshall, Peter
Mindszenty, Jozsef
Niccacci, Rufino
O'Flaherty, Hugh
Pagano, Bernard
Peale, Norman Vincent
Rasputin, Grigori Efimovich
Richelieu, Armand
Romero, Oscar
Seton, Elizabeth
Teresa, Mother
Wasson, William

Clowns
  See Comedians

Coaches, Athletic
Brooks, Herb
Bryant, Paul
Cavanaugh, Frank
Dobkin, Mary
Karolyi, Bela
Robinson, Eddie
Rockne, Knute

Colonists
  See Explorers; Frontiersmen; Political figures; Presidents, American

Columnists
  See Journalists; Writers

Comedians
  See also Actors and Ac-
  tresses
Abbott, Bud
Aykroyd, Dan
Belushi, John
Brice, Fanny
Bruce, Lenny
Cantor, Eddie
Costello, Lou
Fields, W.C.
Foy, Eddie
Keaton, Joseph
Kovacs, Ernie
Lewis, Joe E.
Linder, Max
Marx, Julius H.
Prinze, Freddie
Pryor, Richard
Reiner, Rob
Rogers, Will
Thum, Jack

Composers
  See also Songwriters
Bach, Johann Sebastian
Ball, Ernest R.
Beethoven, Ludwig van
Brahms, Johannes
Chopin, Frederic
Debussy, Claude
Gershwin, George
Grieg, Edvard
Handel, George Frideric
Handy, W.C.
Herbert, Victor
Jones, Quincy
Joplin, Scott
Kern, Jerome
Komitas

Levant, Oscar
Liszt, Franz
Mahler, Gustav
Monk, Thelonious
Mozart, Wolfgang Amadeus
Nordraak, Rikard
Ravel, Maurice
Rimsky-Korsakov, Nikolai
Rodgers, Richard
Romberg, Sigmund
Salieri, Antonio
Schubert, Franz
Schumann, Clara
Schumann, Robert
Sousa, John Philip
Strauss, Johann, Jr.
Sullivan, Arthur
Tchaikovsky, Peter
Wagner, Richard

Concentration camp inmates
   See also Prisoners of war
Arouch, Salamo
Fenelon, Fania
Frank, Anne
Frank, Otto
Mermelstein, Mel
Wiesenthal, Simon

Conductors (Music)
Brico, Antonia
Herbert, Victor
Mahler, Gustav
Strauss, Johann

Congressmen/women
   See Political figures

Conquerors
   See also Emperors
Cortez, Hernando
Khan, Genghis
Pizarro, Francisco

Conscientious objectors
   See Activists

Conservationists
   See also Naturalists
Adamson, George
Adamson, Joy
Fossey, Dian

Conspirators
   See Spies and traitors

Criminals
   See also Assassins and mur-
   derers; Outlaws; Pirates;
   Spies and traitors
Anglin, Clarence
Anglin, John
Barker, Arizona
Barrow, Clyde
Biddle, Ed
Buchalter, Louis
Capone, Alphonse
Carnes, Clarence
Chapman, Edward
Charriere, Henri
Chessman, Caryl W.
Cimo, Tony
Coll, Vincent
Demara, Ferdinand
Dennis, Gerard Graham
Diamond, Jack
Dillinger, John
Edwards, Buster
Eichmann, Adolf
Floyd, Charles
Fugate, Caril Ann
Gallo, Joe
Giancana, Salvatore
Gideon, Clarence
Gilmore, Gary
Haggart, David
Hayes, Billy

Hearst, Patty
Helmsley, Leona
Jackson, George
Johnson, Ray
Karpis, Alvin
Kelly, George R.
Kray, Reginald
Kray, Ronald
Lansky, Meyer
Latour, Marie
Lepke, Louis
Luciano, Charles
McVicar, John
Miller, Vernon C.
Miner, William
Morris, Frank
Murieta, Joaquin
Nelson, George
Nitti, Francesco
Parker, Bonnie
Raynor, Charles
Rosenberg, Jerry
Rothstein, Arnold
Schultz, Arthur
Sheppard, Jack
Siegel, Benjamin
Snyder, Martin
Soffel, Kate
Starr, Belle
Stavisky, Serge
Stroud, Robert
Taylor, Leslie
Touhy, Roger
Valachi, Joseph
Villa, Pancho
Villon, Francois

Cult leaders
Gurdjieff, Georges Ivano-
    vitch
Jones, Jim
Manson, Charles

Dancers
Ashley, Merrill
Baker, Josephine
Bruce, Honey Harlowe
Castle, Irene
Castle, Vernon
D'Amboise, Jacques
Dolly, Jennie
Dolly, Rosie
Donahue, Jack
Duncan, Isadora
Fosse, Bob
Foy, Eddie
Gypsy Rose Lee
Hayden, Melissa
Kent, Allegra
Kistler, Darci
Macleod, Margaret
Montes, Lola
Moylan, Mary Ellen
Nijinsky, Waslaw
Norworth, Jack
Nureyev, Rudolf
Starr, Blaze
Tallchief, Maria

Daredevils
Knievel, Evel

Deaf persons
    See Handicapped persons

Defectors
    See also Spies and traitors
Gauzenko, Igor
Kudirka, Simas

Detectives
    See Police officers

Dictators
Amin, Idi

Hitler, Adolf
Mussolini, Benito
Stalin, Joseph

Diplomats
See also Ambassadors; En-
voys; Political figures
De Lesseps, Ferdinand

Directors
Curtiz, Michael
Fassbinder, Rainer Werner
Fosse, Bob
Huston, John
Malle, Louis
Ozu, Yasuiro
Renoir, Jean
Stevens, George
Tarkovsky, Andrei
Wallis, Hal
Walsh, Raoul

Disk jockeys
Freed, Alan

District attorneys
See Lawyers

Doctors
See Physicians

Dramatists
See Playwrights

Drug addicts
Bronte, Bramwell
Bruce, Lenny
Diener, George Richard
F., Christiane
Ross, Barney

Drummers
See Musicians

Editors
See also Writers
Bradlee, Ben
Cousins, Norman

Educators
Ashton-Warner, Sylvia
Campbell, Joseph
Clark, Joe
Collins, Marva
Conroy, Pat
Crandall, Prudence
Dupuy, Diane
Escalante, Jaime
Harris, Jean
Holder, Maryse
Huckaby, Elizabeth
Johnston, Reginald
Lamson, David
Leonowens, Anna Harriette
MacCracken, Mary
McKenna, George
Morrow, Barry
Place, Etta
Schumann, Clara
Sullivan, Anne
Wilson, Woodrow

Emperors
See also Kings
Caesar, Julius, Emperor of
Rome
Caligula, Emperor of Rome
Constantine I, Emperor of
Rome
Franz Josef, Emperor of Aus-
tria
Ivan IV, ''the Terrible,'' Em-
peror of Russia
Joseph II, Emperor of Austria
Maximilian, Emperor of Mex-
ico

Napoleon Bonaparte, Emperor of France
Nicholas II, Emperor of Russia
Peter III, Emperor of Russia
Pu Yi, Emperor of China

Empresses
See also Queens
Alexandra, Empress of Russia
Carlotta, Empress of Mexico
Catherine I, Empress of Russia
Catherine II, Empress of Russia
Elizabeth, Empress of Austria
Elizabeth, Empress of Russia
Eudoxie Fedorovna, Empress of Russia
Eugenie, Empress of France
Josephine, Empress of France
Wan-jung, Empress of China
Wen Hsiu, Empress of China

Engineers
See also Scientists
Geter, Lenell
Gilbreth, Frank Bunker
Gilbreth, Lillian

Entertainers
See also Actors and actresses; Aerialists; Composers; Dancers; Daredevils; Musicians; Showmen; Singers; Songwriters
Brice, Fanny
Bruce, Honey Harlowe
Crabtree, Lotta
Dolly, Jenny
Dolly, Rosie

Fields, Benny
Foy, Eddie
Guinan, Mary
Gypsy Rose Lee
Houdini, Harry
Lorraine, Lillian
Norworth, Jack
Oakley, Annie
Seeley, Blossom

Entrepreneurs
See Business and financial figures

Envoys
Mesta, Perle

Evangelists
See also Clergy; Religious leaders
Gortner, Marjoe
McPherson, Aimee Semple
Swaggart, Jimmy

Explorers
See also Frontiersmen/women
Amundsen, Roald
Andree, Salomon August
Bridger, Jim
Burke, Robert O'Hara
Burton, Richard Francis
Byrd, Richard
Carson, Kit
Clark, William
Columbus, Christopher
Cook, Frederick Albert
Cortez, Hernando
De Soto, Hernando
Finch Hatton, Denys
Fraenkel, Knut
Fremont, John Charles
Lewis, Meriwether

Nobile, Umberto
Peary, Robert Edwin
Pizarro, Francisco
Polo, Marco
Powell, John Wesley
Radisson, Pierre Esprit
Scott, Robert Falcon
Smith, John
Speke, John Hanning
Stanley, Henry
Strindberg, Nils
Wills, William John

Fantasists
Demara, Ferdinand

Farmers
Fray, Ivan
Fray, Lucile
Halbert, Frederic
Halbert, Sandra

Fashion designers
Chanel, Coco
Vanderbilt, Gloria

Fathers
See Parents of prominent
figures

Fatima visionaries
Dos Santos, Lucia
Marto, Francisco
Marto, Jacinta

F.B.I agents
See Police officers

Feminists
See Activists

Field marshals
See Generals

Financiers
See Business and financial
figures

Firefighters
Fralick, Cindy

Flutists
See Musicians

Football coaches
See Coaches, Athletic

Football players
See also Olympic athletes
Bleier, Robert Patrick
Cappelletti, John
Gregory, Jim
Hirsch, Elroy
Maida, Tami
Piccolo, Brian
Sayers, Gale

Frontiersmen/women
See also Explorers
Boone, Daniel
Bowie, Jim
Canary, Martha Jane
Crockett, Davy
Hickok, James Butler

Fur traders
Radisson, Pierre Esprit

Gangsters
See Assassins and murderers; Criminals

Generals
See also Soldiers
Anthony, Marc
Arnold, Benedict
Bradley, Omar

Brutus
Caesar, Julius
Cardigan, James Thomas
  Brudenell
Chapayev, Vasilii Ivanovich
Chennault, Claire Lee
Custer, George Armstrong
Doolittle, James
Eisenhower, Dwight
Gordon, Charles
Groves, Leslie R.
Hannibal
Jackson, Andrew
Lafayette, Marie Joseph Paul
  Roch Gilbert du Motier
MacArthur, Douglas
Mitchell, Billy
Napoleon Bonaparte
Patton, George
Raglan, Fitzroy James Henry
  Somerset
Rommel, Erwin
Santa Ana, Antonio
Washington, George
Wellington, Arthur

Goldsmiths
Cellini, Benvenuto

Golf players
Hogan, Ben
Zaharias, Babe Didrickson

Gossip columnists
  See Journalists

Gymnastic coaches
  See Coaches, Athletic

Gymnasts
Comaneci, Nadia

Handicapped persons
Brimmer, Gabriela
Carney, Bill
Davis, Nan
Dennis, Rocky
Eareckson, Joni
Fox, Terry
Frank, Morris
Gray, Pete
Keller, Helen
Kennedy, Edward Moore, Jr.
Kinmont, Jill
Krents, Harold
Kutcher, James
Lang, Donald
Lee, Ethel
Lee, James
McDonald, Anne
Merrick, John
Myers, Lowell
O'Neil, Kitty
Sackter, Bill
Schmid, Albert
Stratton, Monty
Sullivan, Tom

Heads of state
  See Dictators; Emperors;
  Empresses; Kings; Political
  figures; Presidents; Presidents, American; Prime
  ministers; Queens; Sultans

Hockey coaches
  See Coaches, Athletic

Hockey players
Eruzione, Mike

**Homeopathic medicine prac-
titioner**
Hoxsey, Harry

Humorists
  See also Writers
Crockett, Davy
Rogers, Will
Twain, Mark

Husbands of prominent women
Blixen, Bror
Bothwell, James Hepburn
Chamberlin, Michael
Dick, Charlie
DiMaggio, Joe
Donahue, Jack
Garcia, Andy
Hargitay, Mickey
Jones, George
Lynn, Oliver
Macy, John
Mollison, Jim
O'Reilly, Johnny
Pierson, Harold
Ponti, Carlo
Roosevelt, Franklin Delano
Snyder, Martin
Zaharias, George

Illnesses
  See Patients

Impresarios
Balanchine, George
Diaghilev, Serge
Edwards, George
Hurok, Sol

Indian chiefs
  See Native American leaders.

Inventors
  See also Scientists
Bell, Alexander Graham

Bowie, James
Edison, Thomas Alva
Friese-Greene, William
Fulton, Robert
Maxim, Hiram Stephen
Mitchell, R.J.
Porter, Edwin S.
Von Braun, Werner
Wallis, Barnes
Wright, Orville
Wright, Wilbur

Japanese-American detention camp inmates
Houston, Jeanne Wakatuski

Jazz musicians
  See Musicians

Jockeys
Champion, Bob

Joggers
  See Runners

Journalists
  See also Writers
Barthel, Joan
Bernstein, Carl
Bly, Nellie
Boyle, Richard
Bradlee, Ben
Brady, James S.
Cox, Jack
Everingham, John
First, Ruth
Gage, Nicholas
Graham, Sheilah
Gunther, Frances
Gunther, John
Hecht, Ben
Hopper, Hedda
Mencken, H.L.

Mitchell, Cathy
Mitchell, Dave
Parsons, Louella
Plimpton, George
Pyle, Ernie
Reed, John
Richardson, Robert
Schanberg, Sydney
Sheehy, Gail
Stanley, Henry M.
Stone, I.F.
Thompson, Hunter S.
White, William Allen
Wicker, Tom
Winchell, Walter
Woods, Donald
Woodward, Bob

Judges
Holmes, Oliver Wendell
Horton, James Edwin
Marshall, Thurgood
Warren, Earl

Justice of the peace
Bean, Roy

Kidnap victims
Hearst, Patty

Kidnappers
See Criminals

Kings
See also Emperors; Empresses; Queens; Sultans
Ahasuerus, King of Persia
Alexander the Great, King of Macedonia
Alfred the Great, King of England
Attila the Hun
Charles I, King of England

Charles II, King of England
Charles VII, King of France
Charles XII, King of Sweden
David, King of Israel
Edward IV, King of England
Edward VII, King of England
George III, King of England
Henry II, King of England
Henry V, King of England
Henry VIII, King of England
Herod the Great
Louis XI, King of France
Louis XIII, King of France
Louis XV, King of France
Louis XVI, King of France
Ludwig II, King of Bavaria
Mongkut, King of Siam
Philip II, King of Spain
Richard I, King of England
Richard III, King of England

Labor leaders
See also Business and financial figures
Boyle, William Anthony
Hoffa, Jimmy
Yablonski, Joseph A.

Lawyers
See also Judges
Bailey, F. Lee
Binder, Alvin
Bryan, William Jennings
Bugliosi, Vincent
Cohn, Roy
Darrow, Clarence
Davis, John William
Dershowitz, Alan M.
Fortas, Abe
Hardin, John Wesley
Kennedy, Robert F.
Krents, Harold
Lincoln, Abraham

Mandela, Nelson
Marshall, Thurgood
Mitchell, John
Myers, Lowell
Nizer, Louis
O'Donnell, Lawrence, Sr.
Rose, Mason
Slaton, Lewis
Smith, James

Literary agents
Ramsay, Peggy

Litigants
Anderson, Anna
Carney, Bill
Dummar, Melvin
Gideon, Clarence
Painter, Hal W.
Pulitzer, Herbert
Pulitzer, Roxanne
Rideout, Greta
Rideout, John
Roy, Julie
Vanderbilt, Gloria Morgan
Whitney, Gertrude

Lovers and mistresses
Abelard, Peter
Albaret, Celeste
Baker, Nicole
Barrows, Sydney Biddle
Beach, Sylvia
Bonaparte, Paolina
Broughton, Diana
Bryant, Louise
Brzeska, Sophie
Carver, Ellsworth
Casanova, Enrico
Clairmont, Clara
Claudel, Camille
Cusimano, Judy
Davies, Marion

Don Juan
Dubarry, Marie
Elder, Kate
Essex, Robert Devereux, Earl
  of
Finch Hatton, Denys
Glatt, Francine
Graham, Sheilah
Gwyn, Nell
Halliwell, Kenneth
Hamilton, Emma
Hastings, Beatrice
Heloise
Hill, Virginia
Lamb, Caroline
Martin, Ellen
Montes, Lola
Monti, Carlotta
Nesbit, Evelyn
Petacci, Claretta
Place, Etta
Raleigh, Walter
Rice-Davies, Mandy
Silva, Chica da
Sirisomphene, Keo
Soffel, Kate
Spungen, Nancy
Starr, Blaze
Stein, Gertrude
Summersby, Kay
Toklas, Alice B.
Vetsera, Maria
Walewska, Maria

Lyricists
  See Composers; Songwriters

Madams
  See Lovers and mistresses

Magicians
  See Entertainers
Houdini, Harry

Managers (Entertainment)
Diaghilev, Serge
Epstein, Brian
Hurok, Sol
Marcucci, Robert
Mathis, June

Marines
See Generals; Soldiers

Martial arts
Dux, Frank

Mayors
See Political figures

Missionaries
See also Clergy; Religious
leaders
Aylward, Gladys
Damien, Father
Donovan, Jean
Liddell, Eric

Mistresses
See Lovers and mistresses

Models
Hanson, Marla

Monks
See Clergy

Mothers
See Parents of prominent
people

Musicians
See also Composers; Sing-
ers; Songwriters
Armstrong, Louis
Bach, Johann Sebastian
Baker, Chet

Beach Boys
Beatles, The
Beethoven, Ludwig van
Beiderbecke, Leon Bismarck
Berry, Chuck
Best, Pete
Big Bopper
Blades, Ruben
Chopin, Frederic
Clapton, Eric
Cole, Nat King
Dalley, John
Daltrey, Roger
Doors, The
Dorsey, Jimmy
Dorsey, Tommy
Duchin, Eddy
Emerson, Keith
Entwistle, John
Fenelon, Fania
Gillespie, Dizzy
Goodman, Benny
Guarneri String Quartet
Handy, W.C.
Harrison, George
Hendrix, Jimi
Horowitz, Vladmir
Jardine, Al
Jones, Quincy
Joplin, Scott
Krupa, Gene
Lake, Greg
Ledbetter, Huddie
Lennon, John
Levant, Oscar
Liszt, Franz
Love, Mike
McCartney, Paul
Miller, Glenn
Monk, Thelonious
Moon, Keith
Morrison, Jim
Nichols, Ernest Loring

Paganini, Nicolo
Palmer, Carl
Parker, Charlie
Schumann, Clara
Sousa, John Philip
Soyer, David
Starr, Ringo
Steinhardt, Arnold
Stern, Isaac
Strauss, Johann, Jr.
Torrance, Dean
Townshend, Pete
Tree, Michael
Wilson, Brian
Wilson, Carl
Wilson, Dennis

Native American leaders
Atahualpa
Cochise
Crazy Horse
Geronimo
Ishi
Joseph
Pocahontas
Sitting Bull

Naturalists
  See also Conservationists
Adamson, George
Adamson, Joy
Darwin, Charles
Leslie-Melville, Betty

Naval officers
  See Admirals; Sailors

Nazi leaders
Eichmann, Adolf
Goebbels, Joseph
Heydrich, Reinhard
Hitler, Adolf

Nazi war crime investigators
Klarsfeld, Beate
Wiesenthal, Simon

Neurologists
  See Physicians

Newscasters
Faulk, John Henry

Newsmen
  See Journalists; Writers

Newspaper executives
  See Business and financial
  figures

Nobility
Alexander, Grand-Duke of
  Vladimir
John of Gaunt, Duke of Lan-
  caster
O'Donnell, Hugh
Sofia Alekseevna
Von Bulow, Claus
Windsor, Edward
Windsor, Wallis Warfield
  Simpson

Novelists
  See Writers

Nuns
  See Clergy

Nurses
Canada, Lena
Cavell, Edith
Harmon, Leola Mae
Kenny, Elizabeth
Nightingale, Florence
Sanger, Margaret
Ufema, Joy

Olympic atheletes
See also Boxers; Golf play-
ers; Gymnasts; Hockey
players; Runners; Skiers;
Swimmers
Abrahams, Harold
Liddell, Eric
Mathias, Robert
Mills, Billy
Owens, Jesse
Thorpe, Jim
Zaharias, Babe

Opera singers
See Singers

Orphans
Reynolds, Andre

Outlaws
See also Assassins and mur-
derers; Criminals
Bass, Sam
Bonney, William
Cassidy, Robert Parker
Cortez, Gregorio
Dalton, Bob
Dalton, Emmett
Dalton, Gratton
Ford, Bob
Hardin, John Wesley
Holliday, John H.
James, Frank
James, Jesse
Kelly, Ned
Longabaugh, Harry
Morgan, Daniel
Younger, Cole
Younger, James
Younger, John
Younger, Robert

Pacifists
See Activists

Painters
See Artists

Parents of prominent figures
Beethoven, Johanna
Brimmer, Michael
Brimmer, Sari
Delford, Carole
Delford, Frank
Dennis, Rusty
Farmer, Lillian
Frank, Otto
Horman, Edmund
Jahnke, Richard, Sr.
Kacew, Nina
Kassab, Freddy
Kaufman, Barry
Kaufman, Suzie
Kennedy, Edward Moore
Kennedy, Joan
Kennedy, Joseph P.
Kennedy, Rose
Lund, Doris
Miller, Barbara
Miller, Larry
Miraldo, Marianna
Osmond, George
Osmond, Olive
Quinlan, Joe
Quinlan, Julie
Roosevelt, Sara Delano
Villani, Romilda
Webster, Billie
Webster, John
Williams, Audrey
Williams, Hank

Patients
See also Victims (Crime)
Baker, John
Balter, Marie
Brimmer, Gabriela
Brown, Christy

Cappelletti, Joey
Delford, Alexandra
Dennis, Rocky
Fox, Terry
Frame, Janet
Fray, Lucile
Gehrig, Lou
Gunther, John, Jr.
Hawksworth, Henry
Helton, Jacquelyn
Kennedy, Edward Moore, Jr.
Lee, Laurel
Lund, Eric
McDonald, Anne
Miller, Kathy
Morris, Kathy
Piccolo, Brian
Piersall, Jimmy
Quinlan, Karen Ann
Roy, Julie
Sackter, Bill
Stokes, Maurice
White, Marian Rose

Patrons of the arts
Borgia, Lucretia

Pediatricians
See Physicians

Photographers
See also Artists
Boyle, Richard
Everingham, John

Physicians
Bethune, Norman
Bonner, Elena
Caldicott, Helen
Cook, Frederick
Cowley, R. Adams
Crippen, Hawley Harvey
Dafoe, Allan Roy

Ehrlich, Paul
Filartiga, Joel
Freud, Sigmund
Groda-Lewis, Mary
Hill, John Robert
Hitzig, William
Itard, Jean
Lear, Harold
Lesser, Anna Maria
Livingstone, David
MacDonald, Jeffrey
Morton, William Thomas
    Green
Mudd, Samuel
Polidori, John
Raynor, Charles
Sacks, Oliver
Sheppard, Sam
Stallings, James O.
Wassell, Roydon M.

Physicists
See Scientists

Pianists
See Musicians

Pilots
See also Astronauts
Bader, Douglas
Barnes, Florence
Brown, A. Roy
Corrigan, Douglas
Denton, Jeremiah
Earhart, Amelia
Gibson, Guy
Hassan, Concetta
Johnson, Amy
Kennedy, Joseph, Jr.
Lawson, Ted
Lindbergh, Charles
Markham, Beryl
McConnell, Joseph

Mollison, Jim
Powers, Francis
Richthofen, Manfred von
Rickenbacker, Eddie
Scott, Robert Lee
Tibbets, Paul
Wead, Frank

Pioneers
See also Frontiersmen/
women
Gunn, Mrs. Aeneas
Wilder, Laura Ingalls

Pirates
Bonney, Anne
Kidd, William
Lafitte, Jean
Morgan, Henry
Teach, Edward

Playwrights
See also Writers
Beckett, Samuel
Behan, Brendan
Cohan, George M.
Coward, Noel
Ephron, Nora
Frisch, Max
Gilbert, W.S.
Hart, Moss
Hellman, Lillian
Ibsen, Henrik
Kaufman, George S.
Miller, Arthur
O'Casey, Sean
O'Neill, Eugene
Orton, Joe
Simon, Neil
Skinner, Cornelia

Poets
See Writers

Police officers
Abberline, Frederick
Bates, Charles
Campbell, Ian
Earp, Wyatt
Egan, Eddie
Foster, Gregory
Garcia, Andy
Garrett, Pat
Gibson, Johnnie Mae
Gilmore, Thomas E.
Glatzle, Mary
Grafton, John
Greenberg, Dave
Grosso, Salvatore
Hantz, Bob
Hettinger, Karl
Hickok, James
Hoover, J. Edgar
Kelly, Hugh
Laurie, Rocco
Martinez, Ramiero
Masterson, William Barclay
Ness, Eliot
Potts, Lamar
Purvis, Melvin
Pusser, Buford
Rodriguez, Alberto
Serpico, Frank
Sieber, Al
Toma, Dave
Torres, Martha
Zigo, Ed

Political figures
See also Dictators; Emper-
ors; Empresses; Kings;
Presidential aides; Presi-
dents; Presidents, Ameri-
can; Prime ministers;
Princes; Princesses;
Queens; Revolutionaries
Adams, John

Benton, Thomas Hart
Borgia, Cesare
Burr, Aaron
Cassius
Cermak, Anton
Churchill, Winston
Ciano, Galeazzo
Crockett, Davy
Cromwell, Oliver
Curley, James M.
Danton, Georges
Davies, Joseph E.
Franklin, Benjamin
Gandhi, Mahatma
Goebbels, Joseph
Grimble, Arthur
Hamilton, Alexander
Hiss, Alger
Hitler, Adolf
Houston, Sam
Jay, John
Jefferson, Thomas
Kennedy, Edward Moore
Kennedy, Joseph P.
Kennedy, Robert F.
Kublai Khan
Lafayette, Marie Joseph Paul
    Yves Roch Gilbert du Mo-
    tier
Lodge, Henry Cabot
Long, Earl
Long, Huey
McCarthy, Joseph
Milk, Harvey
Mitchell, John
More, Thomas
Moscone, George
Mussolini, Benito
Nasser, Gamal Abdel
Parnell, Charles
Penn, William
Peron, Juan
Pontius Pilate

Profumo, John
Rayburn, Sam
Rasputin, Grigori Efimovich
Richelieu, Armand
Roosevelt, Eleanor
Ryan, Leo J.
Slaton, John M.
Smith, James
Stalin, Joseph
Stanford, Sally
Terasaki, Hidenari
Trotsky, Leon
Walker, James
Wallenberg, Raoul

Political prisoners
Gatzoyiannis, Eleni
Herman, Victor
Horman, Charles
London, Arthur
Mindszenty, Jozsef
Powers, Francis Gary
Timerman, Jacobo

Popes
    See also Clergy
Innocent III
John XXIII
John Paul II
Julius II
Peter
Pius XII

Presidential aides
Colson, Charles
Dean, John
Ehrlichman, John
Haldeman, H.R.
Liddy, G. Gordon
Magruder, Jeb

Presidents
Amin, Idi

Juarez, Benito
Moro, Aldo
Nasser, Gamal Abdel
Sadat, Anwar
Somoza, Anastasio
Villa, Pancho
Walker, William

Presidents, American
Adams, John
Eisenhower, Dwight
Jackson, Andrew
Jefferson, Thomas
Johnson, Andrew
Johnson, Lyndon B.
Kennedy, John F.
Lincoln, Abraham
Madison, James
Monroe, James
Nixon, Richard M.
Reagan, Ronald
Roosevelt, Franklin Delano
Roosevelt, Theodore
Truman, Harry S
Washington, George
Wilson, Woodrow

Priests
   See Clergy

Primatologists
   See Scientists

Prime ministers
   See also Political figures
Castro, Fidel
Churchill, Winston
Disraeli, Benjamin
Gandhi, Mahatma
Gladstone, William Ewart
Meir, Golda
Pitt, William
Rhodes, Cecil

Princes
Albert, Prince
Alexander, Grand-Duke of
   Vladimir
Alexis, Czarevitch
Borgia, Cesare
Charles, Prince of Wales
Edward, the Black Prince
George, Prince of Wales
Philip, Prince
Rainier III, Prince of Monaco
Rudolph, Crown Prince of
   Austria
Stuart, Charles

Princesses
Borgia, Lucretia
Kelly, Grace
Spencer, Diana
Tudor, Mary

Prisoners
   See Political prisoners; Prisoners of war

Prisoners of war
   See also Concentration
   camp inmates; Political
   prisoners
Coward, Charlie
Denton, Jeremiah
Frank, Anne
Keith, Agnes Newton

Prizefighters
   See Boxers

Producers
Belasco, David
Cohan, George M.
Diaghilev, Serge
Edwards, George
Friendly, Fred

Gordon, Barbara
Hayward, Leland
Landon, Michael
Marcucci, Robert
Mayer, Louis B.
Rose, Billy
Selznick, David O.
Selznick, Myron
Warner, Jack
Ziegfeld, Florenz

Prostitutes
Adler, Polly
Barrow, Sydney Biddle
F., Christiane
Hamilton, Polly
Hollander, Xaviera
Keeler, Christine
Sage, Anna
Stanford, Sally

Psychiatrists
    See also Physicians
Freud, Sigmund
Jung, Carl

Psychologists
Leary, Timothy
Lee, Lois
Ofshe, Richard

Publishers
Hearst, William Randolph
Hefner, Hugh
Mitchell, Dave
Stone, I.F.
Timerman, Jacobo

Queens
    See also Empresses
Anne of Cleves
Boleyn, Anne
Catherine of Aragon

Catherine of Valois
Christina, Queen of Sweden
Cleopatra, Queen of Egypt
Desideria, Queen of Sweden
    and Norway
Eleanor of Aquitaine
Elizabeth I, Queen of En-
    gland
Elizabeth II, Queen of En-
    gland
Esther, Queen of Persia
Grey, Jane
Howard, Catherine
Isabella I, Queen of Spain
Marie Antoinette, Queen of
    France
Mary, Queen of England
Mary Stuart, Queen of Scot-
    land
Parr, Catherine
Seymour, Jane
Tudor, Mary
Victoria, Queen of England

Racketeers
    See Criminals

Radio personalities
    See Broadcasters; Disk jock-
    eys

Ranchers
Chisum, John

Reformers
    See Activists

Religious leaders
    See also Biblical figures;
    Clergy; Evangelists; Mis-
    sionaries; Popes; Saints
Jesus Christ
Luther, Martin

Mohammad
Smith, Joseph
Wycliffe, John
Young, Brigham

Reporters
See Journalists

Revolutionaries
See also Activists; Political
figures
Devlin, Anne
Giuliano, Salvatore
Guevarra, Ernesto
Luxemburg, Rosa
Mahdi
Malcolm X
Pugachev, Emelyan
Robespierre, Maximilien de
Spartacus
Stuart, Charles
Trotsky, Leon
Villa, Pancho
Zapata, Emiliano

Rock musicians
See Musicians

Rodeo performers
Lyne, Phil
Mahan, Larry
Pirtle, Sue

Rowing
Hanlan, Edward

Royalty
See Emperors; Empresses;
Kings; Nobility; Princes;
Princesses; Queens; Sul-
tans

Runners
See also Olympic athletes

Abrahams, Harold
Baker, John
Fox, Terry
Liddell, Eric
Mills, Billy
Owens, Jesse
Rudolph, Wilma

Safari guides
Leslie-Melville, Jock

Sailors
See also Admirals
Bligh, William
Christian, Fletcher
Drake, Francis
Graham, Calvin L.
Jensen, Andrew
Jones, John Paul
Kennedy, John F.
Kudirka, Simas
Langsdorff, Hans
Sullivan, Albert
Sullivan, Francis
Sullivan, George
Sullivan, Joseph
Sullivan, Madison
Trapp, Georg
Tweed, George R.
Zumwalt, Elmo, III

Saints
See also Fatima visionaries
Becket, Thomas
Bernadette
Clare of Assisi
Francis of Assisi
Joan of Arc
Joseph
Joseph of Cupertino
More, Thomas
Paul
Peter

Seton, Elizabeth Bayley
Therese of Lisieux

Scientists
See also Engineers; Physicians
Bell, Alexander Graham
Crick, Francis
Curie, Marie
Curie, Pierre
Darwin, Charles
Edson, Thomas Alva
Ehrlich, Paul
Fossey, Dian
Franklin, Rosalind
Galilei, Galileo
Leakey, Louis
Oppenheimer, J. Robert
Pasteur, Louis
Petrofsky, Jerrold
Powell, John
Sakharov, Andrei
Szilard, Leo
Von Braun, Werner
Wallis, Barnes
Watson, James D.
Wilkins, Maurice

Scouts
See also Frontiersmen/women
Boone, Daniel
Cody, William
Hickok, James

Sculptors
See also Artists
Bartholdi, Frederic Auguste
Buonarroti, Michelangelo
Cellini, Benvenuto
Christo
Claudel, Camille
Gaudier-Brzeska, Henri

Rodin, Auguste
Whitney, Gertrude Vanderbilt

Sea captains
See Admirals; Sailors

Secret agents
See Spies and traitors

Senators
See Political figures; Presidents, American

Sheriffs
See Police officers

Showmen
Bailey, James Anthony
Barnum, P.T.
Cody, William
Edwards, Gus
Ziegfeld, Florenz

Singers
See also Actors and actresses; Musicians
Adams, Edie
Avalon, Frankie
Barry, Jan
Baynes, Nora
Beach Boys
Beatles, The
Big Bopper
Brice, Fanny
Callas, Maria
Caruso, Enrico
Cash, Johnny
Christy, Edwin P.
Clapton, Eric
Cline, Patsy
Clooney, Rosemary
Cole, Nat King

Crabtree, Lotta
Daltrey, Roger
Destinn, Emma
Doors, The
Emerson, Keith
Emerson, Lake & Palmer
Entwistle, John
Etting, Ruth
Fabian
Froman, Jane
Garland, Judy
Gilbert, Ronnie
Guthrie, Woody
Harrison, George
Hays, Lee
Hellerman, Fred
Hendrix, Jimi
Holiday, Billie
Holly, Buddy
Jardine, Al
Jillian, Ann
Jolson, Al
Jones, George
Joplin, Janis
Lake, Greg
Lawrence, Gertrude
Lawrence, Marjorie
Ledbetter, Huddie
Lennon, John
Lewis, Jerry Lee
Lind, Jenny
Love, Mike
Lynn, Loretta
Madonna
McCartney, Paul
Melba, Nellie
Miller, Marilyn
Moon, Keith
Moore, Grace
Morgan, Helen
Morris, Kathy
Morrison, Jim
Ono, Yoko

Palmer, Carl
Pavarotti, Luciano
Piaf, Edith
Presley, Elvis
Roth, Lillian
Russell, Lillian
Seeger, Pete
Starr, Ringo
Tanguay, Eva
Tilley, Vesta
Torrance, Dean
Townshend, Pete
Valens, Richie
Vicious, Sid
Weavers, The
Who, The
Williams, Hank
Williams, Hank, Jr.
Wilson, Brian
Wilson, Carl
Wilson, Dennis
Wynette, Tammy

Skiers
Johnson, Bill
Kinmont, Jill

Smugglers
Hayes, Billy
Worker, Dwight

Social reformers
See Activists

Social workers
Butterfield, Tom
Duco, Joyce
Flanagan, Edward

Soldiers
See also Generals
Alexander, Grand-Duke of
Vladimir

Andrews, James J.
Bingham, George Charles
Caputo, Philip
Cavanaugh, Frank
Chapman, Edward
Clive, Robert
Cortez, Hernando
Coward, Charles
Darby, William
De Soto, Hernando
Diaz, Rodrigo
Dreyfus, Alfred
Essex, Robert Devereux, Earl of
Gordon, Patrick
Graziani, Rodolfo
Hambleton, Iceal E.
Hassan, Concetta
Hayes, Ira Hamilton
Hensler, Paul G.
Joan of Arc, Saint
Kappler, Herbert
Kovic, Ron
Kutcher, James
Lawrence, T.E.
Leonski, Edward J.
Lucan, George
MacDonald, Jeffrey
Marcus, David
Mathias, Robert
Matlovich, Leonard
Morant, Harry
Mukhtar, Omar
Murphy, Audie
Pelosi, James
Pizarro, Francisco
Pugachev, Emelyan Ivanovich
Raleigh, Walter
Redl, Alfred
Ross, Barney
Schmid, Albert Andrew
Scruggs, Jan C.

Shaw, Robert
Slovik, Eddie
Thornwell, James
Travis, William
York, Alvin
Youssoupoff, Felix

Songwriters
See also Composers
Ball, Ernest R.
Brown, Lew
DeSylva, Buddy
Dresser, Paul
Edwards, Gus
Emmett, Dan
Fisher, Fred
Foster, Stephen
Gershwin, George
Gershwin, Ira
Hart, Lorenz
Henderson, Ray
Howard, Joseph E.
Kahn, Gus
Kalmar, Bert
Lennon, John
Madonna
Marcucci, Robert
McCartney, Paul
Olcott, Chauncey
Porter, Cole
Ruby, Harry
Stuart, Leslie

Spelling champions
Yann, Linn

Spies and traitors
Andre, John
Andrews, James J.
Arnold, Benedict
Bazna, Elyesa
Blunt, Anthony
Boyce, Christopher John

Burgess, Guy
Burr, Aaron
Canaris, Wilhelm
Chambers, Whittaker
Chapman, Edward
Churchill, Odette
Cohen, Elie
Cvetic, Matthew
Lee, Andrew Daulton
Maclean, Donald
MacLeod, Margaret Zelle
Morros, Boris
Powers, Francis Gary
Redl, Alfred
Szabo, Violette

Statesmen/women
See Political figures

Stunt persons
O'Neil, Kitty

Sultans
Saladin, Sultan of Egypt and
Syria

Supreme Court justices
See Judges

Surgeons
See Physicians

Swimmers
Fraser, Dawn
Kellerman, Annette

Teachers
See Educators

Tennis players
Connolly, Maureen
Richards, Renee

Theologians
See Clergy; Popes; Religious leaders

Track athletes
See Olympic athletes; Runners

Translators
Pran, Dith
Pudaite, Rochunga
Wycliffe, John

Transsexuals
Jorgensen, Christine
Richards, Renee

Trappers
See also Frontiersmen
Johnson, Albert

Treasure hunters
Fisher, Mel

Trumpeters
See Musicians

UFO observers
Hill, Barney
Hill, Betty

Undercover agents
Rowe, Gary Thomas
Torres, Martha

Union leaders
See Labor leaders

Veterinarians
Farnon, Siegfried
Herriot, James

Victims (Crime)
Becket, Thomas
Brady, James S.
Erroll, Josslyn Hay
Foster, Gregory
Gatzoyiannis, Eleni
Hanson, Marla
Hearst, Patty
Hill, Joan Robinson
Holder, Maryse
Hughes, Francine
Jahnke, Richard, Sr.
Masters, Hope
Milk, Harvey
Moscone, George
Phagan, Mary
Roy, Julie
Ryan, Leo J.
Saldana, Theresa
Spungen, Nancy
Stratten, Dorothy
Stuart, Carol
Walsh, Adam
Webster, Randy
Yablonski, Joseph A.
Yablonski, Margaret

Violinists
See Musicians

Vocalists
See Singers

War
See Admirals; Generals; Pilots; Prisoners of war; Sailors; Soldiers; War criminals

War criminals
Barbie, Klaus
Eichmann, Adolf
Hitler, Adolf

War heroes
Alexander, Grand-Duke of Vladimir
Andrews, James J.
Brown, A. Roy
Chapayev, Vasilii Ivanovich
Graham, Calvin L.
Hayes, Ira Hamilton
Jones, John Paul
Kennedy, John F.
Murphy, Audie
Richthofen, Manfred von
Rickenbacker, Eddie
York, Alvin

War, Prisoners of
See Prisoners of war

Wardens
Duffy, Clinton T.

Wives of prominent men
Bacall, Lauren
Bach, Anna Magdalena
Barrett, Elizabeth
Biko, Ntsiki
Bonner, Elena
Brady, Sarah
Braun, Eva
Bruce, Honey Harlowe
Burke, Billie
Cassady, Carolyn
Cavanaugh, Florence
Ciano, Edda Mussolini
Clemens, Olivia
Davidman, Joy
Dean, Maureen
Doss, Helen
Earp, Josephine Marcus
Eaton, Peggy
Fitzgerald, Zelda
Fremont, Jessie Benton

Gehrig, Eleanor
Grieg, Nina Hagerup
Gunther, Frances
Holmes, Fanny
Horman, Beth
Houdini, Bess
Jackson, Rachel
Johnson, Claudia
Joyce, Nora Barnacle
Kennedy, Ethel
Kennedy, Jacqueline Bouvier
Kennedy, Joan
King, Coretta Scott
Lawrence, Frieda
Lee, Linda
Lewis, Myra Gale
Lincoln, Mary
Lindbergh, Anne Morrow
Madison, Dolley
Mason, Marsha
McConnell, Pearl
Miller, Helen Burger
Mussolini, Rachele
Peron, Eva
Presley, Priscilla
Pulitzer, Roxanne
Raynor, Katherine
Rogers, Betty
Roosevelt, Eleanor
Ryan, Kathryn
Sadat, Jihan
Schumann, Clara
Stratton, Ethel
Tchaikovsky, Nina Milyu-
  kova
Thrash, Prissy
Thum, Shirlee
Timerman, Risha
Vanderbilt, Alice
Von Bulow, Martha
Wagner, Cosima

Walsh, Reve
Washington, Martha
Williams, Audrey
Wilson, Edith
Wilson, Ellen
Windsor, Wallis Warfield
  Simpson
Yablonski, Margaret

Women's rights activists
  See Activists

Wrestlers
Zaharias, George

Writers
  See also Journalists; Play-
  wrights
Abubadika, Mwlina Imiri
Amory, Cleveland
Andersen, Hans Christian
Angelou, Maya
Barrett, Elizabeth
Bast, William
Blixen, Karen
Brimmer, Gabriela
Bronte, Anne
Bronte, Charlotte
Bronte, Emily
Brown, Christy
Browning, Robert
Burroughs, William S.
Byron, George
Campbell, Alan
Caputo, Philip
Carroll, Lewis
Carson, Sonny
Cervantes, Miguel de
Chessman, Caryl W.
Christie, Agatha
Claudel, Paul

Cousins, Norman
Crawford, Christina
Dahl, Roald
Davis, Angela
Day, Clarence, Jr.
De Sade, Marquis
Delford, Frank
Doss, Helen
Eareckson, Joni
Ephron, Nora
Fitzgerald, F. Scott
Fitzgerald, Zelda
Frame, Janet
Frank, Anne
Gary, Romain
Ginsberg, Allen
Goldman, Emma
Green, Hannah
Greenberg, Stanley
Grimm, Jacob
Grimm, Wilhelm
Gunther, Frances
Gunther, John
Hammett, Dashiell
Hanff, Helene
Harris, Frank
Harte, Bret
Hastings, Beatrice
Hayward, Brooke
Hecht, Ben
Hellman, Lillian
Hemingway, Ernest
Hill, Ann Kurth
Holder, Maryse
Houston, Jeanne Wakatuski
Hughes, Langston
Ibsen, Henrik
Joyce, James
Kaufman, Barry
Keith, Agnes Newton
Keller, Helen

Kennedy, John F.
Kerouac, Jack
Lamb, Caroline
Lawrence, D.H.
Lear, Martha
Levi, Carlo
Lewis, C.S.
Lindbergh, Anne Morrow
London, Jack
Luhan, Mabel Dodge
Lund, Doris
Masterson, William
Mathis, June
Maugham, Somerset
Mishima, Yukio
Morrow, Barry
Mowat, Farley
O'Donnell, Lawrence, Jr.
Omar Khayyam
Painter, Hal W.
Parker, Dorothy
Peale, Norman Vincent
Pepys, Samuel
Pierson, Louise
Plath, Sylvia
Poe, Edgar Allan
Proust, Marcel
Rawlings, Marjorie Kinnan
Reed, John
Rousseau, Jean-Jacques
Ryan, Cornelius
Ryan, Kathryn
Sand, George
Shelley, Mary Wollstonecraft
Shelley, Percy Bysshe
Skinner, Cornelia Otis
Smith, Florence Margaret
Stein, Gertrude
Strindberg, August
Twain, Mark
Villon, Francois

Voltaire, Francois
Wead, Frank
Weaver, Harriet Shaw
Weisman, Mary-Lou
Wells, H.G.

Wilde, Oscar
Wilder, Laura Ingalls
Woods, Wendy
Yeats, William Butler
Zola, Emile

DATE OF RELEASE INDEX

1926
Don Juan 252

1927
The Beloved Rogue 976

1929
Disraeli 247

1930
Abraham Lincoln 624
Billy The Kid 63
Dubarry, Woman Of Passion 263
A Lady's Morals 627
The Vagabond King 978

1931
Alexander Hamilton 401

1932
Law And Order 278
Mata Hari 652
Rasputin And The Empress 823a
Silver Dollar 934

1933
The Man Who Dared 141
The Private Life Of Henry VIII 433
Queen Christina 160
Voltaire 980

1934
The Affairs Of Cellini 140
The Barretts Of Wimpole Street 32
Catherine The Great 134
Chapayev 145a
Cleopatra 167
The Great Waltz 922
The House Of Rothschild 859
Madame Dubarry 264
The Mighty Barnum 31
Nell Gwyn 396
The Private Life Of Don Juan 253
The Scarlet Empress 137
Viva Villa 975

1935
Annie Oakley 752
Cardinal Richelieu 836
Clive Of India 171
The Crusades 832
Diamond Jim 85
Drake Of England 259
Mutiny On The Bounty 54
Peg Of Old Drury 1006

1936
Beethoven's Great Love 45b
The Country Doctor 211
Daniel Boone 73
The Gorgeous Hussy 281
The Great Ziegfeld 1018
Mary Of Scotland 670

Mayerling 864
The Prisoner Of Shark Island 724
Reunion 213
Rhodes 831a
The Robin Hood Of El Dorado 731
The Story Of Louis Pasteur 772
Sutter's Gold 932
The White Angel 747

1937
Conquest 735
Fire Over England 294
The Life Of Emile Zola 1021
Parnell 770
The Plainsman 447
Rembrandt 830
The Toast Of New York 313
Under The Red Robe 837
Victoria The Great 971
We Who Are About To Die 594

1938
The Adventures Of Marco Polo 795
Alexander Nevsky 7a
Billy The Kid Returns 65
Boys Town 317
The Buccaneer 589
Five Of A Kind 212
Frontier Scout 445
The Great Waltz 923
If I Were King 977
Marie Antoinette 665
Sixty Glorious Years 970
Suez 227

1939
Allegheny Uprising 902
Flying Irishman 191

Frontier Marshal 275
Geronimo 356
The Great Victor Herbert 435
Jesse James 510
Juarez 546
The Mad Empress 122
Man Of Conquest 487
Nurse Edith Cavell 139
The Private Lives Of Elizabeth And Essex 295
Rose Of Washington Square 88
Stanley And Livingstone 910
The Star Maker 286
The Story Of Alexander Graham Bell 48
The Story Of Vernon And Irene Castle 133
Swanee River 325
Tower Of London 835
Young Mr. Lincoln 626

1940
Abe Lincoln In Illinois 623
Brigham Young—Frontiersman 1012
Dispatch From Reuters 831
Dr. Ehrlich's Magic Bullet 289
Edison The Man 282
Hudson's Bay 819
In Old New York 341
Kit Carson 125
Knute Rockne—All American 843
Lillian Russell 867
The Return Of Frank James 506
The Westerner 40
Young Bill Hickok 452
Young Buffalo Bill 179
Young Tom Edison 283

1941
Bad Men Of Missouri 1013
Badlands Of Dakota 444
Belle Starr 912
Billy The Kid 64
Blossoms In The Dust 368
Courageous Mr. Penn 777
The Lady With Red Hair 127
New Wine 881
Sergeant York 1016
That Hamilton Woman 403
You Will Remember 928

1942
The Black Swan 712
Gentleman Jim 190
The Great Mr. Handel 405
The Loves Of Edgar Allan
    Poe 794
Mad Dog Coll 181
The Moon And Sixpence 353
My Gal Sal 261
The Pride Of The Yankees
    355
The Prime Minister 248
Tennessee Johnson 532
They Died With Their Boots
    On 209
Tombstone, The Town Too
    Tough To Die 280
Wild Bill Hickok 451
Wings And The Woman 531
Yankee Doodle Dandy 180
Young Mr. Pitt 789

1943
Dixie 300
Flight For Freedom 273
Hangmen Also Die 441
Hitler—Dead Or Alive 461
Hitler's Hangman 442
The Iron Major 138
Ivan The Terrible, Part 1 497

Jack London 633
Madame Curie 205
Mission To Moscow 224
The Outlaw 70
The Song Of Bernadette 50
Spitfire 698
The Strange Death Of Adolf
    Hitler 466
The Woman Of The Town
    675

1944
The Adventures Of Mark
    Twain 960
Buffalo Bill 175
Champagne Charlie 619
Enemy Of Women 370
The Great Moment 717
The Hitler Gang 462
Irish Eyes Are Smiling 28
The Lodger 500
Our Hearts Were Young And
    Gay 899
Roger Touhy—Gangster 952
Shine On Harvest Moon 36
The Story Of Dr. Wassell 989
The Sullivans 929
Thirty Seconds Over Tokyo
    255
Wilson 1004

1945
Captain Eddie 839
Captain Kidd 576
Dillinger 244
The Dolly Sisters 250
God Is My Co-Pilot 884
The Great John L. 930
Henry V 431
Incendiary Blonde 392
Pride Of The Marines 880
Rhapsody In Blue 358
Roughly Speaking 787

A Royal Scandal 136
A Song To Remember 156
The Story Of G.I. Joe 817

1946
Caesar And Cleopatra 166
Devotion 93
Gaiety George 285
Ivan The Terrible, Part 2
  498
The Jolson Story 538
Magnificent Doll 653
My Darling Clementine 279
Night And Day 800
Our Hearts Were Growing
  Up 900
Sister Kenny 571
So Goes My Love 678
Till The Clouds Roll By 572

1947
Bonnie Prince Charlie 927
Buffalo Bill Rides Again 178
Captain From Castile 193
The Exile 147
The Fabulous Dorseys 256
Forever Amber 148
I Wonder Who's Kissing Her
  Now 488
Life With Father 226
The Magic Bow 764
My Wild Irish Rose 756
The Perils Of Pauline 998
Song Of Love 882
Song Of Scheherezade 841

1948
The Adventures Of Casa-
  nova 129
The Babe Ruth Story 869
Eternal Melodies 722
Iron Curtain 353b
Joan Of Arc 525

Look For The Silver Lining
  692
Scott Of The Antarctic 883
The Secret Land 103
Song Of My Heart 938
Words And Music 844

1949
The Adventures Of Don Juan
  251
All The King's Men 634
Bride Of Vengeance 78
Calamity Jane And Sam Bass
  115
Christopher Columbus 184
Guilty Of Treason 694
I Shot Jesse James 321
Madeleine 903a
Oh You Beautiful Doll 312
Prince Of Foxes 79
Samson And Delilah 877a
The Stratton Story 921
The Younger Brothers 1015

1950
Annie Get Your Gun 751
Broken Arrow 173
Cheaper By The Dozen 364
Comanche Territory 82
Davy Crockett, Indian Scout
  202
The First Texan 486
The Great Jewel Robber 234
The Great Missouri Raid 508
The Jackie Robinson Story
  842
Jolson Sings Again 537
Julius Caesar 106
The Kansas Raiders 511
The Kid From Texas 67
The Last Of The Buccaneers
  591
The Magnificent Yankee 475

Three Came Home 553
Three Little Words 548
Young Daniel Boone 75
Young Man With A Horn 47

1951
Anne Of The Indies 62
Bad Lord Byron 104
David And Bathsheba 220
The Desert Fox 849
Follow The Sun 469
Golden Girl 198
The Great Caruso 128
I Dream Of Jeannie 324
I Was A Communist For The FBI 210
Jim Thorpe—All American 943
The Lady With A Lamp 746
The Magic Box 338
Odette 161
Valentino 966

1952
Above And Beyond 946
Belles On Their Toes 365
Blackbeard The Pirate 939
Five Fingers 37
Hans Christian Andersen 16
I'll See You In My Dreams 547a
The Iron Mistress 83
The Lawless Breed 408
Lucretia Borgia 80
The Million Dollar Mermaid 557
The Miracle Of Our Lady Of Fatima 257
Montana Belle 914
Moulin Rouge 953
The Pride Of St. Louis 231
Somebody Loves Me 887
Stars And Stripes Forever 906

The Story Of Will Rogers 846
Viva Zapata! 1017
The Winning Team 9
With A Song In My Heart 340

1953
The Actress 374
Calamity Jane 113
Call Me Madam 688
Captain John Smith And Pocahontas 903
Conquest Of Conchise 174
Crazylegs 457
The Desert Rats 850
The Eddie Cantor Story 116
The Great Gilbert And Sullivan 363
The Great Jesse James Raid 507
Houdini 484
The I Don't Care Girl 935
The Joe Louis Story 639
Julius Caesar 107
A Lion In The Streets 637
Martin Luther 645
Melba 685
Pony Express 449
The President's Lady 505
Salome 877
Serpent Of The Nile 169
So This Is Love 707
The Sword And The Rose 959
Tonight We Sing 493
Young Bess 297

1954
Beau Brummel 96
The Bob Mathias Story 676
Canaris, Master Spy 112a
Deep In My Heart 848
Desiree 736
Duffy Of San Quentin 267
The Eternal Sea 482

The Glenn Miller Story 690
King Richard And The Cru-
  sades 833
The Law Vs. Billy The Kid
  68
The Man In The Attic 501
Masterson Of Kansas 674
The Sign Of The Pagan 23
Sitting Bull 897

1955
The Benny Goodman Story
  371
Cell 2455, Death Row 153
Chief Crazy Horse 200
The Court-Martial Of Billy
  Mitchell 697
The Dam Busters 351
Davy Crockett, King Of The
  Wild Frontier 203
The Far Horizons 618
The Girl In The Red Velvet
  Swing 742
I'll Cry Tomorrow 858
Interrupted Melody 602
The King's Thief 149
Lola Montes 706
Love Me Or Leave Me 304
A Man Called Peter 667
Marie Antoinette 666
The McConnell Story 680
Prince Of Players 76
The Scarlet Coat 21
The Seven Little Foys 327
That Lady 686
To Hell And Back 732
The Virgin Queen 296
The Warriors 284

1956
Alexander The Great 8
The Barretts Of Wimpole
  Street 33

The Battle Of The River Plate
  599
The Best Things In Life Are
  Free 239
The Conqueror 574
Daniel Boone, Trail Blazer 74
Davy Crockett And The River
  Pirates 201
The Eddy Duchin Story 265
The Great Locomotive Chase
  18
I Killed Wild Bill Hickok 446
The Last Ten Days 464
Lust For Life 968
Magic Fire 982
The Mystery Of Picasso 784
Pacific Destiny 388
Reach For The Sky 25
Richard III 834
Somebody Up There Likes
  Me 380
The Ten Commandments 719
The Vagabond King 979

1957
After The Ball 948
Baby Face Nelson 740
Beau James 984
The Buster Keaton Story 551a
Fear Strikes Out 786
Gunfight At The O.K. Corral
  276
The Helen Morgan Story 711
The James Dean Story 230
Jeanne Eagels 270
The Joker Is Wild 617
The Lovers Of Montparnasse
  699
Man Of A Thousand Faces
  145
A Monkey On My Back 857
Mr. Rock And Roll 336
Omar Khayyam 757

The Parson And The Outlaw 71

Saint Joan 526

The Spirit Of St. Louis 629

The True Story Of Jesse James 514

The Wings Of Eagles 991

1958

The Barbarian And The Geisha 415

The Bonnie Parker Story 769

The Buccaneer 590

Carve Her Name With Pride 933

Cole Younger, Gunfighter 1014

Cowboy 413

Darby's Rangers 217

I Accuse 262

I Want To Live 378

The Inn Of The Sixth Happiness 24

The Last Hurrah 206

The Left-Handed Gun 69

Machine Gun Kelly 558

St. Louis Blues 406

Too Much Too Soon 35

Villa 973

1959

Al Capone 117

Beloved Infidel 314

The Big Fisherman 779

The Diary Of Anne Frank 330

Five Pennies 744

The Gene Krupa Story 585

Gunfight At Dodge City 673

Herod The Great 437

Jack The Ripper 499

John Paul Jones 541

The Naked Maja 376

Tempest 810

1960

The Alamo 81

Bluebeard's Ten Honeymoons 596

Esther And The King 303

The Gallant Hours 400

The Great Imposter 232

Hannibal 407

I Aim At The Stars 981

Inherit The Wind 218

Man On A String 716

Nights Of Rasputin 822

Oscar Wilde 1000c

Pretty Boy Floyd 319

The Rise And Fall Of Legs Diamond 241

Song Without End 631

Spartacus 907

The Story Of Ruth 868

Sunrise At Campobello 856

Ten Who Dared 802

The Trials Of Oscar Wilde 1000d

The Waltz King 925

Young Jesse James 515

1961

Bernadette Of Lourdes 49

Bridge To The Sun 940

David And Goliath 221

El Cid 242

Francis Of Assisi 329

The George Raft Story 820

The Hoodlum Priest 164

King Of Kings 524

King Of The Roaring 20's—The Story Of Arnold Rothstein 860

Morgan The Pirate 713

Operation Eichmann 291

The Outsider 419

Salvatore Giuliano 367b

The Trapp Family 955

1962
The Black Fox 458
Caesar The Conqueror 105
Constantine And The Cross
188
Forever My Love 333
Freud 337
Geronimo 357
Gypsy 397
Hemingway's Adventures Of
A Young Man 428
Hitler 460
Imperial Venus 61
Landru 597
Lawrence Of Arabia 603
The Legend Of Valentino 964
The Magnificent Rebel 46
Marco Polo 797
The Miracle Worker 555
Mutiny On The Bounty 55
No Man Is An Island 961
The Password Is Courage 195
The Reluctant Saint 545a
The Trial Of Joan Of Arc 526a

1963
Act One 416
Buffalo Bill 176
Cleopatra 168
Dr. Crippen 200b
Lafayette 588
Marilyn 702
Papa's Delicate Condition
387
PT 109 567
Seven Seas To Calais 260
The Wonderful Word Of The
Brothers Grimm 389

1964
Becket 45
The Christine Keeler Affair
552

The Finest Hours 161a
Four Days In November 562
A House Is Not A Home 6
One Man's Way 774
Your Cheatin' Heart 1002

1965
The Agony And The Ecstasy
98
The Eleanor Roosevelt Story
852
Genghis Khan 575
The Greatest Story Ever Told
520
Harlow 410–411
Murieta 730
The Sound Of Music 954
A Study In Terror 503
Young Cassidy 753
Young Dillinger 246

1966
Born Free 3
Cast A Giant Shadow 664
The Daydreamer 15
El Greco 381
The Fighting Prince Of Done-
gal 754
The Gospel According To St.
Matthew 518
John F. Kennedy: Years Of
Lightning, Days Of Drums
563
Khartoum 373
A Man For All Seasons 709
Marco The Magnificent 798
The Plainsman 448
Pontius Pilate 799
Rasputin—The Mad Monk
824

1967
Bonnie And Clyde 768

Hour Of The Gun 277
In Cold Blood 904
Jean Renoir, The Boss
     830a
A King's Story 1005
The St. Valentine's Day Mas-
     sacre 119
Triple Cross 146

1968
The Boston Strangler 228a
Cervantes 142
The Charge Of The Light Bri-
     gade 121
Custer Of The West 208
Funny Girl 86
The Great Catherine 135
The Lion In Winter 430
A Man Named John 527
Paper Lion 793
Star! 601
Villa Rides 974

1969
Alfred The Great 10
Anne Of The Thousand Days
     60
Butch Cassidy And The Sun-
     dance Kid 132
Che 391
De Sade 228
Fraulein Doktor 614
Gaily, Gaily 425
I Killed Rasputin 1015a
Isadora 269
Lady Hamilton 402
Mayerling 865
The Royal Hunt Of The Sun
     790
Sinful Davy 398
The Unfinished Journey Of
     Robert Kennedy 570
Where's Jack? 893

1970
AKA Cassius Clay 11
Bloody Mama 29
Brian's Song 785
A Bullet For Pretty Boy 318
Chisum 155
The Christine Jorgensen
     Story 544
The Confession 632
Cromwell 204
Elvis That's The Way It Is 806
The Great White Hope 534
The Honeymoon Killers 44a
Johnny Cash! The Man, His
     World, His Music 130a
Julius Caesar 108
King: A Filmed Record . . .
     Montgomery To Memphis
     578
Let It Be 44
Ned Kelly 560
Patton 773a
Song Of Norway 386
The Wild Child 496

1971
The Desperate Mission 729
Doc 473
Eagle In A Cage 737
The French Connection 288
The Great Man's Whiskers
     625
Jack Johnson 535
Joe Hill 454
Mary, Queen Of Scots 671
The Murder Of Fred Hamp-
     ton 403a
The Music Lovers 937
Nicholas And Alexandra 743
No Drums, No Bugles 350a
The Red Tent 14
Sacco And Vanzetti 871
10 Rillington Place 158

Von Richthofen And Brown 838
Waterloo 738

1972
Antony And Cleopatra 165
Arruza 22
The Assassination Of Trotsky 956
The Darwin Adventure 219
Dirty Little Billy 66
Elvis On Tour 805
Evel Knievel 582
The Great Northfield Minnesota Raid 509
The Great Waltz 924
Lady Caroline Lamb 592
Lady Sings The Blues 470
The Life And Times Of Judge Roy Bean 39
Living Free 5
Ludwig 642
Malcolm X 658
Marjoe 375
Pancho Villa 972
Savage Messiah 351
1776 2
Toma 950
The Trial Of The Catonsville Nine 51a
The Valachi Papers 963
The Weekend Nun 266
Young Winston 162

1973
Badge 373
Brother Sun, Sister Moon 328
Ciao! Manhattan 886
Dillinger 245
Galileo 344
Gospel Road 519
Henry VIII And His Six Wives 432

Hitler: The Last Ten Days 463
I Am A Dancer 750
I.F. Stone's Weekly 918
Jesus Christ Superstar 522
Jimi Hendrix 429
Marco 796
Maurie 917
The Nelson Affair 741
Papillon 152
Pat Garrett And Billy The Kid 72
Serpico 889
Sunshine 427
Walking Tall 815

1974
The Abdication 159
All Creatures Great And Small 438
Antonia: A Portrait Of The Woman 89
Badlands 911
A Bigger Splash 467
Conrack 187
Crazy Joe 345
The Education Of Sonny Carson 126
The Execution Of Private Slovik 900
The FBI Story: The FBI Versus Alvin Karpis 549
F. Scott Fitzgerald And "The Last Of The Belles" 315
General Idi Amin Dada 13a
The Great American Cowboy 654
It's Good To Be Alive 111
Lenny 95
Little House On The Prairie 1001
Lucky Luciano 641
Luther 644
Mahler 656

Melvin Purvis—G Man 812
Missiles Of October 565
Mrs. Sundance 791
My Pleasure Is My Business 472
The Sex Symbol 704
Stavinsky 914a
The Story Of Jacob And Joseph 505a
The Story Of Pretty Boy Floyd 320
The Super Cops 383
The Virginia Hill Story 456

1975
Babe 1016
Capone 118
Collision Course 647
The Deadly Tower 999
Death Be Not Proud 394
Delancey Street: The Crisis Within 655
Eric 643
The Family Nobody Wanted 258
Fear On Trial 309
Foster And Laurie 323
Funny Lady 87
Give 'Em Hell, Harry! 957
Guilty Or Innocent: The Sam Sheppard Murder Case 894
The Happy Hooker 471
Hey, I'm Alive 581
A Home Of Our Own 990
Hustling 892
I Will Fight No More Forever 545
Janis 542
The Kansas City Massacre 811
The Legend Of Lizzie Borden 77
The Legend Of Valentino 965

Lisztomania 630
The Man In The Glass Booth 290
Moses 718
The Mystery Of Kasper Hauser 416b
Operation Daybreak 443
The Other Side Of The Mountain 579
Rasputin 823
The Silence 775
The Trial Of Chaplain Jensen 516
The UFO Incident 453
Walking Tall, Part 2 816

1976
All The President's Men 1007
Amelia Earhart 272
Bound For Glory 395
Bridger 90
Buffalo Bill And The Indians 177
Christian The Lion 4
The Disappearance Of Aimee 682
Edvard Munch 728
Eleanor And Franklin 853
F. Scott Fitzgerald In Hollywood 316
Farewell To Manzanar 485
Francis Gary Powers: The True Story Of The U-2 Spy Incident 803
Gable And Lombard 342
Goodbye, Norma Jean 701
The Great Houdinis 483
Grey Gardens 38
Helter Skelter 661
Homage To Chagall—The Colours Of Love 142a
The Incredible Sarah 51
James Dean 229

Jesus Of Nazareth 523
Judge Horton And The
  Scottsboro Boys 481
Leadbelly 604
The Lindbergh Kidnapping
  Case 628
Louis Armstrong, Chicago
  Style 20
Mad Dog Morgan 710
Return To Earth 7
Serpico: The Deadly Game
  890
The Story Of Adele H 492
The Story Of David 223
W.C. Fields And Me 311
Xica 895a

1977
The Amazing Howard
  Hughes 491
Bethune 51c
Brothers 225
Circle Of Children 649
The Death Of Richie 243
Eleanor And Franklin: The
  White House Years 854
Fellini's Casanova 130
Final Chapter, Walking Tall
  813
Greased Lightning 885
The Greatest 12
I Never Promised You A Rose
  Garden 382
Johnny, We Hardly Knew Ye
  564
Julia 426
Kill Me If You Can 154
King 577
The Last Hurrah 207
The Life And Assassination
  Of The Kingfish 636
MacArthur 648
Mary White 997

Mohammad, Messenger Of
  God 700
The Picture Show Man 776
The Private Files Of J. Edgar
  Hoover 476
Scott Joplin 543
Something For Joey 120
Tail Gunner Joe 679
The Trial Of Lee Harvey
  Oswald 762
Valentino 967
The White Buffalo 450
Wilma 866
Young Joe, The Forgotten
  Kennedy 568

1978
American Hot Wax 335
And I Alone Survived 293
Betrayal 862
Born Again 183
Bud And Lou 1
The Buddy Holly Story 474
Deadman's Curve 34
A Death In Canaan 828
The Defection Of Simas
  Kudirka 586
First, You Cry 847
The Great Wallendas 987
Ike: The War Years 292
Ishi: The Last Of His Tribe
  495
Lady Of The House 909
Little Mo 186
A Love Affair: The Eleanor
  And Lou Gehrig Story 354
Lovey: A Circle Of Children,
  Part II 650
Midnight Express 418
More Than Friends 829
The Nativity 669
One In A Million: The Ron
  LeFlore Story 606

The Other Side Of The Mountain, Part 2 580
A Real American Hero 814
Ring Of Passion 640
Ruby And Oswald 863
Sergeant Matlovich Vs. The U.S. Air Force 677
Stevie 901
The Winds Of Kitty Hawk 1009
A Woman Called Moses 958
Ziegfeld: The Man And His Women 1019

1979
Agatha 157
All That Jazz 322
All Things Bright And Beautiful 439
Aunt Mary 249
The Bell Jar 792
The Birth Of The Beatles 42
Blind Ambition 231a
Breaker Morant 708
The Bronte Sisters 92
Butch And Sundance: The Early Days 131
Can You Hear The Laughter? The Story Of Freddie Prinze 808
Chapter Two 896
Dawn 333a
Dummy 598
Eboli 615
Elvis 804
Escape From Alcatraz 714
Friendly Fire 727
The House On Garibaldi Street 409
I Know Why The Caged Bird Sings 19
Jesus 521
The Kids Are Alright 1000

The Lady In Red 874
The Last Giraffe 613
The Last Ride Of The Dalton Gang 214
Marciano 662
Mary And Joseph: A Story Of Faith 668
Meetings With Remarkable Men 394a
The Miracle Worker 556
Mr. Horn 479
Murder By Degree 502
The Onion Field 440
The Ordeal Of Patty Hearst 422
A Shining Season 26
Silent Victory: The Kitty O'Neil Story 758
Son Rise: A Miracle Of Love 550
This Man Stands Alone 367
Time After Time 504
Undercover With The KKK 861a
Walking Through The Fire 605
When Hell Was In Session 236

1980
Alcatraz: The Whole Shocking Story 123
Attica 1000a
Belle Starr 913
Bogie 59
Caligula 110
The Children Of An Lac 27
Coal Miner's Daughter 646
The Day Christ Died 517
The Diary Of Anne Frank 331
The Elephant Man 687

Enola Gay: The Men, The Mission, The Atomic Bomb 947

Escape 1008

FDR: The Last Year 855

Fighting Back 52

From Mao To Mozart: Isaac Stern In China 915

Gauguin The Savage 352

Gideon's Trumpet 362

Guyana: Cult Of The Damned 539

The Guyana Tragedy: The Story Of Jim Jones 540

Haywire 420

Heart Beat 573

The Hunter 944

The Idolmaker 663

The Jayne Mansfield Story 660

Jimmy B And Andre 101

Joni 271

The Long Riders 513

Marilyn: The Untold Story 703

Mark, I Love You 767

McVicar 683

Melvin And Howard 268

Nijinsky 748

The Ordeal Of Dr. Mudd 723

Our Hitler 465

Playing For Time 310

Portrait Of A Rebel: The Re-markable Mrs. Sanger 878

Power 468

A Private Battle 870

Raging Bull 593

Rape And Marriage: The Rid-eout Case 840

Rodeo Girl 788

A Rumor Of War 120a

The Scarlett O'Hara War 888

Seizure: The Story Of Kathy Morris 715

Sophia Loren: Her Own Story 638

This Year's Blonde 705

A Time For Miracles 891

To Race The Wind 584

Tom Horn 480

The Trials Of Alger Hiss 457a

Where The Buffalo Roam 941

1981

The Adventures Of Nellie Bly 58

Amin, The Rise And Fall 13

Beatlemania 41

Bill 872a

Bitter Harvest 399

The Bunker 459

The Case Of The Legless Vet-eran 587

Celeste 809

Chanel Solitaire 144

Chariots Of Fire 620

The Children Nobody Wanted 102

Crisis At Central High 489

The Day After Trinity: J. Robert Oppenheimer And The Atomic Bomb 759

Death Hunt 530

Death Of A Centerfold: The Dorothy Stratten Story 919

Don't Cry, It's Only Thunder 434

Don't Look Back: The Story Of Leroy "Satchel" Paige 766

Eight Minutes To Midnight 109

Emerson, Lake & Palmer In Concert 299

Eric Clapton And His Rolling
Hotel 163
Escape From Iran: The Cana-
dian Caper 936
Evita Peron 778
The Five Of Me 417
From A Far Country: John
Paul II 528
The Gentleman Bandit 765
Grambling's White Tiger
384
Hopper's Silence 477
Jacqueline Bouvier Kennedy
561
John Heartfield, Photomon-
tagist 424
The Killing Of Randy Web-
ster 993
Leave 'Em Laughing 945
Lion Of The Desert 725
The Marva Collins Story 182
A Matter Of Life And Death
962
Max Frisch: Journal I-III 339
The Miracle Of Kathy Miller
691
Miracle On Ice 94
Mommie Dearest 199
Murder In Texas 455
The Ordeal Of Bill Carney
124
The Patricia Neal Story 739
The People Vs. Jean Harris
414
Peter And Paul 780
The Priest Of Love 600
Reds 827
The Roads Of Exile 861
Stand By Your Man 1010
This Is Elvis 807
Thornwell 942
Three Hundred Miles For
Stephanie 845

1982
The Ballad Of Gregorio
Cortez 192
Charles And Diana: A Royal
Love Story 150
Coming Out Of The Ice 436
The Compleat Beatles 43
Damien, The Leper Priest
215
Dangerous Company 536
Danton 216
Eleanor, First Lady Of The
World 851
The Executioner's Song 366
The Flight Of The Eagle 17
Frances 307
Gabe Kaplan As Groucho
667b
Gandhi 346
The Grey Fox 695
If You Could See What I Hear
931
I'm Dancing As Fast As I Can
372
Inside The Third Reich 908
Life Of The Party: The Story
Of Beatrice 760
Little Gloria . . . Happy At
Last 969
Lois Gibb And The Love Ca-
nal 360
Mae West 995
Marco Polo 797a
Marian Rose White 996
Marianne And Juliane 301
Missing 478
Muggable Mary, Street Cop
369
Piaf—The Early Years 783
The Return Of Martin Guerre
390
Rosie: The Rosemary
Clooney Story 172

The Royal Romance Of Charles And Diana 151
Shocktrauma 196
Side By Side: The True Story Of The Osmond Family 761
Wasn't That A Time! 992
The White Rose 880a
Will, G. Gordon Liddy 621
The Wizard Of Babylon 308a
A Woman Called Golda 684

1983
Adam 988
Before The Nickelodeon: The Early Cinema Of Edwin S. Porter 801
Bill: On His Own 872b
Blood Feud 569
Bronte 91
Champions 143
Choices Of The Heart 254
Cook & Peary: The Race To The Pole 189
Cross Creek 825
Dempsey 232
The Divine Emma 238
Edith And Marcel 782
For Us The Living: The Medgar Evers Story 305a
Grace Kelly 559
Hammett 404
He Makes Me Feel Like Dancin' 214a
Heart Like A Wheel 726
I Married Wyatt Earp 274
I Want To Live 379
Jacobo Timerman: Prisoner Without A Name, Cell Without A Number 949
John Wycliffe: The Morning Star 1009a
Kennedy 564a

Living Proof: The Hank Williams, Jr., Story 1003
Love Is Forever 305
M.A.D.D.: Mothers Against Drunk Drivers 622
The Man In The Silk Hat 629a
Murder In Coweta County 985
Never Cry Wolf 720
Quarterback Princess 657
Return Engagement 603c
Rita Hayworth: The Love Goddess 421
Running Brave 693
Sadat 873
The Scarlet And The Black 755
Silkwood 895
Star 80 920
The Terry Fox Story 326
Trackdown: Finding The Goodbar Killer 377
Wagner 983
We Of The Never-Never 393
Who Will Love My Children? 334
Will There Really Be A Morning? 308

1984
Amadeus 721
Anatomy Of An Illness 194
Anne Devlin 240
Another Country 99
Antonio Gaudi 350b
The Assisi Underground 742b
Attack On Fear 697a
The Bear 97
Beyond The Next Mountain 809c
The Bounty 53
Burroughs 100

Calamity Jane 114
Christiane F. 306
Ernie Kovacs: Between The Laughter 583
Fatal Vision 651
George Stevens: A Film-maker's Journey 916
George Washington 988d
Heartsounds 603b
Helen Keller: The Miracle Continues 554
The Jesse Owens Story 763
Kerouac 573a
The Killing Fields 879
The Last Of Mrs. Lincoln 626a
Last Plane Out 197
Love Leads The Way 332
Marlene 243a
Mrs. Soffel 905
Nadia 185
Pope John Paul II 529
Prince Jack 566
Raoul Wallenberg: Between The Lines 986
Sakharov 875
Sam's Son 595
Samson And Delilah 877b
Secret Honor 749
Shattered Vows 365b
Special People 269a
Spring Symphony 882a
Squizzy Taylor 936a
A Test Of Love 681
The Times Of Harvey Milk 689
Touched By Love 112
Victims For Victims: The Theresa Saldana Story 876
Why Me? 412

1985
The Atlanta Child Murders 1003a

The Beach Boys: An American Band 37a
Beethoven's Nephew 45c
A Bunny's Tale 914b
The Burning Bed 490
Children Of The Night 605a
Christopher Columbus 184a
Colonel Redl 826
Dance With A Stranger 298
Deadly Intentions 825a
A Death In California 672
Dreamchild 409a
Eleni 343
An Englishman Abroad 99a
The Falcon And The Snowman 83a
First Steps 781
Florence Nightingale 745
Going For The Gold: The Bill Johnson Story 533
The Hearst And Davies Affair 423
Heart Of A Champion: The Ray Mancini Story 659
Huey Long 635
Hungry Feeling: The Life And Death Of Brendan Behan 46a
James Joyce's Women 545b
John And Yoko: A Love Story 607a
King David 222
Lady Jane 385
Love, Mary 389a
Malice In Wonderland 771
Marie 821
Mask 235
Mata Hari 652a
Mishima 696
Mussolini: The Decline And Fall Of Il Duce 734
Mussolini: The Untold Story 734a

My Wicked, Wicked Ways
320a
Out Of Africa 56
Out Of The Darkness 1020
The Return Of Ruben Blades
51f
Right To Kill? 505b
Robert Kennedy And His
Times 569a
Shadowlands 616
Sweet Dreams 170
Sylvia 22a
A Time To Live 994
Vladmir Horowitz, The Last
Romantic 480a
Wallenberg: A Hero's Story
986a

1986
Act Of Vengeance 1011
Adam: His Song Continues
988a
Alex: The Life Of A Child
231a
Anastasia: The Mystery Of
Anna 16a
Barnum 30
Blunt 57
The Boy In Blue 406b
Caravaggio 120b
A Case Of Deadly Force
754a
Courage 951
Death Of A Soldier 607b
The Deliberate Stranger
97a
Doing Life 856a
Dream West 336a
Dreams Of Gold: The Mel
Fisher Story 312a
Firefighter 327a
The George McKenna Story
681a

George Washington II: The
Forging Of A Nation
988e
The Girl Who Spelled Free-
dom 1011a
Heartburn
Houston: The Legend Of
Texas 486a
I Lived, But . . . 763a
Jo Jo Dancer, Your Life Is
Calling 809a
Johnnie Mae Gibson: FBI
361a
The Last Days Of Frank And
Jesse James 512
The Last Days Of Patton 773
Liberty 35a
Mafia Princess 359
Manhunt For Claude Dallas
213a
A Matter Of Heart 546a
The Moro Affair 713a
Mother Teresa 940a
Murrow 733
Nazi Hunter: The Beate
Klarsfeld Story 581a
Nobody's Child 28a
On Wings Of Eagles 778a
Peter The Great 778b
Salvador 84
Samaritan: The Mitch Snyder
Story 904a
Second Serve 835a
Sid And Nancy 969a
The Ted Kennedy, Jr., Story
560a
Therese 940b
A Time To Triumph 416a
Vengeance: The Story Of
Tony Cimo 162a
What Happened To Kerouac?
573b
A Winner Never Quits 379c

1987

The Alamo: Thirteen Days To Glory 81a
Andy Warhol 988b
The Ann Jillian Story 524b
Au Revoir Les Enfants 658a
Bad Blood 379b
Bloodsport 269b
Burke and Wills 99b
Buster Keaton: A Hard Act To Follow 551
Caspar David Friedrich 337a
Chuck Berry Hail! Hail! Rock'N'Roll 51b
Cry Freedom 51e
Distant Harmony: Pavarotti In China 773b
Dorothy And Alan At Norma Place 769b
The Double Helix 200a
84 Charing Cross Road 406a
Elvis And Me 807a
Eye On The Sparrow 604a
Gaby—A True Story 90a
Guilty Of Innocence: The Lenell Geter Story 358a
A Hero's Journey: The World Of Joseph Campbell 111a
Hotel Terminus: The Life And Times Of Klaus Barbie 26b
I Would Be Called John 526b
The Impossible Spy 180a
In The Mood 128a
Islands 160a
J. Edgar Hoover 475a
John Huston And The Dubliners 493a
La Bamba 963a
The Last Emperor 809b
The Man Who Broke 1,000 Chains 99c
Mandela 659a
Maria 110a
Mayflower Madam 33a
The Murder Of Mary Phagan 331a
Murderers Among Us 1000b
My Life For Zarah Leander 603a
Prick Up Your Ears 760a
Rosa Luxemburg 645a
Samuel Beckett: Silence To Silence 45a
The Sicilian 367c
To Heal A Nation 885a
The Untouchables 742a
Vincent 968b
Waiting For The Moon 949a
Wolf At The Door 353a
Young Harry Houdini 484a

1988

The Attic: The Hiding Of Anne Frank 362a
Bat 21 400a
Beryl Markham: A Shadow On The Sun 666a
Bird 769a
Buster 285a
Camille Claudel 164b
A Cry In The Dark 142b
Fat Man And Little Boy 759b
Frida: Naturaleza Vida 547
Glory 891a
Gore Vidal's Lincoln 624a
Gorillas In The Mist 322a
Hanna's War 888a
Hoxsey: Quacks Who Cure Cancer 488a
Imagine: John Lennon 607
Jack The Ripper 499a
Komitas 582a
The Last Temptation Of Christ 524a
Murder One 494a

My Father, My Son 1022
Nitti: The Enforcer 748a
Pancho Barnes 29a
Patty Hearst 422a
Stand And Deliver 302b
The Thin Blue Line 2a
Too Young The Hero 379a
Tucker: The Man And His
  Dream 958a
Used Innocence 48b
Verne Miller 692a
A Vision Shared: A Tribute
  To Woody Guthrie And
  Leadbelly 395a
Walker 984a
White Mischief 302a
A Winter Tan 469a
The Woman He Loved 896a
A World Apart 311b
Young Guns 72a

1989
An Angel At My Table 327b
Blaze 633a
Born On The Fourth Of July
  583a
Champions Forever 11a
Day One 759a
Directed By Andrei
  Tarkovsky 935a
Goodnight, Sweet Marilyn
  701a
Gore Vidal's Billy The Kid 66a
Great Balls Of Fire 616a
Growing Up In America 367a
Haunted Summer 892a
Henry V 431a
High Fidelity—The Adven-
  tures Of The Guarneri
  String Quartet 398b
Jimi Plays Monterey 429a
LBJ: The Early Years 535a
Lean On Me 164a

Looking For Langston 491a
My Left Foot 94a
Night In Havana: Dizzy Gil-
  lespie In Cuba 365a
Romero 848a
Roxanne: The Prize Pulitzer
  810a
Scandal 552a
Small Sacrifices 258a
Stealing Heaven 1a
Story Of Women 599a
Thelonious Monk: Straight
  No Chaser 700a
Triumph Of The Spirit 21a
The Unforgettable Nat King
  Cole 180c
Wired 48a

1990
Awakenings 872
Bethune, The Making Of A
  Hero 51d
Good Night, Sweet Wife: A
  Murder In Boston 927a
Heat Wave 835b
Impromptu 877c
The Krays 583b
Leona Helmsley: The Queen
  Of Mean 426a
Listen Up: The Lives Of
  Quincy Jones 541a
Mountains Of The Moon
  100a
Reversal Of Fortune 981a
Vincent & Theo 968c

1991
Bugsy 894a
The Doors 715a
Madonna: Truth Or Dare
  653a
The Marla Hanson Story 407a
Never Forget 686a

One Man's War 311a
Separate But Equal 667a
She Stood Alone 198a
Son Of The Morning Star 208a
Superstar: The Life And
    Times Of Andy Warhol
    988c

Van Gogh 968a
Without Warning: The James
    Brady Story 85a
Young Catherine 137a

1992
Citizen Cohn 180b

ABOUT THE AUTHOR

Eileen Karsten is a graduate of Barat College. She earned her MALS from Rosary College. Ms. Karsten is currently Head of Technical Services and Assistant Professor of Bibliography at North Park College and Theological Seminary in Chicago. Her research for this book was initiated by a reference question which could not be answered in any current reference source. *From Real Life to Reel Life* is Ms. Karsten's first book.